IN THE BALANCE

IN THE
BALANCE

Speeches 1949 and 1950

WINSTON S. CHURCHILL

Edited by Randolph S. Churchill

1 9 5 2

HOUGHTON MIFFLIN COMPANY BOSTON

THE RIVERSIDE PRESS CAMBRIDGE

FIRST PUBLISHED 1951
FIRST PUBLISHED IN THE UNITED STATES 1952
L.C. CARD NO. 52-5251

PRINTED IN GREAT BRITAIN BY
THE SHENVAL PRESS, LONDON AND HERTFORD
F.851

INTRODUCTION

THE SPEECHES contained in this volume were delivered in
1949 and 1950. They cover a wide range of topics, both domestic
and foreign, and, as in previous volumes, provide a running com-
mentary on political events in the age in which we live. The outstanding events of this two-year period were the devaluation of the
£ sterling, the General Election of February 1950, the outbreak of the
Korean war, the establishment of the North Atlantic Treaty Organization, and the immense rearmament programmes of the United States.
These events constitute the background against which these speeches
were made.

Up to February 1950 the Socialist Government had a majority of
140. The last General Election cut this down to 6. Already in 1949
the impending Election had cast its shadow upon the Government:
since the Election their minute majority has made it impossible for
them to legislate, and the political fortunes of the Government have
remorselessly ebbed. With the General Election taking place half-way
through the period covered by this volume, it is natural that many
of these speeches should be concerned with domestic issues and Party
politics, but it will be found that foreign affairs are still a major theme.
In addition to many speeches in the House of Commons on foreign
topics, this volume includes speeches made by Mr Churchill in the
United States, in France, in Belgium, and in Denmark.

The years 1949 and 1950 saw the acceptance and realization of many
of the arguments contained in the previous volume *Europe Unite*.
August 1949 saw the opening session of the European Assembly in
Strasbourg and throughout this period a steady advance on many
fronts towards the goal of a United Europe. Mr Churchill's other
major post-war theme, the 'fraternal association of the English-
speaking peoples', for which he pleaded at Fulton in March 1946, also
finds itself close to achievement with the setting-up of the North
Atlantic Treaty Organization and with the appointment, at the end of
1950, of General of the Army Dwight D. Eisenhower to command
the forces of the twelve North Atlantic Powers.

While during these two years dangers have grown, the Western
Powers have made steady if belated progress along the paths of safety

which Mr Churchill has persistently sign-posted not only in *Europe Unite* but in the preceding volume, *The Sinews of Peace*. The Western world is becoming daily more united, and under the leadership and with the aid of the United States is rearming at a formidable rate. These healthy processes have continued during the first six months of 1951. Though the peace of the world is far from assured there is an increasingly wide acceptance of the view that time may yet be allowed in which perseverance with these policies may achieve the safety of Western civilization.

RANDOLPH S. CHURCHILL

July 1951

CONTENTS

CONTENTS

CONTENTS

CONTENTS

PALESTINE

11 *December—Agreement signed in Ottawa for entry of Newfoundland into the Canadian Confederation.*

27 *December—Australia makes a gift of £10,000,000 to Great Britain as a contribution towards helping her to overcome her serious economic difficulties.*

28 *December—Egyptian Prime Minister, Nokrashy Pasha, assassinated in Cairo.*

1 *January—US Government extends full diplomatic recognition to South Korean Government.*

 Eire Government announce the grant of reciprocal citizenship between Eire and Great Britain (including the British Colonies) and Eire and New Zealand.

3 *January—Mr Ivor Thomas, MP, leaves the Labour Party and joins the Conservative Party as a protest against the Government decision to nationalize the Iron and Steel Industry.*

5 *January—Figures published by the Jewish Agency show that over 130,000 Jewish immigrants have entered Israel in 1948.*

7 *January—Announcement of the composition of the Monopolies and Restrictive Practices Commission set up by the Board of Trade.*

9 *January—Sir Stafford Cripps, addressing a Labour meeting in Cumberland, warns against wage claims.*

 Soviet News Bureau in Berlin accuses the British, French and US Governments of entering into a 'secret agreement' to prevent the repatriation of German POWs in order that they can be sent to forced labour camps.

12 *January—The Treasury announces that the 1948 gold and dollar deficit of the Sterling Area amounts to £423,000,000.*

14 *January—M. Robert Schuman, French Premier, arrives in London at Mr Bevin's invitation to exchange views on current international problems affecting the two Governments and in particular Germany, European Union, the Atlantic Pact, the Mediterranean, Middle East, South-East Asia and the Far East.*

19 *January—US Export-Import Bank announces that an immediate loan of $35,000,000 has been made available to the provisional Government of Israel for the purpose of purchasing in the USA equipment,*

materials and services for the development of Israel's agriculture, and a further credit of $65,000,000 for the development of transport communications, public works, manufacturing industries.

20 *January—Generalissimo Chiang Kai-shek resigns office of President of China.*

President Truman commences his second term as President of the US.

21 *January—Canada announces her agreement to 'unfreeze' the balance of $235,000,000 of the $1,250,000,000 loan to Britain at the rate of $10,000,000 monthly to finance Canadian exports to Britain.*

Marshal Tito attacks the Soviet Union's anti-Yugoslav campaign.

22 *January—Peking surrendered to the Communists.*

23 *January—Meat ration reduced to 10d. worth per week, plus 2d. worth of corned meat.*

25 *January—Elections in Israel result in a victory for the Labour Party.*

25 *January—Findings of the Lynskey Tribunal published, reporting adversely on Mr Belcher (Parliamentary Secretary to the Board of Trade) and Mr George Gibson (Director of the Bank of England and the North-Western Electricity Board).*

26 *January—German de-Nazification Tribunal at Nuremberg classifies Franz von Papen as a 'second-degree' Nazi and orders his release.*

26 *January—Nationalist Government of China announces that the Government headquarters will be transferred to Canton in February.*

[26 *January* 1949

The right hon Gentleman [Mr Ernest Bevin] has covered a wide field, both in the extent of the topics with which he has dealt and in the period of history which he has taken into consideration. But I have been asking myself, as I listened to this statement of historical facts and so many arguments which one approves of as such and in their places, what was the conclusion that the Foreign Secretary was asking the House to draw from the statement which he has just made. It seems to me that it would not be doing him any injustice if I said that the conclusion to which he wishes to lead us is that the conduct of this matter and the policy pursued by the Government for the last three and a half years could hardly have been bettered. All is for the best in the best of all possible worlds, and all kinds of arguments can be used with all kinds of varying emphasis at every stage and aspect of the story.

I shall have to tell some of this story, though I trust at not undue length. But before I plunge into it I must make one general remark about the right hon Gentleman and his policy. We have supported the main principles and structure of the foreign policy of the right hon

Gentleman, and everyone is glad that he has had the patriotism and courage to take a firm stand in these last years against the vile and wicked brutalities and manoeuvres of Communism which threaten not only the peace of the world, but even more important, its life and freedom. In this connection I see that one of Mr Ramsay MacDonald's bishops, or perhaps his only bishop,* has lately been eulogizing the humanistic virtues of Soviet Communism, while all the time at least 12,000,000 people are being toiled to death as slaves in the Soviet concentration camps. Such an example of mental and moral obliquity on the part of a prelate deserves at least the passing notice of thinking men. As this might be considered to reflect upon a Member of the other House, I shall avoid your rebukes, Mr Speaker, by not pursuing the topic or the prelate any further. We must not forget, and we do not forget, that the Foreign Secretary, supported by the British trade union movement and by the present Socialist Administration and Labour Party, has not hesitated or failed to draw an impassable line between the professional Communist adept and other human beings.

We are glad of that. We also respect the Foreign Secretary's British outlook. He represents many of the virtues and some of the weaknesses which have enabled our people to make a tolerably collective presentation of their character to the rest of the world in many years of history. There is also, of course, the sense of war comradeship, which although it must not be allowed to interfere with the proper, due discussion of current affairs or with party strife at a time like this, is nevertheless a subsisting element between many of those who sit on the Front Benches of this House.

I wish to say that because I make it perfectly clear that in the general policy which the right hon Gentleman has pursued—I am not talking about the methods but the spirit of the general policy he has pursued—in resisting the Communist menace and encroachment, and in cultivating ever closer and more friendly relations with the United States, we have given him our support, and we do not withdraw our support at the present time. But it is on this basis and with this background that we are forced this afternoon to consider the right hon Gentleman's astounding mishandling of the Palestine problem. We feel that this has been so gross and glaring that we should fail in our duty if we did not expose it in the plainest terms. We shall not only do that in Debate; we shall support our criticism in the Lobby. Only in this way can we make an effective protest and lead public opinion to the true conclusions.

* The Right Rev Ernest William Barnes, Bishop of Birmingham. Appointed by Mr Ramsay MacDonald in 1924.

3

The right hon Gentleman's Palestine plight is indeed melancholy and cannot be covered up with wide generalities. No one ever made such sweeping declarations of confidence in himself on this point as the right hon Gentleman, and no one has been proved by events to be more consistently wrong on every turning-point and at every moment than he. Every opportunity for obtaining a satisfactory settlement was thrown away. Immediately after the end of the Japanese war, we had the troops in the Middle East and we had the world prestige to impose a settlement on both sides. That chance was missed. Instead, an Anglo-American Committee of Inquiry was set up to examine the problem. It was on that occasion that the right hon Gentleman staked his political future on solving the Palestine problem. No more rash bet has ever been recorded in the annals of the British turf. Luckily, it is not intended that the wager shall be paid.

Mr BEVIN: May I ask whether it was greater than that which the right hon Gentleman undertook when he went after Denikin and Koltchak?

Mr CHURCHILL: I certainly did not stake my political reputation upon the successes which those generals would have, but I think the day will come when it will be recognized without doubt, not only on one side of the House but throughout the civilized world, that the strangling of Bolshevism at its birth would have been an untold blessing to the human race.

Mr COCKS (Broxtowe): If that had happened we should have lost the last war.

Mr CHURCHILL: No, it would have prevented the last war. Let me return to the more peaceful paths of Palestine and leave these furious controversies of a bygone period. When this Anglo-American Committee reported, its recommendations, although accepted by Mr Truman, were rejected by His Majesty's Government.

Mr BEVIN: No.

Mr CHURCHILL: Well, were not effectively accepted.

Mr BEVIN: We accepted the ten points. Mr Truman only accepted one—the 100,000. We accepted the lot.

Mr CHURCHILL: If I may quote the right hon Gentleman, 'This is my speech.' No agreement was reached upon this issue. At length, in February 1947, the right hon Gentleman announced that he had decided to refer the matter to the United Nations. But having done so, what happened? A United Nations Committee was set up to examine the matter. It recommended the termination of the Mandate, and, by a majority vote, it recommended the policy of the partition of Palestine. This decision was endorsed by the United Nations Assembly on

29 November 1947. Yet, though they had referred the matter to the United Nations for a solution, His Majesty's Government were not prepared to accept their decision. Indeed, they refused to allow the United Nations Palestine Commission to enter the territory of Palestine until a fortnight before the termination of the Mandate. And so it went on. His Majesty's Government were always one, or even two, and sometimes three, steps behind.

THE SECRETARY OF STATE FOR THE COLONIES [MR CREECH JONES]: I think that, for the sake of accuracy, this rumour, which has been so often repeated, should be denied. The British Government suggested that it would not be wise for the Palestine Commission to go to Palestine more than a fortnight before the Mandate came to an end. [HON MEMBERS: 'Why?'] I met the Palestine Commission on behalf of the Government and discussed their entrance into Palestine, and it was understood that they would come to London at the end of March and discuss with us their entrance into Palestine which would probably be sometime in the early part of April. That was four or five, possibly six weeks before the Mandate expired.

MR CHURCHILL: What happened?

MR CREECH JONES: I think this untruth ought to be completely repudiated. What happened was that the Palestine Commission reported to the Security Council that they could not implement the Resolution of 29 November. Subsequently, the Security Council summoned a Special General Assembly in order that the whole Resolution of 29 November should be brought into review.

MR CHURCHILL: The Foreign Secretary will be grateful for the chivalrous aid which his colleague from the Colonial Office has brought to his notice. In the long interruption which he made, I did not gather from him at what date before the evacuation the United Nations Commission actually began to travel about Palestine.

MR CREECH JONES: The Palestine Commission reported to the Security Council that it was quite unable to implement the Resolution of 29 November and accordingly remained in New York because it could not implement the Resolution which had been passed.

MR CHURCHILL: It is quite simple. They did not go. And so it went on. I am sorry if hon Gentlemen do not like the argument I have to unfold. They must not shrink from bearing these strokes. We bear with what fortitude we can summon the heavy blows struck us by the Foreign Secretary, the Prime Minister and others, and similar equanimity and toleration should prevail in the ranks of our opponents. His Majesty's Government, in the whole of this matter, have always been one, or even two, and sometimes three, steps behind the march of events. When the State of Israel was proclaimed, it was recognized at once by the Americans. His Majesty's Government could at least have accepted the principle of partition laid down in the United Nations Resolution. When they finally accepted that principle in the Bernadotte Report of September last, why could they not have faced reality and accorded *de facto* recognition to Israel?

I have told the tale of different aspects of this story so often that I cannot but mention today the salient features. These have led us, through vast waste of money, to the repeated loss of British lives, to humiliation of every kind, to the fomenting of injurious hatreds, to a position where Britain has given up every interest she possessed and abandoned the task for which all parties in this island had laboured for a quarter of a century, and has quitted—or half quitted, because in some ways we have not; we still manage to get the disadvantages— the scene of so much valuable work and achievement, amid the scorn and hatred of Arab and Jew and the contemptuous disdain of the civilized world. That is what we are asked to believe deserves our general confidence and approbation—the victory of patience and phlegm in the long run.

But with us it is not a case of being wise after the event. It was more than a year before I realized that the Foreign Secretary and the Government had no plan or policy. It took another year after I had urged the Government to quit Palestine, if they had no plan, for them to take the decision to go. They took it a year later when everything was more difficult. Great opportunities were cast away. They took it in such a way as to render themselves unable to bring perfectly legitimate pressure to bear upon the United States to leave the side-lines and come into the arena of helpful action. They lost the opportunities of that year since they were told they had better go. And we paid the bill of £80,000,000 for the troops alone for maintaining order under most trying conditions and facing the horrible murder of many of our brave soldiers.

All that is in the past. We have at length evacuated Palestine. Yet we still find ourselves involved in its problems. This fact has furnished the Foreign Secretary with the opportunity for making further public blunders and committing himself to more painfully obvious misjudgments. There never has been, in my belief, the slightest comprehension of the Palestine problems by the right hon Gentleman. Every word that he says in his speech is known, by those of us who have lived our lives with this great problem for many years, to be subject to wrong emphasis. Nor will he take advice.

It is six weeks ago that we formally advised the Government to make a *de facto* recognition of the Israeli Government. The right hon Gentleman brushed our proposal aside. What is he going to do now? It is difficult to discover, from what he said, what he is going to do. Perhaps he has not yet made up his mind? Perhaps it is a question of how much pressure is brought to bear upon him before he does so? He has lost opportunities and argued for delay and for putting off the action which the great majority of the people know it would have been wise and practicable to take.

I am quite sure that the right hon Gentleman will have to recognize the Israeli Government, and that cannot be long delayed. I regret that he has not had the manliness to tell us in plain terms tonight, and that he preferred to retire under a cloud of inky water and vapour, like a cuttlefish, to some obscure retreat. *De facto* recognition has never depended upon an exact definition of territorial frontiers. There are half a dozen countries in Europe which are recognized today whose territorial frontiers are not finally settled. Surely, Poland is one. It is only with the general Peace Treaty that a final settlement can be made. Whoever said, 'How can we recognize a country whose limits and boundaries are not carefully defined?' I am astonished to find the right hon Gentleman giving any countenance to it. What trouble, what inconvenience, what humbling rebuffs should we have avoided if the Foreign Secretary had taken the sincere advice tendered to him from this side of the House. The only reason, or, certainly, one particular reason, offered by him was irrelevant and incorrect. He talked about the mistakes which some countries have made in hastily recognizing Indonesia. Recognition, or hasty recognition, he thought, would be a bad precedent, but how absurd it is to compare the so-called Republic of Indonesia with the setting-up in Tel Aviv of a Government of the State of Israel, with an effective organization and a victorious army.

Whether the right hon Gentleman likes it or not, and whether we like it or not, the coming into being of a Jewish State in Palestine is an event in world history to be viewed in the perspective, not of a generation or a century, but in the perspective of a thousand, two thousand or even three thousand years. That is a standard of temporal values or time values which seems very much out of accord with the perpetual click-clack of our rapidly-changing moods and of the age in which we live. This is an event in world history. How vain it is to compare it with the recognition, or the claims to recognition, by certain countries, of the Communist banditti which we are resisting in Malaya or of the anarchic forces which the Dutch are trying to restrain in Indonesia.

No one has done more to build up a Jewish National Home in

Palestine than the Conservative Party, and many of us have always had in mind that this might some day develop into a Jewish State. [*Interruption.*] I am speaking for myself, anyhow. The hon Gentleman always seems to be faced with the difficulty of knowing which side he is on in any controversy, and of always being faced with the danger of trying to be on both sides at once. I will not discuss the matter any further, but I warn him to be a little more careful. I say that the Conservative Party has done a great task over twenty-five years, with Parliaments which had a Conservative majority, in trying to build a Jewish National Home in Palestine, and, now that it has come into being, it is England that refuses to recognize it, and, by our actions, we find ourselves regarded as its most bitter enemies. All this is due, not only to mental inertia or lack of grip on the part of the Ministers concerned, but also, I am afraid, to the very strong and direct streak of bias and prejudice on the part of the Foreign Secretary.

I do not feel any great confidence that he has not got a prejudice against the Jews in Palestine. I am sure that he thought the Arab League was stronger and that it would win if fighting broke out, but I do not suggest for a moment that he wished to provoke war. He was quite right in saying, in effect, that, in that particular quarrel, they needed very little provocation, but the course he took led inevitably and directly to a trial of strength, and the result was opposite to what I believe he expected it to be. I will say no more than that. Everyone has his feelings on this subject, and there is no unanimity of opinion on either side of the House, but, at any rate, the course he took led directly to a trial of strength and it turned out in the opposite way in which he expected, acting on the advice of his military advisers, I have no doubt, and against the recorded opinion of Lord Wavell, as to which side was the stronger.

I certainly felt that the spectacle of the Jewish settlements being invaded from all sides—from Syria, Transjordan and Egypt—and with a lot of our tanks and modern tackle was, on the face of it, most formidable, but I believed that that combination would fall to pieces at the first check, and I adhered to the estimate I had formed in the war of the measure of the fighting qualities and the tough fibre of the Zionist community, and the support which it would receive from Zionists all over the world. But the Foreign Secretary was wrong, wrong in his facts, wrong in the mood, wrong in the method and wrong in the result, and we are very sorry about it for his sake and still more sorry about it for our own.

We have so managed our affairs as to find ourselves arrayed in this matter on the opposite side to the United States, to Soviet Russia, to the Palestine settlers and to Zionist supporters all over the world, and without—and I want my hon Friends on this side to realize this—doing the slightest service to the Arab countries to whom we have very serious obligations. This is not at all a favourable conjunction for British interests, and it should have been the careful aim of the Foreign Office to avoid its being brought into being. It makes our position a very weak one and it predisposes UNO against us on numbers alone. Our influence is therefore at a minimum as a result of our improvident diplomacy.

This is a poor and undeserved result of all that we have created and built up in Palestine by the goodwill and solid work of twenty-five years. We have lost the friendship of the Palestine Jews for the time being. I was glad to read a statement from Dr Weizmann the other day pleading for friendship between the new Israeli State and the Western world. I believe that will be its destiny. He was an old friend of mine for many years. His son was killed in the war fighting with us. I trust his influence may grow and that we shall do what we can, subject to our other obligations—because we cannot forget those other obligations—to add to his influence. I hope that later on a truer comprehension of the Zionist debt to this country will revive. Here I am in agreement with the right hon Gentleman—I trust it will revive; but for the present we seem to have deprived ourselves of all the fruits of the past. Moreover, as I mentioned just now, the Foreign Secretary's policy has been the worst possible for the Arabs. I am sure we could have agreed immediately after the war upon a partition scheme which would have been more favourable to the Arabs.

THE PRIME MINISTER [MR ATTLEE]: May I ask the right hon Gentleman, if he thought that could have been done, why did he not do it after the war? He was in power.

MR CHURCHILL: No. The world and the nation had the inestimable blessing of the right hon Gentleman's guidance. I am sure that we could have agreed immediately after the war upon a partition scheme which would have been more favourable to the Arabs than that which will now follow their unsuccessful recourse to arms.

MR THOMAS REID (Swindon): Agreed with whom? Would it not have led to a major war in the Near East if partition had been pursued?

MR CHURCHILL: I give my opinion. I am sure we could have made better arrangements for the Arabs at that time—I am not talking of the Jews—than will be possible after there has been this unfortunate recourse to arms. Indeed, the scheme of partition proposed by UNO was better than what they will get now, after their defeat. We are evidently in the presence here of prolonged, repeated and serious miscalculations on the part of the Foreign Secretary and his advisers and colleagues.

I do not propose to enter tonight upon the drawing of frontier lines or the details of any partition for which we should use our remaining influence, such as it is. I will, however, say that we ought not to grudge a fair share of the deserts of the Negeb to the Jews. It is nearly thirty years since I came officially and responsibly into this story. I have always felt that the Negeb should afford a means of expansion to the Jewish settlers in Palestine and offer future prospects to Zionist movements. But it is impossible to fly over these regions low down, as I did before the Second Great War, or travel through them to Petra and other places without seeing how fierce and barren these regions of the Negeb are. And yet they once held great cities and nourished important populations. The Jews, by the gift they have and by the means which they do not lack, have a way of making the desert bloom. Those who have seen it can testify. The Arabs, with all their dignity and grace, are primarily the children of the desert, and where they dwell, in this part of the world at least, and for the most part, the desert lands do not become reclaimed while the Arab control is complete over them.

Here let me say a word about how the British have treated the Arabs. I take up the cudgels not for one party or Government; I speak of twenty-five years of British policy and the settlement made after the First World War, supported by a Parliament with a great Conservative majority, in which I was prominently concerned, and which placed Feisal on the throne of Iraq and his dynasty is there today. I myself, with the advice and guidance of Lawrence, took steps to put Emir Abdullah at Amman, where he is still after twenty-five years of shock and strain, always a good friend. We took all pains when we liberated Syria during a difficult moment in the last war to make sure that the Syrian Arabs had their full rights and independence, and although it meant bitter controversy with General de Gaulle we insisted upon that at a moment when, as everyone knows, our margin of control and subsistence was not large.

I will not have it said that we have not behaved with loyalty to the Arabs or that what has been asked for the Jews, which was supported and sustained by the Conservative Party for so many years, to say nothing of the party opposite, has gone beyond what was just and fair, having regard to the fact that both these races have lived in Palestine for thousands of years side by side. Hon Gentlemen do not seem to realize that Jew and Arab have always been there. They say,

'How would you like to have a piece of Scotland taken away and to have a lot of other races put in?' The two races have always been there, and I trust always will be there, happily.

In the Negeb there is at least an opportunity and indeed a hope of affording a refuge to the survivors of the Jewish community who have been massacred in so many parts of Europe and letting them try their best—and their efforts are amazing—to bring back into economic usefulness lands which the world cannot afford to leave lying idle. It is obvious that both Jews and Arabs must have access to the Red Sea through the Gulf of Aqaba. This has figured in most of the schemes of partition and it should be possible to reconcile competing claims with justice. The Gulf of Aqaba is in fact to the Red Sea, although on a smaller scale, what Trieste is to the Adriatic. The outlet here should certainly not be monopolized by either of the races who have dwelt together so long in this vast hinterland. It is therefore a place of special significance.

I do not intend today to try to judge whether the Government were right in the prevailing circumstances and in the aftermath of their evacuation of Palestine to send an armed British force to Aqaba. However, in view of our obligation to Abdullah and our treaty with him, I entirely agree that we could not disinterest ourselves in his fate or in that of his country. I should not like to see us repeat in Transjordania the behaviour the Government adopted in respect of our treaty obligations with the Indian Princes, and in particular with the Nizam of Hyderabad. I hope the Emir of Transjordania will have a better tale to tell of us. The act of sending a force to Aqaba did, however, wear an aspect of decision unusual in recent British policy in Palestine. I hope that, having gone there, we shall stay there, and keep an ample margin of force there, until the whole question has been finally decided by the United Nations organization and until their award has been accepted and obeyed by both Jews and Arabs. We should support any steps taken to that end. We feel bound to make our protests and to dissociate ourselves from a policy of folly, fatuity and futility the like of which it is not easy to find in modern experience, for which the right hon Gentleman and the present Cabinet are responsible. But inside this large parade and presentation of mismanagement and misfortune there is an inset, a cameo, of inconsequence and muddle which cannot, I think, be matched. Here we have wrong thinking and imprudent acting presenting in miniature a working model—a working model of what all persons concerned in public affairs should strive to avoid by all means. A truce had been arranged and a cease fire was to take place at 2 p.m. that afternoon.

Yet in the morning the Government—the Prime Minister very properly took full responsibility—sent a reconnaissance into the battle area or the fighting area of Royal Air Force planes which had on preceding days been flying in conjunction with Egyptian planes which were hostile to the other side, the Jewish forces. The pilots were, I am told, to a large extent, trainees—we shall know more about that from the inquiry—and were the product of the Air Ministry in its decline since the war. They were sent out under conditions which exposed them to the maximum danger.

This was no high altitude photographic operation. They were to fly low over areas where they knew hostilities were in progress. No warning had been sent to the Israeli forces, but restrictive orders were given to our pilots about not firing their guns except after having been fired upon effectively by others. The first reconnaissance was sent out on a wholly unnecessary mission, because there was a cease fire that evening. The second reconnaissance was sent out in order to ascertain what had happened to the first, but before the second could have got back the cease fire between Jews and Arabs had already taken place. Why expose our Forces, our young men, to such risks as that? It was in these circumstances that we had to endure the affront and injury for which our two young airmen lost their lives.

When we turn to seek redress from UNO or from the Commissions on the spot, the international bodies, when we look to other nations for sympathy in the matter, we are asked certain questions. For instance, why should we go—this is one question—why should we go out over this area at the very moment of the cease fire? It is said on our behalf in reply that the Jews were invading Egypt and that they had no business to be there. But had not the Egyptians already invaded Palestine some time before? We are told also that the Jews had refused the United Nations observers the right to go to the area to see for themselves. I am told—I may not be correctly informed—but I am told on good information, as far as I can judge it, that the United Nations Palestine Commission has special aeroplanes painted white and known to both sides as entirely neutral and outside the conflict. Is that so? If it is so, why were they not used? Why were our planes used? A British reconnaissance at this moment was very inconsistent with the general purposes of the United Nations and detrimental to a peaceful settlement.

Then it is said the Americans encouraged us to find out what was going on. But is that, if true, a wholly convincing reason? If I criticize His Majesty's Government it is by no means to declare that the action of the United States in all these months has been impeccable. Considering the interests, sentimental and other, which they have in Palestine and Arabia they should have come to our aid two or three years ago, and I believe that if our policy had been wise and wisely conducted, and proper contacts made and developed, we should have had their assistance, as an alternative to the evacuation to which we were eventually forced. Curiosity to know what was going on would certainly not justify doing a thing so improvident as this sortie of aircraft at such a moment. I say it was the quintessence of maladresse of which the right hon Gentleman and the Prime Minister, who takes the responsibility, were guilty. And now poor old Britain—Tories, Socialists, Liberals, Zionists, anti-Zionists, non-Zionists alike, we find ourselves shot down in an air skirmish, snubbed by the Israeli Government, who said, 'We understand you do not recognize us,' and with a marked lack of support from the international bodies upon which we depend so greatly and whose opinions we value so highly.

During all this period the Foreign Secretary has not been able to inform Abdullah, our faithful adherent, where he stood or what he would be wise to do. He has had to wait and guess. I am sure Abdullah would have done everything in his power to work for a peaceful solution with the Jews. I believe that the Government of Transjordan would have been glad to see His Majesty's Government having an effective representative in Tel Aviv during these difficult times. I am sure that Abdullah has done everything to work for a peaceful solution, which is in his interests, and to maintain his loyalty to the British who placed him in his seat at Amman and his brother on the throne of Iraq. No fault can be alleged against him. If any attack were made across the Jordan we should be bound to go to his aid by every obligation of treaty and of honour.

There is this question—I think the last important one to which I wish to refer—of the Arab refugees, on which the right hon Gentleman dwelt with emphasis and with indignant eloquence. Certainly, it involves much human suffering. The right hon Gentleman's remark about the policy I put in a memorandum in 1922 shows how very superficial is his knowledge of this question. The whole point of our settlement was that immigration was to be free, but not beyond the limits of economic absorptive power. We could not have had it said that newcomers were coming in, pushing out those who had lived there for centuries. But the newcomers who were coming in brought work and employment with them, and the means of sustaining a much larger population than had lived in Palestine and Transjordan. They brought the hope with them of a far larger population than existed in Palestine at the time of Our Lord. One has only to look up

13

to the hills that once were cultivated and then were defaced by centuries of medieval barbarism, to see what has been accomplished.

In twenty-five years the Jewish population of Palestine doubled or more than doubled, but so did the Arab population of the same areas of Palestine. As the Jews continued to reclaim the country, plant the orange groves, develop the water system, electricity and so forth, employment and means of livelihood were found for ever-larger numbers of Arabs—400,000 or 500,000 more Arabs found their living there—and the relations of the two races in the Jewish areas were tolerable in spite of external distractions and all kinds of disturbances. General prosperity grew. The idea that only a limited number of people can live in a country is a profound illusion; it all depends on their co-operative and inventive power. There are more people today living twenty storeys above the ground in New York than were living on the ground in New York 100 years ago. There is no limit to the ingenuity of man if it is properly and vigorously applied under conditions of peace and justice.

When the British Government quitted the scene and the Arab armies from Syria, Transjordania and finally in considerable strength from Egypt rolled forward to extinguish the Jewish National Home, all this Arab population fled in terror to behind the advancing forces of their own religion. Their condition is most grievous, and I agree that it should certainly not be neglected by the Government. The one great remedial measure is peace and a lasting settlement. The Jews need the Arabs. If we can get peace the problem of the refugees will be reduced to one-third, possibly one-quarter, perhaps it will disappear altogether. I do not think we shall find—I make this prediction—that there will be, once fighting stops and some kind of partition is arranged, any difficulty in the great bulk of the present refugees returning to do work essential to the growing prosperity and development of the Jewish settlement in Palestine.

I thank the House very much for allowing me to speak at such length on this topic with which I have been connected for so many years, and on which I feel so very strongly and have always tried to form my own opinions. All this Debate is, of course, on a small scale compared with the sombre march of events throughout the world. But it is a disquieting thought that the mismanagement we notice here in the working model may perhaps be typical of what is proceeding over much wider spheres under the present Government. However that may be, His Majesty's Opposition cannot allow themselves to be involved in this Palestine fiasco and muddle. We must take this opportunity of severing ourselves beyond all doubt or question from these latest acts of mismanagement on the Palestine question. But also we must tonight make our protest against the course of action prolonged over nearly four years which has deprived Britain of the credit she had earned, and of the rights and interests she had acquired, and made her at once the mockery and scapegoat of so many States who have never made any positive contribution of their own.

LYNSKEY TRIBUNAL

---

27 *January—The Minister of Fuel and Power announces that consumers will have freedom of choice in their suppliers of coal as from 1 May.*

29 *January—Soviet Foreign Ministry issue a statement denouncing the Western Union and the proposed North Atlantic Pact, and accusing America and Britain of seeking 'world domination' through such pacts.*

28-29 *January—De facto recognition accorded to Israel by Great Britain, France, Belgium, Holland, Luxembourg, Australia and New Zealand.*

29 *January—Soviet Union, in a Note, requests Norway to clarify her attitude towards the proposed Atlantic Pact.*

30 *January—Weekly bacon ration restored to 2 oz.*

31 *January—US accords de jure recognition of Israel and Transjordan.*

2 *February—Debate on relations between Spain and Great Britain.*

3 *February—In a statement before the debate in the House of Commons on the report of the Lynskey Tribunal, Mr George Belcher states that he will resign from his seat in Parliament.*

[3 *February* 1949

I do not feel it necessary this afternoon to trespass long upon the attention of the House. I cannot feel that any party issue is involved. This House of Commons has shown itself vigilant in the protection of its honour, and has realized that it is with its honour that the dignity and strength of democratic Parliamentary institutions are concerned. The honour of the Labour Party, of the Conservative Party, of the Liberal Party are not the interests of those parties alone but of the British nation, whom all parties try to serve according to their light— or want of lights. Many odd things happen abroad, but we are all glad today to feel that there is no difference between us and the Socialist Government or between us and the Labour Party, or the great trade union institutions of our country upon the need to keep our public life clean and healthy and to root out corruption in any form.

The course and procedure which the Government adopted when these matters were brought to their notice were not prompted by any party interest. Indeed, it might well be thought that the procedure which they adopted was the least suited to their interests, and also most severe upon the persons concerned. Nevertheless, it is our considered view that the right course was to invoke the 1921 Act and have these matters examined by the statutory Tribunal.

We accept the recommendations and the Report of the statutory Tribunal. The Tribunal, in its good faith, impartiality, competence and independence cannot be impugned or challenged. There is no need for the House, in my view, to add to what they have said, and no need for them to subtract from it. The conduct of the Attorney-General, although a Minister of the Government involved, has been correct and unbiased. There is, therefore, no difference between the Government and the Opposition upon the steps which were taken by the Prime Minister and his colleagues in dealing with the lamentable matters with which they were confronted. Still less is there any suggestion that the Labour Government have not done their best to sustain those standards of decent behaviour and to condemn and punish any departure from those standards of which we have always been proud in this island. I have some other remarks to make, but these are definitely subordinated to the major premises which I have submitted to the House.

I am sorry that I cannot avoid making some comments on the personal issues involved. I am personally acquainted with Mr Gibson, who was recommended to me some time ago on high authority as a most suitable representative of the trade unions to help in the movement with which I and others were concerned for United Europe. When party trouble came, Mr Gibson did not desert us. I grieve indeed to see him fall into all this trouble. I cannot say, in the face of the Report, that he does not deserve to suffer, but we all feel that he has paid a very heavy penalty after all his long years of good service. He has acted with propriety in resigning his directorship of the Bank of England and also his position on the nationalized Electricity Board. This action on his part renders it unnecessary, it seems to me, for such issues to be further discussed in this House. We accept the Attorney-General's view that a criminal prosecution is not required by the process of law, and one is certainly glad to feel that it is not required for any other purpose. I should also like to make it clear that the Conservative Party will not tolerate any suggestion that the leaders of the great trade unions in this country are susceptible to the temptations of corruption, or that these vital organs in our system of government are not conducted in accordance with British traditions and standards.

I come now to the case of the hon Member for Sowerby (Mr

Belcher), to whose speech we could not listen without pain. He was a Minister of the Crown and a Member of this House. We are all glad that he has chosen himself to resign not only his office but his seat in Parliament. I do not feel that I can do otherwise in this matter than recall to the House the precedents which we followed on the last occasion when the procedure of the special statutory Tribunal was used. This special procedure of law was prescribed to deal, not only with matters where common criminalities and specific charges were involved, but with the special position, obligations and behaviour of Ministers of the Crown.

There is a gulf fixed between private conduct and that of persons in an official, and, above all, in a Ministerial position. The abuse or misuse for personal gain of the special powers and privileges which attach to office under the State is rightly deemed most culpable, and, quite apart from any question of prosecution under the law, is decisive in respect of Ministers. I do not think I can do better than quote the words which the Prime Minister himself used when Leader of the Opposition in 1936, thirteen years ago, on the J. H. Thomas case—the last occasion, I think, when this particular procedure of the statutory Tribunal was invoked. The right hon Gentleman said:

'The Debate today does not raise in any way at all a party issue. It is a mere House of Commons matter, concerning the honour of Members of this House . . . and the two Members concerned have been found by the Tribunal to have acted in a manner inconsistent with the position which they held in public life. I agree entirely with the Prime Minister that that alone is a very heavy punishment. Other consequences have followed, such as the necessity, which they have rightly realized, that they must vacate their seats, and I do not think that anyone of us would wish, by any word of ours, to add to this punishment. . . . We must all sympathize with the families of the Members who necessarily suffer, though entirely innocent, and I think we all have a very natural reluctance to pass judgment on others. We are all conscious of our own faults; at the same time, we must not allow our personal sympathy for men who are down to lead us to condone in any way the seriousness of the offences committed. It is our clear duty to vindicate the honour of this House. We owe that duty not only to this House but to democratic government and to the servants of the State. There are many attacks made on democratic government today, and any action of the nature of utilization of a public position for private gain cuts at the root of democratic government. The corruption which accompanies dictatorships is generally hidden; the corruption which enters into a democracy is brought to light and must be dealt with drastically, and if there is any suggestion at all, it is that, as a democratic assembly, we are bound to take action.'

That is what the Prime Minister, the then Leader of the Opposition, said thirteen years ago, and I must say that he has certainly lived up to his well-chosen words. [HON MEMBERS: 'Hear, hear.'] Holding the position which I do, and which he then held, I cannot find any better words upon this subject, which incidentally, in my opinion, dispose of the question of whether or not the seat of the hon Member for Sowerby should have been vacated by him. We are ready to accept the Government view that no prosecution is necessary in the case of the hon Member for Sowerby.

We are glad that the Tribunal has declared that no taint or reproach of corruption lies upon the various other Ministers whose names were mentioned during—to repeat the phrase which the right hon Gentleman has already quoted from Mr Baldwin—'the unthinking cruelty of modern publicity'. It certainly has been very unpleasant to see our papers clouded by these continuous accounts. It was, perhaps, their duty to report the Tribunal proceedings, but the pain that it must have caused to individuals whose names were mentioned casually and whose characters have been completely cleared, is one which we can most easily comprehend. I am bound to say that whereas the honour of those Ministers has been effectively cleared, the competence of some of them in the discharge of their departmental duties is not free from criticism in all respects and would seem to require at a later stage the attention of the Prime Minister. I must say that I think the head of a Department ought to know pretty well how his immediate Parliamentary subordinates are carrying on.

The right hon Gentleman at the end of his speech made certain proposals. There is to be a committee to inquire into how guidance can be given to Ministers in various respects, and the right hon Gentleman then spoke of some conversation which I gather he had had with you, Mr Speaker.

THE PRIME MINISTER [MR ATTLEE]: I think the right hon Gentleman has confused two things. One thing I said was that I propose to give guidance in a certain matter; the other was a question of an inquiry by a committee.

MR CHURCHILL: Yes, a committee to inquire into contact men. In addition there was a question of some change in the rules affecting entry of strangers and others into this House, and hospitalities which are shared or given here. We on this side of the House have not noticed the need for such changes, and it is very difficult to change the freedom which has been indulged in by Members of all parties in the House of

Commons. If it is abused, this is the kind of occasion which cleanses that abuse and makes it very unlikely that it will continue. If at times persons outside the House have come in as guests and paid for refreshments and so forth, all this will undoubtedly be stiffened up by what has occurred.

I am doubtful myself whether we should do well to take steps which, after all, do imply a reflection on the conduct of Members of the House of Commons as a whole. I do not like that. I should warn the Prime Minister that a great many more difficulties may be found in dealing with any evils of this kind that exist than there are in discerning cases when they have occurred. I therefore hope, before any decision should be taken with regard to making rules, that there will be some consultation between the leaders of all parties. After all, we are Members of Parliament, and if we cannot manage the conduct of our personal relationships within this building in a decent and reasonable manner, we have smudged ourselves in a manner which no statutory Tribunal has ever done.

I have said all I wish to say upon the Parliamentary and personal aspects of this painful incident which, as I have indicated, has already in my opinion received an amount of publicity beyond what was required for the strict cleanliness of our public life. I trust, however, that the most severe methods open to the law will be used against the disreputable persons who have been concerned in attempts to corrupt our public men or have been concerned in the processes which the Tribunal have censured. The House will have regretted to hear from the Attorney-General, though I cannot blame him, that he saw grave difficulty in prosecuting some of these figures, particularly the notorious figure, the so-called Stanley. The House will accept the assurance of the right hon and learned Gentleman that the full rigour of the law, such as it may be, will be applied to any persons who have been found by this Tribunal to be dabbling in corruption. By this I do not mean a measure of deportation but the subjection of the persons involved to whatever prosecution for criminal offences the law renders possible, subject, of course, to the full protection of the rights of the accused. If it is found that nothing can be done, I think it will be a disadvantage of our course of affairs to have people going around trying to suborn and attempting to lead people into evil courses, worming their way into their confidence, and so forth, and offering bribes from motives of corruption. Whether that sort of conduct succeeds or not, it should be visited with the utmost severity that the law allows. If we are told that the law does not allow, I am no judge there.

All this leads me to the last series of comments which I shall venture to offer to the House. We are all Britons and we are all brothers, and we are proud of our decent, tolerant, comprehending life at home. We have been brought up to believe that our standards are certainly not inferior to any other long-established or newly-formed system of society in the world, but we must beware of putting too great a strain on British human nature. Some time ago I ventured to remind the House of the French proverb: 'Chase Nature away, and she returns at the gallop.' If you destroy a free market you create a black market. If you make 10,000 regulations you destroy all respect for the law. As Burke said, although I have not been able before this Debate to find his exact words: 'Those who make professions above the ordinary customs of society will often be found in practice to fall far below them.'

This unpleasant case which has riveted the attention of the public, and which is before us now, warns us of perils to our society which cannot be warded off merely by inflicting severe penalties on those who are found guilty. There are the laws of the land—the ancient common law of England—which still remain to guide the vast English-speaking world. There is the immense force of public opinion in free and civilized countries. There are the honest and honourable conventions of British business life without the observance of which few men can obtain or maintain any position of responsibility in the commercial world. All these are needed to maintain a healthy, democratic civilization. If a whole vast catalogue of new crimes and penalties is suddenly brought into being, and a whole series of actions hitherto free and unchallenged in the ordinary play of daily life are to be judged shameful and punishable, Parliament must be careful to carry the public conscience with it. If the permission of State officials has to be sought in innumerable cases for all kinds of trivial but necessary and unavoidable transactions hitherto entirely untrammelled, you will be opening the door to difficulties, stresses and strains to which our social system has not hitherto been exposed. I was in the United States more than once during Prohibition. I saw there, with some complacency, a general breakdown and contempt of a law, imposed no doubt from the highest motives, but which did not carry with it the support of public opinion or fit the ordinary needs of the people.

We, on this side of the House, are convinced that the enforcement, or the attempted enforcement, as a peace-time policy, of thousands of war-time regulations by scores of thousands of war-time or post-war officials, whatever penalties Parliament may decree, will result in a breaking down of that respect for law, custom and tradition which has played so large a part in the reputation of our peoples and was so vital a factor in our survival during the period of mortal peril through which we have passed. That is no doubt a theme which will play its part in our future discussions, and its lessons must be impressed upon the nation. I wish to end where I began, namely, that we approve the course which the Government have taken in appointing the Tribunal; that we accept the measured and carefully limited conclusions to which it has come; that we are glad to see so many public men whose names have been mentioned, as I feared they would be by idle or malicious gossip, cleared from reproach; and above all that we repudiate all slanders upon the general conduct of British public life where questions of tolerating personal corruption and dishonour are concerned.

RECRUITING FOR THE FORCES

A BROADCAST TALK
17 FEBRUARY 1949

---

4 *February—Attempted assassination of Shah of Persia in Teheran.*

5 *February—Provisional recommendations as to the form and functions of the Council of Europe issued by the Permanent Commission of the Brussels Treaty Powers.*

6 *February—Ban on political processions in Metropolitan area of London lifted.*

5-10 *February—Professor Ernst Reuter, Oberburgermeister of the Western Sectors of Berlin, visits London for discussions with Mr Bevin, and Paris for discussions with M. Schuman.*

8 *February—Cardinal Mindszenty found guilty by the Hungarian Court of treason, espionage and currency offences and sentenced to life imprisonment.*

9 *February—Supplementary estimates presented to the House of Commons showing that an increase of £58,455,000 will be required for the National Health Services.*

10 *February—Prime Minister announces that a Royal Commission on Lotteries, Betting and Gambling will be set up.*
  All-party Parliamentary group formed to support European Movement.

12 *February—The Irish High Commissioner in London issues a statement to the effect that while Eire is in sympathy with the aims of the Atlantic Pact, she could not co-operate in it while the Partition issue is still outstanding.*

14 *February—The First Assembly of the State of Israel held in Jerusalem.*

15 *February—White paper published of the Government's statement on defence for 1949-50 showing that provision had been made for a defence budget of £759,860,000 compared with the 1948-1949 estimates of £692,000,000.*

[17 *February* 1949

I come forward tonight to support the Prime Minister, Sir Stafford Cripps, Mr Eden and many others who have spoken on this subject, in the effort His Majesty's Government are making to help recruiting for the Regular Army and the Territorials and indeed for all the Services. The action which the Socialist Government have taken in establishing compulsory national service in this island in time of peace commands the respect of all parties, not least for the reason that it was not particularly popular. But the introduction of compulsory service for the fighting forces makes a very heavy impact upon our pre-war system. It raises many problems, particularly for the Regular Army, and very few of these have so far been solved.

The Regular Army has not only to provide the spearhead of our defence against a sudden attack, but now it must be the training-machine for large numbers of young men who are called up or who may be called up under the National Service Act. This means that our Regular Army must have a very strong professional structure of teachers and leaders in order at once to preserve its glorious traditions and keep abreast of the times. It also means that the Regular Army can provide for the serious-minded, experienced soldier a professional career, which should constitute his life's work and be a guarantee of his later years. When I think of all the youngish men, many in their early prime, that are going around today, men who have dared, endured and learned so much on the field of battle, I cannot doubt that numbers will be willing and will be forthcoming to join on a long-service basis the Regular Army, and make their way and rise in a profession honour-able to its members and vital to the State.

The Territorial Army, which succeeded the old volunteers of the nineteenth century, is equally indispensable to any plan made by any Government in these present dangerous times. It is a citizens' army of men who have to earn their livelihood before they do their military work. They will form the structure in time of peace upon which in time of war—and no one wants war; we wish to prevent war—the trained reserves arising from national service will be moulded into many famous regiments which represent to us and remind us of the great deeds of the past. There can be no effective Territorial Army without a strong volunteer element made up of the best kind of men and women we have got—and we have got some good ones still. I earnestly appeal to the young veterans of the late war to come for-ward and join their Territorial units. People say the times are hard. There are many things we do not like. The Government have com-pulsory powers. If they want us, why do they not issue their orders? But that is not the way in which the victorious British soldiers of the last war should approach their decision. The volunteer element in our national life, the willingness, nay the urge to do more than is required by law, or required just to keep your head above water is a character-istic of the British spirit without which we should not have survived.

Some have told you of the advantages of joining the Territorials:

good comrades, jolly pals, pleasant holiday camps. That is all true, but in my opinion our recruiting campaign for the Territorial Army will only be a success if it makes its appeal to the men who wish to fortify their lives by a special sacrifice for our country, which we love so dearly and which so many of those to whom I now appeal saved from shame and ruin. A suitable man with the right gifts and turn of mind who joins his Territorial battalion or battery now would add to his own stature among his fellow men. It is true that he volunteers to face heavier risks than he otherwise would, but so do the fire brigades and the lifeboat men, and so do lots of people when honour's call rings clear.

The fact of making an extra sacrifice of leisure and life's strength and of undertaking a special obligation to bear a bit of the extra weight gives a man a rightful status of dignity and self-respect. It is a matter which each must settle with his conscience. The more awkward or dreary many things may be in our life, the brighter shine these acts of the spirit. Here is the flame which enabled us, as I firmly believe, to save the freedom of the world and the life of our island in the war. It must not die now or we shall all die with it. A man may well be proud in himself, though he must tell it to none, if, regardless whether things fall well or ill, or whether he likes them or not, he comes forward to do his bit—and a bit more, too.

COUNCIL OF THE EUROPEAN MOVEMENT

A SPEECH AT THE SALLE DES BEAUX ARTS, BRUSSELS
26 FEBRUARY 1949

---

16 *February—Announcement made in London and Washington of agreement for an additional loan of $3,000,000 (£750,000) to the UK under ERP bringing ECA loans to Britain in the first year of the Marshall Plan to $313,000,000 (£78,250,000).*

17 *February—Debate on the Supplementary Estimates for the Ministry of Health.*

18 *February—Total supplies flown to Berlin by the RAF and USAF air lift reaches 1,000,000 tons during the 253 days of blockade.*

22 *February—Economic Secretary to the Treasury states that the yield from purchase tax for the year 1948 amounted to £300,000,000.*

23 *February—Mr Christopher Mayhew, British Under-Secretary for Foreign Affairs, speaking at Lake Success, says that the United Kingdom is within sight of balancing its total overseas payments and that she has long passed the stage of talking about recovery.*

25–28 *February—Inaugural Session of the International Council of the European Movement held in Brussels.*

26 *February—Sir Stafford Cripps repudiates Mr Mayhew's speech at Lake Success and issues a statement pointing out that Britain's recovery is not complete and that she still needs US assistance.*

[26 February 1949

After each of the fearful wars which have ravaged the lives and homes of mankind, the hopes of humanity have centred upon the creation of an instrument of world government capable, at least, of maintaining peace and law among men. We have all been grieved and alarmed by the fact that the new United Nations Organization should have been so torn and broken. It has made a far less hopeful start in these first four years than its predecessor, the League of Nations.

In spite of the faithful efforts that have been made by the representatives of many countries, great and small, the new organization, to which we had looked for guidance in our problems and guardianship in our dangers, has already been reduced to a brawling cockpit where taunts and insults may be flung back and forth. An institution in this condition cannot have the authority to prevent the approach of a new war and is in danger of losing the confidence and even the respect of those who were most ardent for its creation.

The main cause of this disaster is, of course, the fact that the world is sundered by the aggression of the Communist ideology supported by the armed power of Soviet Russia. But there are also fundamental defects in the structure of the United Nations Organization which must be corrected if any progress is to be made. I had always felt during the war that the structure of world security could only be founded on regional organizations. Regional organizations are encouraged by the constitution of the United Nations, but they have so far played no effective part. In consequence, the supreme body has been cumbered and confused by a mass of questions, great and small, about which only a babel of harsh voices can be heard. Large regional units are the necessary elements in any scheme of world government. It is vain to build the dome of the temple of peace without the pillars on which alone it can stand.

Just as in a great army it is necessary to have army groups; just as in a division it is necessary to have battalions, so there must be these intermediate organizations to make coherent and effective action possible at the supreme summit. What would happen to a military system where there was nothing between the supreme HQ and the commanders of all the different divisions? What plan could emerge from such a concourse? Such a method could only lead through chaos to defeat. Therefore, I believe that the creation of regional organisms is an inseparable part of any structure of world security.

It is the task and duty of the regional bodies to settle a vast number of regional questions among themselves within their own circle and to send representatives of the highest authority from their unit to the supreme world instrument. Unless and until this is done the United Nations Organization will be a failure and even a mockery.

Tonight we meet here, working patiently together, for the building of one and, in some respects, the greatest of the regional organizations. We work here for European Unity and for the creation of the necessary apparatus by which United Europe can become a principal factor in the life and peace of the world, and a worthy member of the world organization. If we are striving to raise Europe from the awful welter of misery and ruin into which we have been plunged, it is not only for the sake of Europe but for the sake of the whole world that we toil. It is not only to the regional organization but to the cause of world government that our loyalties are directed.

We are all encouraged by the progress which the European Movement is making. We feel conscious of the inherent force of the cause we serve and the idea which guides us. It shines like a bright, steady light. In the confusion and exhaustion of our age it shines all the brighter because of the storms which gather. Although we are a regional organism, it is not only geography that unites us. We find our principle of union in the moral sphere. We take our stand on human rights, as set forth in the Charter of Human Rights proclaimed by the United Nations Organization. Any European country that sincerely accepts and adopts the principles there set forth will be welcomed by the European Union.

Alas, there are a number of ancient and famous European States which are no longer free to take their stand for those human rights of which they have so great need. The yoke of the Kremlin oligarchy has descended upon them and they are the victims of a tyranny more subtle and merciless than any hitherto known to history. We are glad to see them represented here by men and women who have escaped from the trap that has closed upon their fellow-countrymen. It is this moral bond which first of all unites us.

In the report of the Executive Committee, our principles are set forth with clarity: love of freedom; hostility to totalitarianism of every kind; the humble and conscientious search for truth; respect for the human personality and for the individual as an individual. These moral values, founded alike on Christian faith and charity and on the critical spirit of rationalism, are the message of our 2,000-year-old European civilization and culture. Let us make sure that, enjoying as we do this common inheritance, we take all necessary steps lest it be wasted or cast away.

At The Hague Congress in May, two proposals for practical action were made: the creation of a European Assembly; and the setting up of a European Court for the enforcement of Human Rights. The European Assembly is now on the point of being achieved. The responsible governments of all our countries have reached their agreements. We have now to take the second step forward and to try to establish, as the practical result of our meeting here, the setting up of a European Court of Human Rights. Such a court in no way challenges the authority of a world court, but it may well be that the principles laid down by the United Nations will be better and more effectively interpreted by courts in the more limited and homogeneous area of regional units: Let Europe judge Europe.

We have the Charter of Human Rights, and we must have a European means of defending and enforcing it. It must not be possible that, within the boundaries of United Europe, such a legal atrocity could be perpetrated as that which has confronted us all in the case of

Cardinal Mindszenty. Here you have the crime of religious persecution committed on an innocent man under the direct orders of Moscow, and carried through with all those features of police government with which we are familiar in trials under the Soviets.

There must be means by which such events in any of the countries with which we can consort can be brought to the test of impartial justice. We cannot rest content with the division of Europe into two parts—the free and the unfree. The Europe we seek to unite is *all* Europe; and in our Movement we must strive, by every means in our power, to help bring about conditions in which our fellow-Europeans, now living in the satellite States of Russia, will be united with us.

The task of our Movement is to foster, encourage and develop the sense of being Europeans, a pride in Europe and what she has stood for, and confidence in the greatness of our common mission in the future. These sentiments can only be brought about by Europeans in different countries learning to know each other better. In all this work the new European Assembly can play a vital part. By its discussions, which will be reported in the Press and on the radio, it can create and express a European public opinion, a common European point of view, and the sense of all that we have in common.

We are all agreed that our ultimate aim—the unity and freedom of the whole of Europe—can only be achieved by stages. Our first task is to unite the free countries which are working together under the Marshall Plan. We recognize that individual countries have special problems for which solutions must be found. In Switzerland, in Sweden, in Germany, there are special conditions which must be patiently studied. Great Britain is herself the centre of a free and world-wide commonwealth of States. We are sure in our country that a satisfactory solution can be found whereby we can develop our new association with Europe without in the slightest degree weakening the sacred ties which unite Britain with her daughter States across the oceans.

Europe, which we are striving to revive, must be independent but not isolationist. We desire that our regional structure all be harmoniously fitted into a system of world government, but we stretch our hands out in gratitude and goodwill across the ocean to the other half of the free world, whose generous help has been forthcoming to assist our stricken continent on the path of recovery. We express our admiration of the great United States and of the part they are playing, not only in the restoration of European economy, but also in our security and defence.

The Brussels Pact united the five Western democracies in a scheme of common defence, and we in Britain are glad once again to take our stand with the gallant Belgian Army against the perils of the future. The Atlantic Pact will give us all the guarantee that the cause of freedom in the Old World will not be aggressively assailed without effective aid from the great Republic across the ocean.

This, therefore, is the hour in which we should move forward with confidence, offering to all the men in all the lands the human rights and freedom which we ourselves enjoy and for the preservation of which— if ever it should be necessary—we should be prepared to do our duty whatever the cost might be.

NEW YORK

A SPEECH AT A DINNER GIVEN BY MR HENRY R. LUCE
AT THE RITZ–CARLTON HOTEL
25 MARCH 1949

---

27 *February—Communist Party in London announce their intention of putting forward* 100 *candidates at the next general election.*

4 *March—Security Council at Lake Success approve Israel's application for membership of the United Nations by* 9 *votes to* 1 *and* 1 *abstention; the USA, Soviet Union, France, China, Canada, Argentine, Norway, Cuba and the Ukraine voting in favour; Egypt opposing, and Great Britain abstaining.*

Application for membership of the United Nations Organization by North Korea rejected by 8 *votes to* 2 *(USSR and Ukraine).*

Announcement from Moscow that M. Vyshinsky is to succeed M. Molotov as Foreign Minister, and M. Gromyko is to succeed M. Vyshinsky as Deputy Foreign Minister.

6 *March—End of trial in Bulgaria of* 15 *pastors who had 'confessed' to espionage for Britain and USA.*

12 *March—British Note presented to the Bulgarian Government protesting against the trial of the pastors and stating the 'confessions' are viewed with suspicion by HM Government.*

14 *March—Debate in the House of Commons on the East African Groundnuts Scheme on an Opposition motion to reduce the Civil Vote on Account by £1,000,000. Motion defeated by* 231 *votes to* 113.

15 *March—Air Estimates debate in the House of Commons, during which the Air Minister makes a statement on the policy of increasing the striking force of the RAF.*

Clothes rationing ends after nearly eight years.

16 *March—Australian House of Representatives passes a Bill to be called the Commonwealth Scientific and Industrial Research Organization for the purpose of preventing the leakage of research and defence secrets.*

18 *March—The text of the North Atlantic Treaty issued.*

20 *March—The three Western Military Governments in Berlin announce that the 'West Mark' is to be the only legal tender in Western Berlin.*

21 *March—The Home Secretary, Mr Chuter Ede, reimposes the political processions ban in the Metropolitan Police district.*

I am extremely complimented to be invited here tonight and to find myself your guest amidst a gathering of Americans among whom I can discern many doughty comrades in our common struggle and who, taken together, represent a powerful living element in the future and in the power of the United States. I thank you very much for all the kind things that you have said.

You yourself have rendered great services. The wonderful publications which spread so widely through the land and put quality and art and point and pith and so forth in their vanguard, these are in themselves great contributions to the life and strength not only of the United States but of the English-speaking world. This great company, these old friends and comrades, gives me confidence and I am glad to come here and express my profound thanks on behalf of Britain and on behalf of Western Europe, of free Europe, as I have some credentials to do—for all you have done and are doing.

Gentlemen—many nations have arrived at the summit of the world but none, before the United States, on this occasion, has chosen that moment of triumph, not for aggrandizement, but for further self-sacrifice—sacrifice for the causes by which the life and strength of mankind is refreshed. The United States has shown itself more worthy of trust and honour than any government of men or associations of nations, that has ever reached pre-eminence by their action on the morrow of the common victory won by all. I wish to express the thanks of my own dear island and of its Empire, Commonwealth and also of the many countries in Western Europe who are drawing together on the broad ideals of Anglo-Saxon, British-American, call it what you will, unity, which alone gives an opportunity for the further advance of the human race.

Gentlemen, some time ago, you may possibly remember, I made a speech in Missouri at Fulton—I got into great trouble for that. But now not so much. Now it is thought better of. And I was very glad to see that General Marshall, that great statesman and soldier—I do not know whether you put soldier or statesman first in regard to so eminent a man—General Marshall has created this policy of the Marshall Aid, which shall ever bear his name—not because of what happens in the three or four years of the Aid but because of its effect as a turning point in the history of the world. General Marshall played his part, and then, we have now come to the Atlantic Pact, which when Mr Attlee kindly showed it to me before it became public—but after it was settled—I thought it was one of the most important documents ever signed by large communities of human beings and certainly indicates a very considerable advance in opinion as far as the United States of America are concerned. Well, there you are—you're in it now, because there's no way out, but still if we pool our luck and share our fortunes I think you will have no reason to regret it.

But what has brought this great change from the time when I was so scolded three years ago for what I said at Fulton? And I do remember Governor Dewey coming down here to back me up at that rather bleak and raw moment when I spoke here in New York. The Governor knows how to take a bump and I've had some of that, too. My father— I remember some words that my father spake when I was an urchin —I remember that he said a man who can't take a knockdown blow isn't worth a damn. Well, I've always tried to live up to that and on the whole it's quite a healthy process. How has this great change from the atmosphere three years ago, when I spoke at Fulton, and now address you here—this distinguished gathering here—how has that great change been accomplished? No one could possibly have done it but Mr Stalin. He is the one. No enemy of Russia, no—and I was never an enemy of Russia—no anti-Communist or no Conservative Republican gathering, missionaries, agitators, propaganda—none of them—if they worked night and day could ever have achieved the extraordinary change of opinion, change of conviction, change of mood, change of attitude and policy which has taken place in the last two years except the Soviet Government.

And that brings me to a question which we must ask ourselves. What is the explanation of the Soviet policy? Why have they deliberately united the free world against them? I will hazard the answer. These men in the Kremlin are very capable men; they do not act on the spur of the moment; profound deliberations take place in conclaves long welded together and any mistake made by any member of the company may be seriously viewed and punished. Yes—they do not let themselves go like some of us politicians do in the democratic countries. Well, how is it then—that they have deliberately united the free world against them? It is, I am sure, because they feared the friendship of the West more than they do its hostility. They can't afford to allow free and friendly intercourse between their country and those they control, and the rest of the world. They daren't see it develop—the coming and going and all the easements and tolerances which come from the agreeable contacts of nations and of individuals. They can't afford it. The Russians must not see what goes on outside and the world must not see what goes on inside the Soviet domain. That is, in my opinion, the explanation. After all if you were one of the fourteen men in the Kremlin—holding down hundreds of millions of people, aiming at the rule of the world—you might well feel that your prime interest was, at all costs, to keep up the barriers. I believe that their motive is self-preservation—not for Russia—but for themselves. Of course going out of office in Russia isn't quite as easy a business as it may be here or over the other side of the ocean. You lose the election, you may lose your life. It's very high stakes they play for—these fourteen men—and I'm sure that self-preservation for themselves lies at the root of this strange, extraordinary, unreasonable policy which has caused them deliberately to alienate all the generous sympathy there was for the brave Russian armies who fought so nobly in the war.

And thus we have come to what is called the cold war, a form of relationship between nations unprecedented in history, unparalleled in history. Never have there been such things that are happening now published all over the world. The insults, the taunts, the affronts, the ultimatums, the holdings up and so forth, and American bombers based in British airports and Soviet plans being pushed in every country to undermine or overthrow the existing state of civilization. All this— never in peace has been possible, but it is going on now and it is called the cold war.

You would like me to examine some of these questions with you tonight because I don't want to trespass upon so important an audience except to put to them points of real vital consequence. And I put this question. Are we winning the cold war?

It's a very important one for all of us, and for our families and our children. We wonder what world they will inherit and come into. Are we winning the cold war? Well this can't be decided, I think, by looking at Europe alone. We must first look to the East. The worst event, I'm sure Mr Luce will agree with me in this—I'm sure the worst event since the fighting stopped has been the subjugation of a large part of China by Communism. There's your most formidable event. Now mind you, I think you have done quite right not to be diverted to make great undue efforts there at this moment, but the American interest in China is enormous. I was very much astonished when I came over here after Pearl Harbour to find the estimate of values which seemed to prevail in high American quarters, even in the highest, about China. Some of them thought that China would make as great a contribution to victory in the war as the whole British Empire together. Well, that astonished me very much. Nothing that I picked up afterwards led me to think that my astonishment was ill-founded. And it was said to me—well, China is an immense factor in the world, an immense population of intelligent, gifted, cultivated people, charming people with so many virtues, and so on. Well, I was thinking what part they would be able to play in our victory. I think on the whole you will not find a large profit item entered on that side of the ledger, but that doesn't alter our regard for the Chinese people. But what has happened now? It's very important, and while I think the decision of the United States is quite right, I am astonished they are not more concerned about it than they appear to be. Here I would like to congratulate you upon, and pay a tribute to, the work of General MacArthur in Japan. [*Applause.*] He has seemed to show a genius in peace equal to the high renown he gained in war.

In my view you don't want to knock a man down except to pick him up in a better frame of mind. That is my view about all these things that happen in the world—and you may pick him up in a better frame of mind. And that is a thing to think about. I say that the Atlantic Pact, in my view, would naturally be followed at no lengthy interval by a Pacific Pact which would deal with that immense portion of the globe.

Well, so much for the East. But a great advance has been made in the West in this cold war. Take the success of the Berlin Airlift, which arose largely from American conviction that it could be done. I will say, quite frankly, without any special knowledge, I wondered really whether it could be done and on the face of it, it seemed rather odd— I mean, carrying coal by air, and so on. But still it has been a great success. Time has been gained for peace. The efficiency of the American and British air forces has been greatly sustained by the enormous practice in almost active service conditions which they have had and are having over all these long months, not without their sacrifices in life. And lastly, and this I care about very much, the airlift into Berlin has won the heart of Germany—gathered the heart of Germany over to us—as nothing else could have done and shown them that their choice should be with the Western Nations and with progress and with freedom and that they should not be drawn into the hideous, Communist entanglement which many of them might in their despair otherwise have succumbed to. I think it is a wonderful thing, although when we look at the record of crimes that have been brought out, it seems hard to forget at all the past. I assure you you must forget the past. You must obliterate all parts of the past which are not useful to the future. You must regard the re-entry of Germany into the family of European nations as an event which the Western World must desire and must, if possible, achieve.

Gentlemen—three weeks ago I was in Brussels. I was addressing a meeting of 30,000 people—very friendly, even enthusiastic; 250 Communists were removed or thought it better to be silent—but there were these 30,000 people in this great square at Brussels, and I could feel their anxiety. I could feel, as I spoke, their anxiety—their fear. After all, they haven't got the Atlantic Ocean between them and danger. They haven't even got the Channel and the Channel is pretty good, as we showed you in the last war—and showed others. In ten days—in ten days perhaps the Soviet armour might be in Brussels. Here were these 30,000 people—good, faithful, decent people—naturally they know about it all. The Soviets have a new technique developing for what they do to countries they overrun, and what they will do to the countries they expect to overrun. It is a very elaborate technique—a Swedish professor came and explained it to me at length —he's writing a book about it—it is to liquidate all outstanding personalities in every class and walk of life. To liquidate them so as to have nothing below but a mass of ordinary people whom they can rule like the Communist Party in Russia rules the enormous mass of unfortunate Russian serfs. That is their technique, and they have got lists all made out of the different countries outside the Iron Curtain and of the people and so on. I don't suppose they've troubled to make a list here but they might find quite a lot in this room. But it's a grim thing to have that peril so little away. And while I was talking to these people—in the beautiful surroundings there—I could feel their fear and anxiety, but when I spoke of the United States being with us in this matter of European freedom, I felt a wave of hope in this great concourse and I know you will not let them down in regard to any matter in which you have pledged the word of the great Republic.

Well, gentlemen, it isn't only in Belgium. You look at Europe. The hideous process of the subjugation of Czechoslovakia should be studied in the utmost detail. It's a work of art—the methods and so on. Well, the Czechs live on and no nation in bondage should despair, but I was glad to see the American veterans tonight displaying a placard on which is written 'Uncle Joe, what happened to Masaryk?'— a friend of ours and fighter in the war, a struggler for freedom. There is terrible danger and peril and if you have not got these great barriers of salt water or short effective barriers, fear must come into their hearts, but that fear is removed because they are relying upon the valour, virtue and the giant strength of the United States.

And France—they have a situation with Thorez, this deserter, saying that this third of the population who vote Communist will fight against their country if the Russians have to invade it or have a chance of invading it. Italy—shattered and ruined in many ways but making a great recovery. In all these countries under direst peril they do look to you to give them the strength, not only to protect them, but to give them the strength to stand up for their own liberties. I don't want to have the whole of the world, of Britain and all that hanging on to the United States to be kept going by them, but you must do enough to animate them—that is what you are doing and that is what the Marshall Aid and the Atlantic Pact have done—is to animate these countries and enable them to come forward more and more in their own strength.

If it was not for the aid of the United States and, I will say, of Great Britain (which counts), they would all go down like ninepins before the Communist menace. I tell you—it's no use arguing with a Communist. It's no good trying to convert a Communist, or persuade him. You can only deal with them on the following basis. I have had some experience in direct contact with the highest authorities, under the most favourable conditions, and I can tell you that you can only do it by having superior force on your side on the matter in question—and they must also be convinced that you will use—you will not hesitate to use—these forces, if necessary, in the most ruthless manner. You have not only to convince the Soviet Government that you have superior force—that they are confronted by superior force—but that you are not restrained by any moral consideration if the case arose from using that force with complete material ruthlessness. And that is the greatest chance of peace, the surest road to peace. Then the Communists will make a bargain—I have made bargains with them and they will keep the bargains so long as it suits them—and a good bargain—I mean good in the best sense of the word—may well last for quite a long time—may well suit both parties for quite a long time. I cannot tell how it will go but this I am sure, that if you wish for peace, it is absolutely necessary that you should be the stronger—I say you—we, all of us, we're in it—we should be the stronger and that they should know that we stop at nothing that honour allows. But you will ask—I will press this a little more if you will permit me, and my argument is a whole, is integral—you will ask: Is time on our side and the question whether more decided action should be taken?— Now I have reached a conclusion for the moment upon that. And I do not think any violent or precipitate action should be taken now. I do not regard war as inevitable. I do not think so. I think we still have control to preserve our cause without the world being plunged in another frightful struggle.

Well, now, do not let us however delude ourselves with the idea that we can make armies strong enough in the next year or two which could hold the front of civilization in Europe. I do not think we can. But they're all getting welded together under this pressure.

Unities are being formed which would never otherwise have been formed. Give them a little time to knit and set. Let us have it. Our forces are getting stronger, actually and relatively, than they were a year ago. We have probably a year or two before other people are able to make the atomic bomb. And once they are able to make it, then they have to make it, which is another phase, measured by considerable time periods. Well, I heard a lot about that. But—gentlemen, it is sad after all our victory and triumph and all that we hoped for and so on, to find not peace and ease and hope and comfort, but only the summons to further endeavour. But that is life! After our great victory we did hope that the struggle for freedom would be decided in our time, but however long the struggle lasts, British and American peoples will not weary of it, or if weary of it, they will not desist from it, because victory or defeat are things which happen, but duty is a thing which is compulsory and has to go on irrespective, and carries with it its own rewards whatever the upshot of the struggle may be.

We are now confronted with something which is quite as wicked but much more formidable than Hitler, because Hitler had only the Herrenvolk stuff and anti-Semitism. Well, somebody said about that —a good starter, but a bad stayer. That's all he had. He had no theme. But these fourteen men in the Kremlin have their hierarchy and a church of Communist adepts whose missionaries are in every country as a fifth column, and not only a fifth column, in your country, ours, everywhere, and so on, with a feeling that they may be running a risk, but if their gamble comes off they will be the masters of the whole land in which they are a minority at the present time. They will be the Quislings with power to rule and dominate all the rest of their fellow countrymen. Therefore they have a good prospective advantage. It is certain in my opinion that Europe would have been communized and London would have been under bombardment some time ago, but for the deterrent of the atomic bomb in the hands of the United States. That is my firm belief and that governs the situation today. Sometimes one looks at the terrible alternative. Fancy if they had got it first. Well, I feel that sense that we all should have in our troubled journey—pilgrimage—that Divine protection has shielded those who faithfully sustained the causes of freedom and of justice.

One comfort I've got today is that the democratic nations are not fooled so easily by Stalin as they were by Hitler. You must have noticed that. Whenever Hitler said 'this is the last territorial claim I shall make, I need no more Czechs' and so on—they all used to turn around upon me in those days and say, there are you, now you see how wrong you were! Now you see it's all settled, it's all happy!

38

Look, this is a peace move, it's all friendly, and so on. Well, once bit, twice shy—and I notice now that a very different and far more critical mood about manoeuvring offers by dictators prevails in the most enlightened circles on this side of the Atlantic.

I will say just a word about my own country before I sit down— a word or two about the British scene. Now I'm opposed to the— you might have heard perhaps—I'm opposed to the present Government. But that's our own affair. Like you, we settle our own affairs in our own way by our own political system. We don't want foreigners interfering any more than you would like any of us to interfere with you. That's all right. And I'm grateful for all the aid you have given to my country, but I say—do not underrate the strength of Britain. And do not ever lose sight of the fact that Britain is an absolutely vital necessity to the strength and future of the United States.

You may be larger and we may be the older. You may be the stronger, sometimes we may be the wiser. But let us talk it out like friends and brothers, as we shall, and as we can, because we can understand each other with greater perfection than any two great groupings of the human race have ever been able to before. I said at this speech I made at Fulton, which I got scolded for, I said—don't suppose that half a century from now you will not see 70,000,000 or 80,000,000 of Britons spread about the world and united in defence of our traditions, our way of life and the world causes which you and we espouse. Well, added to all that, you have of power in this world, that fraternal association of the English-speaking world which I plead, far greater than alliances and not so formal, that fraternal association will give the freedom and security that is needed, that we demand for ourselves, and that we together, perhaps alone, can bestow on other mortals.

Forward then! Forward, let us go forward, without fear into the future and let us dread naught when duty calls!

THE TWENTIETH CENTURY—ITS PROMISE AND ITS REALIZATION

A SPEECH AT THE MASSACHUSETTS INSTITUTE OF TECHNOLOGY, BOSTON
31 MARCH 1949

24-26 March—At the Liberal Party Assembly at Hastings it is announced that the Liberal Party will put 600 candidates into the field at the next general election.
31 March—Newfoundland officially enters the Canadian Confederation.
  Soviet Union issues a memorandum protesting against the North Atlantic Treaty.

[31 *March* 1949

I am honoured by your wish that I should take part in the discussions of the Massachusetts Institute of Technology. We have suffered in Great Britain by the lack of colleges of university rank in which engineering and the allied subjects are taught. Industrial production depends on technology and it is because the Americans, like the pre-war Germans, have realized this and created institutions for the advanced training of large numbers of high-grade engineers to translate the advances of pure science into industrial technique, it is for that reason that their output per head and consequent standard of life are so high. It is surprising that England, which was the first country to be industrialized, has nothing of comparable stature. If tonight I strike other notes than those of material progress, it implies no want of admiration for all the work you have done and are doing. My aim, like yours, is to be guided by balance and proportion.

The outstanding feature of the twentieth century has been the enormous expansion in the numbers who are given the opportunity to share in the larger and more varied life which in previous periods was reserved for the few and for the very few. This process must continue at an increasing rate. If we are to bring the broad masses of the people in every land to the table of abundance, it can only be by the tireless improvement of all our means of technical production, and by the diffusion in every form of education of an improved quality to scores of millions of men and women. Yea, even in this darkling

40

hour I have faith that this process will go on. I rejoice in Tennyson's celebrated lines:

> Men, my brothers, men, the workers,
>   ever reaping something new;
> That which they have done but earnest of the
>   things that they shall do.

I was, however, a little disquieted, I must admit, that you find it necessary to debate the question, to quote Dean Burchard's opening address, 'whether the problem of world production yielding at least a minimum living to the whole population can be solved, and whether man has so destroyed the resources of his world that he may be doomed to die of starvation'. If, with all the resources of modern science, we find ourselves unable to avert world famine, we shall all be to blame, but a peculiar responsibility would rest upon the scientists. I do not believe they will fail, but if they do, or perhaps were not allowed to succeed, the consequences would be very unpleasant because it is quite certain that mankind would not agree to starve equally, and there might be some very sharp disagreements about how the last crust was to be shared. This would simplify our problem, as our greatest intellectual authorities here will readily admit, in an unduly primordial manner.

I frankly confess that I feel somewhat overawed in addressing this vast scientific and learned audience on the subject which your panels are discussing. I have no technical and no university education, and have just had to pick up a few things as I went along. Therefore I speak with a diffidence, which I hope to overcome as I proceed, on these profound scientific, social and philosophic issues, each of which claims a lifelong study for itself, and are now to be examined, as schoolmen would say, not only in their integrity but in their relationship, meaning thereby not only one by one but all together.

I was so glad that in the first instance you asked me to talk about the past rather than to peer into the future, because I know more about the past than I do about the future, and I was well content that the President of the United States, whose gift of prophecy was so remarkably vindicated by recent electoral results, should have accepted that task. We all regret that his heavy State duties prevent him from being here tonight. I shall therefore have to try to do a little of the peering myself.

For us in Britain, the nineteenth century ended amid the glories of the Victorian era, and we entered upon the dawn of the twentieth in high hope for our country, our Empire and the world. The latter and larger part of the nineteenth century had been the period of liberal advance (liberal with a small 'l'). In 1900 a sense of moving hopefully forward to brighter, broader, easier days predominated. Little did we guess that what has been called the Century of the Common Man would witness as its outstanding feature more common men killing each other with greater facilities than any other five centuries put together in the history of the world. But we entered this terrible twentieth century with confidence. We thought that with improving transportation nations would get to know each other better. We believed that as they got to know each other better they would like each other more, and that national rivalries would fade in a growing international consciousness. We took it almost for granted that science would confer continual boons and blessings upon us, would give us better meals, better garments and better dwellings for less trouble, and thus steadily shorten the hours of labour and leave more time for play and culture. In the name of ordered but unceasing progress, we saluted the age of democracy expressing itself ever more widely through parliaments freely and fairly elected on a broad or universal franchise. We saw no reason then why men and women should not shape their own home life and careers without being cramped by the growing complexity of the State, which was to be their servant and the protector of their rights. You had the famous American maxim 'Governments derive their just powers from the consent of the governed', and we both noticed that the world was divided into peoples that owned the governments and governments that owned the peoples. At least I heard all this around that time and liked some of it very much.

I was a Minister in the British Liberal Government (with a large 'L' please this time), returned with a great majority in 1906. That new Liberal Government arrived in power with much of its message already delivered and most of its aims already achieved. The days of hereditary aristocratic privilege were ended or numbered. The path was opened for talent in every field of endeavour. Primary education was compulsory, universal and free, or was about to become so. New problems arising, as problems do from former successes, awaited the new administration. The independence of the proletariat from thraldom involved at least a minimum standard of life and labour, and security for old age, sickness and the death of the family breadwinner. It was to these tasks of social reform and insurance that we addressed ourselves. The name of Lloyd George will ever be associated in Great Britain with this new departure, and I am proud to have been his lieutenant in this work and also, later, as a Conservative Chancellor of the

Exchequer and later, still, as head of the wartime National Coalition to have carried these same themes forward on a magnified scale.

That is how we began the century. Science presently placed novel and dangerous facilities in the hands of the most powerful countries. Humanity was informed that it could make machines that would fly through the air and vessels which could swim beneath the surface of the seas. The conquest of the air and the perfection of the art of flying fulfilled the dream which for thousands of years had glittered in human imagination. Certainly it was a marvellous and romantic event. Whether the bestowal of this gift upon an immature civilization composed of competing nations whose nationalization grew with every advance of democracy and who were as yet devoid of international organization, whether this gift was a blessing or a curse has yet to be proved. On the whole I remain an optimist. For good, or for ill, air mastery is today the supreme expression of military power, and fleets and armies, however vital and important, must accept a subordinate rank. This is a memorable milestone in the march of man.

The submarine, to do it justice, has never made any claim to be a blessing or even a convenience. I well remember when it became an accomplished fact of peculiar military significance to the British Isles and to the British Navy, there was a general belief even in the Admiralty where I presided, that no nation would ever be so wicked as to use these underwater vessels to sink merchantmen at sea. How could a submarine, it was asked, provide for the safety of the crews of the merchant ships it sank, and public opinion was shocked when old Admiral Fisher bluntly declared that this would be no bar to the submarine being used by the new and growing German Navy in the most ruthless manner. His prediction was certainly not stultified by what was soon to happen.

Here then we have these two novel and potent weapons placed in the hands of highly nationalized sovereign States in the early part of the twentieth century, and both of them dwell with us today for our future edification. A third unmeasured sphere opened to us as the years passed, which, for the sake of comprehensive brevity, I will describe as radar. This radar, with its innumerable variants and possibilities, has so far been the handmaiden of the air, but it has also been the enemy of the submarine, and in alliance with the air may well prove its exterminator. Thus we see the changes which were wrought upon our society.

In the first half of the twentieth century, fanned by the crimson wings of war, the conquest of the air affected profoundly human affairs. It made the globe seem much bigger to the mind and much smaller to the body. The human biped was able to travel about far more quickly. This greatly reduced the size of his estate, while at the same time creating an even keener sense of its exploitable value. In the nineteenth century Jules Verne wrote *Round the World in Eighty Days*. It seemed a prodigy. Now you can get around it in four; but you do not see much of it on the way. The whole prospect and outlook of mankind grew immeasurably larger, and the multiplication of ideas also proceeded at an incredible rate. This vast expansion was unhappily not accompanied by any noticeable advance in the stature of man, either in his mental faculties, or his moral character. His brain got no better, but it buzzed the more. The scale of events around him assumed gigantic proportions while he remained about the same size. By comparison therefore he actually became much smaller. We no longer had great men directing manageable affairs. Our need was to discipline an array of gigantic and turbulent facts. To this task we have certainly so far proved unequal. Science bestowed immense new powers on man, and, at the same time, created conditions which were largely beyond his comprehension and still more beyond his control. While he nursed the illusion of growing mastery and exulted in his new trappings, he became the sport and presently the victim of tides, and currents, of whirlpools and tornadoes amid which he was far more helpless than he had been for a long time.

Hopeful developments in many directions were proceeding in 1914 on both sides of the Atlantic and they seemed to point to an age of peace and plenty when suddenly violent events broke in upon them. A spirit of adventure stirred the minds of men and was by no means allayed by the general advance of prosperity and science. On the contrary prosperity meant power, and science offered weapons. We read in the Bible, and I hope you still read the Bible, 'Jeshurun waxed fat and kicked'.

For several generations Britannia had ruled the waves—for long periods at less cost annually than that of a single modern battleship. History, I think, will say that this great trust was not abused. American testimony about the early period of the Monroe Doctrine is upon record. There was the suppression of the slave trade. During our prolonged naval supremacy undeterred by the rise of foreign tariffs, we kept our ports freely open to the commerce of the world. Our Colonial and Oriental Empire, even our coastal trade, was free to the shipping of all the nations on equal terms. We in no way sought to obstruct the rise of other States or navies. For nearly the whole of the nineteenth century the monopoly of sea power in British hands was a trust discharged faithfully in the general interest. But in the first decade of the twentieth century with new patterns of warships, naval rivalries became acute and fierce. Civilized governments began to think in dreadnoughts. It was in such a setting very difficult to prevent the First World War, far more difficult than it would have been to prevent the second.

There was of course one way to prevent it—one way then as now—the creation of an international instrument strong enough to adjust the disputes of nations and enforce its decisions against an aggressor. Much wisdom, eloquence and earnest effort was devoted to this theme in which the United States took the lead, but they only got as far as the World Court at The Hague and improvements in the Geneva Convention. The impulses toward a trial of strength in Europe were far stronger at this time. Germany, demanding her 'place in the sun', was faced by a resolute France with her military honour to regain. England, in accordance with her foreign policy of 300 years, sustained the weaker side. France found an ally in the Russia of the Czars and Germany in the crumbling Empire of the Hapsburgs. The United States, for reasons which were natural and traditional, but no longer so valid as in the past, stood aloof and expected to be able to watch as a spectator, the thrilling, fearful drama unfold from across what was then called 'the broad Atlantic'. These expectations, as you perhaps may remember, were not borne out by what happened.

After four and a half years of hideous mechanical slaughter, illuminated by infinite sacrifice, but not remarkably relieved by strategy or generalship, high hopes and spacious opportunities awaited the victorious Allies when they assembled at Versailles. War, stripped of every pretension of glamour or romance had been brought home to the masses of the peoples and brought home in forms never before experienced except by the defeated. To stop another war was the supreme object and duty of the statesmen who met as friends and allies around the Peace Table. They made great errors. The doctrine of self-determination was not the remedy for Europe, which needed then, above all things, unity and larger groupings. The idea that the vanquished could pay the expenses of the victors was a destructive and crazy delusion. The failure to strangle Bolshevism at its birth and to bring Russia, then prostrate, by one means or another, into the general democratic system lies heavy upon us today. Nevertheless, the statesmen of Versailles, largely at the inspiration of President Wilson, an inspiration implemented effectively by British thought, created the League of Nations. This is their defence before history, and had the League been resolutely sustained and used, it would have saved us all.

This was not to be. Another ordeal even more appalling than the first lay before us. Even when so much else had failed we could have obtained a prolonged peace, lasting all our lives at least, simply by keeping Germany disarmed in accordance with the Treaty, and by treating her with justice and magnanimity. This latter condition was very nearly achieved at Locarno in 1925, but the failure to enforce the disarmament clauses and above all to sustain the League of Nations, both of which purposes could easily have been accomplished, brought upon us the Second World War. Once again the English-speaking world gloriously but narrowly emerged, bleeding and breathless, but united as we never were before. This unity is our present salvation, because after all our victories, we are now faced by perils, both grave and near, and by problems more dire than have ever confronted Christian civilization, even in this twentieth century of storm and change.

There remains however a key of deliverance. It is the same key which was searched for by those who laboured to set up the World Court at The Hague in the early years of the century. It is the same conception which animated President Wilson and his colleagues at Versailles, namely the creation of a world instrument capable at least of giving to all its members security against aggression. The United Nations Organization which has been erected under the inspiring leadership of my great wartime friend, President Roosevelt, which took the place of the former League, has so far been rent and distracted by the antagonism of Soviet Russia and by the fundamental schism which has opened between Communism and the rest of mankind. But we must not despair. We must persevere, and if the gulf continues to widen, we must make sure that the cause of freedom is defended by all the resources of combined forethought and superior science. Here lies the best hope of averting a third world struggle.

One of the questions which you are debating here is defined as 'the failure of social and political institutions to keep pace with material and technical change'. Scientists should never underrate the deep-seated qualities of human nature and how, repressed in one direction, they will certainly break out in another. The *genus homo*—if I may display my Latin—is a tough creature who has travelled here by a very long road. His nature has been shaped and his virtues ingrained by many millions of years of struggle, fear and pain, and his spirit has, from the earliest dawn of history, shown itself upon occasion capable of mounting to the sublime, far above material conditions or mortal terrors. He still remains man—still remains as Pope described him 200 years ago.

> Placed on this Isthmus of a middle State,
> A being darkly wise and rudely great, . . .
> Created half to rise and half to fall;
> Great Lord of all things, yet a prey to all;
> Sole judge of truth, in endless error hurled;
> The glory, jest and riddle of the world.

In his introductory address, Mr Burchard, the Dean of Humanities, spoke with awe of 'an approaching scientific ability to control men's thoughts with precision'. I shall be very content personally if my task in this world is done before that happens. Laws just or unjust may govern men's actions. Tyrannies may restrain or regulate their words. The machinery of propaganda may pack their minds with falsehood and deny them truth for many generations of time. But the soul of man thus held in trance or frozen in a long night can be awakened by a spark coming from God knows where and in a moment the whole structure of lies and oppression is on trial for its life. Peoples in bondage need never despair. Let them hope and trust in the genius of mankind. Science no doubt could if sufficiently perverted exterminate us all, but it is not in the power of material forces in any period which the youngest here tonight need take into practical account, to alter the main elements in human nature or restrict the infinite variety of forms in which the soul and genius of the human race can and will express itself.

How right you are, Dr Compton, in this great institution of technical study and achievement, to keep a dean of humanities in the gaining of which philosophy and history walk hand in hand. Our inheritance of well-founded, slowly conceived codes of honour, morals and manners, the passionate convictions which so many hundreds of millions share together of the principles of freedom and justice, are far more precious to us than anything which scientific discoveries could bestow. Those whose minds are attracted or compelled to rigid and symmetrical systems of government should remember that logic, like science, must be the servant and not the master of man. Human beings and human societies are not structures that are built or machines that are forged. They are plants that grow and must be tended as such. Life is a test and this world a place of trial. Always the problems, or it may be the same problem, will be presented to every generation in different forms. The problems of victory may be even more baffling than those of defeat. However much the conditions change, the supreme question is how we live and grow and bloom and die, and how far each human life conforms to standards which are not wholly related to space or time.

And here I speak not only to those who enjoy the blessings and consolation of revealed religion but also to those who face the mysteries of human destiny alone. The flame of Christian ethics is still our highest guide. To guard and cherish it is our first interest, both spiritually and materially. The fulfilment of spiritual duty in our daily life is vital to our survival. Only by bringing it into perfect application can we hope to solve for ourselves the problems of this world and not of this world alone.

I cannot speak to you here tonight without expressing to the United States—as I have perhaps some right to do—the thanks of Britain and of Europe for the splendid part America is playing in the world. Many nations have risen to the summit of human affairs, but here is a great example where new-won supremacy has not been used for self-aggrandizement but only for further sacrifice.

Three years ago I made a speech at Fulton under the auspices of President Truman. Many people here and in my own country were startled and even shocked by what I said. But events have vindicated and fulfilled in much detail the warnings which I deemed it my duty to give at that time. Today there is a very different climate of opinion. I am in cordial accord with much that is being done. We have, as dominating facts, the famous Marshall Aid, the new unity in Western Europe and now the Atlantic Pact. Let us inquire into that. The responsible ministers in all the countries concerned deserve high credit. There is credit enough for all. In my own country the Foreign Secretary, Mr Bevin, who has come here to sign the Atlantic Pact, has shown himself indifferent to mere party popularity in dealing with these great national issues. He has shown himself, like many American public men, above mere partisan interest in dealing with these national and world issues. No one could, however, have brought about these immense changes in the feeling of the United States, Great Britain and Europe but for the astounding policy of the Russian Soviet Government. We may well ask: 'Why have they deliberately acted so as to unite the free world against them?' It is certainly not because there are not very able men among them. Why have they done it? It is because they fear the friendship of the West more than its hostility. They cannot afford to allow free and friendly intercourse to grow up between the vast areas they control and the civilized nations of the West. The Russian people must not see what is going on outside, and the world must not see what goes on inside the Soviet domain. Thirteen or fourteen men in the Kremlin, holding down hundreds of millions of people and aiming at the rule of the world, feel that at all costs they must keep up the barriers. Self-preservation, not for Russia but for themselves, lies at the root and is the explanation of their sinister and malignant policy.

In consequence of the Soviet conduct the relations of Communist Russia with the other great powers of the world are without precedent in history. Measures and countermeasures have been taken on many occasions which in any previous period could only have meant or accompanied armed conflict. The situation has been well described by distinguished Americans as the 'cold war'. And the question is asked: 'Are we winning the cold war?' Well, this cannot be decided by looking at Europe alone. We must also look at Asia. The worst disaster since our victory has been the collapse of China under Communist attack and intrigue. China, in which the United States has always taken a high interest, comprises an immense part of the population of the world. The absorption of China and of India into the Kremlin-controlled Communist Empire, would certainly bring measureless bloodshed and misery to 800,000,000 or 900,000,000 people.

On the other hand the position in Europe has so far been successfully maintained. The prodigious effort of the Berlin Airlift has carried us through the winter. Time, though dearly bought, has been gained for peace. The efficiency of the American and British Air Forces has been proved and improved. Most of all, the spectacle of the British and Americans trying to feed the 2,000,000 Germans in Berlin, in their zone in Berlin, while the Soviet Government was trying to starve them out, has been an object lesson to the German people far beyond anything that words could convey. I trust that small and needless provocations of German sentiment may be avoided by the Western Powers. The revival and union of Europe cannot be achieved without the earnest and freely given aid of the German people.

This has certainly been demonstrated by the Berlin Airlift, which has fully justified itself. Nevertheless, fear and its shadows brood over Western Europe today. A month ago in Brussels I spoke to a meeting of 30,000 Belgians. I could feel at once their friendship and anxiety. They have no Atlantic Ocean, no English Channel, between them and the Russian Communist armoured divisions. Yet they bravely and ardently support the cause of United Europe. I was also conscious of the hope and faith which they, like the Greek people, place in the United States. I can see the movement of this vast crowd when I spoke of the hands—strong hands—stretched out across the ocean. You have great responsibilities there for much faith is placed upon you.

We are now confronted with something quite as wicked but in some ways more formidable than Hitler, because Hitler had only the

Herrenvolk pride and anti-Semitic hatred to exploit. He had no fundamental theme. But these thirteen men in the Kremlin have their hierarchy and a church of Communist adepts, whose missionaries are in every country as a fifth column, obscure people, but awaiting the day when they hope to be the absolute masters of their fellow countrymen and pay off old scores. They have their anti-God religion and their Communist doctrine of the entire subjugation of the individual to the State and behind this stands the largest army in the world, in the hands of a Government pursuing imperialist expansion, as no Czar or Kaiser has ever done. I must not conceal from you tonight the truth as I see it. It is certain that Europe would have been Communized, like Czechoslovakia, and London under bombardment some time ago but for the deterrent of the atomic bomb in the hands of the United States.

Another question is also asked. Is time on our side? This is not a question that can be answered except within strict limits. We have certainly not an unlimited period of time before a settlement should be achieved. The utmost vigilance should be practised but I do not think myself that violent or precipitate action should be taken now. War is not inevitable. The Germans have a wise saying, 'The trees do not grow up to the sky.'

Often something happens to turn or mitigate the course of events. Four or five hundred years ago Europe seemed about to be conquered by the Mongols. Two great battles were fought almost on the same day near Vienna and in Poland. In both of these the chivalry and armed power of Europe were completely shattered by the Asiatic hordes and mounted archers. It seemed that nothing could avert the doom of the famous continent from which modern civilization and culture had spread throughout the world. But at the critical moment the Great Khan died. The succession was vacant and the Mongol armies and their leaders trooped back on their ponies across the 7,000 miles which separated them from their capital in order to choose a successor. They never returned till now.

We need not abandon hope or patience. Many favourable processes are on foot. Under the impact of Communism all the free nations are being welded together as they never have been before and never could be, but for the harsh external pressure to which they are being subjected. We have no hostility to the Russian people and no desire to deny them their legitimate rights and security. I hoped that Russia, after the war, would have access, through unfrozen waters, into every ocean, guaranteed by the world organization of which she would be a leading member; I hoped that she should have the freest access, which indeed she has at the present time, to raw materials of every kind;

and that the Russians everywhere would be received as brothers in the human family. That still remains our aim and ideal. We seek nothing from Russia but goodwill and fair play. If, however, there is to be a war of nerves let us make sure our nerves are strong and are fortified by the deepest convictions of our hearts. If we persevere steadfastly together, and allow no appeasement of tyranny and wrong-doing in any form, it may not be our nerve or the structure of our civilization which will break, and peace may yet be preserved.

This is a hard experience in the life of the world. After our great victory, which we believed would decide the struggle for freedom for our time at least, we thought we had deserved better of fortune. But unities and associations are being established by many nations through-out the free world with a speed and reality which would not have been achieved perhaps for generations. Of all these unities the one most precious to me is, to use an expression I used first at Harvard six years ago, and one most precious to me, the fraternal association between the British Commonwealth of Nations and the United States. Do not, my friends, I beg of you, underrate the strength of Britain. As I said at Fulton, 'Do not suppose that half a century from now you will not see 70,000,000 or 80,000,000 of Britons spread about the world and united in defence of our traditions, our way of life, and the world causes which you and we espouse.' United we stand secure. Let us then move forward together in discharge of our mission and our duty, fearing God and nothing else.

INDIA (COMMONWEALTH RELATIONS)

A SPEECH TO THE HOUSE OF COMMONS
28 APRIL 1949

1 April—Soviet Union sends Notes of protest to the signatories of the Atlantic Pact.

2 April—Britain and the USA present Notes to the Governments of Bulgaria, Hungary and Rumania accusing them of repeatedly violating the Peace Treaties.

4 April—North Atlantic Treaty signed at the State Department in Washington by Belgium, Canada, Denmark, France, Iceland, Italy, Luxembourg, Netherlands, Norway, Portugal, United Kingdom and United States.

6 April—Sir Stafford Cripps introduces the Budget.

8 April—Dr Malan, Premier of South Africa, speaking in the Union Senate, says that South Africa does not intend to leave the British Commonwealth of Nations.

9 April—International Court of Justice at The Hague finds Albania responsible under International Law for the damage and loss of life suffered when the British destroyers 'Volage' and 'Saumarez' were mined in the Corfu Channel on 22 October 1946.

Marshal Tito denounces the Cominform for anti-Yugoslav campaign.

4-9 April—County Council Elections result in sweeping Conservative gains and corresponding Labour losses. London County Council results:

64 Conservatives
64 Labour
1 Liberal

10 April—Mr Attlee, speaking at a Labour Party demonstration in Glasgow, attacks the Soviet Government's foreign policy and the methods of Communism.

The text of the Occupation Statute for Western Germany is communicated to German Parliamentary Council at Bonn. The Statute sets out the desire and intention of the three Western Powers that the German people shall enjoy self-government to a degree consistent with the occupation.

13 April—British Government issue a strongly worded reply to the Soviet Union's protest against the North Atlantic Treaty.

Details announced of tripartite agreements between Britain, the USA and France regarding the dismantling in Western Germany of industry for reparations.

16 *April—Twenty-year Pact of Friendship and Mutual Assistance signed in Budapest between Hungary and Czechoslovakia.*

18 *April—Republic of Ireland Act comes into force, thus severing the remaining link with the United Kingdom and the British Commonwealth and Empire.*

20 *April—The tenth report of the US Economic Co-operation Administration states that from the commencement of ERP on 3 April 1948 to 31 March 1949 purchases have been authorized to the value of $1,259,800,000 for the United Kingdom.*

24 *April—Sweets and chocolates de-rationed.*

Board of Trade allows newspapers to increase their size by one page.

26 *April—Mr Attlee makes a statement in the House of Commons on the shelling of British warships in the Yangtse by Chinese Communists and with special reference to the incident of the 'Amethyst'.*

Tass Agency announce that the Soviet Government have informed the US Government of their willingness to raise the blockade of Berlin if the Western Powers' counter-measures are lifted simultaneously.

21-28 *April—London Conference of Commonwealth Premiers decides that India shall remain in the Commonwealth as an Independent Republic.*

[28 *April* 1949

Perhaps I may be allowed to ask whether the Lord President is aware of the deep interest with which we have listened to his statement. I am well aware of the difficulties of clock time and sun time throughout the British Empire and Commonwealth of Nations, and I cannot say that they have been satisfactorily solved on this occasion, which seems to assign to London and Great Britain 2 a.m. as the moment of release for an important declaration. One would think this might be a matter for further consideration on future occasions. But I am all the more glad that His Majesty's Government have met the request which I made to them with the full support of my right hon and learned Friend the Leader of the Liberal Party, that the joint declaration of the Commonwealth Prime Ministers should be reported formally to the House and thus take its place not only in the newspapers, but in our Parliamentary records. Any other course, I feel, would be derogatory to Parliament and especially to the Mother of Parliaments.

Final judgment on matters of such gravity and far-reaching merit is impossible today. Debates have to take place not only here, but in the Parliaments which are concerned and which are located in the five continents of the globe. There are many questions which arise which are unanswered, and there are possible consequences, some of them potentially adverse, which cannot yet be measured. Nevertheless, I feel that I should be failing in my duty as Leader of the Conservative Party if on this occasion I failed to express under all proper and necessary reserves a definite view. The test question which, it seems to me, we ought to ask ourselves, and which I have asked myself is, do we wish India to remain of her own free will and desire within the Commonwealth or not? I have no doubt whatever that nearly all of us in all parts of the House would answer that question 'Aye'.

I do not in any way retract or regret the views I have expressed over so many years, and I am very glad not to be responsible for much that has been done in the past—[Hon Members: 'Hear, hear']—and in the recent past. But we are all of us governed by events which we cannot control, and by the actions of majorities duly elected to the House of Commons. Six months ago I said in this House in the Debate on the King's Speech:

'We must look forward. It is our duty, whatever part we have taken in the past, to hope and pray for the well-being and happiness of all the peoples of India, of whatever race, religion, social condition or historic character they may be. We must wish them all well and do what we can to help them on their road. Sorrow may lie in our hearts but bitterness and malice must be purged from them, and in our future more remote relations with India we must rise above all prejudice and partiality and not allow our vision to be clouded by memories of glories that are gone for ever.'

The present attitude of India seems to me more favourable to continued association than it did when those words were spoken. [Hon Members: 'Hear, hear.'] I am unfeignedly glad that an impassable gulf has not opened between the new India and the British Empire and Commonwealth of Nations or between our famous past in India and our anxious present all over the world. I am sure that this will be a help for all in the future. I am well aware of the arguments about equal sacrifices and contributions, belonging to the club and taking the advantages and not contributing to the rules but, as the Bible says, 'It is more blessed to give than to receive.' It is certainly more agreeable to have the power to give rather than the need to receive. We do not always find ourselves in that position in respect to some other countries in the world. If, on the whole, we most of us feel able to answer the test question in the affirmative and wish to have India associated with us in the future, it is fortunate that the institution of the Monarchy, never more deeply enshrined in the hearts of its proud and willing subjects and citizens all over the world than at the present time, should not have been a barrier to the inclusion of India as a Republic in the Commonwealth.

Some time ago, when by courtesy of Ministers I had some indication of what was afoot, I foresaw some danger that the symbol of the Crown, which had hitherto been the circle of unity for the whole British Empire and Commonwealth of Nations, might become an exclusive instrument in respect of India in its new guise. I am sure it has been wise to avoid any chance of that. I cannot feel that either the majesty of the Crown or the personal dignity of the King is impaired by the conditions under which India remains in the Commonwealth. On the contrary, the final significance, the vital significance and value of the Monarchy, seems to be enhanced both by the latest proofs of its enduring importance to the other Dominions, as testified by their responsible Prime Ministers, and to the fact—[HON MEMBERS: 'This is out of Order.'] I take it that it is in the public interest, when an important statement is made in the House by the Government, that the views of other parties should be ascertained, and I have no doubt that the Adjournment could be moved if that were desired by the Government.

It seems to me that the personal dignity of the King is not impaired by the conditions under which India remains in the Commonwealth. The final significance and value of the Monarchy seems to be enhanced by the way in which the King is acknowledged by the Republic of India and by the Commonwealth monarchies alike. [*Interruption.*] It is astonishing how far below the level of events hon Gentlemen are showing themselves to fall.

MR WARBY (Luton): On a point of Order, Mr Speaker. May I ask your guidance whether we are to have a series of extensive comments on this statement and, if so, on what Motion those comments are to be made?

MR SPEAKER: One knows perfectly well that on these formal occasions it is the right of leaders of political parties to state their party's point of view. Rather than have an Adjournment, I gave my consent to this, and I take full responsibility for it. Realizing that the guillotine has to fall at 5.30 and that, therefore, there is little time for discussion on the Steel Bill, I thought this was the quickest way out: that statements should be made by the responsible leaders of the Opposition parties. It is not for me to tell them how long or how short they should be.

MR CHURCHILL: I should like to put this point. It seems to me that, far from being any derogation of the Monarchy, the proof of the attachment and importance that all the Dominions give to it has shown the strength and vitality of that institution.

We cannot, of course, tell how all this will work out in practice, and obviously there are many difficult questions and dangers to be surmounted. There is no doubt however—this I say to all my friends on this side—that it is the duty of us all, wherever we sit, to try our best to make this new expression of the unity of the world-wide association of States and nations a practical and lasting success, and that that is the course which we on this side of the House intend to steer. I feel that the tides of the world are favourable to our voyage. The pressure of dangers and duties that are shared in common by all of us in these days may well make new harmonies with India and, indeed, with large parts of Asia. We may also see coming into view an even larger and wider synthesis of States and nations comprising both the United States of America and United Europe which may one day, and perhaps not a distant day, bring to harassed and struggling humanity real security for peace and freedom and for hearth and home.

THE NORTH ATLANTIC TREATY

A SPEECH TO THE HOUSE OF COMMONS
12 MAY 1949

---

29 *April—Details issued of concert hall to be erected on the south bank of the Thames at a cost of £2,000,000.*

1 *May—Britain's gas industry passes into State ownership.*

5 *May—Council of Europe set up. Mr Herbert Morrison announces in the House of Commons that British representation in the European Consultative Assembly will include Members of the Opposition, and that only Members of the Houses of Parliament will be nominated.*

Lord Henderson, British Under-Secretary for Foreign Affairs, announces in the House of Lords that war crimes charges against Marshal von Runstedt and General Strauss will be dropped on medical grounds, and that after the trial of Field-Marshal von Manstein no further war crimes trials will be held in the British zone of Germany.

11 *May—Strong criticism of the Labour Party's nationalization policy made at the meeting of the Federation of British Industries.*

Riots in Tripoli on publication and adoption by the Political Committee of United Nations General Assembly of the Bevin-Sforza plan for Italian trusteeship of Tripolitania.

12 *May—Blockade of Berlin ends.*

House of Commons adopts by 333 votes to 6 Motion approving the North Atlantic Treaty.

[12 *May* 1949

The House will not be surprised if I begin by saying that I find myself in very general agreement with the sombre speech which the Foreign Secretary has just made. I am glad that the lifting by the Soviet Government of the blockade of Berlin has not been taken by him as an occasion for proclaiming that an important peace gesture has been made. Before the last war, I do remember how, every time Herr Hitler made some reassuring statement, such as 'This is my last territorial demand', people came to me and said, 'There, now, you see how wrong you have been; he says it is his last territorial demand'; but the bitter experience we have all gone through in so many countries, on this side and on the other side of the Atlantic, has made us more wary of these premature rejoicings upon mere words and gestures. We give our cordial welcome to the Atlantic Pact. We give our thanks to the United States for the splendid part they are playing in the world. As I said when over there the other day:

'Many nations have risen to the summit of world affairs, but here is a great example where new-won supremacy has not been used for self-aggrandizement, but only further sacrifices.'

The sacrifices are very great. In addition to the enormous sums sent to Europe under Marshall Aid, the Atlantic Pact entails further subsidies for military supplies which are estimated at over $1,000,000,000 up to the year 1950. All this has to be raised by taxation from the annual production of the hard-working American people, who are not all Wall Street millionaires, but are living their lives in very different parts of the country than Wall Street. I say that nothing like this process of providing these enormous sums for defence and assistance to Europe—nothing like this has ever been seen in all history. We acknowledge it with gratitude, and we must continue to play our part as we are doing in a worthy manner and to the best of our abilities.

Our differences with the Soviet Government began before the war ended. Their unfriendly attitude to the Western Allies was obvious before the end of 1945, and, at the meeting of the United Nations organization in London in January 1946, Anglo-Russian relations had already reached a point where the Foreign Secretary had to give the word 'lie' in open conference to Mr Vyshinsky. I was impressed with that indication, which I read in the newspapers, and I was also very much impressed with the statements made at that time by Mr Vandenberg, that great American statesman, as I will not hesitate to call him. His whole career in recent years has been to carry world security and righteous causes far above the level of the fierce and repeated American political contentions and elections.

I have always myself looked forward to the fraternal association of the English-speaking world and also to the union of Europe. It is only in this way, in my view, that the peace and progress of mankind can be maintained. I gave expression to these views at Fulton in March 1946, after the remarks to which I have referred had shown the differences which had arisen with Russia. Although what I said then reads very tamely today, and falls far short of what has actually been done, and far short of what the House actually has to vote at the present time, a Motion of Censure against me was placed on the Order Paper in the name of the hon Member for Luton [Mr Warbey] in the following terms:

'World Peace and Security.—That this House considers that proposals for a military alliance between the British Commonwealth and the United States of America for the purpose of combating the spread of Communism, such as were put forward in a speech at Fulton, Missouri, USA, by the right hon Gentleman the Member for Woodford are calculated to do injury to good relations between Great Britain, USA and the USSR, and are inimical to the cause of world peace.'

That is the operative part. It is quite unusual, when a Private Member is out of office, that a Motion of that kind should be placed upon the Order Paper with regard to a speech made on his own responsibility, but no fewer than 105 hon Members of the party opposite put their names to it. I do not see them all here today; some of them are here, but, of course, I feel that there has been a large-scale process of conversion, and, naturally, I welcome converts, and so do His Majesty's Government. They say that there is more joy over one sinner who repenteth than over ninety and nine just persons who need no repentance. Here, we have got about a hundred in a bunch, so far as I can make out, although some of them have emphasized the change of heart which they have gone through by a suitable act of penance by abstaining from attending this Debate.

MR SYDNEY SILVERMAN (Nelson and Colne) *rose——*

MR CHURCHILL: Far be it from me to refuse an opportunity to a penitent.

MR SILVERMAN: I was only going to say in all humility to the right hon Gentleman that because a number of people are prepared to support the calling in of the fire brigade, that does not mean that they withdraw one word of censure from those who contributed to the setting of the house on fire.

MR CHURCHILL: I did not expect that such a condemnation of the Soviet Government's policy would be forthcoming from the hon Gentleman. For all these reasons, it is most certainly true that the occasion is not entirely unmingled with joy, for the country sees so many who have changed their courses, but I say that we are now asked to approve this Atlantic Pact, and the only opposition to it is expected from that small band of Communists, crypto-Communists and fellow-travellers whose dimensions have been very accurately ascertained in recent times. In all this matter, the policy of the Foreign Secretary has been wise and prudent. We have given it our fullest support, and we shall continue to do so. There is, of course, a difference between what a private Member of Parliament may say, even if his words carry far, and what a Minister has to do. To perceive a path and to point it out is one thing, but to blaze the trail and labour to construct the path is a harder task, and, personally, I do not grudge the right hon Gentleman any credit for the contribution which he has made to bringing about the Atlantic Pact. It entitles him, and the Government he represents, to the congratulations of the House which will be formally signified tonight by the passing of this Motion.

We must not, however, lose sight of the fact that the prime agent is the United States. I agree with what the Foreign Secretary said, that if the United States had acted in this way at an earlier period in their history they might well have averted the first world war, and could certainly, by sustaining the League of Nations from its birth, have warded off the second. The hope of mankind is that by their present valiant and self-sacrificing policy they will be the means of preventing a third world war. The future is, however, shrouded in obscurity.

As I have said on former occasions, we are dealing with absolutely incalculable factors in dealing with the present rulers of Russia. No one knows what action they will take, or to what internal pressures they will respond. He would be a bold, and, I think, an imprudent man who embarked upon detailed prophecies about what will be the future course of events. But it is absolutely certain that the strengthening by every means in our power of the growing ties which unite the signatories of the Atlantic Pact, of the Brussels Treaty, and the signatories of the Statute of the Council of Europe—on all of which there is overwhelming agreement in this House—is our surest guarantee of peace and safety. Now we must persevere faithfully and resolutely along these courses.

While I like the strong note which was struck by the Foreign Secretary in his speech this afternoon, we must persevere along these courses. It has been said that democracy suffers from the weakness of chopping and changing, that it can never pursue any course for any length of time, especially Parliamentary democracy. But I think that may prove to be a phase from which we are shaking ourselves free. At any rate, persistence at this time and a perseverance which is emphasized in the speech of the Foreign Secretary is, we on this side are quite certain, the safest course for us to follow and also the most right and honourable course for us to follow. It has been said that the Atlantic Pact and the European Union are purely defensive conceptions. The Foreign Secretary has claimed that they are not aggressive in any way. How could they be? When we consider the great disparity of military strength on the continent of Europe, no one can doubt that these measures are of a defensive and non-aggressive character. The military forces of the Soviet Union are at least three or four times as great as those which can be set against them on land. Besides this, they have their fifth column in many countries, waiting eagerly for the moment when they can play the quisling and pay off old scores against the rest of their fellow countrymen. Nothing that can be provided in the Atlantic Pact or the Western Union Agreement on land can make our position and policy other than purely defensive. It remains the first duty of all the signatory Powers to do their utmost to make Europe, and for us here to make Britain, self-supporting and independently secure. For this we must all labour.

I have only a word or two of detail to say upon the subject. It seems that our first duty is to put our own defences in order. I cannot feel—none of us can feel—that any adequate return in actual fighting power is being received for the vast sums of money and the very great numbers of men which Parliament is voting at the request of the Government. There seems, also, to be no close integration of military plans and forces on the Continent. There is no system comparable to that which was created at SHAEF, the Supreme Headquarters of the Allied Expeditionary Force. There, there was great unity under the wise guidance of General Eisenhower. But, according to unofficial reports which we hear, national considerations are playing far too great a part in the present discussions which are taking place.

Thirdly, in view of the inevitable delay in the ratification of the Treaty and the need for speed, I have heard the suggestion that it might be desirable to broaden the activities of the Western Union Military Committee by inviting representatives of the other Atlantic Treaty powers, namely, the Italians, Portuguese, Danes, Norwegians and Icelanders, at any rate occasionally, to attend the Western Union Committee at Fontainebleau as observers. However, I should not wish to impede the precision of their work by the mere addition of numbers. Nevertheless, this might be an advantage.

The absence of Spain from the Atlantic Pact involves, of course, a serious gap in the strategic arrangements for Western Europe. I was glad to hear the right hon Gentleman, not this afternoon, but the other day, express himself in a favourable sense to the return of ambassadors. I do not ask more than that at the present time. I think it is better to have ambassadors than to carry it all on through the back door, as it all has to be carried on—a sort of black market diplomacy. Also, I do not think it a good thing to appear to insult and to appear to treat with lack of ceremony a people so proud and haughty as the Spaniards, living in their stony peninsula, have always shown themselves to be.

The services rendered by Spain to us in the war were not all negative. First of all, we had a most fertile and serviceable trade with Spain which, in one way or another, the Germans did not dare to interfere with. Products of the greatest value, both to our armaments and to our nourishment, were brought in, but it was at the time of the landing in North Africa—Operation 'Torch'—that the greatest forbearance was shown by Spain in allowing us to use, far beyond any treaty rights, the harbour of Algeciras and the neutral ground between Gibraltar and the mainland for our aeroplanes and for the gathering of our transports. It was a most anxious period for us because the whole of that great operation—the first great Anglo-American joint operation—would have been jeopardized if they had chosen, as they so easily could have done, to plant cannon on the hills overlooking the harbour, and fire them upon the shipping crowded therein.

I cannot feel at all that they did us harm in the war and I personally agree with what Senator Connally said in the American Senate the other day, that he could not see the sense of having relations with Soviet Russia and refusing to have any relations with Spain. As a matter of fact, the conditions under which people live in Spain give far greater freedom to the individual than those under which they live in Russia or, I may say, Bulgaria or Rumania or other countries which have fallen into the grip of——

MR SKEFFINGTON-LODGE (Bedford): The right hon Gentleman said that he agrees with the expression of opinion of an American Senator. Does he also agree with the expression of opinion which appeared in *The Times* today and which comes from Mr Acheson, the Secretary of State, in which Mr Acheson says that the Franco Government was set up by Hitler and Mussolini and that it is patterned on Germany and Italy, and in which he adds that the judiciary is not independent in Spain today and Habeas Corpus is quite unknown?

MR CHURCHILL: I should not like to live under the present Spanish regime, but I would rather live there than under the governments of the various countries I have just mentioned, and I imagine that would be the opinion of almost every Member of this House who is not either blinded by fanaticism or sure he would get most favoured treatment in the circumstances which might arise.

As I say, I am not suggesting that we should go further at all at the present time than to have the interchange of ambassadors. At the time of Potsdam, I agreed that Spain should not be a member of the United Nations Organization because I felt it was more important to gather together other elements, nor do we include Spain in our United Europe movement, but let us at least take the step of abandoning insult and boycott and exchange formal ambassadors with that country. I am sure that the attitude and policy which has been pursued in the last three years has been a great service to Franco and has enabled him to secure his hold, which might otherwise have been greatly mitigated.

Those are the only points of detail which I venture to mention. This may be an occasion for satisfaction, but it is not an occasion for triumph or for exultation. We are on the eve of the Four-Power Conference out of which we may hope a peace treaty with Germany may come. We must give that conference the best possible chance and be careful not to use language at this juncture which would hamper its discussions or compromise its chances of success. At the same time, I am glad that the Foreign Secretary is not under any illusions and that we shall not be deceived by gestures unaccompanied by action. It is deeds, not words, which are wanted. Any deed done by the Russian Soviet Government which really makes for the peaceful and friendly intercourse of mankind will have its immediate response, but mere manoeuvres must be watched with the utmost vigilance.

Moreover, there can be no assurance of permanent peace in Europe while Asia is on the Elbe or while so many ancient States and famous capitals of Eastern Europe are held in the grip of the thirteen men who form the oligarchy of the Kremlin. The Communist gains in China and the disturbances, all springing from the same source, which are causing so much misery in South-East Asia, all bring home to us the magnitude of the great struggle for freedom which is going on under the conditions of what is called the 'cold war'. We are confronted with a mighty oligarchy disposing not only of vast armies and important armaments by sea and in the air, but which has a theme, almost a religion, in the Communist doctrine and propaganda which claims its devotees in so many countries and makes them, over a large portion of the globe, the enemies of the lands of their birth.

There is this fear which the Soviet dictators have of a friendly intercourse with the Western democracies and their hitherto inflexible resolve to isolate the enormous populations they control. They even fear words on the broadcast. Everyone in this country is free to tune in to the Russian broadcasts at any hour of the day, and I am bound to say I am very glad that they should be free to do so. It would be a terrible thing if we were afraid of anything that might be said about us on the broadcasts. It is a woeful admission of a guilty conscience or a defective political system when you are afraid to let your people listen to what goes on abroad. We soon got used to 'Lord Haw-Haw' during the war, and we never feared what he might have said about us. It is astonishing that there should be this terror in the hearts of these men, wielding such immense material and physical power, merely of words let out by our fairly harmless BBC upon the ether. They must have very poor nerves to get alarmed by that. But the fact remains that there is this fear—fear of friendship and fear of words, and it acts upon men who wield the most terrible agencies of military force.

The situation is, therefore, from many points of view unprecedented and incalculable. Over the whole scene reigns the power of the atomic bomb, ever growing in the hands of the United States. It is this, in my view, and this alone that has given us time to take the measures of self-protection and to develop the units which make those measures possible, one of which is before us this afternoon. I have said that we must rise above that weakness of democratic and Parliamentary Governments, in not being able to pursue a steady policy for a long time, so as to get results. It is surely our plain duty to persevere steadfastly, irrespective of party feelings or national diversities, for only in this way have we good chances of securing that lasting world peace under a sovereign world instrument of security on which our hearts are set. We shall, therefore, support His Majesty's Government in the Motion which the right hon Gentleman has just commended to us.

GENERAL SIKORSKI

A SPEECH AT THE OPENING OF THE SIKORSKI INSTITUTE
5 JULY 1949

---

14 *May—Dock strikes commence.*

17 *May—Indian Constituent Assembly approves the decision of the Government of India to remain within the Commonwealth of Nations with the status of an independent Republic.*

66·1 per cent of electors in Soviet Zone of Germany vote for a new 'People's Congress' to be elected on a single list of candidates.

2 *June—Mr Bustamente, Labour leader in British West Indies, declares that he will 'organize and lead a general strike' if the British Socialist Government nationalize the sugar industry.*

3 *June—Announcement made that the strength of the US Air Force in Britain will shortly be increased from the present 8,000 to 12,000 men.*

6 *June—Mr A. V. Alexander, Minister of Defence, arrives in Hong Kong to consult with the local commanders on the defence measures to be taken in the colony in view of Communist advances in the Chinese civil war.*

7 *June—Great Britain ratifies the North Atlantic Treaty.*

6-10 *June—Annual Conference of the Labour Party held in Blackpool.*

12-14 *June—Dockers return to work.*

16 *June—The American Military Government in Germany announces that according to public opinion surveys there is a revival of Nazism in Germany.*

19 *June—Conference of Freemasons from the Western Zones of Germany decide to revive freemasonry in Western Germany on a national scale.*

23 *June—Lord Milverton announces his resignation from the Labour Party as a protest against the nationalization of steel.*

27 *June—Mr Mayhew, Under-Secretary for Foreign Affairs, states in the House of Commons that the cost of the Berlin airlift to the British taxpayer to 15 June 1949 was approximately £8,600,000, and that British aircraft handled 23½ per cent of the total weight carried during the airlift.*

Dockers decide to resume unofficial strike.

3 *July—Mr Attlee, addressing a Labour rally in Manchester, condemns unofficial strikes.*

4-7 *July—Combined naval exercises by Fleets of Western Union—Great Britain, France, Netherlands and Belgium.*

Sir JOHN ANDERSON, My Lords, Ladies and Gentlemen:

We are met here to invest with structural strength the undying memory of a great and gallant man. In General Sikorski the cause of world freedom found a champion whose activities ranged far beyond the limits of his own country. He was a great Pole; but he was greater as a citizen of the whole world. He understood, deeply and intensely, the causes which were at stake in the struggle through which we have passed, and for which we are still contending.

I had the pleasure—the honour—of meeting him in the early years of the war when he took me to inspect the magnificent Polish Division we had in Scotland, and often and often I saw him when we conferred upon the difficult questions which he and I and my friend Mr Eden had to decide and discuss together. And I remember, as if it were yesterday, the shock which came to us both—Mr Eden and myself— when the news of his sudden, tragic, untoward death came in upon us. The aeroplane crashed, taking off at that restricted landing-ground at Gibraltar, where many of us had to go several times, and so a great figure fell out of the Allied line of battle.

I am glad this Institute is here being definitely established. I earnestly hope it will receive all the support that is necessary to invest it with permanent strength. The name of Sikorski should be preserved—I say it in the presence of his gracious widow who is here with us today— should be preserved as an inspiration for all who care about the future of Europe and the future of the world.

I have been speaking about General Sikorski. I knew beforehand that other great Pole, Marshal Pilsudski, who played so fine a part in the years after the late struggle in the first world war was over, and who suffered so much in the period before victory was attained. These are the names which Poland will cherish. I come to a thought, if you will permit me, of Poland itself. In hearts throughout Poland, how long—how many times—are they to suffer? How long, how many times are they to win their freedom and deliverance, and find it only a mockery? But they must never despair. In all the qualities of the Polish nation, there is none which stands out more strongly than this unconquerable quality of always renewing and refreshing the life strength of the nation from generation to generation; from disaster to disaster; from one tragedy to another—always with gleams of triumph and victory.

Then, after all that was suffered and all that was endured—and all that was achieved—it was found they had but exchanged one form of oppression for another. But that will pass. The great forces of the world are growing in strength. Recession marks the front of the forces of tyranny in every land. Far and wide throughout the world, modern methods and intelligence, swift and easy intercourse which, in spite of all their efforts, is taking place between human minds all over the world, show that the forces of freedom have formed a broad front and are advancing steadily. And I am sure the day will come when we shall see that the causes that General Sikorski fought for, and for which he gave his life cheerfully, are causes which will not fall to the ground and perish by the wayside or perish in the wilderness.

No, the day will come undoubtedly, when Poland will enter into the full inheritance which her readiness to endure sacrifice and martyrdom and her unfailing spirit of revival have entitled her to, and when we shall be able to feel that all of us who, in our different ways, have worked for the freedom and independence and the lasting glory of Poland, will find that our efforts have played their definite part in the history of the world, and are consolidated by the event. When that day comes there are many names in Polish history which will be honoured. There is none, I feel, on which the glint of fame and gratitude will fall more than on that of the famous soldier and statesman, General Sikorski, the Institute to whose memory we are here to consecrate tonight. I earnestly hope everyone will try their best to make a great and lasting practical success of our efforts. But all over the world there are thoughts. Far off in America and all over the world, there are thoughts which flow here and find their centre in this room. Let them be made effective and fruitful.

FOREIGN AFFAIRS

---

6 *July—Sir Stafford Cripps announces in the House of Commons that the sterling area gold and dollar reserves have fallen from £471,000,000 to £406,000,000 in the quarter ended 30 June. In reply to a question he says that he has not the slightest intention of devaluing the £.*

9 *July—Cardinal Mindszenty's appeal against the sentence of life imprisonment rejected by the highest judicial court in Hungary.*

10-18 *July—Conference in London of Commonwealth Finance Ministers.*

11 *July—Owing to failure of dockers to end strike, a state of emergency is declared.*

    At Trades Union Conference at Scarborough a resolution is passed by 426-208 votes to exclude members of the Communist Party from holding office in the Union either as members or as full-time officers.

13 *July—Government and Opposition meeting to consider defence problems.*

    Warning of ex-communication issued by Vatican to Catholics supporting Communism.

14 *July—Sir Stafford Cripps announces in the House of Commons that the dollar deficit in the second three months of this year is £157,000,000. In order that 'rumours may be laid' he gives a reassurance that the suggestion of devaluation is not entertained.*

15 *July—Field-Marshal Lord Montgomery, in a speech to the Royal Netherlands Army Society in The Hague, denounces Communism.*

20 *July—Food rationing abolished in Italy.*

21 *July—Debate in House of Commons on Foreign Affairs during which Mr Ernest Bevin strongly criticizes the policy of 'unconditional surrender' adopted during the war by War Cabinet of which he was a member.*

[21 July 1949

MR CHURCHILL (Woodford): I shall venture to trespass for only a very few minutes upon the Committee, but topics have been referred to by the right hon Gentleman in his speech which, perhaps, require some comment from me. The right hon Gentleman is, I am sure, uneasy in his mind about the belated, persistent dismantling that is going on in Germany. He is uneasy in his mind about the very belated —or he should be uneasy in his mind—about the very belated bringing to trial of German generals, and in the mood that he is in he takes,

I think, an altogether exaggerated view of any criticisms that were made by my right hon Friend the Member for Bromley [Mr H. Macmillan] in his very restrained and carefully phrased speech.

HON MEMBERS: Oh!

MR S. SILVERMAN: I wonder what the right hon Gentleman would say if he abandoned restraint.

MR CHURCHILL: The hon Gentleman is always intervening. On this occasion he did not even hop off his perch. I should not have risen at all had it not been that the right hon Gentleman felt so uneasy about those criticisms on the two points I have mentioned that he floated back across the years into the history of the war, and touched upon some large and important matters affecting our relations with the United States, with a view to throwing some invidious burden upon me personally.

I was a person very responsible in these matters, and I must say that the phrase 'unconditional surrender' was not brought before me to agree to in any way before it was uttered by our great friend, our august and powerful ally President Roosevelt. But I did concur with him after he had said it, and I reported the matter to the Cabinet, who accepted the position. Whether if we had all discussed it at home we should have proposed such a settlement is another matter. Still, they did accept the position, as I, in my turn, on the spot, thought it right to do. I cannot feel that there can be any separation of responsibility between us in the matter, having regard to the long years in which we subsequently acted together.*

Then the right hon Gentleman rather used this episode to suggest that the difficulties in Germany were greatly aggravated by the use of this phrase. I am not at all sure that that is true. I am not going to plunge into a lengthy argument, but I am not at all sure that, if Hitler had been murdered by some of the plots which were levelled against him by men whom I do not hesitate to call patriotic Germans, a new situation would have arisen. I believe there was the force and vigour to carry on the fight, as it was carried on, to the very last gasp. He and the band of guilty men around him were in the position that they could not look for any pardon or any safety for their lives and they would certainly have fought to the death.

MR ZILLIACUS (Gateshead) rose——

MR CHURCHILL: I do not wish to give way, if the hon Gentleman will permit me to continue. I have been rather seriously criticized by the Foreign Secretary trying, as it were, to throw all the discredit for unconditional surrender upon me. [HON MEMBERS: 'No.'] If he did

* See pp. 137—139.

not mean that he did not mean anything. He is doing that because he is vexed with what my right hon Friend said, though I thought my right hon Friend's statement was very mildly expressed. It cannot be said that the decisions to which the Foreign Secretary has come about the prolongation of dismantling are connected in any way with the use of the phrase 'unconditional surrender' by President Roosevelt, so why bring it in and extend the Debate into other circles, and into matters of really very great gravity?

Another matter to which the Foreign Secretary referred, about which I do not by any means feel so confident in my conscience as to the judgment of my actions, is the Morgenthau Agreement at the second conference—the document published by Mr Morgenthau of the conference. There is an agreement; it was initialed by President Roosevelt and by me, and it undoubtedly proposed treatment of Germany which was a harsh treatment, in respect of largely limiting her to an agricultural country. But that was not a decision taken over the heads of the Cabinet. It was not one that ever reached the Cabinet. It never reached the Cabinet because it was only *ad referendum*; it was disapproved by the State Department on the one hand and by my right hon Friend and the Foreign Office Committee on the other, and it just dropped on one side. I must say that it never required a Cabinet negative; it never had any validity of any sort or kind.

Nevertheless, I must say that I do not agree with this paper, for which I none the less bear a responsibility. I do not agree with it, but I can only say that when fighting for life in a fierce struggle with an enemy I feel quite differently towards him than when that enemy is beaten to the ground and is suing for mercy. Anyhow, if the document is ever brought up to me I shall certainly say, 'I do not agree with that, and I am sorry that I put my initials to it.' I cannot do more than that. Of course, many things happen with great rapidity, but to say it was done over the heads of the Cabinet, or anything like that, is quite untrue, and the Cabinet never agreed to it for a moment.

These two matters of great importance were brought in in order to justify the right hon Gentleman in pursuing the policy of dismantling, and some incidents connected with the trial of the German generals. I do not think the right hon Gentleman need have brought such artillery back from the past to fire at me on such matters. I do not put the case with hostility against him. I consider that in the airlift and the treatment of the Berlin difficulty the Government and the Foreign Office—no one more than he—showed the very greatest determination, skill, good judgment and tenacity, and their exertions over a long period were crowned by unmistakable success which has been of the greatest advantage to Europe, and very likely played a part in the closer drawing together of Britain and the United States, which has found its manifestation in the Atlantic Pact.

I was very much struck at the way in which all Germany watched the airlift, and how all Germany saw the British and American planes flying to carry food to 2,500,000 Germans whom the Soviet Government were trying to starve. I thought that was worth all the speeches that could have been made by all the peace leaders of Europe to turn the eyes of Germany to where her true destiny lies: namely, in peaceful and honourable association with the Western democracies and with the future into which they hope to lead the world under the auspices of the United Nations organization. I indeed thought that was a very great advantage.

I must say that I personally was instinctively disappointed and chilled when I saw the dismantling policy, which has draggled and straggled on for four years, being a cause of upsetting this strong drift and tide of German sentiment which may be of very great value in the future. I could not help feeling that it was untoward. Of course, these things must in some cases be done. They should have been done, or could have been done, two years ago. That would have been all right.

But now, four years after, when Europe is in the midst of all this feeling of hardship and pressure, and of hopes of coming out of it again, to go on tearing down these buildings and solemnly proceeding with methodical routine on some agreement which now no longer has any validity or application to current affairs was, I thought, an error: not an error of major criminality, but a bad touch. I should have hoped that it would have been possible to have let that go. I should have thought it should have been brought to an end. I have said so several times in the last months, and I do not think it is a wrong thing for us to put that view.

Nor do I think that because I was present and supported President Roosevelt when he used the phrase 'unconditional surrender' I am debarred from saying that at any time there should be a little give and take, and a different touch and handling in a sensitive manner of our relations with the German people. I am sure that the munitions which could be made by these factories which still remain to be dismantled would never do half the harm to the cause of peace, or to any future victory of the Allies against aggression, as is done by the great setting back and discouragement, out of all proportion, of the German movement towards Western civilization and Western ideas. I will not put it at more than that.

As for the generals and so on, that, I think, should have been settled within a year or two of the end of the fighting; but to go on dragging these things out is simply feeding all the forces against peaceful solution and against passing the sponge across the past with opportunities for making up ill-will and bad feeling. I do not make this a serious case of indictment against the right hon Gentleman. In the main we approve of his policy, but he really must not get so very upset and angry when certain points and notes are struck, even though when they are struck from this side they awaken a very immediate echo on the benches behind him.

I have only one other thing to say, which I should not have referred to at all had I not felt it right to refer to the important topics which the right hon Gentleman raised, and that is this question of our future meetings at Strasbourg. There will be a European Assembly at Strasbourg representing ten nations.

MR BEVIN: More than that.

MR CHURCHILL: Maybe more. They will not necessarily consider themselves forced to agree with every dictate, ukase or regulation which is made by the Council of Ministers. They may not have any executive powers, but they will not be forced necessarily to accept the directions which come down to them from on high. Maybe, in the course of time, some method of adjusting quarrels, disputes and differences between the European Assembly and the European Council will be devised. Maybe we shall have a sort of Parliament Act and pass it to and fro to overthrow eventually the veto of the upper chamber. Anyhow, I think this had much better be left until we get there.

What questions we should be allowed to discuss is not a matter on which they must not express an opinion. Personally, I should be very sorry to see military matters discussed, but I am bound to say that a European Assembly meeting together in these conditions should have a wide latitude to discuss matters of general interest not affecting the national safety of their countries and the combination of all the countries that there are. You will have to reckon on the views of the Assembly. You have called it into being reluctantly, and it is a fact, which I hope will not be easily removed from European affairs. I think it would be better for us to wait until we are assembled there and see how the Assembly chooses to act, what its thoughts are and what its political divisions are and may be. I hope and trust that the right hon Gentleman will make sure that if there is a desire expressed, not only in the Assembly but in the Council of Ministers, that broad views shall be taken and good latitude given to the Assembly; he will not be the principal person to offer resistance, because he may not find himself possessed, either in the Council of Ministers or in the Assembly, of the large majority he commands in this House.

MR BEVIN: Perhaps I may be allowed to make an explanation, because this is very important internationally. In regard to unconditional surrender, I want the House and the right hon Gentleman to be clear that what I was saying was that the use of that phrase meant that the whole constitution was smashed and that our military governor and the military governors of the Allies have had to build up right from the bottom. Therefore, I do not think the criticism of the right hon Gentleman the Member for Bromley [Mr H. Macmillan] was justified—he did not take that into account. I do not complain at all of Mr Roosevelt making the statement, and I do not complain at all of the right hon Gentleman agreeing. I do not complain, because I agreed that in the circumstances the right hon Gentleman could do nothing else but agree; I stood by that and never said a word in spite of all the criticisms of my own party that followed. I do not think the right hon Gentleman will accuse me of ever being disloyal to a Cabinet decision in the end.

In regard to the European Assembly, all I shall say is this: That it is an infant institution and that I am not laying down any laws or rules as to what should be discussed or not discussed. What I beg of the right hon Gentleman is that we should learn to walk in the European Assembly before trying to run. This is really a very delicate instrument which I have nothing to do with except as a member of the Committee of Ministers. It is in a very complicated stage, as we are involved in OEEC and the other things, and all of us, including the right hon Gentleman in his wise old age and myself in my infancy, I hope may combine together to steer it along the right lines.

MR CHURCHILL: I did not have this quotation on the subject of unconditional surrender when I first made my speech, but perhaps the House will allow me now to give it. Here is what I said:

'The principle of unconditional surrender was proclaimed by the President of the United States at Casablanca, and I endorsed it there and then on behalf of this country. I am sure it was right at the time it was used, when many things hung in the balance against us which are all decided in our favour now. Should we then modify this declaration which was made in days of comparative weakness and lack of success now that we have reached a period of mastery and power?

'I am clear that nothing should induce us to abandon the principle of unconditional surrender or enter into any form of negotiation with Germany or Japan, under whatever guise such suggestions may present themselves, until the act of unconditional surrender has been formally executed. But the President of the United States and I, in your name, have repeatedly declared that the enforcement of unconditional surrender upon the enemy in no way relieves the victorious Powers of their obligations to humanity, or of their duties as civilized and Christian nations. I read somewhere that when the ancient Athenians, on one occasion, overpowered a tribe in the Peloponnesus which had wrought them great injury by base, treacherous means, and they had the hostile army herded on a beach naked for slaughter, they forgave them and set them free, and they said:

' "This was not because they were men;
"It was done because of the nature of Man."

'Similarly, in this temper we may now say to our foes, "We demand unconditional surrender, but you well know how strict are the moral limits within which our action is confined. We are no extirpators of nations, or butchers of peoples. We make no bargain with you. We accord you nothing as a right. Abandon your resistance unconditionally. We remain bound by our customs and our nature." '*

I venture to rest on that.

---

* House of Commons, 18 January 1945.

UNITED EUROPE

A SPEECH AT AN OPEN-AIR MEETING, PLACE KLEBER, STRASBOURG
12 AUGUST 1949

---

23 *July—Conservative Party publish statement of policy for the next General Election.*

25 *July—Dockers decide to resume work.*
President Truman signs the ratification of the North Atlantic Treaty.

26 *July—Debate on dock strike in House of Commons. State of emergency revoked by HM the King.*

27 *July—Mr Lester Hutchinson, Labour Member for the Rusholme Division of Manchester, expelled from the party for persistent opposition to the Government's foreign policy. He declares that he can no longer support the 'disastrous policy' of the Socialist Government.*

28 *July—It is estimated by the Ministry of Health that 4,500,000 pairs of spectacles have been supplied under the National Health Scheme in the past twelve months, and 3,000,000 to 4,000,000 are on order. Also 8,000 wigs have been ordered under the Scheme at an average cost of £12 each.*

10 *August—Civil Defence Regulations, recently approved by Parliament, come into force.*
First session of Council of Europe meets at Strasbourg.

[12 *August* 1949

Prener-garde! Je vais parler en Français.

Dans cette ville ancienne, et encore marquée par les blessures de la guerre, nous sommes réunis pour former une Assemblée qui, nous l'espérons, serâ un jour le Parlement de l'Europe. Nous avons fait le premier pas et c'est le premier pas qui coûte. Ce magnifique rassemblement des citoyens de Strasbourg a été convoqué par le Mouvement Européen pour montrer au monde quelle force a l'idée de l'Europe Unie, quelle puissance elle a, non seulement sur les esprits des penseurs politiques, mais dans les cœurs des larges masses populaires, dans tous les pays d'Europe où les peuples sont libres d'exprimer leur opinion.

Je me sens encouragé, mais je suis étonné aussi, en voyant quels remarquables résultats nous avons obtenus en si peu de temps. Il n'y a pas beaucoup plus d'une année que nous avons, à notre Congrés de La Haye, demandé la création d'une Assemblée Européenne. Il fallait ·

mobiliser l'opinion publique pour persuader de puissants gouvernements de transformer nos demandes en réalités. Il fallait surmonter de sérieuses hésitations.

Mais nous avons aussi, de notre côté, avec nous, bien des amis de cette grande cause de l'Europe Unie, et parmi eux des amis qui étaient au pouvoir ministériel. Aucun de ces amis n'a fait plus pour le Mouvement Européen que M. Spaak, qui depuis longtemps a été le champion d'un Parlement Européen, et qui a été hier, ici, dans cette cité élu à l'unanimité comme son premier Président.

Nous sommes réunis ici, dans cette Assemblée nouvelle, non pas comme représentants de nos divers pays ou de différents partis politiques, mais comme des Européens, marchant en avant, la main dans la main, et s'il le faut au coude à coude, pour faire revivre les gloires anciennes de l'Europe et permettre à cet illustre continent de reprendre, dans une organisation mondiale, sa place de membre indépendant et se suffisant à lui-même.

Cette fidélité première et sacrée que l'on doit à son propre pays, il n'est pas difficile de la réconcilier avec ce sentiment, plus vaste, de camaraderie européenne. Au contraire, on constatera que tous les intérêts *légitimes* s'accordent harmonieusement, et que chacun de nous servira le mieux les intérêts réels et la sécurité de son pays si nous élargissons notre sentiment à la fois de citoyenneté et de souveraineté communes, si nous englobons dans ce sentiment tout ce continent d'Etats et de nations qui ont la même manière de vivre.

Ces principes qui nous gouvernent sont définis dans la Constitution des Nations-Unies, dont l'Europe devrait être un élément vigoureux et dirigeant; ces principes sont aussi, en termes généraux, formulés dans la Déclaration des Droits de l'Homme proclamée par les Nations-Unies (à Genève). Ainsi, non seulement nous trouverons le chemin de la renaissance, et de la prospérité de l'Europe, mais en même temps nous nous protégerons nous-mêmes contre tout risque d'être piétinés, d'être écrasés par n'importe quelle forme de tyrannie totalitaire, que ce soit la domination détestée des Nazis, que nous avons balayée, ou tout autre forme de despotisme.

Pour ma part, je ne suis l'ennemi d'aucune race et d'aucune nation du monde. Ce n'est pas contre une race, ce n'est pas contre une nation quelconque que nous nous rassemblons. C'est contre la tyrannie sous toutes ses formes, anciennes ou modernes, que nous nous dressons résolument. La tyrannie reste toujours la même, quelles que soient ses fausses promesses, quel que soit le nom qu'elle adopte, quels que soient les déguisements dont elle habille ses valets.

Mais si nous voulons conquérir notre suprême récompense, nous devons écarter tous nos empêchements, et devenir les maîtres de nous-mêmes. Nous devons nous élever au dessus de ces passions qui ont ravagé l'Europe et l'ont mise en ruines. Il faut en finir avec nos vieilles querelles; il faut renoncer aux ambitions territoriales; il faut que les rivalités nationales deviennent une émulation créatrice dans tous les domaines où nous pouvons rendre les services les plus réels à notre cause commune.

En outre, nous devons prendre toutes les mesures et toutes les pré-cautions nécessaires pour être bien sûrs que nous aurons le pouvoir, et que nous aurons le temps, de réaliser cette transformation de l'Europe dans laquelle l'Assemblée Européenne (maintenant effectivement réunie à Strasbourg) a un si grand rôle à jouer. Elle ne pourra jouer ce rôle que si elle montre qu'elle possède ces qualités de bon sens, de tolérance, d'indépendance, et surtout de courage, sans lesquelles rien de grand ne se fait dans ce monde.

Et pour finir, je demande l'aide de ce vaste rassemblement de citoyens de Strasbourg; vous faites partie de ces énormes masses d'hommes que nous affirmons représenter et dont nous avons le devoir de défendre les droits et les intérêts. Il y a, en Europe, des deux côtés du rideau de fer, des millions de simple foyers dont tous les cœurs sont avec nous. Ne leur donnera-t-on jamais une chance de prospérer et de fleurir? Ne vivront-ils jamais dans la sécurité? Ne pourront-ils jamais jouir des simples joies et des libertés que Dieu et la Nature leur ont accordées? L'homme qui gagne honnêtement son pain, ne pourra-t-il jamais récolter les fruits de son travail? Ne pourra-t-il jamais élever des enfants bien portants, heureux, avec l'espoir de jour meilleurs?

Ne sera-t-il jamais libéré de la peur, peur de l'invasion étrangère, peur de l'éclatement des bombes et des obus, peur du pas lourd de la patrouille ennemie, et surtout, et c'est celle-là qui est la pire, peur des coups frappés à la porte par la police politique, qui vient enlever un père ou un frère hors de la protection normale de la Loi et de la Justice—alors que chaque jour, par un seul effort spontané de sa volonté, cet homme, cet Européen pourrait se réveiller de ce cauchemar et se dresser libre et viril dans la grande lumière du jour?

Dans notre longue histoire, nous avons triomphé des dangers des guerres de religion et des guerres dynastiques; après trente ans de luttes, j'ai confiance que nous sommes arrivés à la fin des guerres nationalistes. Après toutes nos victoires et toutes nos souffrances, allons-nous maintenant sombrer dans un dernier chaos, dans des guerres idéologiques déclanchées parmi nous par des oligarchies barbares et criminelles, préparées par les agitateurs de la cinquième colonne qui s'infiltrent et conspirent dans tant de pays?

Non, je suis certain qu'il est en notre pouvoir de traverser les dangers qui sont encore devant nous, si nous le voulons. Nos espoirs et notre travail tendent vers une époque de paix, de prospérité, de plénitude, ou l'inépuisable richesse et génie de l'Europe feront d'elle, une fois de plus, la source même et l'inspiration de la vie du monde. Dans tout cela, nous avançons avec le soutien de la puissante République au-delà de l'Atlantique, et des Etats souverains qui sont membres de l'Empire et du Commonwealth des Nations britanniques.

Les dangers qui nous menacent sont grands, mais grande aussi est notre force, et il n'y a aucune raison de ne pas réussir à réaliser le but et à établir la structure de cette Europe Unie dont les conceptions morales pourront recueillir le respect et la reconnaisance de l'humanité, et dont la force physique sera telle que personne n'osera la molester dans sa tranquille marche vers l'avenir.

CONSULTATIVE ASSEMBLY OF THE COUNCIL OF EUROPE

A SPEECH AT STRASBOURG
17 AUGUST 1949

MR PRESIDENT, and colleagues:

I must congratulate the Assembly upon the high level maintained during this Debate. Not only have the speeches been full of thoughts which have their own particular value because they have been contributed from so many angles, but also there have been successful attempts at oratory which have triumphed over the acoustic conditions which, I must tell you, are none too good and which will, I trust, be subject to development, like all the rest of our proceedings. We are engaged in the process of creating a European unit in the world organization of the United Nations. I hope that we shall become one of several continental units which will form the pillars of the world instrument for maintaining security, and be the best guarantee of maintaining peace. I hope that in due course these continental units will be represented in the world organization collectively, rather than by individual States as in the present system, and that we shall be able to settle a great mass of our problems among ourselves in Europe before they are brought, or instead of them being brought, to the world council for decision.

We are not in any way the rival of the world organization. We are a subordinate but essential element in its ultimate structure. The progress of our first meeting has so far been encouraging. Our relations with the Committee of Ministers show a desire on both sides to reach a working harmony. That should not be difficult if we recognize clearly what our respective functions are. We are a deliberative Assembly, and we must have full freedom of discussion on all questions except defence. We must assert our right to this freedom and we must have our own Parliamentary officers to assist us in our debates. I trust that the necessary Amendments to the Statute will be made by the Committee of Ministers on this point as the result of our first session here at Strasbourg.

But while I feel that we should insist upon full freedom of debate, and choice of subjects, we do not possess executive power, and at this stage in our development we could not possibly claim it. Our foundation by selection by the Governments of the day from the various parliaments is not such as to give us authority at this stage to take decisions. We claim, however, to make proposals. It is not for us to make decisions which would require executive authority. We may discuss European problems and try to bring about a sense of unity. We must feel our way forward and, by our good sense, build up an increasing strength and reputation. But we must not attempt on our present electoral basis to change the powers which belong to the duly constituted national parliaments founded directly upon universal suffrage. Such a course would be premature. It would be detrimental to our long-term interests. We should, however, do our utmost to secure that these national parliaments examine and let us know their views upon any recommendation on European problems that we may make. That, I think, we may require of them. Each of us, in our respective parliaments, should take the opportunity to raise points according to the procedure which prevails.

I touch upon some of the points which are upon our agenda. I am not myself committed to a federal or any other particular solution at this stage. We must thoroughly explore all the various possibilities, and a committee, working coolly and without haste, should, in a few months, be able to show the practical steps which would be most helpful to us. I will not prejudge the work of the committee, but I hope they will remember Napoleon's saying: 'A constitution must be short and obscure.' Until that committee reports, I think we should be well advised to reserve our judgment. I am in accord with what Mr Morrison has said on this subject. I share his view that we would be wise to see what are the recommendations of our committee which, I hope, will sit permanently and not be broken up by our departure. To take a homely and familiar test, we may just as well see what the girl looks like before we marry her. It is to our advantage to have an opportunity of making a detailed examination of these problems.

Then there is the question of human rights, which is the second subject set down on our agenda. We attach great importance to this, Mr President, and are glad that the obstacles to discussion by the Assembly have now been removed by the Committee of Ministers. A European Assembly forbidden to discuss human rights would indeed have been a ludicrous proposition to put to the world. Again, I should like to see the report of the committee on this subject before we put forward our proposals to the Committee of Ministers. There is an urgency about this, because once the foundation of human rights is agreed on the lines of the decisions of the United Nations at Geneva—but I trust in much shorter form—we hope that a European Court might be set up, before which cases of violation of these rights in our own body of twelve nations might be brought to the judgment of the civilized world. Such a court, of course, would have no sanctions and would depend for the enforcement of its judgments on the individual decisions of the States now banded together in this Council of Europe. But these States would have subscribed beforehand to the process, and I have no doubt that the great body of public opinion in all these countries would press for action in accordance with the freely given decision.

I now come to the question of the empty seats, which was put before us by M. André Philip. Ten ancient capitals of Europe are behind the Iron Curtain. A large part of this continent is held in bondage. They have escaped from Nazism only to fall into the other extreme of Communism. It is like making a long and agonizing journey to leave the North Pole only to find out that, as a result, you have woken up in the South Pole. All around are only ice and snow and bitter piercing winds. We should certainly make some provision for association with representatives of these countries, who are deprived of ordinary democratic freedom but who will surely regain it in the long march of time. This is a matter which should be carefully considered by the Assembly, and I agree with all those, and there are many, who have spoken in favour of setting aside some seats in the Assembly as a symbol of proof of our intention that the Assembly shall some day represent all Europe, or all Europe west of the Curzon Line.

I now come, sir, to the greatest and most important of all the questions that are before us. A united Europe cannot live without the help and strength of Germany. This has always been foreseen by the European Movement to whose exertions our presence here is due. At The Hague, fourteen months ago, where we resolved to press for the formation of this Assembly, a German delegation was present and was welcomed by all, especially by the representatives of France. One of the most practical reasons for pressing forward with the creation of a European Assembly was that it provided an effective means, and possibly the only effective means, of associating a democratic and free Germany with the Western democracies.

It is too early to judge the results of the German election; but so far as we can yet appreciate the results, many of us, apart from party considerations, may have felt encouraged by the evident size and validity of the poll and by the general results. We cannot part at the end of this month on the basis that we do nothing more to bring Germany into our circle until a year has passed. That year is too precious to lose. If lost, it might be lost for ever. It might not be a year, but it might be the year.

On the other hand, I am assured—and here I must break the rule which Mr Harold Macmillan laid down this morning, that the word 'impossible' must never be used again—that it is physically impossible for any German Government that may emerge in the next few weeks to be represented here before we separate. I need scarcely say that I should be very glad if a way could be found. If, however, this cannot be found, then we must draw the attention of the Committee of Ministers to Article 34 of the Statute, which says: 'The Committee of Ministers may convoke an Extraordinary Session of the Consultative Assembly at such time and place as the Committee, with the concurrence of the President of the Assembly, shall decide.' I think we must ask that an assurance shall be given to us before we separate that the Committee of Ministers will convoke an Extraordinary Session of the Consultative Assembly at the earliest suitable date. If we could be told that we should meet again for an Extraordinary Session under this Article 34 in December or in January, I personally should be content to leave the matter in the hands of the Committee of Ministers, and even to forgo our claim for a debate upon this subject at this juncture.

I would ask that we should receive an assurance that an Extraordinary Session will be convened and I appeal to you, Mr Vice-President, personally to place yourself in communication with M. Spaak and urge him to confer with the Committee of Ministers upon this subject, so that we may have an answer and know what course we should take in the limited number of days and weeks which are at our disposal. When we meet in the Extraordinary Session—if one is granted—in December or January next, it is my hope that we shall find ourselves already joined by a German delegation similar to that of other Member States; but if this cannot be done, then will be the time for us to debate the issue in full freedom.

Mr Vice-President, I earnestly hope that an agreement on this matter may be reached along these lines, and that we may be informed of it as soon as possible. It would enable us to avoid various serious difficulties at the present moment and would, I think, give the best chance for the future development of the European Assembly, and the best chance of making sure that the peace of Europe will be given every opportunity to consolidate itself. Such an event as the arrival in our midst of a German delegation as a result of our work here this month would certainly crown our first Session with a solid and memorable achievement, and would have a highly beneficial result in the cause of world peace and European security.

I have only ventured to deal with these particularly important practical points, and I have not attempted to speak of the sentimental and moral aspects of our work. I hope that we shall not put our trust in formulae or in machinery. There are plenty of formulae—'slogans' I think Mr Morrison called them—and, in spite of all the misfortunes which have occurred, there is still plenty of machinery in the political field. It is by the spirit that we shall establish our force, and it is by the growth and gathering of the united sentiment of Europeanism, vocal here and listened to all over the world, that we shall succeed in taking, not executive decisions, but in taking a leading and active part in the revival of the greatest of continents which has fallen into the worst of misery.

STERLING EXCHANGE RATE (DEVALUATION OF £)

A SPEECH TO THE HOUSE OF COMMONS
28 SEPTEMBER 1949

---

19 *August—Communist Party announces its intention to put 100 candidates in the field at the next general election.*

20 *August—Mr Alfred Edwards, expelled from the Labour Party in 1948 for opposing the nationalization of steel, joins the Conservative Party.*

31 *August—British Military Government survey states that the People's Police Force in the Soviet Zone of Germany is on a military rather than a police basis.*

4 *September—Maiden flight of world's largest civil airliner, the 130-ton Bristol Brabazon 1.*

6 *September—Ethiopia demands the surrender of Marshal Badoglio and Marshal Graziani as war criminals. Italy refuses to accept the Note.*

7 *September—Australia makes a further gift of £A10,000,000 (£8,000,000) to Britain.*

   First meeting of the Parliament of the Federal Republic of Germany at Bonn.

   The Transport Commission's report discloses a deficit on the 1948 operations of £4,732,824.

8 *September—Trades Union Congress passes a Resolution calling for the greatest possible measure of restraint on wage claims.*

17 *September—At the conclusion of Washington Financial Conference, Sir Stafford Cripps says that the meeting with American and Canadian Ministers has been the most successful they have ever had.*

   First session in Washington of North Atlantic Treaty Powers.

   Sir Stafford Cripps announces the devaluation of the £ to $2.80.

   Similar measure announced by Australia, New Zealand, South Africa, Canada, India and Ceylon.

19 *September—Mr Churchill and Mr Clement Davies ask the Prime Minister for recall of Parliament to consider the situation arising from the devaluation of the £.*

21 *September—Currency devaluation announced by Belgium, Denmark, Eire, Finland, France, Greece, Iceland, Luxembourg, Netherlands, Norway, Portugal and Sweden in relation to the US dollar.*

22 *September—Statements issued by American, British and Canadian Governments that Soviet Russia is in possession of the atomic bomb.*

24 *September—Sentences passed in Hungary on Laszlo Rajk (former*

Foreign Minister) and others accused of conspiracy, with the help of Yugoslavia, to overthrow the Hungarian Government.

27 *September—Recall of both Houses of Parliament to debate the Government's decision to devalue the* £.

[28 *September* 1949

Order read for resuming Adjourned Debate on Question [27 *September* 1949]:

'That this House approves the action taken by His Majesty's Government in relation to the exchange value of the pound sterling, supports the measures agreed upon at Washington by the Ministers of the United States, Canada and the United Kingdom which are designed to assist in restoring equilibrium in the sterling–dollar balance of trade for the purpose of enabling the economy of the sterling area to maintain stability independent of external aid; and calls upon the people for their full co-operation with the Government in achieving this aim, whilst maintaining full employment and safeguarding the social services.'—[*Sir S. Cripps.*]

Question again proposed.

MR CHURCHILL (Woodford): I beg to move, in line 1, to leave out from 'House', to the end of the Question, and to add

'welcomes the measures agreed upon in Washington but regrets that His Majesty's Government, as a result of four years' financial mismanagement, should now be brought to a drastic devaluation of the pound sterling, contrary to all the assurances given by the Chancellor of the Exchequer, and considers that a return to national prosperity, the maintenance of full employment and the safeguarding of the social services can never be assured under the present Administration, which, instead of proposing fundamental cures for our economic ills, resorts to one temporary expedient after another.'

We have reached a point in our post-war story and fortunes which is both serious and strange. We have before us this afternoon the financial measures which have to be taken as a result of four years' government by the Socialist Party. It is our common interest and our first duty in the pass to which we have come to decide what it is best to do and to help it to be done in the most effective manner.

There also lies before us a General Election, the date of which will be settled in accordance with what the party opposite consider to be in their tactical interest. All political thought and party machinery is affected by this. We are, I think, most of us agreed that it is high time for another Parliament and that all our difficulties will have a better chance of being solved in a new House of Commons. We are a

Parliamentary democracy—[HON MEMBERS: 'Hear, hear.']—created before the Labour Party was born, or thought of. We are organized on a two-party basis—[An HON MEMBER: 'Two?']—in the main, and an appeal to the nation is due and overdue. There can be no doubt that this Election overlays all our domestic affairs and also, I am sorry to say, it looks as if it will be fought out with more fundamental divergencies at every grade and in every part of our society than have been known in our lifetime.

Finally over all there looms and broods the atomic bomb which the Russian Soviet, for reasons not yet explained, have got before the British, though happily not before the Americans. If you take these three factors together, the financial crisis, the party conflict and the atom bomb, it will, I think, be generally agreed that the hour is grave.

The Socialist Government ask for a vote of confidence in their financial and economic policy during the last four years and in the measures they have adopted in the present crisis and they call upon the people for their full co-operation with the Government. This is a considerable demand, this vote of confidence, and it forces us to look back on the past conduct and record of the Socialist Party who, with almost absolute power, have ruled us during this difficult and harassing period. No one must underrate the task which fell upon these Labour Ministers as the consequence of the Election of 1945. Britain and her Empire were in the war from the start and ran at full gallop, keeping nothing back, aiming only at victory till the finish. Britain had great claims on the respect of the world and on the goodwill of the United States. At the end there was an inevitable phase of national exhaustion, physical and psychical which required time to repair. There was also the tremendous transition from war to peace to be accomplished.

Under the unchallenged working of our Constitution a new Parliament was brought into being by the free choice of our people. Of course the circumstances were exceptional. There had not been a General Election for ten years; 3,000,000 or 4,000,000 of our men were with our armies abroad. The present Government were the result. They were the heirs not only of the problems of that grievous but triumphant hour, but also of all the slowly gathered treasures, customs, qualities and traditions of the ancient and famous British State.

How have they done? That is the question which by their Motion they ask us to consider this afternoon, and that is the question upon which the electors will have to pronounce at no distant date. I think it will be generally admitted that we are not in a very good position as a result of all we have done and put up with since the fighting stopped. In these last four lavish years the Socialist Government have exacted upwards of £16,000,000,000 and spent them—over four times as much every year as was the cost of running the country in our richer days before the war. They have used up every national asset or reserve upon which they could lay their hands; they have taken 40 per cent of the national income for the purposes of Governmental administration. Our taxation has been the highest in the world. It oppresses every effort and transaction of daily life.

Large incomes are virtually confiscated. The exertions and rewards of the most active class of wage-earners and craftsmen have been burdened in times of peace by the harsh direct taxation which in war, when we are fighting for life, may be a matter of pride to bear, but which in victory is at least a disappointment, and I believe has been a definite deterrent to production. Every capital reserve we had has been gobbled up. As has been well said, we ate the Argentine railways—£110,000,000—last year as a mere side dish. Our reserves of gold and hard currency which at the end of 1946 were £650,000,000 have been draining away until we are brought together here and brought up against the fact that only £300,000,000 at the old rate are left and that this would hardly last for a few months. It is because we are now brought to the verge of national and international bankruptcy after the dissipation of all this wealth that this emergency Session has been called.

MR SHURMER (Birmingham, Sparkbrook): Let the right hon Gentleman sell his horse.

MR CHURCHILL: I could sell him for a great deal more than I bought him for but I am trying to rise above the profit motive. Let us see how great is the help we have received from the productive efforts and generosity of countries outside this small crowded island which has been led so far astray. We have been given or loaned— and have spent—about £1,750,000,000 sterling by the United States. We have been helped to the extent of over £300,000,000 by Canada, Australia and New Zealand. In addition, at the end of the war Australia owed us £220,000,000 and we now owe them £10,000,000, a turnover of about £230,000,000; and there are other very considerable items which could be mentioned.

In all history no community has ever been helped and kept by gratuitous overseas aid, that is to say, by the labour of other hardworking peoples, to anything approaching the degree which we have been under the present Socialist Government. And where are we at the end of it all? That is the emergency which we have been called together here to face.

After these preliminary observations I come to the actual Motion and Amendment which are before us, and the measure which has given rise to them, namely, the devaluation of the pound sterling from 4.03 down to 2.80 of the American dollar. The Government declare that this was all they could do in the extremity to which we have come or to which we have been brought by them. Nay more—they even try to represent it as a benefit and a fine shrewd stroke of timely policy. Here again in this matter I will venture to recur to first principles and seek for realities. One must be careful not to be baffled and bewildered by technical jargon. There is no sphere of human thought in which it is easier for a man to show superficial cleverness and the appearance of superior wisdom than in discussing questions of currency and exchange. I saw a very good cartoon in a newspaper the other day of a hospital ward filled with patients who had become demented through trying to explain the devaluation problem to their wives.

But I will submit to the House some simple propositions which they may deem worthy of consideration and which are at any rate easy to understand. The reduction of the rate of dollar exchange from 4.03 to 2.80 means, subject to certain minor abatements, that we may have to pay up to nearly half as much again, some say 35 per cent, some 40 per cent, for what we buy—much of it necessaries without which we cannot live—from the dollar area. We may have to pay up to nearly half as much again over an area of almost one-fifth of our imports—actually 17 per cent.

That cannot be good for us. It can only mean that we are forced to give much more of our life energy, that is to say toil, sweat, physical fatigue, craftsmanship, ingenuity, enterprise and good management, to buy the same quantity of indispensable products outside this country as we had before. We have to do more work and draw more upon our spirits and our carcasses to win back the same amount of food, raw materials and other goods without which we cannot carry on. That is bad for us; it is a new blow to our economic health and a new burden which we have to bear.

Now, the life thrust of the British nation, if not impeded, is magnificent, but we have been, as I said at the beginning, exhausted by our glorious efforts in the war. Great exertions are made by the people, but we can ill afford to make a new drain upon our latent strength and remaining motive power. We are not in a state of health to become a blood donor on a large scale at the present time. We are already a blood donor on a tremendous scale through our unrequited exports to India, Egypt and other countries to whom we became indebted for local supplies while we were defending them from being conquered by the Italians, the Germans or the Japanese. The *Manchester Guardian*, perhaps at this moment a better guide on economics than on ethics, has estimated these unrequited exports at nearly one-fifth of our total exports. That is a lot.

Many hundreds of thousands of our skilled or semi-skilled wage earners are toiling today to make desirable things for those countries which are paid for simply by somebody scratching something off with his pen from what is described by the misleading term 'sterling balances', which really means British debts. Nothing comes back in return to nourish the productive energies of the island. Trade is exchange, but here is neither trade nor exchange. An intense effort goes out and nothing comes back. I am not at this moment arguing the rights and wrongs, though I am quite willing to do so on a suitable occasion. I think that an amount for our expenses for the defence of those countries should have been set against the local supplies, but it would be a long argument and much could be said. I am not arguing it at the moment; I am only setting forth the brutal fact.

On the top of all this the devaluation of the pound sterling draws a further draft in life blood and initial energy not only from the wage-earning masses but from all that constitutes the productive fertility of Britain. We are to give anything up to 45 per cent more products of our own toil for the same amount of dollar imports. That cannot be a good thing, it cannot be something to rejoice about, it cannot be something to parade as a triumph or to boast over as some new benefit bestowed by the Socialist Government upon our struggling community. It is a hard and heavy blow. However necessary it may be at the point to which we have been led, even if it be the best step open to us to take in the plight into which we have fallen—and all that is arguable—the hard, blunt, simple conclusion remains; it cannot be a good thing. We have suffered a serious disaster. In all this my mind would have marched step by step with that of the Chancellor of the Exchequer until a fortnight ago. Now, he probably finds these notions revolting and reactionary. So much for the first of the realities of devaluation. I must not again make the joke about revaluation. The delicacy of the point will I am sure be fully respected.

Now I come to the second reality which is more complicated. Anybody can understand that it is not good for a man in a weak state of health with an overstrained vitality to be tapped month by month for his life blood for the good of others across the oceans, be they stronger or weaker, in order to win his daily bread and that of his wife and children. But this second point concerns the whole sterling area of which the British Empire and Commonwealth is the foundation; and also it concerns all the mighty regions of Europe outside the Iron Curtain.

I see it said that the effect of our devaluation of the pound and its consequences on European and on sterling currencies is to erect something like a 40 per cent tariff wall against the United States. I am myself a supporter of Imperial Preference, of European Unity and of the sterling area and I am glad to see all these vast regions and forces becoming conscious of a common identity. I cannot regret in itself the drawing of a girdle or *zollverein* around themselves. But here it is a question of degree. Up to a certain point it would be a help. It would help world recovery. But beyond that point it may well be a hindrance.

I think of course as a free trader. I may have adopted some variations and modifications, as we all have in the course of years, but still that is the basis on which my thought was formed many years ago. If we pierce down to the economic roots of world production and human material and creative power, the erection of a new barrier in addition to the political and economic barrier of the Iron Curtain in the modern world of today cannot be deemed a stimulus. Restriction is never a stimulus in itself. It may in a crisis make for order, but it is not a stimulus. It may on a long-term view promote a wider harmony and more equal bargaining power, but in so far as world trade is restricted this is a contrary force to the ideal of plenty. Abundance or plenty is the aim of mankind. Plenty is within its power. Plenty should be its inheritance. Plenty is hope for all. Restriction is inevitably the enemy of plenty.

It has been stated that the United States Government have pressed us to devaluate the pound. The Chancellor need not even shake his head. I was not going to omit the point. The Chancellor told us yesterday that he did it of his own free will when the time came. I do not suppose that the United States, this gigantic capitalist organization, with its vast and super-abundant productive power—millions of people animated by the profit motive—I do not suppose that it will be seriously injured by a moderate wire fence being placed around the British Empire, the sterling area and United Europe. But I cannot believe that American manufacturers will see in such a development any immediate inducement to reduce their own highly protective tariff behind which they have built up their unrivalled economic power and which tariff is backed—as all tariffs are—by potent political interests.

I should be very glad to be contradicted by events. I have always hoped for a large reduction in American tariffs, but this is no time to nurse illusions or delusions. We must seek the truth even if we cannot give full effect to it at this particular moment, and we must face it when found however ugly it may be. I cannot feel that what has taken place—namely, the erection of a 40 per cent tariff around the European area and the sterling area is likely to promote in itself the probability of an important United States change from her present protective policy. I hope, however, that they will rise above the considerations which obviously present themselves at this stage.

I come to my third point, my third reality, upon this issue of devaluation and it centres upon the word 'truth'. Whatever the currency experts may say—and they say all sorts of things and with learned grimaces change their views very frequently—but whatever they may say, the true exchange value between pound and dollar, or between all other currencies and the dollar or the pound, the true one is the right one; and the one at which we ought to aim. In the present circumstances if the Chancellor of the Exchequer felt it necessary to devaluate the pound to a fixed figure, I think it was right to go the whole hog; and that it was better to cut down the rate of exchange to this level in the hopes of a later revival than to take half measures which would soon have been overtaken and overwhelmed by the true and real forces which are relentlessly at work.

Now the matter is done, and when we have had to give up our exchange position which we had maintained so long I feel entitled to take a fresh view. I am all for a free market and a true market. As I told the House two or three years ago, it is only a false and untrue market officially supported that breeds a black market. A sham market can no more escape a black market than a man can escape from his own shadow. Therefore I should myself have been more inclined, had I been in any way responsible, to set the pound free under regular and necessary safeguards and control—[*Laughter*]—certainly, and accept the results, than to the present rigid method of pegging the exchange at the very lowest rate which anyone could possibly conceive.

The Chancellor of the Exchequer argued at some length against this yesterday, and it is obvious that anything that is free or largely unregulated is obnoxious to the Socialist mentality. But this was what we did in 1931—the last time we had to clear up the Socialist financial mess—[*Interruption*]—Oh, I remember it well. Quite soon we had a natural exchange rate of 3.30 which through the actions of both countries rested fairly stable until the war came. I do not think that the idea of the liberation of the pound should be ruled out by any Government which can command confidence abroad. That may be the decisive reason for the Chancellor of the Exchequer rejecting it at the present time.

I believe that great strength still resides in the sterling area of which Britain is the centre. That has to some extent been proved by the many countries which, roughly as they were used, and little though they were consulted, have had to conform to our action. I believe that this strength, working freely and backed by the intense productive effort of all the communities concerned, would in a short while achieve a far better rate of exchange against the dollar than the present figure of 2.80 to which we have been condemned. I believe further that in its intrinsic strength under favourable circumstances a free pound might establish itself at a rate which, while far more beneficial for us than the present position, would nevertheless promote and express a natural but conscious affinity throughout the sterling and associated currencies of the world.

To sum up this part of my argument which I am submitting to the House, the devaluation of the pound sterling is a new and serious drain upon the life strength of Britain. We always supported the Chancellor of the Exchequer in resisting it. It might have been better in my view, and may still be better when confidence is restored, to let the pound go free under proper safeguards—[HON MEMBERS: 'What are they?']—control of the sending of large sums of money from this country—all this applied in 1931—[*Laughter*]—what are hon Members laughing at? They had very little to laugh at in 1931. It may have been better, I say, and may well be better when confidence is restored to let the pound go free under proper safeguards and reach its natural level. A free pound would impose a less severe drain upon our conditions of life and labour, and nevertheless, in reaching its true level would afford a girdle to the European and sterling area which, without being unduly restrictive, would afford an effective means of economic as well as political association.

Now I turn from discussing the policy of devaluation to the timing of the act and the sequence of events in which it lies. Judged by the results, the management of our finances has been deplorable. If as a result of that mismanagement the devaluation or liberation of the pound sterling had become inevitable, ought it not to have been taken as part of a general policy of setting our finances in order? A reduction in expenditure—

THE MINISTER OF NATIONAL INSURANCE [MR JAMES GRIFFITHS]: On what?

MR CHURCHILL:—a substantial relief in taxation—[HON MEMBERS: 'On what?']—The Chancellor of the Exchequer does not say there should never be any reduction in expenditure. Hon Members should ask him on what. He has the power to answer the question, and the duty to answer the question—[An Hon Member: 'It is your duty, too.']—I am as good a judge of my duty as the hon Member is of his.

I say that a reduction in expenditure, a substantial relief in taxation applied to increase incentives to production and earnings, especially among the wage-earners liable to direct taxation, widespread relaxation of needless and vexatious controls and interferences with the flexibility of private enterprise, the definite lifting of the shadow of further nationalization from our most active and prosperous industries and, above all, the return to power of a Government commanding national and international confidence—all these would have created and may still create conditions in which the liberation of the pound sterling would have a good chance of opening wide doors of prosperity into the future.

But by one means or another devaluation or liberation, if this step were inevitable, should have been taken as part of a general scheme of financial reform instead of being plunged into as an isolated act forced upon us at the last moment. Again and again the Chancellor was warned from this side of the House and by financial authorities outside that he was living in a fool's paradise. But all these warnings were in vain. I think he made some remark about 'Dismal Desmonds'. Was that his phrase or did one of his colleagues achieve this alliterative gem?

Therefore, whatever may be thought of the relative advantages or disadvantages of devaluing or liberating the pound sterling, the timing of the step was obviously wrong. A drastic alteration in the exchange rate, if proved necessary, should not have been left till the crisis broke upon us but should have been taken in anticipation of it. It is not easy to palliate the right hon and learned Gentleman's blunder. We all know the abilities of the Chancellor of the Exchequer. In his position he had more and better information on the subject at his disposal than anyone else in the world. He ought, surely, to have exercised foresight and decision in good time before our remaining gold reserves had been drained away and he was forced higgledy-piggledy into action which we know he loathed, under the worst possible circumstances.

I am sorry not to see the Lord President of the Council [Mr Herbert Morrison] in his place because I wish to quote with great approval some remarks which he has made on this subject:

'The real problem of statesmanship,' said the Lord President of the Council in June 1946, 'in the field of industry and economics is to see trouble coming and to prevent ourselves getting into the smash. We are determined that we are not going to be caught unawares by blind economic forces under this Administration.'

But that is exactly what has happened to his colleague the Chancellor of the Exchequer. He could not possibly have described it in more precise or harmonious language. In fact, it has almost a prophetic aspect about it.

I come to another point. The question is much discussed in the country of the Chancellor's political honesty. Ordinary people find it difficult to understand how a Minister, with all his knowledge and reputation for integrity, should have felt it right to turn completely around, like a squirrel in its cage, abandon his former convictions and do what he repeatedly said he would never do, and moreover, enforce upon his party and his most faithful followers the humiliating tergiversation which we have witnessed. I am surprised, I must say, that the Chancellor's own self-respect did not make him feel that, however honest and necessary was his change of view, his was not the hand that should carry forward the opposite policy. Certainly he stands woefully weakened in reputation, first by his lack of foresight, and secondly, by having had completely to reverse the reasoned convictions with which he made us familiar. Of course, we know that changes in currency cannot be announced beforehand. The secret had to be kept. It was certainly very well kept, perhaps too well kept considering the position of some of our friendly countries like France. But we congratulate the Chancellor—and he will agree with this—and the Foreign Secretary on the high art which they displayed in the necessary process of deception. The histrionic quality of their performance was indeed remarkable.

But I am not speaking of the last month but of the position three and four months ago. I have been shown nine quotations from the Chancellor's speeches declaring himself the inveterate opponent of devaluation. It is very important that our Chancellor of the Exchequer should have foresight. It is also desirable that he should have consistency, as far as possible. It is important that Parliament and the country should believe that when he speaks at that box opposite he means what he says. Otherwise, how can people attach the weight to his declarations and pledges without which a Chancellor of the Exchequer is grievously crippled? How he of all men could adopt the policy, 'What I tell you nine times is untrue', is most astonishing.

Although his personal honour and private character are in no wise to be impugned, it will be impossible in the future for anyone to believe or accept with confidence any statements which he may make as Chancellor of the Exchequer from that box. He stands convicted of lamentable lack of foresight. His usefulness, for all his abilities in the great office he holds, has been definitely impaired, and I find it most difficult to believe that he would have been content to stay in office if he had thought the ordeal was likely to be a long one.

It is odd that the Chancellor of the Exchequer in his present weak and vulnerable position should feel entitled to judge his predecessors with so much severity and to impute wrong and unworthy motives to them. The right hon and learned Gentleman referred yesterday to my action in returning to the Gold Standard a quarter of a century ago. He said that his policy today was a substitution for the alternative policy of severe deflation.

'That policy'—I quote his words from *Hansard*—'was pursued at one time under the aegis of the right hon Gentleman the Leader of the Opposition and depended for its efficacy upon a massive extension of unemployment, with the accompanying lowering of wage rates and so the impoverishment of the employed and unemployed.'

There were loud cheers from hon Gentlemen opposite.

This was a very aggressive and I may even say offensive reference to past history. To suggest that people would like to see other people unemployed is I think deserving—[*Interruption*]. I will pick my epithets with care, and I have a large collection of them—is I think deserving of the word 'offensive'. I think that the whole passage in which he referred to me is singularly out of keeping with the governess and sermon-like passages of some other parts of his discourse. I must say that I am obliged to him for making his accusations here, where they can be answered, instead of circulating them, as is no doubt being done far and wide at this present moment by his party propaganda machine.

The House must pardon me if I make a short digression——

MR GEORGE THOMAS (Cardiff, Central): This whole speech has been a digression.

MR CHURCHILL: The hon Gentleman is very talkative. One of the strongest claims that the party opposite have is that with their great majority they have never hampered free speech, however detrimental they might find it to themselves.

I will cite only one quotation in answer to the Chancellor. It is by Mr Snowden, Chancellor of the Exchequer in the first Socialist Government in 1924, and Chancellor again in 1929. In the interval he led the Socialist Opposition in all financial matters. He was one of their most respected and influential founder members.

On the Second Reading of the Gold Standard Bill he said that while the Government had acted with undue precipitancy, he and his Socialist colleagues were in favour of a return to the Gold Standard at the earliest possible moment. The Socialist Opposition thereupon refrained from voting against what, in the right hon and learned Gentleman's words of yesterday, was a policy which:

'. . . depended for its efficacy upon a massive extension of unemployment with the accompanying lowering of wage rates.'

Later on, in December 1926, Mr Snowden wrote an article in the *Financial Times* in which he said:

'All the facts do not support the impression that the return to gold has been detrimental to industry. The bank rate has not been raised; unemployment has not risen; real wages have not fallen; and the price level has been fairly well maintained.'

I am rather astonished that the right hon and learned Gentleman, before he went out of his way to attack me about transactions long buried in the past, should not have acquainted himself with these declarations of Mr Snowden's in the heyday of his power and influence with the Labour Party. I must also state, since the matter has been raised, that during my four and a half years' tenure of the Chancellorship, the cost of living declined by at least 18 points, while money wages remained stable. That certainly compares very favourably with what has occurred in the last four years, what is occurring now, and what is going to recur in a harder degree.

Secondly, I may remind the House that when I am charged with seeking a massive extension of unemployment, it was not until I left the Exchequer in 1929 that, under the Socialist administration, the rate of unemployment doubled and overtopped the 2,000,000 figure. It really is remarkable that the accusation of being callous about unemployment or the welfare of the people should be launched against me, the author of the labour exchanges and of the first Unemployment Insurance Act, and, as Conservative Chancellor of the Exchequer, of the Old Age Pensions age being lowered from 70 to 65 and the institution of the Widows' and Orphans' Act.

When the right hon and learned Gentleman or anybody on those benches can show services rendered to the working classes equal to those I have mentioned they will be more free to throw stones at others. All the benevolent and beneficial aspects of this Parliament— apart, that is to say, from sterile controversial party measures—were actually planned in great detail by the National Coalition Government. [*Interruption.*] The right hon Gentleman the Minister of Health was not a member of that Government; he was otherwise occupied in those days. That legislation was actually planned by the National Coalition Government of which I was the head and which rested on an overall Conservative majority in the House of Commons of 150.

I noticed by the way—the right hon and learned Gentleman in his difficult position is showing himself not unruffled—that the Chancellor yesterday used a new term of prejudice and opprobrium. He spoke with disdain of doing anything which would start a period of freedom for the profit earners. What is this prejudice against profit earners? 'Profiteer' is the word which all may abhor, but the stigma in that term is not 'profit earner' but unfair exploitation. How can a country like this live without its profit earners? How could the Chancellor of the Exchequer collect his revenues without taking, as he admits, 50 or 60 per cent of the profits that they earn? How can anything stand without the profit earners? How wrong it is for a statesman in his position to cast his censures upon them, and, presumably, reserve his tributes for the disinterested loss-makers who manage our nationalized industries?

In the closing sentence of our Amendment, which I am now moving, we have given prominence to the Chancellor of the Exchequer's own words. He has certainly been candid in his confession. He has admitted that the financial policy of the Government he is supposed to be defending has been 'the resort to one temporary expedient after another'. That is certainly a frank confession, and it is, to a large extent, an explanation of our continued drift and slide downhill. I can only say confession is good for the soul, but after confession comes penance, not power.

His Majesty's Government in their Motion appeal for the co-operation of the whole people. It is certainly the duty of everyone to help in every way to increase our production and improve its efficiency. But surely it is not for the present Government to appeal to us on the grounds of national interest. Of our own accord, in spite of many provocations and insults, we have helped them throughout their long four years of power in all that we believed was necessary in the public interest.

First there was the American Loan of £1,000,000,000. Not without some doubts and differences, and some criticism in our own party, I and my colleagues on this bench helped them all we could, both here and in the United States, to obtain the loan, little though we liked its terms. Secondly, the Marshall Aid Plan on which the Government are now living was stated by General Marshall to have arisen in his mind out of the movement for United Europe which he directly associated with my name. This, he said, had led him to what we all acclaim as his wise and generous policy without which, according to the Lord President of the Council at Manchester on 17 April 1948, 'we should be facing cuts in rations and a million or two people on the dole'. And the Minister of Health on 18 May 1948, in a momentary lapse, which he has no doubt greatly regretted since, said: 'But for Marshall Aid, unemployment in this country would at once rise by 1,500,000.' That the Socialist Government have been spared the distress, nay the agony, of an immense rise in unemployment which would have been fatal to them and for many years to their party, has been directly due, and provedly due, to the aid which the Conservative Opposition have given, irrespective of party interests.

I think that some acknowledgment of these facts by Ministers in this Debate would have been becoming. We cannot, of course, forgo our right or neglect our duty to criticize the maladministration of our affairs or fail to warn the people of what lies before them if they allow themselves again to be misled by promises and fallacies. At one moment we were told—it now appears, from the account given by the Chancellor of the Exchequer, none too accurately—that the mission which the Chancellor and the Foreign Secretary were carrying out in the United States was concerned with matters vital to our financial interests, and that it all hung in the balance. From that moment we used all our influence to silence all criticism, and we only resume it now that these matters have been settled and because a new policy has been declared.

At every moment throughout this Parliament we have urged all those with whom we have influence—probably the majority of the workers and producers of the nation, employers and employees alike—to do their utmost to stimulate production. We have supported, at the request of the Prime Minister, on the public platform the savings campaign and the recruiting campaign, and we shall continue to do so. We have done this because though we are party men, we feel bound to put country before party.

But how does His Majesty's Government behave in this field? I will admit that they have done many unpopular things, some of which were in the public interest. But, on the whole, they have played the party game with national stakes in a manner which no other Government I can remember in my long life or read about in modern history have ever done. They perpetuated a mass of wartime controls to give them that power of interference in the daily life of the country which is a characteristic of Socialism. They reasserted by regulation the wartime control of the severest form of direction of labour. They have the power today to take anyone and send them anywhere they will. Though they took these powers, they have not dared to enforce them, but the insult to national and personal liberty remains unreduced. As a mere act of party spite the Chancellor of the Exchequer abolished, at substantial annual loss, the Liverpool Cotton Exchange. The Government thrust upon the nation struggling out of its wartime exhaustion the evils of nationalization and of their party doctrines.

It is some consolation, I must admit, that the miners and the railwaymen should have learned, and learned by practical experience, what the nationalization of great industries means in practice to the workers in them and to the public at large. The whole policy of nationalization is being proved every day more clearly to be a costly failure and a further drain upon our life blood. Now at this moment when we are brought to this melancholy pass, and now that we are in this position of grave difficulty, the Government still proclaim their intention to nationalize the steel industry, and, should they be returned to power, they proclaim their resolve to nationalize insurance, cement and sugar. Never have a Government or a party more completely divested themselves of the title deeds to speak in the name of the nation.

But all this ill-usage in no way relieves us of our duty to encourage everyone to do his or her utmost to improve the national effort in these days of crisis, and thus to preserve to the British nation the power to regain in the future the great position in the world which it has held in the past. Nor must we allow the insults which have been hurled at us to provoke us into similar taunts. [*Laughter.*] Hon Members opposite laugh. Personally, I do not think that a large part of the British people are lower than vermin. I think that the British nation is good all through.

More than forty years ago I sat myself in a Left-wing Government with a majority even greater than that of the present one, and I was one of their most prominent and controversial figures. The House returned in 1906 represented, in my view, more or less the same slice of the population, the people who elected it coming very largely from the same homes and from the same areas, as does this majority today. I found them very good people to work with, and I renewed this comradeship in the long and terrible years of the war. But there was a great difference between those days of forty years ago and these in which we are now living. The Liberal Government of 1906 was built around and upon those great principles of Liberalism which have since passed into the possession of every party except the Communists, and are still spreading with irresistible appeal throughout the world. But now those who sit opposite to us are not ranged around the great truths of Liberalism; they are ranged around the fallacy of Socialism, which is in principle contrary to human nature and which I believe can only be enforced upon nations in its entirety in the wholesale fashion of Communism.

At present only 20 per cent of our industries are nationalized, and we have been living upon the other 80 per cent, which the Government eye with so much disfavour and malice. There is indeed a great gulf of thought and conviction between us. 'All men are born equal,' says the American Declaration of Independence. 'They must be kept equal,' say the British Socialist Party. Here is the deadly stroke at the mainspring of life and progress. I grieve that in these perilous years we should be so harshly and needlessly divided. Only an appeal to the people and a new Parliament can relieve the increasing tension.

And let me say this. If at this moment the Government were to drop steel nationalization and their other extreme plans, it would certainly enable the approaching General Election to be conducted in an atmosphere much less dangerous to the underlying national unities on which 50,000,000 in this island depend for their survival. [*Laughter.*] The Chancellor of the Exchequer may lead the cackles opposite at those sentiments if he believes it worthy of his position and of the serious part he has played and is playing in our affairs. It is my duty and that of those whom I lead to warn the country in good time of its dangers. But I thank God that in my old age I preserve an invincible faith that we shall overcome them.

What has been the great characteristic of our age? As I have seen it during my lifetime, it has been the arrival at an ever more bountiful table of millions and tens of millions and scores of millions of people. There is no reason why this march should not continue. There is no reason why the struggle of the masses for a more spacious life, for shorter hours, for constantly improving conditions of labour, should not be crowned with increasing success. Otherwise, what would be the use of all the machinery and improved methods of modern times? There is no reason, I say, why the forward march should not continue, provided that mistaken guides do not enforce the rule that all must come to the table at once or none at all. That indeed would bar the door to that continuous progress and expansion which has been maintained even during the convulsions of our lifetime, and which it is ours to enjoy if we do not wantonly cast it away.

CONSERVATIVE TRADES UNION CONGRESS

A SPEECH AT LONDONDERRY HOUSE
13 OCTOBER 1949

---

30 September—*Berlin airlift officially ended. Total cost of airlift to the British Exchequer was approximately £10,250,000.*

1 October—*Mao Tse-tung announces that the National Government of China has been overthrown and proclaims the People's Republic as the sole Government of China.*

5 October—*Announcement in Berlin of a decision to form a 'German Democratic Republic' in Eastern Germany.*

10 October—*Lord Beaverbrook publishes his 10-point programme which he claims would, if put into operation, 'restore to our country peace and plenty'.*

11 October—*Annual Conference of Conservative Party at Eastbourne. Mr Churchill says Lord Beaverbrook's programme does not represent the considered policy of the Conservative Party.*

Foreign Office issue the text of a Note presented to Moscow rejecting the Soviet charges that the Western Allies had violated the Potsdam Agreement by forming a Western German Government.

12 October—*Civil Aviation reports disclose a deficit of £9,700,000 for the year ending 31 March 1949 by the British Airline Corporations.*

[13 *October* 1949

I am very glad to see you here in Londonderry House. In the bygone aristocratic days it was associated with the glories of the Napoleonic era, in which our island defended not, as it proved, for the last time, the liberties of Europe against tyranny. It is appropriate that Conservative trade unionists should meet here, because the private enterprise of the Londonderry family drove out the great shaft to the coalbeds under the sea, which has been a source of enduring employment and a permanent enrichment to the coal supplies of Britain. The Government have told us today that there is to be no General Election before Christmas. In their announcement they say that this is because of the disturbing effect on trade and industry and on the national effort, which has been caused by the continuance of speculation about the date. There has indeed been disturbance of trade and industry, but whose fault is it? It is the fault of one man, the Prime Minister—

Mr Attlee—who could at any time in the last month by a nod or a gesture have dispersed the rumours that he intended to spring a snap election. He need not even have spoken himself; he could have told his party organ, the *Daily Mirror*. Instead of this, he has held everything in the balance and in suspense until the last moment, and has in fact arranged all kinds of discussion and all kinds of party bargaining while they made up their minds what it would pay them best to do. Any loss there has been, and it may be heavy, has been entirely due to Mr Attlee and to his failure to make up his mind what was the proper course to take. Some say he was waiting for Mr Bevin's return from America; but I did not know that the Labour Party had abolished the electric telegraph. Others will wonder whether he was not awaiting reports from the Party machine as to how the effects produced by devaluation, with its certain rise in the cost of living, had gone down in the constituencies. Perhaps they will come in now that undoubtedly, in the words of the Government communique, 'grave disturbance has been caused to business and to industry at this critical time'.

So far as the Conservative Party is concerned, looking at the matter on purely party grounds, we are quite indifferent as to the date of the election. The only thing we are concerned with, as party men, is that we should be ready whenever it comes, so that we are not taken by surprise and are ready for it in every way—we are pretty sure that Lord Woolton will look after that. But this is not to be judged as a matter of Party advantage or disadvantage. From a national point of view the sooner a new Parliament, the better. A continuance of the present uncertainty and friction can only be an impediment to national revival. I said two years ago there ought to be a new Parliament; had there been one, we should be much better off now in many ways. There is only one course open to the Socialists if they wish to redeem their record. They should do their duty in the intervening months by carrying out the financial reforms that are necessary, however unpopular they may be. But whatever the Government propose that is for the national good will be supported by the Opposition, whether it is popular or not. But above all it is the duty of the Government, if they care for the country, to call an immediate stop to all schemes of nationalization and to concentrate their energies upon the grievous task of saving us from bankruptcy. If they were to do this, great improvements in every direction might be possible. But if they merely continue to falter and show themselves, on this occasion, incapable of decision, and at the same time continue their vague attacks upon the foundations of our national prosperity, they will only make things worse for all and, you may be sure, for themselves.

The Conservative position towards trade unions is well known. We support the principle of collective bargaining between recognized and responsible trade unions and employers, and we include in collective bargaining the right to strike. They have a great part to play in the life of the country and we think they should keep clear of Party politics. We hope that Conservative wage-earners in industry will join the trade unions and will take an effective part in their work not as Party men, but as good trade unionists. I consider myself a trade unionist. When, in the beginning of 1945 there was a great national meeting of the trade union leaders at which I was to be presented by Lord Citrine himself with my trade union ticket, my public duty forced me to go to Yalta, to the talks there, and I am not quite sure when the engagement is postponed to.

I am told about 32 per cent of the trade unionists are Conservatives; the more the better. If we should become responsible for the conduct of affairs it will be our aim, as I said at Wolverhampton, to maintain the closest contact with the trusted and able trade union leaders and to discuss with them all means of improving continually working conditions, and to further those principles of co-operation and profit-sharing which are set out at length in our short book, *The Right Road For Britain*. But we do not wish to compromise their position with their members by trying to make them become the agents of Government-owned monopolies—partisans of any particular political group. I hope trade union leaders will realize that as nationalization proceeds, they lose their position of bargaining on behalf of their members with private employers. I trust they will consider this. In the nationalized industries the trade union leaders, for many of whom I have much respect, are being more and more drawn into the position of being on the side of the State employer, instead of facing a much more flexible private owner while the State stands aside ready to conciliate and mitigate the process of collective bargaining.

Now I am pretty sure in the near future the Conservative Party will become responsible for the government of this country. We were 10,000,000 in the last election; it is more likely to be between 12,000,000 and 14,000,000 in the forthcoming election. We have every intention, if we have to accept responsibility of government, of exercising those responsibilities in no class or party spirit and to do the best for all. In order to do that it will be necessary for the great trade union bodies to play their part in the Councils of State and take their part in bringing forward improvement in new industries and bringing prosperity to our industrial life.

The British nation is one all the world over. No one party has the right to use insulting terms about the other. Like a great family we go forward to more glorious service to our fellow men.

CONSERVATIVE ANNUAL CONFERENCE

A SPEECH AT THE EMPRESS HALL, EARLS COURT, LONDON
14 OCTOBER 1949

We have all been kept on tenterhooks about whether there would be a General Election before Christmas and about when we should be graciously told. The Prime Minister spoke yesterday about the grave disturbance he had caused to trade and industry by his inability to decide. That is quite true.

All over the country, in every form of productive and business activity, people have been kept in needless uncertainty, waiting about from day to day. At the very moment when we should all be driving full steam ahead, we all had to wait until the Cabinet could agree among themselves what would pay their Party best. Now at last they have made up their minds.

What part have we in all these twittering calculations? How glad we are that we have nothing to do with them at all. We are indifferent as to when the election comes. Whenever it comes we are ready. On Party grounds alone we can certainly afford to wait. But on national grounds, a very grave, practical question arises. Can Britain, in the pass to which she has been led, or has been brought, afford to spend three or four, or five months' manoeuvring about Party tactics and electioneering, with a Parliament which is not only dead but decomposing, with divisions growing ever deeper and passions rising ever higher in the bosom of our hard-pressed people by whose actions in this crisis the fortunes of our world-wide Empire and of many other lands are affected?

I said two years ago that we ought to have a new Parliament in view of the unrepresentative character of the House of Commons resulting from the last election, the first for ten years, with many of our men abroad and so on. It is certain now that if we had had a new Parliament two years ago we should be in a very much better position in the world tonight than we are at this moment. All our reserves and resources would not have been used up. We should be a stronger, a richer, and it might well be a more united nation in the deepening crisis of our own and world affairs.

We have now before us a period of several months more Socialist rule, at the end of which an election must come. It would be in the public interest that Ministers should make up their minds and announce to the public at least the month in which they intend to appeal to the country; that would be in the public interest, and I have just put in a plea for that. If they do not do so, it is inevitable that all our affairs, especially our trade, will be hampered every week and every day by the unrest of an impending election, at which so much is at stake, and which may pounce out upon us at some moment tactically selected by the Socialist Party. We have got to live through these months on the alert for any blow that may be struck; but what a way to treat the serious situation in this country! If the Socialists repeat in the New Year the uncertainty, which Mr Attlee told us yesterday had already done harm in this year, theirs will be the responsibility, and on them will fall the censure of the nation.

What then should be our attitude in the intervening period? We shall support the Government in all measures which we consider necessary to restore the national finances and economy, however unpopular they may be. We shall not grudge them any advantages which they may gain by doing their duty to the country. But we, too, are bound to discharge our duty as an Opposition and to labour ceaselessly to explain to the nation the evils that have been brought upon us and to convince the elector that these are only a foretaste of what full Socialism would bring upon the British people.

In Parliament, for instance, we have now to meet two of the most controversial measures—the mutilation of the Parliament Act and the crowning stroke at British trade recovery, the steel nationalization Bill; these are coming upon us—they are being thrust upon us. We shall make our most earnest protest and resistance against these acts of party spite and economic sabotage. They completely strip the Socialist Ministers of the slightest right to appeal for national unity. If these two Bills are driven through Parliament in this economic crisis, the gulf between the two parties will become wider and deeper than ever before. And here again the blame will fall on the heads of those who give this renewed provocation.

But let me say this. We are here a Party straining at the leash to drive from power the men who we think have done our country so much harm and robbed it in a large measure of the fruits of our hardwon victory. I know Conservatives will never allow our Party feelings and natural righteous desires to lead us into welcoming bad news or hoping that the misfortunes of our country will help our return to power. We are Party men, but we shall be all the stronger if in every action we show ourselves capable, even in this period of stress and provocation, of maintaining the division—where there is a division—between national and Party interests. And it is in this way that we shall prove to our fellow countrymen that Conservative interests are identical with national interests, that we stand for the nation and its fortunes as a whole, and that if we fight as partisans it is only because we deserve and desire to serve not one class or one party but the whole of our dear island.

We are often asked what we should do ourselves if we had the power. Today the Conservative Party has neither the power nor the responsibility to decide the policy and shape the fortunes of the State. All the instruments of Government and much of the machinery of propaganda are in Socialist hands. At this moment we can only utter words, but the national safety requires deeds. It is not propaganda but action which is required and for action we must have both responsibility and power. The advantage and significance of deeds is that they bring consequences. A number of well-considered actions might each one of them be unpopular or even painful in itself, but if all were taken at the same moment as part of a general design might quite soon bring about a widespread improvement which would more than compensate for what we have had to endure or give up.

A programme of words can be pulled to pieces bit by bit without there being any compensating results to show in the general welfare of the State. That is why I have advised you consistently during these last four years not to commit yourselves to detailed rigid programmes, but to let the nation learn as it is learning from its own experience— the hard teaching of facts. That is what we have done. Two years ago at our Conference at Brighton I ventured to give the Government some advice. I said then:

'The wasteful and needless expenditure which we see on all sides must be reduced by several hundred million pounds a year, and this must, when saved, be immediately given in relief of taxation in such a way as to increase the incentives to diligence, to thrift, to ingenuity and profit-making.'

Well, I say the same tonight. Of course the Socialists answer: 'Show us in detail what economies you intend.' But how could we do this without knowledge and without control of the great departments and machinery of State? Of course the Socialists only ask the question with the sole object of enabling their canvassers to go around from house to house appealing to individual and personal local self-interest of the narrowest kind. Now, two years too late, they have to start to cut expenditure themselves. It will be interesting to see what their plans are, but whatever they are we may already say that there is nothing they can do now which would not have been much better done two years ago, when they were advised to do it by us.

In our statement on Tory outlook and aspiration, which we have called *The Right Road For Britain*, we have set forth in much detail the mood and temper in which our half of the nation, and it may well be the better half—and it may well prove to be the larger half —approach the future. *The Right Road For Britain* shows where we want to go. It offers a broad, tolerant, progressive and hopeful prospect to the British people. I am very glad that this little book, for which Mr Butler deserves much credit, should already have gone into 2,000,000 British homes. It constitutes an overwhelming repudiation of the taunt that we are a class Party seeking to defend abuses or willing to tolerate the exploitation of the mass of the people by vested interests, by monopolies or by bygone ideas. Here then is the right road for Britain, that is the road we shall strive to tread.

But there is one thing which I want to make clear tonight above all else and that is the position of the Conservative Party whenever the election comes. We are not going to try to get into office by offering bribes and promises of immediate material benefits to our people. The Socialists did that in 1945. We offer no smooth or easy path to the British nation now fighting for its life almost as it did in the war. We do not know what will be the facts with which we shall be confronted should we be returned to power. Certainly they have gravely worsened in the last few months and we have found out much more about them only in the last few weeks. Nothing will induce me as your leader at this election to bid for office by competing with the Socialists in promises of Utopias around the corner or of easy escape from the hard facts by which we are surrounded. It would be far better for us to lose the election than to win it on false pretences.

All I will promise to the British electorate in your name and the only pledge that I will give on behalf of the Conservative Party is that if the Government of Britain is entrusted to us at this crisis in her fate we will do our best for all, without fear or favour, without class or party bias, without rancour or spite, but with the clear and faithful simplicity that we showed in the days of Dunkirk. We did not think then about party scores. We did not divide the men we rescued from the beaches into those we cared about and those for whom, to quote a Ministerial utterance, we did not care a tinker's curse. The rescuing ships that set out from Britain did not regard a large part of the wearied and hard-pressed army we were bringing back to safety, and as it proved in the end to victory—we did not regard them as 'lower than vermin'.

However the voting may go in this part or that, in this district or the other, in the town or the country, our sole aim will be to act for all our fellow countrymen and bring them out of the perils and privations by which they are now oppressed and surrounded. Above all we shall go forward without fear and with unconquerable hope that our ancient and mighty people which, as I believe and declare, saved the world in the early stages of the war, are not confronted with any problem they cannot solve, or with any difficulty or danger they cannot overcome.

The Socialists claim that they have cured unemployment and they seek to make this a prime issue. Devaluation is defended by Sir Stafford Cripps as a means of stopping unemployment and he makes the cruel charge against the Conservative Party and against me of all men, who am, after all, responsible for more anti-unemployment legislation than anyone alive, of seeking to use mass unemployment as a means of spurring on the efforts of those who are employed. Well, he is very touchy himself, this Chancellor of the Exchequer—nervous about his reputation for political integrity. He has given up all hope of having one for political consistency.

But let us see how this matter stands. In 1944 when I was Prime Minister of a National Government, resting upon a Conservative House of Commons with a majority over all Parties of 150, I set up a committee to inquire into the ways of preventing unemployment after the war. The principal members of the present Socialist Government and the principal members of the present Conservative Opposition were upon it; the chairman was Lord Woolton. This document gives a most fresh, strong and ingenious view of what should be done on all occasions when a world slump threatens to affect the daily life of our island. It is published and can be read—and should be read; it expresses our policy today. The foreword to their report begins:

'The Government accept as one of their primary aims and responsibilities the maintenance of a high and stable level of employment after the war.'

It goes on:

'There will, however, be no problem of general unemployment in the years immediately after the end of the war in Europe. The total manpower available will be insufficient to satisfy the total demands for goods and services.'

This was the joint declaration of Socialist and Conservative Ministers and of Sir Archibald Sinclair representing the Liberals, all serving side by side in a national administration, and with no conceivable motive except to find and tell the truth. They foresaw with remarkable accuracy that fact that in the years immediately after the war there would be no problem of general unemployment and they all declared jointly that one of the primary aims and responsibilities of the Government was the maintenance of a high and stable level of employment. This historic document, for the preparation of which no one was more responsible than the chairman of the committee, Lord Woolton, was approved by the War Cabinet and was presented to Parliament in May 1944.

Now it is not hard to believe that men like Mr Attlee, Mr Bevin, Mr Herbert Morrison and Sir Stafford Cripps, can have the face to go about propagating the double falsehood, first, that it is they who have prevented unemployment after the war, and secondly, that their Conservative colleagues—now their opponents—would deliberately use mass unemployment as an economic weapon. Yet all these four high Ministers now holding power appear ready to spread the exact opposite of what they know to be the truth and what they are on record as having said they knew would be the truth—in order to gain votes in the hope of securing their return to office in the next few months. I hope these statements which I have read to you, and the names of those who approved them in all three Parties, I hope they will be placarded throughout the length and breadth of the country, in order that Socialist charges about the Conservative attitude towards unemployment may be refuted and Socialist claims to have cured it with what they did in the last few years may be disproved out of their own mouths.

There is another legend which the Socialist leaders have invented and are spreading. It is that between the wars, unemployment was worse under Conservative Government than under Socialist Government. Why it was under the disastrous Socialist administration of 1931, which lasted from 1929-1931, that unemployment bounded upwards to the figure never before reached of nearly 3,000,000. The National Government, which succeeded the Socialists and was sustained by the enormous Conservative majority gained in 1931, grappled with the evil. At the beginning of 1933, the sinister curve turned downwards. From then until the outbreak of the war it fell steadily, until in 1939, before the outbreak, the number of unemployed was less than half the total recorded at the date the Socialists ended their lamentable term of office.

Here again these facts should be placed before the nation in every constituency and on every platform, not just to those who are here who have special duties and responsibilities for making sure the people know the truth. Those who have the special duties and responsibilities will make it their business to see that the people in the constituencies where they live are acquainted with the facts and are not swept away with the lie. It is part of the Communist-Socialist theory that the repetition of an untruth long enough makes it a truth. Let us be very careful not to be subjugated by such base methods.

When Mr Attlee and his present principal colleagues subscribed to and helped compose our joint statement that there would be no problem of general unemployment in the years immediately after the war, none of us knew of the generous American aid that was to be forthcoming in these four years. This up to date, I mean up to the end of the current Marshall Aid year, amounts to £1,750,000,000 sterling. All this vast sum of money which has been pouring into this island from the United States was a makeweight, which should have made employment still more secure. They are not all Wall Street millionaires in the United States; they are as hard-working people as are found anywhere in the world. But after we had had nearly three years of Socialist Government, Mr Herbert Morrison in fact confessed at Manchester in April 1948, that but for the American aid 'we should be faced with a million or two people on the dole'. Yet it is with these facts proving the case, staring them in the face, that the Socialist leaders whose names I have mentioned have the effrontery to try to dupe the people into believing that it is they and their policy which has prevented unemployment, and to spread the falsehood—I refrain from using any other word—that the Conservatives would have used unemployment as a means of spurring the exertions of labour. Now, I think this is some proof of the ill-treatment in public behaviour that we are receiving from the leading Socialist Ministers.

For what then, we are asked, will be the employment policy of a Conservative Government, if returned to power in the present crisis now everything has become or has been made much more difficult, and the years immediately after the war when the whole world wanted to buy all kinds of things—what they call a sellers' market—have come to an end. Our policy is exactly the same as we laid before the nation and laid before a Conservative House of Commons in 1944. Any Conservative Government would accept 'as one of their primary aims and responsibilities the maintenance of a high and stable level of employment'. Of course, I cannot tell what the future will bring forth. It is not now possible after four years of Socialist rule, to speak with the same confidence about the future as Conservative and Socialist Ministers were able together to do in 1944. But our purpose and intention remains unchanged. And the first of all conditions that will help us is a restoration of confidence and enterprise, impossible under Socialist Government.

One thing I will say now. We shall not rely upon the compulsory direction of labour in time of peace. The regulations which the

Socialist Government reintroduced two years ago for the compulsory direction of labour, which in my opinion are an insult to the rights and liberties of the British people, will be abolished and the present insurance benefits will stand, as a powerful aid and help to every man and woman entitled to draw them.

The four years of this Government have been, from beginning to end, a rake's progress of unbridled expenditure. In these four years the Socialist Government have begged, borrowed—or exacted—and have spent £16,000,000,000 or nearly as much as was spent in the twenty years between the two wars. That is a fact which takes some thinking about. They have used up almost every national asset or reserve upon which they could lay their hands. They have taken 40 per cent of the national income for the purposes of governmental administration. Our taxation has been the highest in the world. It oppresses every transaction of daily life. Besides the £1,750,000,000 from the United States, they have had over £300,000,000 advanced by Canada, and £50,000,000 of gifts from the other Dominions. They have eaten up our Argentine Railways, and many other foreign investments, and £350,000,000, or more than half our gold and hard currency reserves, the last reserves, our sacred treasure, have all gone down the drain. Whilst all this riot of spending has been going on, the spendthrifts themselves have exhorted us to save more, to work harder, and to endure austerities. Great efforts have been made by the British people in their loyalty, but at the end all we have is devaluation—that is all we have come to at the end of all these years and all these efforts. The £ sterling, which Lord Woolton well called 'Our financial Union Jack', has been hauled down to half-mast, or almost. It is not only our money which has been devaluated. Our prestige and reputation abroad have been devaluated. What is thought about us in Germany? I am going to quote you what the Socialists say themselves about that:

'There is no doubt it is said that whereas in 1945-6 British prestige in Germany was higher than that of the Americans and French, the position is now reversed.'

Whose words do you think I am quoting? These are the words of two of the leading intellectuals of the Socialist Party, Sir Richard Acland and Mr Richard Crossman, who have been travelling in Germany this year, and this is what they wrote to *The Times* newspaper. What is the position in France? Anyone can see what must be the effect in France of Sir Stafford Cripps' devaluation, giving them hardly a moment to prepare, as the result of which an exceptionally stable Government has been overthrown.

But I could multiply these examples of our loss of the prestige, influence and esteem we had won abroad by our conduct in the war, which never stood so high as when the Socialists rollicked into power in 1945. But there is one bit of devaluation which is a comfort. The false theories of Socialism and the mischievous policy of nationalizing our industries have been, like those industries themselves, devaluated too.

And, when they, our opponents, ask us will the Conservatives cut the social services or the food subsidies, why they have already been cut by the Socialist Government and are being cut more every day. Every increase in the cost of living is a direct reduction in the social services. Every step to devaluate the money we spend and every increase in the cost of living is a slashing cut to the social services of all kinds. Now we are to have more—that is the work which lies immediately before us—how much more our people will find out in the months that lie ahead.

I said at Wolverhampton that nationalization had already been exposed as a failure. Every major industry which the Socialists have nationalized without exception has passed from the profit-earning or self-supporting side of our national balance sheet to the loss-making or debit side. The Government speakers denied this. The Economic Secretary to the Treasury, Mr Jay, said that the Bank of England and the Cables and Wireless Company were not making losses. Who has ever suggested that the Bank of England and Cables and Wireless Company were major British industries. I was of course speaking about the great branches of our industrial life—coal, railways, road transport, gas and electricity and, on a smaller scale, air transport. The Prime Minister, Mr Attlee, himself has challenged me on this. As usual, I cannot feel he has been right. We must not look only at the balance-sheets presented by the uneasy boards of officials and Party nominees who now manage these industries. It is easy when you have a State monopoly and can charge the public what you like and what you dare to show a paper profit. The Coal Board boast that they have made the enormous profit of nearly £2,000,000 last year, but Mr Attlee must take into consideration the great increase of cost to the public. Since coal has been nationalized the price has gone up by 6s. 6d. a ton. On an annual output of about 200,000,000 tons that has meant nearly £100,000,000 more has been paid by the consumer directly or indirectly, and forms a definite part of that higher cost of living and of manufacture expressed in a devaluated currency.

I must, however, say this, that the great part of that increase has gone in the higher wages of the coal miners, and I have always drawn a distinction between the work of men underground and those who work in the light of the sun. There is no question of our going back on that. What we hope is that a proportionate increase of production will follow from this heavy addition to the public burden.

About the railways, I said the paper deficit might be over £20,000,000. We now know the figures. It is £13,000,000. Not £20,000,000, only £13,000,000 deficit. What a triumph! Something to celebrate! But this takes no account of what the report of the Transport Commission calls 'that marked deterioration in 1949'; nor of the fact that fares were raised very substantially immediately before nationalization began. I cannot refer to the railways without paying my tribute to the restraint of that splendid body of railway workers who, in spite of the disappointments and disillusionments they have sustained by nationalization, which they have been urged to ask for year after year, have nevertheless shown their earnest desire not to add to our many difficulties at this time.

Then there are gas and electricity about which no financial statement has yet been presented. Prices have, however, been heavily marked up against the housewife and the general consumer, and they only have to compare their electricity bills for this last Easter with those of the year before to see what happens when an industry of this kind is run from Whitehall. The State-run airlines have now declared, with an air of pride and glee, that they have only lost £9,000,000 this year, compared with £11,000,000 last year. Here is another triumph for the Socialist nationalizers to parade. Despite Mr Attlee, I repeat my carefully measured assertion that all major nationalized industries have ceased to be assets to the public, and have become instead burdens upon it, and that the losses they make will be paid for either by the taxpayer, through the Exchequer, or by the consumer in higher prices or by both. You are both.

We are asked what a Conservative Government would do with these nationalized industries. It is physically impossible to undo much that has been done. You cannot thrust the coal mines and the railways back upon the private owners. They would not take them. All that can be done in these two basic services is to decentralize and cut down the enormously swollen costs of management. We have already stated in detail in *The Right Road For Britain* what a Conservative Government will do for road transport. We are now threatened, besides the nationalization of steel, with that of insurance, sugar and cement. All of these thriving industries are to be disturbed, mauled and finally chilled and largely paralysed by the clumsy and costly grip of State bureaucracy, infected by Party patronage and manipulation.

Ministers call, and they are going to call, for further sacrifices from all classes. Why do they not set the example themselves? Why do they not sacrifice to the general welfare some of these wrong-headed partisan indulgences of Socialist theory, and concentrate their efforts upon their plain duty to save our country from approaching bankruptcy? They talk of economy. Why do not they try to save themselves? Perhaps they are to make some suggestions on that subject; at any rate we shall have some few suggestions of our own. There is no doubt what the policy of the Conservative Party will be. It will be to put a full-stop—here and now—to all further nationalization. This, of course, will be one of the major issues on which the electors will have to pronounce.

Now I turn to another aspect of the same problem and must ask your indulgence if I unfold these matters to you as this is an occasion of great importance. The question is asked: 'Are Conservatives opposed to planning?' There is nothing new in planning. Every Government, ancient or modern, must look ahead and plan. Did not Joseph advise Pharaoh to build granaries and fill them for the lean years when the Nile waters failed? He followed the opposite course to the present Government, which is to waste the favourable period of getting the country on to its feet and meanwhile squander all the accumulated resources. But of course we are in favour of planning. But planning what for?

We hold that in these modern times planning, with all the resources of science at its disposal, should aim at giving the individual citizen as many choices as possible of what to do in all the ups and downs of daily life. The more a man's choice is free, the more likely it is to be wise and fruitful, not only to the chooser but to the community in which he dwells. Now there is an important distinction between the quality and kind of planning. This kind of planning differs fundamentally from the collectivist theme of grinding them all up in a vast State mill which must certainly destroy in the process the freedom and independence which are the foundation of our way of life and the famous characteristic of our race.

The Socialist policy and aim is to flatten out all those differentials—to use an important trade union expression—which result from the efforts and qualities of individuals and at all costs to establish a dead level above which no one but Socialist lackeys and politicians shall be allowed to rise. Of course they can only bring this about gradually, but that is the goal they seek, and that is the only goal that their political philosophy can reach.

I am glad to see that responsible trade union leaders, Socialists though they may call themselves, who are in daily contact with the realities of industry and of labour, do not hesitate to resist this ironing-out process. That process would be fatal to all those forces which make for more abundant and progressive production, and would deny to every man that right to make the best of himself and his abilities for the benefit not only of his family but of his fellow countrymen, within the limits set by the old broad and well-known laws upon which our way of life in this island has been built.

We should certainly plan for the future. And let me tell you what we should plan first of all. We should plan first of all how to keep alive in the next ten years 50,000,000 of people in Britain. In my lifetime our population has nearly doubled. Under cheap imported food given us in return for the sale of our manufactures, we brought nearly 25,000,000 more people into being. Without that we should not have been a great power. Without that we might not have turned the balance in the world struggle against tyranny when we were all alone. But now we cannot be sure that foreign countries will wish to buy our manufactures to the same extent, nor as in Victorian times that the food they have to sell us will be cheap. There is no possibility of emigrating such great numbers of our population in the next ten years or in the next twenty. The first thing we must do to establish our national independence is to increase our production of home-grown food.

In *The Right Road For Britain* we have set out clearly how we propose to set about this task. I wish to repeat here this evening our cardinal principle, that first place in the home market must be reserved for the home farmer. Next to him must come the Empire producer.

If long-term plans for the production of food and raw materials are made now in our Empire and Commonwealth of Nations there is no reason why our main supplies should not, after a period of years, flow in steadily from these widespread, trusty sources under the British flag.

We can, I am sure, depend upon our farming community to do all that lies in their power to increase production if the Government provides them with the necessary means. They need clear guarantees on which they can rely. In particular the horticulturists who have suffered so much recently from destructive foreign imports of a temporary and freak kind must in future receive the fair treatment they deserve. The livestock population of the country can be greatly increased. To do this we shall provide the farmers with the feeding-stuffs which the Socialist Government have so lamentably failed to procure. We shall extend the Hill Farming Act to provide for the reclamation of marginal land.

No less urgent is the need for improvement in the conditions of life in our countryside. The Socialists have delayed or obstructed the reconditioning of rural houses and the extension of rural water supplies. We shall see that proper priority is given to these and other essential rural requirements. The machinery of the County Agricultural Committees must be overhauled. The recent report of the Select Committee on Estimates shows that losses on the trading services operated by these committees alone have amounted to over £17,000,000. There is a great need for team-work and leadership in the countryside and an example could well be set at the top, by more team-work between the Ministries of Food and Agriculture. But in all matters of good housekeeping the Socialists have proved themselves an effective substitute for some of the evils we overcame in the war. I expect there is many a housewife who looks back to those hard days with reflection, as she only wishes old Woolton had it in his hands again. I was, of course, only quoting the housewife, because as a matter of fact he is quite a young fellow compared to me. But going back from food and agriculture to general topics, freedom of choice and variety of method are also the main solutions of the urgent problem of housing our people. In this Mr Bevan has been his own and our worst enemy. Our Conservative policy is to give greater freedom to the private builder. We shall sweep away the hindrances and restrictions that at present impede private enterprise in creating the vast number of dwellings needed, which hindrances have kept the building of houses in these years of frustration so much below the level quite naturally and normally maintained in the days of Mr Chamberlain's Conservative Government before the war.

Mr Bevan insists that for every one house built for sale four must be built to be let by the local authorities at rents subsidized out of the pockets of taxpayers and ratepayers. There is still a great need for council houses, but surely it is nonsense that four out of every five families who are going into new houses should be subsidized by their fellow citizens. Building costs are now so high that the rents of some council houses, despite the subsidy, are too high for those to whom they are offered and many of the poorest families have to stay where they are, mocked by the fact that, through their rates and taxes, they provide subsidies for others who are richer. Planning is indeed needed in our housing sphere, but it is planning to remove the burdens and restrictions that cramp and hobble the building industry today.

And I sum up the picture at home, control, devaluate and flatten out. That is the message of the Socialist Government and to it we oppose our Conservative policy. Liberate the genius and initiative of our race. Revive and stabilize the value of the money on which wages, pensions and social services are based. Build with enterprise and courage the forward and everchanging structure of our industrial and agricultural life without which this island cannot live, or its population be sustained. There is the contrast between the two policies which lie before you.

It is a relief to turn from the hard and, I fear, darkening scene at home to the inspiring spheres into which this conference soared yesterday. The Empire: that is the word we use, nor are we ashamed of the word 'British'. The British Empire: its unity, its development, and its consolidated strength. I hope all Conservatives will call it the British Empire and Commonwealth of Nations, and let other Parties imitate us as they learn. But there is our first thought and dream and aim. Then there is our fraternal association with the United States in what is called the English-speaking world. And thirdly, there is this grand design of a free and United Europe in which we are resolved to play our part. I rejoice at the wisdom of this conference which did not allow itself to be led astray by arguments that these were divergent or contradictory objectives, and declared almost unanimously in favour of pursuing them all at once. As I see it there are these three circles in each of which we have a vital share. And these may all be linked together by Britain, if we in this island prove ourselves worthy of it.

Great progress is being made in all these directions, and we shall move forward earnestly and resolutely upon all of them. The unity of the Empire is no longer a Party question. Friendship with the United States grows in spite of the abuse of the Communist Party and their fellow travellers in the House of Commons. The policy of United Europe, out of which Marshall Aid originated, has made steady headway in spite of jealousies and prejudices in high Socialist quarters.

All is moving forward. When we are asked: 'What is your policy abroad and overseas?' we can answer: 'It has already been adopted, largely upon our initiative, impulsion and guidance.' We shall carry it forward with all our might and main. Yes, and at home as well as throughout the world, we shall strive to carry forward that great social evolution which has covered the lifetime of the oldest of us here, namely the bringing forward of ever larger numbers of mankind to an ever more bountiful table of moral and material rewards. To this process of unceasing, untiring expansion and advance, the Conservative Party devotes itself and, linking as we do the past with the present, we shall gain for all the mastery of the future.

FOURTH ALAMEIN REUNION

I am glad to come to the fourth, as I came to the first, Reunion of the Eighth Army to celebrate the victory of El Alamein. How right you are to keep together and to preserve that spirit of devotion to duty, of self-sacrifice and daring and of comradeship, that only burns the brighter for all the storms that blow. The toils and trials of war are hard and cruel, but when they are crowned with victory veterans who have shared them together have a common inheritance of brotherhood and of memories which is a treasure to them when they meet in after-years.

By a blessed dispensation, human beings forget physical pain much more quickly than they do their joyous emotions and experiences. A merciful Providence passes the sponge of oblivion across much that is suffered and enables us to cherish the great moments of life and honour which come to us in our march through life. Such meetings as these not only give expression to the deep feelings of those who fought and won, they also are a salute to the memory of those who fell. I hope you will long continue to preserve the fame and the spirit of the Eighth Army.

The story of the Eighth Army does not begin with Alamein. We must not forget the long months of fierce fighting with many surprising turns of fortune which were its record, and that of the Desert Army before it, or that Rommel's advance was brought to a standstill by General Auchinleck before the changes in command were made. When I arrived in Cairo at the beginning of August 1942, I found a grave and critical, but by no means hopeless, situation. I found also a British and Imperial Army that did not know why it had been forced to retreat 400 miles with a loss of 80,000 men. It was an Army in no wise daunted, but an Army bewildered and enraged. My visit came at the same time as the arrival of powerful reinforcements, including the very latest weapons and tanks which we had set in motion around the Cape a good many months before.

As the result of the decisions for which I am proud to be responsible, General Alexander became Commander-in-Chief in the Middle East, with a definite directive to concentrate all his efforts against Rommel, and, after the death of General Gort, who was killed the next day, the illustrious Field-Marshal, who has just spoken to us so movingly, took the command of the Eighth Army into his strong and skilful hands. The appointment of these two great officers, whose names, at the time, were little known outside professional circles, will be acclaimed by history. Neither of these men was ever defeated or long-checked in the intense and bloody fighting in so many different lands in the thirty-three months which still lay between us and our goal. 'Alex' and 'Monty' are now household words. They are beloved by the peoples of the Empire as they were by their soldiers, and their fame will long be cherished by their fellow-countrymen and honoured by the free nations of the world.

And it is to Monty (as he has long allowed me to call him), that we pay our tribute tonight. The advance of the Eighth Army under his command will ever be a glittering episode in the martial annals of Britain, and not only of Britain, but of the mighty array of Empire and Commonwealth which gathered around our island in the days of its mortal peril and found its expression in all the desert battles.

Field-Marshal Montgomery is one of the greatest living masters of the art of war. It has been my fortune and great pleasure often to be with him at important moments in the long march from Alamein to the Rhine. He has always shown himself equal, and more than equal, to the largest operation, and the true and comprehending leader of every unit of the mighty armies in his grip. The Battle of Alamein ranks among the most famous victories in British history. It was the turning-point in our military fortunes during the World War.

Up till then my own experience had been none too agreeable. I had had to face nearly three years of unbroken defeat and disappointment on land. Indeed, it was astonishing that Parliament and the nation put up with me for so long. (They made up for it afterwards.) But now, at Alamein, was the turning of the tide for which we had so carefully prepared in secret. Alamein was the herald of the great Anglo-American invasion of North-West Africa and, from that time forth, although there were ups and downs, we were borne forward irresistibly to complete and final victory. Up till Alamein we survived. After Alamein we conquered.

I do not wonder that those who played a personal part in this ever-famous event rejoice together when they look back upon it; or that, as the Field-Marshal has told us, they should find in it a source of further inspiration to help our dear country to their utmost strength and at every moment in their lives.

Monty has reminded us of all that Britons have in common and how much more precious is this heritage than the differences which are so prominent today. He will excuse me if I say that, from whatever angle you measure them, they are not small—they are in some respects fundamental. It is impossible that public opinion should not remain deeply divided at a time when a General Election is approaching. It is only in countries where tyrants rule and from which freedom is banished that a sham uniformity is imposed and that strong and sharp differences are not expressed. If they were not, the voting would be a mere pretence, as in Soviet Russia and other Communist satellite countries. My own hope is that this period of unavoidable Party strife will be as short as possible. For it is certainly a great and growing hindrance to our national welfare, and a danger to the preservation of all we have to defend in common. Nothing can be more harmful to national unity than a prolonged period of electioneering.

There is one thing I will tell you tonight which I feel is most appropriate to this gathering of men and women of all Parties. You have seen discussions reported in the newspapers which show that there is in all Parties a strong movement for the abolition of national service. No doubt, from many points of view, that would be a popular policy. But it is my conviction that to make such a change at this time would be deeply injurious to the strength of Britain and would reduce our chances of maintaining what we all desire—the peace of the world.

The Field-Marshal holds a position of far-reaching responsibility in Western Europe, and I am sure that no one will agree more when I say that for Britain to abandon the principle of national service at this present anxious time would strike a deadly blow at the great defence combination which has come into being under the Atlantic Pact, and is ever growing stronger—a combination not only of Britain and her Empire and Commonwealth, but of the free nations of Western Europe and of our great Ally across the Atlantic Ocean.

I have therefore assured the Prime Minister, in the name of the Party which I lead, that we shall give His Majesty's Government full support in maintaining national service and, so far as it is in our power, will not allow it to be made a partisan election issue. I feel sure this step will win the approval of the men who fought and conquered in the Battle of Alamein.

ECONOMIC SITUATION (GOVERNMENT PROPOSALS)

A SPEECH TO THE HOUSE OF COMMONS
27 OCTOBER 1949

---

24 October—Corner-stone of permanent headquarters of United Nations Organization laid in New York.

The Prime Minister announces in the House of Commons economy cuts in national expenditure totalling (apart from defence) £250,000,000. Additional saving on defence will amount to £12,500,000 during the remainder of the current financial year, and to £30,000,000 in a full year.

26-27 October—Debate in the House of Commons on Government 'crisis' economy proposals.

[*27 October* 1949

Although my hon Friend the Member for Hertford [Mr Walker-Smith] has set an example in brevity which I trust will never be made uniform and compulsory, he has none the less made a point which has gathered support behind it from all quarters. I regret that, having an engagement in a constituency—constituencies now are becoming very important since they become more alive as the House becomes more dead—I was not fortunate enough to hear the concluding speeches of the Debate last night.

However, I feel sure that the House will realize the full value of the weighty speech of my right hon Friend the Member for the Scottish Universities [Sir J. Anderson]. Although on account of his rank he speaks from this Bench, his was not a party speech and therefore, no doubt, incurred the censure and derision of the supporters of the Government. He gave some openings which cheered up the depressed spirits below the Gangway and were a great relief to the Lord President of the Council who, as usual, was hard put to it to fill in the time which it was his duty to devote to a major political pronouncement. The record of my right hon Friend's experience and action before and during the war, all the high posts he has held with efficiency and courage, all the responsible work he has done, is known to all parties, and the great confidence with which he is regarded should make serious people in the Government, if such there be, and even below the Gangway—weigh carefully his deeply considered opinions.

The speech of the Lord President of the Council to which I also listened was a typical debating performance in which his object was to confine himself to diverting the attention of the House from the grave issues to the solution of which he was expected to make at least some contribution. I did not notice a single point which had any other object but to confuse debate and darken counsel. He dwelt at length upon economies of the National Government which succeeded the Socialist collapse in 1931, and I venture to complete his historical account in one important particular.

The object of the right hon Gentleman in dwelling upon all this—apart from filling in the time—and all the measures taken then was, of course, to create class prejudice and to rouse party cheers. He outlined the economies which were made in those days by a Government sustained during the course of them by the earnest and overwhelming vote of the nation. He tried to pretend that these were the economies which we should introduce should we have the power, although they, obviously, have no relation to the circumstances and facts of today.

There is, however, one point which he did not mention. All but one of these economies, well judged or harsh, had been previously approved, not only by Mr MacDonald and Mr Snowden, then at the head of the Socialist Government, but by the Socialist Cabinet. Every one of these points, with the exception I have mentioned, to which he has referred in such prejudicial terms, were approved by the Cabinet of the Labour Party, carrying their party with them, with the one single exception of the reduction in unemployment pay. [HON MEMBERS: 'Ah!'] I give you that.

MR H. MORRISON: It is a well-known rule that Members of Cabinets and Privy Councillors do not reveal Cabinet proceedings—[*Interruption*]—and I am certainly not going to do so, especially in my present position as Lord President of the Council, but I wish to say that I do not accept the statement which the right hon Gentleman has made.

MR CHURCHILL: Fortunately, I have brought my authority with me. My authority is Mr Snowden, who says in his autobiography that the Labour Cabinet had agreed to cuts in Government expenditure of £56,000,000, of which the unemployment insurance for transitional benefit amounted to £22,000,000, and that the split and division happened not upon the bulk of the cuts, which the right hon Gentleman has enumerated with so much gusto in order to throw upon us the odium which belongs to his own colleagues of the Labour Party, under whom he was so proud and eager—and lucky—to serve, but also, of course, to cast prejudice upon us. All that the right hon

Gentleman has been trying to do this afternoon is to hold up to odium the decisions of the Labour Government of those times. There is a saying: 'It is an ill bird which fouls its own nest.'

The right hon Gentleman made great play with our publication known as *The Right Road For Britain*. It is quite true that it is the road we should like to tread. Perhaps, if the party opposite had not got in our way, it is the road we should have already trodden. The Lord President of the Council greatly exaggerated the cost of these proposals. Apart from the question of equal pay between men and women, to which both parties are equally, or at any rate largely, committed, these proposals in our opinion do not involve an expenditure of more than £10,000,000 a year, or a sum equal, shall we say, to the loss incurred on Civil Aviation alone under its present nationalized system..In any case, I and my colleagues have made it absolutely clear that in present developments we shall not go an inch further than the financial resources of the country warrant and, in view of all that has occurred and is occurring, we shall hold ourselves entirely free to take a new view of the position should we be granted the opportunity.

Parties differ on a great many matters of principle. I was brought up to believe that taxation was a bad thing, but the consuming power of the people was a good thing. The Chancellor of the Exchequer please note—the consuming power of the people is a good thing. Many of his predecessors have opened their Budgets with the statement, 'The consuming power of the people is well maintained', but he adopts a different tone. I was brought up to believe that trade should be regulated mainly by the laws of supply and demand and that, apart from basic necessaries in great emergencies, the price mechanism should adjust and correct undue spending at home, as it does, apart from gifts and subsidies, control spending abroad.

I was also taught that it was one of the first duties of Government to promote that confidence on which credit and thrift, and especially foreign credit, can alone stand and grow. I was taught to believe that these processes, working freely within the limits of well-known laws for correcting monopoly, exploitation and other measures in restraint of trade, as the old phrase had it, that these principles would produce a lively and continuous improvement in prosperity. I still hold to those general principles.

However, between the terrible wars which have rent the world, we were subjected to violent convulsions in world trade. To guard against their coming upon us again when the Second World War was at an end the National Government—my colleagues, in large numbers, are on the Bench opposite—at my suggestion or by our common instinct, set up a formidable inquiry into the means of preventing and forestalling the effect of world fluctuations upon our employment. There is the White Paper of 1944 which was presented to Parliament. The Lord President was a party to it, not in the vague way of being connected with the Government; he followed these things with great perspicacity and attention—he will surely not deny that—and the Chancellor of the Exchequer and the Prime Minister and others of great importance in those days.

This White Paper was praised by the Foreign Secretary only three years ago. It is a modern and enlightened statement of the ways of meeting world-wide fluctuations and preventing the kind of terrible surge of unemployment which wrecked the Socialist Government of 1929-31. I believe that all those ideas and methods, for what they are worth, are an essential part of a wise and up-to-date outlook and policy in economics. I may say that this White Paper said that there would be no problem of general unemployment in the years immediately after the war in Europe, and that the difficulty would be to find the labour to do the jobs. The right hon Gentleman today, finding fault with this, said that his prophecy as well as mine—he is as much involved in it—referred to a statement that we were at the time contemplating a normal rate of 8 per cent unemployment whereas we had had only 2 per cent. That is really not so. It is in the Appendix and is not on the authority of those who prepared the Report. It was in fact a statement by Sir William Beveridge on his plan and on what would be the cost of meeting unemployment if its proportions reached such a point. We must have a little accuracy in these discussions.

But all the principles which I have unfolded on taxation being an evil and consuming power being good, etc., are all violated and repudiated by the policy and outlook of the present Government. Socialists regard taxation as good in itself and as tending to level our society. Come on, give a cheer to that. What a pity the Minister of Health is consistently absenting himself from our Debates. This would have been the point where he might have come in and gathered some followers behind him on the great theme for commercial and hard pressed Britain of having a redistributed taxation based upon retribution, a great contribution to all the work which the Chancellor of the Exchequer has been left to do.

The Socialists rejoice in Government expenditure on a vast scale, and they believe it is a sure method of preventing unemployment, which it may be for a short time. Apparently increased consuming power, except by the Government, even in the home market is an evil which must be curbed by every form of Government intervention.

The laws of supply and demand, regulation of consumption by price mechanism, apart from the basic essentials, are ruled out as part of the devices of outworn capitalism; while exhortations to thrift and saving are reiterated until they have become almost continuous—I mean unceasing. Everything possible is done to discourage and stigmatize the inventor. The Chancellor speaks in slighting terms of profit earners. What a lot of contempt he put into it—'profit earners!' When I pressed him upon the subject he received it with one of his mirthless smiles which is the common form in which his personal philosophy has to express itself.

There was the old Gladstonian expression, 'Let the money fructify in the pockets of the people.' That is regarded as a monstrous device of a decadent capitalist system. As for maintaining confidence and credit what is to be thought when one of the most powerful Ministers, to whom I have already referred, is able to speak about redistribution of wealth in a spirit of retribution, at this junction of all others? And when the Prime Minister under whom he is serving does not feel strong enough to disavow it?

The Prime Minister has not dared to contradict his Minister of Health. But even the Prime Minister's submissive demeanour and docility—unbecoming in one holding such great power and bearing such responsibility—has not, so far as I can see induced this future leader of the Socialist Party and highly claimed spokesman, at the present time to come within the precincts. I want to ask, how are the Government going to restore confidence and credit when they show themselves in every mood and action the enemy of wealth gathered, accumulated or inherited in private hands; when they penalize enterprise and deny thrift and good housekeeping their due reward?

Thus we have been led for four years of unprecedented and unbridled expenditure, of ceaseless interference in every form of private enterprise and activity to taxation unparalleled in times of peace and unequalled throughout the whole world today—[Hon Members: 'We have heard that before.'] Hon Members say they have heard that before; they will hear it again, and over and over again. We see the Government taking 40 per cent of the entire national income into their far from competent hands. We have spent—I have said this before and I will say it again whenever I speak in the country—in the four years since the war we have spent £16,000,000,000; nearly as much as was spent in the whole twenty years between the wars. Are not these among the more important explanations of the plight to which we have been brought?

It must be remembered as we sit here tonight that Britain is a capitalist society, and that 80 per cent of its whole industry is in private hands. It is this part alone which earns the profits which the Chancellor of the Exchequer censures but on which he lives, taking over 60 per cent of them by taxation, and on which the 20 per cent loss-making nationalized industries are at present carried.

Under the Communist system all capital is sequestrated, all capital-owners are liquidated, and society is reduced to a strong hierarchy and army of officials and politicians by whom the proletariat are ruled under a one-party system with absolute tyranny, and a very considerable measure of ease. However abhorrent this conception may be to our spiritual outlook, and our physical resolves, on both sides of the House no one can say that it is not a system which has a hideous and logical symmetry about it. Luckily, that is not an issue in our country today. But what we have here now is a capitalist society on which we are dependent for our daily life and survival, and a Socialist Government which views it with the utmost hostility and is trying continually to gain credit with its own extremists by casting a baleful net over its activities, by denouncing and threatening it all the time and stabbing it with gusto whenever a chance offers.

No one can possibly devise an economic theory that can fit or can even explain such a process. In a progressive and ever-broadening society, many corrections of emphasis can be made and are made as the years pass by. But a deliberate attack on the capitalist system by a Socialist Government, responsible and in power, a Socialist Government which has, I am glad to say, neither the hardihood nor the wickedness to embark on Communism, cannot be reconciled with any theory based on principle or any policy which can be accompanied in peacetime by a wide measure of prosperity and social well-being. Sir, the violent assault of Socialism upon the intricate and artificial economy of Britain at the moment when it was exhausted and quivering from the ordeal of total war has so far been fatal to our recovery.

Two or three years ago on several occasions I asked for a large reduction in Government expenditure. I named the figure of £500,000,000; I will not read out the quotation, because time is short and I have to consider the Prime Minister. We are all waiting to hear from him his views upon the present situation. I named the figure of £500,000,000. What was the reply of the Government? It was the same as they are so anxious to use today, namely, 'Please say exactly what your economies would be.' They do not ask this in order to gain good advice but in order that their canvassers at by-elections, or at a General Election, can go from door to door and endeavour to accuse the Conservative and the Liberal Parties of being the enemies of social welfare and improvement. That has certainly been the atmosphere in this Debate.

Now I find that expert financial opinion agrees that far larger reductions than the £250,000,000 of capital and Government expenditure which the Government propose are the least that can enable us to escape from an unmeasured disaster. If the economies of £500,000,000 a year, for which I asked in the name of the Conservative Party two or three years ago, had been made at that time, we should never have reached the situation in which the ghastly measure of devaluation which the Chancellor announced so jauntily would have been our lot. That £500,000,000 of Government expenditure—current expenditure, apart from capital—would have been saved in the intervening period, and we should have been confronted with a very different situation than that in which we find ourselves—of a great impending collapse, when our reserves are far below what this Government iself declared was the least that could be tolerated.

We are presented now, at the end of all this, with a cut of £90,000,000 in the current national expenditure of over £3,300,000,000. That is really hardly worth making out to be a great achievement. But I had never contemplated that a reduction in expenditure of £500,000,000 should take place without giving more or less corresponding relief to the taxpayer. In the same sentence of my speech in Brighton, I said that the relief in taxation should be used in every way to stimulate incentives to production and should be accompanied by a vast sweeping away of wartime controls, dear to the Socialist heart because they represent the overweening power of the State, but profoundly injurious to the national wealth-producing forces and those elements upon which our finances and economy rest.

I also urged for many years the evil of unrequited exports. I think it is scandalous that we should be made to repay to Egypt, India and some other countries money which we borrowed from them to pay for the supplies which maintained the armies by which they were protected from German, Italian or Japanese invasion. I have always considered that we should make a counter-claim for the services rendered by us to them, and that the one should be set off against the other.

No one hesitated to make this claim about the United States. The United States have repeatedly been reminded by us how we fought alone for two years before they came in. The United States acknowledged this and not only treated all wartime expenditure under Lend-Lease but made these subsequent vast grants, gifts and loans to us which we have been spending so freely during these four profligate years. More than that, United States opinion has been that we had no right to take no steps to deal with our war debts to the countries we defended—sterling balances they are called—while appealing to them continuously for further aid. I was glad to hear the Chancellor of the Exchequer, for the first time yesterday, speaking of the need to curtail on a far greater scale unrequited exports, but no one is more responsible than he for the vast and accelerating scale on which they have been proceeding.

One of the main foundations upon which our standard of living can be maintained is a stable value of money. In theory, though not always in practice, Socialists view money with great disdain. It is, however, the sole means by which the innumerable millions of ordinary transactions of daily life, the exchange of goods and services, all the thought and provision that can be made for the future, all our social services and the like, can be maintained. Surely, the maintenance of this stable rate should be one of the first duties of any civilized and democratic Government?

The Communist Party take a different line. They say: 'Give us control of the currency, and we can overthrow any capitalist country in the world.' We can see in every direction the fall in the value of our money, not only at home, but abroad, and we are now to face a new crop of depression as a result of devaluation. The devaluation of money, arising mainly from the astounding extravagance in Government expenditure, causes anxiety even in those most responsible for it. The word 'disinflation' has been coined in order to avoid the unpopular term 'deflation'.

The Socialist Party are very mealy-mouthed today, and the Chancellor of the Exchequer is very delicate in his language. One must not say 'deflation', but only 'disinflation'. In a similar manner, one must not say 'devaluation', but only 'revaluation', and, finally, there is the farce of saying that there must be no increase in personal incomes when what is meant is no increase in wages. However, the Chancellor felt that a certain broad prejudice attaches to the word 'income' and that consequently no one would mind saying that incomes shall not increase —but wages, no. However, it is wages that he means. I am sure that the British electors will not be taken in by such humbug. I suppose that presently when 'disinflation' also wins its bad name, the Chancellor will call it 'non-undisinflation' and will start again. It is not only the value of money that we are interested in—the purchasing power of money—but the steady and grievous fall in Government securities which is a direct result of the financial mismanagement and the attempt to bring about 'Socialism in our Time'.

In this affair, the two Chancellors of the Exchequer we have known in late years, and whom I see before me and under whom we have suffered, have shared a responsibility which I think I may say is gradually becoming more equal. If I may use a sporting term, it looks as if there will be a 'pretty close finish'. For the consols called 'Daltons', in compliment to the right hon Member for Bishop Auckland (Mr Dalton), which were issued at £100 three years ago, only £66 can be realized today. What an encouragement to saving; what a sinister advertisement of the financial insecurity and depression which have been brought upon us. It cannot even be claimed as part of the policy of the Minister of Health of retributive redistribution. The loss is not redistributed; the value has vanished into thin air. This is a serious matter for the whole country and particularly for the many thousands of people whose savings have been slashed by this fall.

The latest statement of the National Insurance Reserve Fund shows that on 31 March this year the Fund held £201,000,000 worth of these securities. The current value of their stock is now £133,000,000, representing a loss, unless they have been realized, of some £68,000,000. All that is taken out of the subscriptions of the wage-earning population of this country. The Government are continually exhorting the people to save, and we for our part have always lent our support to the National Savings Movement, but how can people be expected to save and invest their savings in Government securities, when they see what is happening? The fact is that the public at large have lost all confidence in this Government's financial administration, and they are pretty clear of what the financial intentions of the party behind the Government are.

I had meant to deal with the cuts proposed by the Government. I have just one word to say on them. I am strongly of the belief that if the great policy and decision of national military service had been used properly and a smaller number called up for a longer time, great economies might have been made and might still be made in the military services. I have no time to elaborate that, although I am not in the least bit afraid to do so. The Government have failed in their duty to the nation and they will be severely judged by it. That is no reason why we for our part should fail. We shall do our utmost to encourage everybody in the country to work as hard as they can in order to get things ready for the day when there will be a Government capable of aiding their efforts.

Anyone who has been in this Debate must feel that the main issue that is before us tonight is the need of a new Parliament. We are indifferent to the date of the election. We do not mind if the Government put it off. Many experts think that the longer the drop the surer the execution, but nothing could be worse for the country than a very long period of electioneering uncertainty. We have before us two malignant Bills, relating to steel and the alteration of the Parliament Act, which are bound to divide this House more than ever and bring into force party fighting. We have apparently to live for three, four or five months in the present state of increasing domestic strife and uncertainty. It is not giving the country a chance if you do not at least curtail this period and impart an element of certainty into it.

I say to the Government: you have the fortunes of this great country in your hands. For four years you have had power and wealth such as no Government have ever possessed. It is not only devaluation but bankruptcy which confronts us now. Here we are concerned only with party manoeuvres and calculations. The Government have devalued the pound and devalued the British nation, but most of all they have devalued themselves and brought us to bankruptcy. They have shown themselves not only financially but mentally and morally bankrupt, and the sooner they appeal to their fellow countrymen the better it will be for all who wish to see this country rise again in its own strength.

IRON AND STEEL BILL (LORDS AMENDMENTS)

A SPEECH TO THE HOUSE OF COMMONS
16 NOVEMBER 1949

---

1 *November—Publication of first annual Report of Overseas Food Corporation, covering the period of thirteen months to 31 March 1949, reveals liabilities amounting to £23,300,000 on the Groundnuts Scheme.*
11 *November—Chancellor of Exchequer gives figure of National Debt for 1949 as £25,267,000,000, being £503 per head of population of United Kingdom.*
15 *November—Commencement of recruiting for Civil Defence.*

[16 *November* 1949

I am sure that no Member of the House, wherever he may sit or whatever views he may hold about the merits of the particular topic now before us, will have envied the right hon Gentleman in the task which it has fallen to his lot to fulfil. About a fortnight ago we were informed that the Government wished to end the deadlock between the two Houses on the Iron and Steel Bill by accepting in principle the House of Lords Amendment delaying its operation until after the people have been consulted. There was no question of a bargain or a compromise. The Government asked a question and the Leader of the Conservative Party in the House of Lords, after consulting with some of his friends in both Houses, gave the answer. The answer was to the effect that if the Amendment the Lords were insisting upon were accepted in principle and substance he, Lord Salisbury, would advise the House of Lords to accept it, even though the form was slightly altered.

We have given most careful consideration to the differences in form between the Lords Amendment and that which is now proposed to us this afternoon by the Socialist Government, and we are satisfied that for all practical purposes they mean the same thing. It would hardly have been in accordance with the manner in which the House of Lords discharges its constitutional duties under the Parliament Act settlement of thirty-five years ago for the Conservative Leader in the House of Lords to advise them to take advantage of minor differences in form in order to reject what is the undoubted acceptance by the Commons of their contention.

It is not for us here this afternoon to forecast what the action of the Lords will be, but in this House we shall not oppose this series of alterations. We shall not oppose them, and I should think it very likely that a similar course will be adopted in another place. Of course, if the House of Lords accept this Amendment, and we here do not vote against it, it in no way alters our opposition to the nationalization of steel. On the contrary, we are very glad that the issue should be presented in so clear-cut a form to the electors. We are content with that; it is almost a referendum on the issue. Should we be returned to power—[AN HON MEMBER: 'Wishful thinking.'] Well, one has to take all things into consideration. Not to do so would be to throw doubts upon the freedom of elections and the intelligence of the electors. Should we be returned to power one of our first steps would be to expunge from the Statute Book this wanton, wasteful and partisan measure, in which many of those associated with it do not, in their hearts, believe, and which strikes this country a bitter blow at a bad time.

It will be one of our first steps to remove it from the Statute Book, and to allow the steel industry to continue its splendid career—to which tribute has even been paid this afternoon—of ever-improving production and efficiency, with unbroken good will between employers and employed, a record almost in this country and almost in the steel industries of the world—without being dragged into party politics by the fanatics of obsolete and discredited Socialistic doctrines. We are very glad that this should be so.

The actual matter before us does not seem to me to be of major importance either way. I rather agree with some sentences which fell from the right hon Gentleman. Some say that if the Government had not bowed, as they have done, to the wishes of the Lords they would not be able to have an election as early as January or February and yet pass the Steel Bill, even under their new Parliament Act. What they are now gaining, it is said, is an opportunity of an early election without what is called losing the Steel Bill. Of course, as the right hon Gentleman's speech has fully admitted, under the Parliament Act—and I am speaking of the great Parliament Act——

THE LORD PRESIDENT OF THE COUNCIL [MR HERBERT MORRISON]: Yours.

MR CHURCHILL: If the right hon Gentleman was ever responsible for social legislation which, thirty-five years later, he could speak of with as calm a conscience as I can about a Parliament Act which has become the foundation of our political system, although much fought at the time, if he has anything like that to show in his records, he will have more to be proud of than anything else that can be found in his past career.

What the Government are gaining by this, it is said, is that they can have an election without losing the Steel Bill. But, as I was saying, under the Parliament Act if they had an early election, and won that election, the Bill would still pass into law with a very few weeks' delay. There would be nothing to affect the general march of events. If this same Bill is renewed after the election, it can resume its progress under the original Parliament Act, *a priori* under this one, from the point which it had reached in the previous Parliament. All that the Government would have lost would be the pleasure of saying, 'We have fulfilled our programme. We have given you the full dose. Would you like another dose?' That is really not controversial. It is in their power to say that anyhow.

It cannot, therefore, be argued that the acceptance of this Amendment has affected in any way the date of the General Election. It is not within our power to do so, and where there is no power there can be no responsibility. However, the question of the date of the General Election, especially if the Steel Bill is out of the way, is undoubtedly in all our minds this afternoon, and it seems to me the only explanation for the tactics which the Socialist Government have pursued. To us on this side of the House as a party the date is a matter of indifference. In fact, however, party strife will rage in this land in its most active form until the votes are counted.

I am glad to see the Prime Minister in his place. In my view it is his duty in all the present circumstances to curtail and limit the uncertainty of when the General Election will come as much as possible. It may flatter his vanity and that of his colleagues to walk around with an air of superior knowledge on a matter which affects so very many people, but against this somewhat feeble satisfaction must be set the inconvenience to the public and the hindrance to our wealth-producing energies involved in a prolonged period of purposeless uncertainty. I suppose that the plans of scores of thousands or even hundreds of thousands of people are affected in their daily lives by not knowing when this inevitably approaching event will occur.

MR WARBEY (Luton): On a point of Order. May I ask what is the relevance of this discussion on the date of the election to the subject matter before us this afternoon?

MR SPEAKER: The reason the Lords gave for insisting on their Amendment was that the electors should have an opportunity of expressing their views on the matter. Therefore, it seems to me that the question when the electors will express their opinion is in Order.

MR WARBEY: But is it in Order to discuss when the General Election should be held?

MR SPEAKER: I should have thought that the whole range of that was in Order on this Debate.

MR CHURCHILL: As I was saying, I believe that very great damage and injury is being done by keeping this uncertainty going unnecessarily. If there is any serious public or even party reason for keeping everyone on tenterhooks and tiptoe it ought to be stated, but there is none apparently, and with some experience of these matters it seems to me a very wrong thing to hamper and injure the national life in this way. If there were a party advantage that would be sensible, but I cannot see that what has been done is an advantage; it is a great national detriment. Therefore it seems to me, as I said a month ago, that the Government would be consulting the national interests, and possibly even their own, by taking the nation into their confidence at the earliest moment. Everyone knows this Parliament is dead, and that on the subject of this Steel Bill a new Parliament would have a much better chance of getting us out of our dangers and difficulties.

All these manoeuvres, which I understand is the term used about this Measure, are an example of the low-grade tactical motives which are the key to Government policy. The Measure mutilating—I should perhaps not use the word 'mutilating'—altering the Parliament Act was forced through the day before yesterday by the Government majority. I am not reflecting on the measure. I am only speaking about the circumstances in which it was passed before it was known to the House that the Government admit, as they have admitted today, that the view of the House of Lords is right—namely, that the Steel Bill should not become law until it has been submitted to the judgment of the electors.

Why, then, we might well ask, should the House of Lords be punished and maltreated for being right? Why, then, we might have asked, should they be stripped of part of their functions for having used them so wisely and so well? How can the Government have the face to recognize the justice of the Lords demand that the people should be consulted on the nationalization of steel—a monstrous tyranny that such a demand should be made, that the people should be consulted on the subject—when at the same time—almost on the very day—they strike a crippling blow at the powers of the Lords under the Parliament Act, which gives them full power to pass this Bill at approximately the same date?

Why should it be necessary to pass into law the Bill for amending the Parliament Act, which contains a special retroactive clause for the express purpose of carrying the nationalization of steel into law before the elections can pronounce upon it, when, after all, it is admitted that they ought to have such an opportunity? I do not often quote to the House the leading article of *The Times*, but I noticed this morning this sentence:

'Judged merely as an episode in Parliamentary tactics, this cynical and over-ingenious business has been badly botched.'

However, out of evil often comes good. I am glad that the House of Lords should once again have vindicated their wisdom and sagacity. Just as on the question of the abolition of capital punishment they prevented an act of folly and voiced the opinion of the vast majority of the nation, so now they render a service in making sure that the people are effectively consulted on the proposals to nationalize steel before those proposals can come into operation. That is the position that they have taken up and which we on this side take up, and to which the Socialist Government have thought it right to bow and to submit. No reasons have been given to us which explain the Government's action other than those of party convenience. I say—and I leave the matter here—that we take our stand on the position that it is not the function of the House of Lords to govern the people but to make sure that the people have the right to govern themselves.

FOREIGN AFFAIRS

---

16 *November—A good-will gift of £A10,000,000 (£8,000,000) made by Australia, this being the third of its kind, and the total amounting to £A45,000,000 (£36,000,000).*

[17 *November* 1949

Before I come to the matter of the speech of the right hon Gentleman the Foreign Secretary, it is my duty to clear up a matter upon which I was misinformed at our last Foreign Affairs Debate in July. The right hon Gentleman introduced into the Debate as a controversial issue the question of responsibility for the introduction for the term 'unconditional surrender' into our policy in the wartime conference at Casablanca. It seemed to me that he cast some of the responsibility on me for the use of that phrase. He seemed to complain that the Cabinet had not been consulted, and he asserted his inveterate opposition to the idea. It had left him, he said, with nothing but a shambles to deal with in Germany—the House will remember the occasion—and from this arose many of the difficulties of his task. This was, of course, the exact opposite of what he had said eighteen months before when—and I entirely agree with him—he said that he did not think unconditional surrender had played an important part in the conditions in which the war was brought to an end.

The right hon Gentleman raised this matter without giving me any notice, and on the spur of the moment I said that the first time I heard the words, 'unconditional surrender'—in regard, of course, to the late war—was when the President used them in his speech to the Press Conference at Casablanca. This was the impression which had been left in my mind and which I had expressed to Mr Robert Sherwood three years before when he raised the point with me in connection with his biography of Mr Harry Hopkins. This impression was confirmed in my mind by what President Roosevelt said himself on the point, which is quoted in the Hopkins' biography. This is the quotation:

> 'Suddenly the Press Conference was on, and Winston and I had no time to prepare for it, and the thought popped into my mind that they had called Grant "Old Unconditional Surrender", and the next thing I knew, I had said it.'

However, there is great danger in quoting from memory when all these things crop up about the tumultuous past. We all remember the advice which the aged tutor gave to his disciples and followers on his death-bed when they came to him—'Verify your quotations.' At any rate, I have now looked up the telegrams and records of the occasion, and I find that undoubtedly the words 'unconditional surrender' were mentioned, probably in informal talks, I think at meal times, between the President and me. At any rate, on 19 January 1942, five days before the end of the Conference, I sent the present Prime Minister, then the Deputy Prime Minister, the following message as part of a long telegram on other matters:

'We propose to draw up a statement of the work of the conference for communication to the Press at the proper time. I should be glad to know what the War Cabinet would think of our including in this statement a declaration of the firm intention of the United States and the British Empire to continue the war relentlessly until we have brought about the "unconditional surrender" of Germany and Japan. The omission of Italy would be to encourage a break-up there. The President liked this idea, and it would stimulate our friends in every country.'

To which the Prime Minister and my right hon Friend the Member for Warwick and Leamington (Mr Eden)—he is not here today; he is absent in his constituency, as many hon Members have to be in present circumstances—replied on the 21st:

'The Cabinet were unanimously of opinion that balance of advantage lay against excluding Italy because of misgivings which would inevitably be aroused in Turkey, in the Balkans and elsewhere. Nor are we convinced that effect on Italians would be good. Knowledge of rough stuff coming to them is surely more likely to have desired effect on Italian morale.'

It is clear, therefore, that the right hon Gentleman was mistaken, I have no doubt quite innocently—and I was in my own way, though not in such an important aspect—in saying that the Cabinet had not been consulted. They not only had been consulted but had expressed a very decided opinion. Also, I think he was mistaken in saying that he was not a party to that opinion before President Roosevelt's speech was given to the Press.

It will be seen that the opinion of the Cabinet was not against the policy of unconditional surrender. They only disapproved of it not being applied to Italy as well. I did not want this, because I hoped—and the hope has not been unfulfilled—that Italy, freed from Mussolini's dictatorship, might fight on our side, which she did for several years of the war, with lasting beneficial results to the state of Europe. I have the strong feeling that I cooled off on the point because I did not want to bring Italy into this sphere; and I thought that that would influence the President, too. This is borne out by the agreed communiqué which was drafted by the Combined Chiefs of Staff and approved by both of us, and which contains no mention of unconditional surrender. As the issue was raised in debate by the right hon Gentleman in his very responsible position, and as my own memory was at fault on the subject, I felt it my duty to place the true facts on record in the journals of the House if only in justice to the memory of President Roosevelt. I apologize for this digression which I think was necessitated by what had already occurred in the House.

I now come to the review of the spacious European scene which the right hon Gentleman has given us in, I might almost say, dulcet tones— at any rate, in a manner which seems to leave it free from all atmosphere of urgency or danger. I will begin with this question of Germany and German dismantlement. We all admire the work which has been done since the war in the British zone in Germany. It has been a great achievement into which, as in the American zone, an immense fund of personal devotion has gone. We have also spent large quantities of British money which we could not properly afford, in enabling our enemies of yesterday to recover after the shattering conditions of defeat, and they have made a very remarkable recovery in many ways. The success of the air-lift into Berlin, where the Allies were trying to feed the German people, and the Soviet Government were trying to starve them was a famous event. What a pity it is that the right hon Gentleman should mar, as I think he has to some extent marred, these sacrifices and achievements by errors which arise from smaller facts and lesser considerations. I cannot speak, of course, now about the trial of German generals four and a half years after the Armistice, because that is at present *sub judice*, but on this side of the House for two years past we have steadily drawn attention to the unwisdom of belated dismantlement. Yet this is what the Foreign Secretary has pursued with astonishing perseverance. It is impossible to reconcile his insistence upon belated dismantlement with the policy which he also supported of free elections in Western Germany.

To bring on the elections and then feed the fires which burn at such times with all this fuel of dismantlement, is an act which cannot be explained by any wise or rational process. To persist in belated dismantlement—after all, the great bulk of it has already been completed—and at the same time to give the German people full freedom to say what they thought about it as an election issue, was to authorize and stimulate every force in Germany hostile to the Western democracies to give full vent to their passions. There was something to be said for finishing up dismantlement; there were serious arguments, certainly. Security against future perils must always be in our minds, and I can assure the right hon Gentleman that it is not excluded from my mind by mere sentiment.

There was something to be said for finishing up dismantlement. There was much also to be said for German self-government, but no human being can find anything in reason to say for the combination and the exact timing of the two processes. It was, I say, a grotesque piece of mismanagement. Now that the harm is largely done, we are to have a new set of proposals probably going halfway or a third of the way, and these are soon to be put before us. There is not an argument for stopping or mitigating dismantlement now which was not valid and even clamant six months, twelve months or even eighteen months ago.

In this matter, as in the Palestine policy, the Foreign Secretary, I regret to say, has succeeded with astonishing precision in securing for our country the worst of both worlds at the same time. It is, indeed, melancholy to find that the fine work of British administration in Germany is blurred over in this way, and needless misunderstandings are created between peoples who, for good or ill, have to live together if the world is to revive. It is really like someone painting, with art and labour, a magnificent picture and then, at the moment when it is about to be exhibited, throwing handfuls of mud all over it. Happily, perhaps the mud can be washed off by other hands.

I say that the right hon Gentleman has made serious mistakes in this. Some of these mistakes have had beneficial reactions. We are, I think, largely indebted to the right hon Gentleman for the present Right-wing complexion of the Government of Western Germany. The House will remember how three years ago His Majesty's Government declared that they would enforce nationalization of German industries throughout the British zone, and specially the Ruhr. Then the United States used its influence and asked them whether it would not be better to allow the Germans to express their own opinion upon a matter of that kind. The right hon Gentleman had to give way, or gave way, and so it was decided that this matter should be left to the first elected Government of Western Germany.

It is said that the speech about dismantling made here by the right hon Gentleman in July when the German elections were about to take place turned a million votes over against the Socialists of Germany. I should not at all mind if any oration which the right hon Gentleman delivered had a similar effect here. At any rate, the Parliament chosen by the German people and the Government based upon it have rejected the policy of nationalization and support that of private enterprise under customary modern controls. Here is a case, and not the only one, when the right hon Gentleman has shot at a pigeon and hit a crow. Which is the pigeon and which is the crow I shall not at this moment attempt to define. I am sure it is a wise decision of the German electorate and the Government resting upon them not to take all these industries into the direct control of the German State but to allow others to exist in their country besides the State itself.

This is not the only case of these difficulties. We have in the main throughout this Parliament supported the foreign policy of the right hon Gentleman, but I must say quite plainly, after fully considering the French position as well as that of the United States, that it seems to me that no Government in this country after the present one is likely to carry the official Socialist policy of dismantling, as it has been pursued up to the present time, very much further.

MRS LEAH MANNING (Epping): What about the French?

MR CHURCHILL: The greatest part of dismantling is in our own British zone. Therefore, we have for a very long time been in the extremely unfortunate position of getting all the unpopularity with the Germans while our friends the French were largely immune from it. [*Interruption.*] I have my opinion, which I have expressed.

Now I come to Strasbourg and United Europe. The right hon Gentleman told us in a previous Session that United Europe was his idea, that he had thought of it twenty, or even thirty, years ago. But the unlucky thing was that the right hon Gentleman forgot to take out a patent for it at the time. If he had only done that, how much smoother the course would have been; and he could have had all the credit to himself, and he might have been much more helpful and friendly to the development of this great idea. Instead, the right hon Gentleman has been forced, as everyone knows, by deep tides of public opinion in Europe and in his own party, to make great concessions to the idea of a United Europe, but he has always done it, it seems to me, in the least possible degree, at the latest moment and in a grudging manner.

This process reached its climax at Strasbourg, where the right hon Gentleman was so ably assisted by the Lord President of the Council and the Chancellor of the Duchy of Lancaster. It was remarkable to me to witness how quickly they lost all effective contact with their own Socialist comrades in Europe. These three Ministers together completely threw away what the British Socialist Party had long greatly desired—namely, the leadership of Social democracy in Europe.

The party opposite, under the control of the right hon Gentleman, have completely lost their influence as a party in Europe and they are regarded with bewilderment by their own best friends. The right hon Gentleman referred to M. Leon Blum. He is a friend of both of us and certainly must be considered one of the most eminent of all the Socialist statesmen of Europe. I was reading in the *Manchester Guardian* yesterday what he had written in *Le Populaire*. Hon Members opposite should take notice of these words by M. Leon Blum, a man of very high elevation in intellect and spirit, who says:

'On various occasions doubt has arisen as to whether our comrades of the [British] Labour movement were not opposing the European movement. Although they declare that these impressions were false a great deal of damage has been done by them already. We have the right to turn to our English comrades and to insist that they should spare no effort to dissipate such an impression.'

That should be weighed by members of the Socialist Party throughout the country. If I were a Socialist—which I am not—I certainly would be rather pained to see, on a great matter like this European Movement, the most prominent European Socialist expressing himself in terms like that, which are all the more powerful because they are so moderately expressed.

Steady progress has, however, been made in this field. At Strasbourg in August I pointed out that the admission of Germany to membership of both the Consultative Assembly and the Council of Europe was a matter of urgent necessity for the future of Europe. This has indeed been my theme since I spoke at Zurich in 1946, when I appealed to France to take Germany by the hand and lead her back into the European family and forget the age-long quarrel which has rent Europe and the world. Everyone present at Strasbourg this summer agreed that the matter was one of primary importance and deserved the gravest consideration, but there were some who thought that it was being raised at too early a date. Since then opinion has advanced by long strides. Two months later nobody considered the matter premature. At the beginning of November the Committee of Foreign Ministers, to which the right hon Gentleman referred, met and gave out to the Press a statement that they were unanimously in favour of the principle of the admission of the Federal Republic of Western Germany as an Associate Member.

The Foreign Ministers did not themselves decide to admit Germany. They decided, very wisely I consider and very courteously to take the opinion of the Standing Committee of the Consultative Assembly.

That committee met and considered the matter and on 9 November, the week before last, it was announced that this committee were also unanimously in favour of the admission of Germany provided that the new German Government indicated its wish and ability to comply with the democratic conditions of membership.

MR HAROLD DAVIES (Leek): May I interrupt the right hon Gentleman? This is of vital importance. I put this question in no partisan spirit whatever. [*Laughter.*] Hon Members opposite need not smile—this is vital to the destiny and peace of the world. Is the right hon Gentleman prepared to take the risk of completely rearming Germany at this juncture, because that is what his proposal really ultimately means?

HON MEMBERS: Nonsense.

MR CHURCHILL: I must leave the House to judge of the total lack of connection between what the hon Member has said and any language being used by me or anything in the immediate circumstances before us in Europe.

It was a very remarkable decision of the Consultative Assembly Standing Committee, and I hope that it may become a milestone on our journey. The Standing Committee contained representatives of nations, including France, whom the Germans did overrun and occupy for long hard years. The representatives of these countries, especially of France, deserve the thanks of every lover of peace and of every good European for their sagacious and tolerant view. There could be no stronger proof of the advance which European opinion has made towards greater unity and, as we know, it is in this greater unity that the best chance and hope resides of the future salvation of the world.

Nevertheless, we must remember that the formal admission has not yet taken effect. I urge His Majesty's Government to make every effort to ensure that no time is lost. Nineteen hundred and fifty may well prove a critical year as to how the minds of Germans will turn; I mean Germans free to express a conviction, outside the Iron Curtain. I am troubled by the thought that even if the admission becomes a fact at once, it may not be until next August, or September, that the Germans will take their seats. I am sure it will be of great benefit if the meeting of the next Assembly could be brought forward, so that the introduction of German representatives to this infant, but vital, democratic body could at the earliest moment become an accomplished fact.

I wish to turn to a kindred, but different topic in the great field that lies before us. There is, I think, some obscurity of thought about the recognition of different countries and diplomatic representation which should be sought with them. I spoke some time ago about Spain.

Fancy having an ambassador in Moscow, but not having one in Madrid. The individual Spaniard has a much happier and freer life than the individual Russian—[Hon Members: 'Oh.']—or Pole or Czechoslovak. I do not suppose that there are ten hon Members in this House who, if it was actually put before them as a decision which they must take tomorrow morning, whether they would rather live the next five years in Franco Spain or in Soviet Russia, would not book their ticket for the south.

Mrs Manning: I can assure the right hon Gentleman that I should not have a chance of living for five years in Spain—nor for five minutes.

Mr Churchill: Happily the hard choice is not thrust before the hon Lady. Other difficulties and interests will confront her over here. She will still have full liberty to remain in this country and to discharge her duties. But the question remains, which I leave for reasonable people to consider, if we have an ambassador to Moscow, why should we not have one in Spain?

Now the question has arisen also of what our attitude should be towards the Chinese Communists who have gained control over so large a part of China. Ought we to recognize them or not? Recognizing a person is not necessarily an act of approval. I will not be personal, or give instances. One has to recognize lots of things and people in this world of sin and woe that one does not like. The reason for having diplomatic relations is not to confer a compliment, but to secure a convenience. When a large and powerful mass of people are organized together and are masters of an immense area and of great populations, it may be necessary to have relations with them. One may even say that when relations are most difficult that is the time when diplomacy is most needed.

We ought certainly to have suitable contacts with this large part of the world's surface and population under the control of the Chinese Communists. We ought to have them on general grounds, quite apart from all the arguments—and they are very important arguments—about the protection of specific British interests. Again I would say it seems difficult to justify having full diplomatic relations with the Soviet Government in Moscow and remaining without even de facto contacts with its enormous offshoots into China. On this side of the House, however, I am speaking of the general principles, the general line of approach to these topics—we agree with the Foreign Secretary in the answers he gave yesterday that no such step should be taken by us, except in consultation with the whole of our Commonwealth and also, of course, with the United States.

Mr Gallacher: Why the United States?

Mr Churchill: We should certainly not be in favour of isolated action in this respect, although, if it could be brought about as a joint policy, as the right hon Gentleman foreshadowed, it would seem to be well worthy of consideration.

A very different issue arises when His Majesty's Government deliberately select a country which is held in Russian bondage, which is not free to express its own opinions and whose Government is a mere Quisling tool of Soviet policy. His Majesty's Government deliberately select such a country to be placed on the Security Council of the United Nations. We all have deep memories about Czechoslovakia and much British blood was shed to save her from German tyranny. As things have turned out, the unhappy people of Czechoslovakia have only exchanged one tyranny for another. Everyone knows that they have been to a large extent robbed of their civic liberties and national independence and that they have become a mere pawn in the Kremlin game.

Mr Ronald Chamberlain (Norwood): Rubbish.

Mr Churchill: Who said 'rubbish'?

Mr Chamberlain: May I ask the right hon Gentleman——

Mr Churchill: No.

Mr Gallacher: The hon Member has just come back from Czechoslovakia.

Mr Churchill: I think the Communist Members and fellow travellers have a pretty good run in this House.

Mr Gallacher: On point of Order, a direct reference has been made to the Communist Members getting 'a good run in this House', by the right hon Gentleman, who never comes to this House except when he is going to make a speech.

Mr Deputy-Speaker [Major Milner]: Order. I hope that all hon Members in this House get 'a good run'.

Mr Churchill: I have been wondering of late years and months whether indeed representation ought not to be made to the Chair on the abuse of raising questions on points of Order which have nothing whatever to do with Order. It is no doubt a fault which is not confined to any one party. That I can well believe, but I certainly think that some more precise definition would be a help to hon Members in the discharge of their duties.

I say that not one of the present representatives of Czechoslovakia has the slightest right to speak in the name of the brave Czechoslovak people, whose love of democracy is as strong as ever.

Mr Chamberlain: Rubbish.

MR CHURCHILL: The right hon Gentleman seems-to have nothing in his head but rubbish.

MR CHAMBERLAIN: On a point of Order.

MR DEPUTY-SPEAKER: No point of Order can arise. The hon Gentleman has made persistent efforts to interrupt the right hon Gentleman who has possession of the House. He is not entitled to do that.

MR CHAMBERLAIN: My point of Order has nothing to do with rubbish. I wish to know if it is in Order for the right hon Gentleman to classify me along with himself by referring to me as 'the right hon Gentleman'?

MR CHURCHILL: I quite agree that my profound apologies are due to the House.

I wish to say a few words about the Czechoslovak people. It has been their fate to live under outside rule for many generations, but in all this time they have learned how to preserve a very great deal of their own national life. They have by their own means of internal and passive resistance presented a kind of subdued but constant opposition to all those who have sought to rule them in the past 300 years. At the present moment they are under extraordinary stress. The Communist form of tyranny is far more efficient than any that has ever been devised in bygone centuries. Many things are happening in Czechoslovakia which must be the cause of anxiety to their foreign overlords and to those persons whom those overlords employ in ministerial offices.

There have been cruel executions, in some cases of men who fought valiantly for the Allied cause during the war. Purges have taken place in every grade of society. There is a tense if partly concealed reign of terror. Large numbers of refugees of every class are making their escape from this Soviet prison camp. We read in the newspapers only yesterday how the whole Czechoslovakian Reparations Commission in Western Germany were seeking asylum and British protection for themselves and their wives and children rather than go back to their native land in the plight into which it has fallen. What a symbol this is of what is actually going on inside Czechoslovakia.

I cannot feel that there is any Government in Europe less deserving of being chosen to be on the Security Council of the United Nations. I cannot think of any step more likely to discourage all the forces in Czechoslovakia who are working so patiently and steadfastly to free their country from the Soviet yoke. The fact that Great Britain, which has always been looked upon with so much regard by the Czechs, should give its vote for placing on the Security Council a Government which at the dictation of the Kremlin is trying to torment them into Communism will be a heavy blow to all those in Czechoslovakia with whom, on both sides of the House, there is a great measure of sympathy.

Yet that is what the right hon Gentleman has done, and that is what he asks the party who sit on the benches opposite to become responsible for. We are told that there was a 'gentlemen's agreement' to the effect that representatives of the Eastern bloc behind the Iron Curtain should in practice be chosen for the Security Council in accordance with the wishes of the majority of those States. But the 'gentlemen's agreement' was in 1946, and since then the revolution in Czechoslovakia has taken place. We have an entirely new situation. Was the fate of Masaryk and Benes covered by the 'gentlemen's agreement'? Was the execution and purging of some of the finest Czechoslovak patriots part of the 'gentlemen's agreement'?

The United States at any rate did not consider themselves bound in this way. They voted for Yugoslavia which has to a large extent freed itself from Kremlin oppression though not from Kremlin menace. [An HON MEMBER: 'It is still Communist.'] I think that the way in which they manage their internal affairs is for them to decide but I certainly do not think that they should be held down under foreign pressure from outside. Even if they be Communist, which I largely question because they are a very free, rough and ready mountain people, the product of centuries of war in the struggles with Turkey— I doubt very much whether they are—I say that it was in those circumstances an extraordinary thing for Great Britain to vote for the election of the present Czechoslovak Government to membership of the Security Council.

I have also heard, although I cannot vouch for it, and I am quite ready to be corrected if I am contradicted, that there was some kind of deal—that if we voted for the Soviet-managed Government in Czechoslovakia the votes of the bloc of satellite States would be given to one of the British Dominions for a seat on the Security Council. If this is true—and I shall be very glad to hear that it is not true—it would seem to be an unworthy transaction reflecting not only upon those concerned, but affecting the dignity of the United Nations institution itself. Be this as it may we are astonished that the right hon Gentleman has lent himself to supporting the controlled, satellite Government of Czechoslovakia rather than the free and independent— in the national sense—Government of Yugoslavia. I am sure that the majority of the party opposite, if they dared express their minds, would condemn such a decision.

It is the sort of behaviour which makes people in many friendly countries in Europe and America feel that they do not know where Britain stands on some of the large issues for which in the past we have fought so hard. It robs the foreign policy of His Majesty's Government of all distinction, and indeed to a very large extent of rational explanation. On both sides of the House, I think, we are glad that Yugoslavia and not Czechoslovakia was elected to the vacancy on the Council of the United Nations in spite of the British vote to the contrary.

The threatened position of Yugoslavia raises directly that of Albania. It is known that the Soviet 'Diplomatic Mission' includes some thousands of military and scientific personnel and that the Russians are in physical possession of the former Italian submarine base at Sassano opposite Valona. The internal development schemes, including oil exploration, which formerly were being carried out with Yugoslav help, are now directly in Russian hands. On the other hand, the land communications with Albania are in the hands of Tito. This certainly seems to be a danger point at the present time. We have no reason to trust the Government of Albania. The regime of Enver Hodja, like other Kremlin-controlled institutions, commands no real national support. Last June, Hodja's Deputy-Premier Xoxe, who also held the position of Minister of the Interior—a very important position—and was also General Secretary of the Communist Party was executed after charges of collaboration with Tito had been made against him.

It is clear that fierce political stresses rack Albania, and I must remind the House before leaving Albania that it is now three years since the mining of the British destroyers in the Corfu Channel proved Albania's complete disregard of international law. Forty British lives were lost for which compensation, adjudged by the International Arbitration Court to which the matter was referred, was accorded and, of course, has not been paid.

MR BEVIN: The point is that compensation has not been assessed. The Court have given the verdict but they have not assessed the compensation and in this case I have to wait for the lawyers.

MR CHURCHILL: I certainly cannot blame the right hon Gentleman for that. The fact remains that we have not yet received any compensation, after three years, for the murder, in defiance of international law, of forty British sailors.

MR BEVIN: I must ask the right hon Gentleman to appreciate that we are in the hands of the International Court——

MR CHURCHILL: Certainly.

MR BEVIN: —and if he is blaming anybody, he is blaming the International Court.

MR CHURCHILL: I was not so much—[HON MEMBERS: 'You

were.'] Hon Gentlemen opposite do not know what I am going to say. I was not so much blaming anybody as deploring what is an undoubted fact.

Albania is, of course, the principal base from which the Communist rebellion in Greece has been sustained, and it has also been the refuge of the Greek Communist forces whenever they have been in difficulties. We must all rejoice that the fortunes of Greece have so greatly improved. High credit is due to the Americans for the strong aid they have given to Greek freedom. They took over, adopted and made their own a policy which Great Britain under the National Coalition— the right hon Gentleman and I were associated in that—initiated in Greece during the war—not without much criticism here and much criticism in the United States.

We are glad that a British Brigade has been kept in Greece all this time. I had myself thought that it would be withdrawn after the General Election in Greece held under inter-Allied supervision in 1946, but I readily agree that circumstances have changed and that the Soviet sponsored Greek Communist rebellion made it desirable for us to continue to associate ourselves with the Greek policy of the American Government in every way. I hope that the date of the withdrawal of the British Brigade, however desirable on other grounds, will not be determined purely on the grounds of expense, but only in due relation to the whole situation in the Balkans and, I may add, generally throughout the world.

The latest attitude of the Soviet Government is curious. They have now asked for a free election in Greece under international supervision. But this was the very proposal which the right hon Gentleman made to the Russians three years ago, and we strongly urged them to join us in seeing that the election was fairly and freely conducted, but they refused. Now they have asked for it. They have also asked for an amnesty for the defeated Greek rebels, but this also was offered by the Greek Government two years ago and spurned. It seems to me that, after all that has happened, the question of holding another supervised election in Greece and also that of extending an amnesty, are measures about the timing of which the Greek Government, after all it has gone through, is entitled to be the prime judge.

I apologize to the House for having kept them so long, but even if one deals only selectively with this vast field there is much to be said. I now reach the end. I have had to make some serious criticisms of the right hon Gentleman, most of which I imagine will have their echo in the breasts of Members of the Socialist Party because in this matter I think he has put a needless strain upon their feelings.

I wish to end on a different note. I have on former occasions paid my tribute to the many characteristic British qualities which the right hon Gentleman possesses and to the courage with which he has faced misunderstanding and unpopularity among his own supporters. We all trust that his public life and personal health may long be preserved. It may be, however, that this is the last Parliamentary Debate on Foreign Affairs we shall see in the present House of Commons, and it may be that so far as the tenure of the Foreign Office by the right hon Gentleman is concerned, we have listened this afternoon to his swan song.

The right hon Gentleman certainly had a great opportunity. When he took up his important office we were the most respected country in Europe and not surpassed by any other country in the world in the esteem in which we were held. Under this administration we have fallen back in many spheres and from this we cannot exclude the foreign sphere. The policy of the right hon Gentleman has not represented the coherent outlook of Socialists or of Liberals or of Conservatives. It cannot be reconciled with any integral theme of thought. It has been swayed, and even at times dominated, by his personal likes and dislikes, strengthened by pride and enforced by obstinacy.

We on this side have done our best to support him. We have sustained him in all aspects of his policy which are a logical and harmonious part of the great causes which Britain has at heart. His manly resistance to Communism, his preservation of good relations with the United States, the Brussels agreement about Western Europe——

Mr Bevin: Good.

Mr Churchill: —the Atlantic Pact——

Mr Bevin: Good.

Mr Churchill: —the air-lift into Berlin——

Mr Bevin: Good.

Mr Churchill: —the policy pursued in Greece, the reinforcement of Hong Kong—are all events of the first magnitude in which the right hon Gentleman has played a prominent part. We are sorry indeed that these achievements do not stand by themselves unclouded by other and lesser actions, but still they stand, and on that note I will take the opportunity of bringing my remarks to a close.

EUROPEAN MOVEMENT

---

21 *November—Debate in House of Commons on Groundnuts Scheme. Opposition move an amendment demanding an urgent and full inquiry into the conduct of the Scheme, but this is defeated by 315 votes to 161.*
22 *November—Discussions by Tripartite Conference in Paris result in decisions to extend wider powers to the German Federal Republic.*
23 *November—TUC General Council recommends restraint in wage claims.*
24 *November—Prime Minister commends the TUC General Council's recommendations to wage claims restraint.*

[*28 November* 1949

Monsieur Spaak, as Prime Minister of Belgium, made the first governmental declaration in support of The Hague Congress demand for a European Assembly, and has throughout, with the French Government, sustained the idea. As one of the Presidents of Honour of the European Movement he has led public opinion in favour of European Union. Now, as President of the European Assembly, he has become the guide and champion of the new Parliament of Europe. We salute him as a great Belgian and, at the same time, as a great European.

You, my Lord Archbishop, have referred to the progress made by the European Movement since you presided at our Albert Hall meeting in May 1947. That progress has indeed been remarkable. Exactly a year later, in May 1948, The Hague Congress demanded the creation of a European Assembly. Exactly a year after that, in May 1949, ten governments signed the Statute of Europe.

In Strasbourg last August delegates to the European Assembly, representing widely differing political tendencies, declared themselves convinced of the urgent necessity for creating a United Europe and the dire consequences of hesitation or delay. The recommendations sent by the Assembly to the Committee of Ministers were bold and challenging. But they cannot be said to have been unrealistic. Whilst people may disagree with a point here or there, these recommendations represent broadly the requirements of the situation which confronts us. The policy enunciated at Strasbourg offers to Europe the only possible means of preserving her peace and freedom and of maintaining and developing the living standards of her peoples.

151

We all recognize, of course, that the policy of European Union raises many serious and practical difficulties which will require solution. But the difficulties are not a reason for inaction. They are rather a justification for the redoubling of our efforts. As we advance we shall hear more and more about these difficulties, but we have no choice but to go on. The alternative is not to remain as we are. The alternative is to face the certainty of wholesale economic collapse as soon as American Aid ceases, accompanied by the spread of misery and Communism.

The French Foreign Minister, M. Schuman, declared in the French Parliament this week that 'Without Britain there can be no Europe'. This is entirely true. But our friends on the Continent need have no misgivings. Britain is an integral part of Europe, and we mean to play our part in the revival of her prosperity and greatness. But Britain cannot be thought of as a single State in isolation. She is the founder and centre of a world-wide Empire and Commonwealth. We shall never do anything to weaken the ties of blood, of sentiment and tradition and common interest which unite us with the other members of the British family of nations. But nobody is asking us to make such desertion. For Britain to enter a European Union from which the Empire and Commonwealth would be excluded would not only be impossible but would, in the eyes of Europe, enormously reduce the value of our participation. The Strasbourg recommendations urged the creation of an economic system which will embrace not only the European States, but all those other States and territories elsewhere which are associated with them.

The British Government have rightly stated that they cannot commit this country to entering any European Union without the agreement of the other members of the British Commonwealth. We all agree with that statement. But no time must be lost in discussing the question with the Dominions and seeking to convince them that their interests as well as ours lie in a United Europe. An opportunity for these consultations offers itself at the Conference of Commonwealth Foreign Ministers at Colombo early next year which Mr Bevin is going to attend—we hope to be a help. We ask that the issue of European Union be placed upon the agenda of this conference. Then when the European Assembly next meets at Strasbourg, the representatives of Britain in the Committee of Ministers and in the Assembly will no longer be restrained as they are now by uncertainty about the opinions and wishes of their partners overseas.

At The Hague, and now this summer at Strasbourg, the importance of admitting the new German Federal Republic as an associate member of the Council of Europe appeared, and we rejoice that this step has now been decided in principle. Understanding and co-operation must be established between Germany and the rest of free Europe. Therefore, although belated, we welcome the recent decision in favour of the partial abandonment of the provocative and, at the same time, ineffective policy of dismantling. Western Germany, overcrowded as she is, with millions of German refugees from the East, cannot hope to restore lasting prosperity except within the framework of a wider unity in which her peoples could find a peaceful outlet for their energies and abilities. Europe needs Germany, but Germany still more needs Europe.

At Zurich I said France has a special responsibility for taking Germany by the hand and leading her back into the European family. I congratulate the French Parliament upon its decision to approve the admission of Germany into the Council of Europe. At The Hague I said: 'For us the German problem is to restore the economic life of Germany and revive the ancient fame of the German race without thereby exposing their neighbours and ourselves to any reassertion of their military power of which we still bear the scars. United Europe provided the only solution to this two-sided problem. It is a solution which can be implemented without delay.'

The basic idea underlying the conception of European Union is the desire to preserve and develop the free way of life of the participating nations. This implies the acceptance of collective responsibility for the defence of liberty and the dignity of man. That was the purpose of the proposal put forward by the European Movement and adopted by the Assembly for the conclusion of a European Convention on Human Rights. We understand that the Government may require to consider carefully the details of such a convention but we ask them, without further delay, to make it clear that they accept the principle of joint responsibility for the maintenance of freedom and that they intend not merely to issue pious declarations but to set up judicial and executive machinery to make this a reality.

We trust that the Government will be in a position to announce the signing of this Convention on Human Rights and the setting-up of the machinery to implement it before the next session of the Assembly. Nothing could give to the Assembly more confidence in the Government's sincerity. Nothing could give greater inspiration to the European peoples than this step. The European Movement must campaign for the Convention on Human Rights as it campaigned so successfully for the creation of the Assembly.

We are at present forced by circumstances to confine our action to the democratic nations of Europe who are free. But let us never for a moment forget that behind the Iron Curtain there are peoples who share our culture and our traditions and who have no greater desire than to be united with us. All our plans for the new Europe must be based on the firm assumption that our fellow Europeans now living under totalitarian domination will, as soon as they are free, come and take their places with us in the Council of Europe.

The European Assembly at Strasbourg, under Monsieur Spaak's leadership, has proved that it is capable of bold initiative. But the decisions rest with governments. The ability of the Assembly to persuade governments to act will depend upon the backing which exists for this idea among the broad masses of the people in every country. To create this body of public interest and public support is one of the main tasks of the European Movement. The union of Europe must be a union not only of governments but of peoples.

The European Movement, an international all-party organization, was the inspiration and motive force which brought the European Assembly into being. It must now build up a vast body of popular support behind the Assembly so that the Assembly's recommendations may be translated by the governments into action. Many of you here are no doubt already supporters of the European Movement. Those of you who are not will have an opportunity during the meeting to enrol tonight. I hope that you will join us and work with us in this historic campaign, the triumph of which will be decisive for the peace and well-being of Europe and the world for generations that are to come.

THE CONSERVATIVE POINT OF VIEW

A PARTY POLITICAL BROADCAST
21 JANUARY 1950

---

6 *December—Decision on final allocation of reparations equipment in Western Germany among Western Powers. As the Soviet Union has failed to fulfil its part of the Potsdam Agreement, no further allocation of this equipment will be made to her.*

10 *December—Australian Labour Party defeated at General Election. Liberal Party returned to power.*

14 *December—Japanese Parliament appeals to the United States for the repatriation of 376,000 Japanese prisoners of war detained in the USSR.*

16 *December—Parliament Bill of 1945 receives Royal Assent.*

21 *December—The Committee of the International Socialist Conference (Comisco) issue a statement denouncing the Cominform as 'the fifth column of an imperialistic tyranny' and accusing it of 'openly fomenting war throughout half the world'.*

27 *December—Holland transfers full political sovereignty to the United States of Indonesia.*

9-14 *January—Colombo Conference of Foreign Ministers.*

10 *January—It is announced from 10 Downing Street that Parliament will be dissolved on Friday, 3 February; and that a General Election will take place on Thursday, 23 February.*

11 *January—Statistics issued by the British Iron and Steel Federation show that 1949 steel production was the highest ever achieved.*

15 *January—Milk rationing ends.*

16 *January—Abolition of food rationing in Western Germany.*

18 *January—Labour Party issues General Election Manifesto 'Let Us Win Through Together'.*

20 *January—Labour Party publishes its proposals for the 'mutualization' of industrial insurance companies.*

[21 *January* 1950

All the world is wondering what is going to happen here at this election. In every country—friend, ally, foe; victor, rescued or vanquished—inquiring or anxious minds are turned to Britain. What is she going to do? That is the question on every lip. The Empire, the English-speaking world, all Europe outside the Iron Curtain are once again looking to us in curiosity and in anxiety. For what it is worth, this is a compliment. We need not shrink at all from this attention. Under our British Constitution, slowly and painfully built but solidly established, and not yet overturned, all can vote and none need fear to discharge their civic duty. Not to vote on what is now at stake for our country—or to vote in a way which wastes the vote—would be a failure to rise to the level of events. The ballot is secret. The votes can be freely recorded and will be fairly counted, and the results will govern our fortunes—it may be for a long time to come.

At this moment everyone ought to consider very carefully what is his duty towards his country, towards the causes he believes in, towards his home and family and to his own personal rights and responsibilities. What then is the supreme and fundamental question which we have to answer and have to answer now? As I see it, the choice before us is whether we should take another plunge into Socialist regimentation, or by a strong effort regain the freedom, initiative and opportunity of British life. I believe that on this decision depends not only our future as a leading nation in world thought and progress, but also our physical ability to maintain our vast population upon decent standards without foreign charity. Let us therefore examine the matter without being confused by the hum and throb of events.

Socialism is based on the idea of an all-powerful State which owns everything, which plans everything, which distributes everything, and thus through its politicians and officials decides the daily life of the individual citizen. We have not of course got this—or anything like it —in Britain at the present time. The process of establishing the Socialist State has only begun. The practical question which we have to settle now is whether we shall take another deep plunge into State ownership and State control, or whether we shall restore a greater measure of freedom of choice and action to our people, and of productive fertility and variety to our industry and trade.

Before deciding upon this, it is well to look around. Except in Scandinavia, Socialism and Socialist parties are on the decline throughout Europe everywhere outside the Iron Curtain. Socialism has been found in all European countries, bond or free, to have been the weakest defence against Communism. In taking another lurch into Socialism at this juncture we should be moving contrary to the general trend and tide of reviving European society. Still more should we be out of harmony with the States and nations of the English-speaking world, the British Dominions and the United States. Mr Attlee at this moment is the head of the only Socialist government to be found anywhere in the whole English-speaking world, the birthplace and the home of parliamentary democracy—the only one.

New Zealand and Australia, which have given a prolonged trial to Socialist governments, though not of course to Socialism in its complete form, have recently shaken themselves free. A young nation, like Australia, dwelling in a continent growing ample food for itself and for export, may try experiments in Socialism without the risk of fatal injury, but the 50,000,000 gathered together in this small island are in a very different position. We are a highly artificial community, balanced precariously at a level of well-being which before the war was superior to anything in Europe, but whose means of existence have been seriously, though not yet irreparably, undermined by changes in the surrounding world, and also by the actions of our own Government during these last critical and difficult years.

No nation of equal size, no society of equal civilization, has ever been in time of peace in the economic peril in which we stand. We do not grow enough food at home to keep ourselves alive, nor have we many of the raw materials which we need to earn our living. I am sure that if we act wisely we can make our way through our dangers as we have done before. But if, through political thoughtlessness or wrong guidance, we make grave mistakes and consume our strength in domestic quarrels and class war, consequences may descend upon us the like of which we have never yet suffered or even imagined.

The main reason why we are not able to earn our living and make our way in the world is because we are not allowed to do so. The whole enterprise, contrivance and genius of the British nation is being increasingly paralysed by the wartime restrictions from which all other free nations have shaken themselves clear, but these are still imposed upon our people here in the name of a mistaken political philosophy and a largely obsolete mode of thought. Our Government is the only one glorying in controls for controls' sake. I am sure that a parliament resolved to set the nation free would soon enable it to earn its own living in the world. I am sure on the other hand that the Socialist policy of equalizing misery and organizing scarcity instead of allowing diligence, self-reliance and ingenuity to produce abundance, has only to be prolonged to be fatal to our British island home.

The scheme of society for which Conservatives and National Liberals stand is the establishment and maintenance of a basic standard of life and labour below which a man or a woman, however old or weak, shall not be allowed to fall. The food they receive, the prices they have to pay for basic necessities, the homes they live in, their employment, must be the first care of the State, and must have priority over all other peace-time needs. Once we have made that standard secure we propose to set the nation free as quickly as possible from the controls and restrictions which now beset our daily life. Above the basic standard there will be free opportunity to rise. Everyone will be allowed to make the best of himself, without jealousy or spite, by all the means that honour and the long respected laws of our country allow.

One of the main pillars of any modern society is a stable value for money. 'Honest money', as it is called, is the only means by which goods and services can be fairly interchanged for mutual benefit between fellow citizens. The Socialist Government has spent every penny which it could lay its hands on, or which it could beg or borrow. They have spent in their term of office over £17,000,000,000, including the enormous sums given or loaned to us from abroad. They have exacted from us the heaviest taxation in the world. We are now paying £500,000,000 more a year even than in the height of the war.

At the same time they have cut down the buying power of every pound we earn in wages, salaries or in trading with one another. The British pound has fallen since the war stopped by no less than 3s. 8d. This has struck a heavy blow at the social services, at pensions of every kind, at every form of national insurance and at all savings. Thus what is given with the one hand is taken away with the other, and Socialist claims about safeguarding or extending the social services are vitiated by the fraud of giving only 16s. 4d. and calling it a pound. This is one of the gravest evils which we have to face and, remember, we still have the consequences of devaluation coming upon us to make it worse. I hope, my friends, you will think carefully about this and what it means to all of us. As head of the wartime Government I proclaimed the Four-Years' Plan of social reform—Education, Family Allowances and the National Health Scheme. Although mauled and twisted a bit by ministerial ineptitude, this programme has now largely been carried through. At that time I summed it up in three words: Food, Work and Homes.

Without food, work is impossible and homes a mockery. I am sorry indeed that Lord Woolton is not looking after our food as he did in the war. We should have a better diet now if he were and at about half the administrative cost. Cheap and abundant food is the foundation of our strength. It will be the foundation of our policy. But this can only come in the long run from the workings of a free market. There is, however, a larger aspect of the food problem. We must grow more food at home. We must set to work forthwith to raise our home-grown food supply. We must also make long-term arrangements inside the Empire for mutual trade, whereby our brothers in their spacious food lands will feel that they have an assured market in the Mother Country and can plan ahead to supply it.

Now I come to work. All parties are agreed that the prevention of unemployment ranks next to food in the duties of any government. The policy on unemployment which all parties will follow was set forth in the commanding scheme of the National Government to which the leading men of all parties bound themselves in 1944. The scheme has not had to be put into operation for two reasons. First, because all the world is still at work and engaged in repairing the damage of the war, and replacing all kinds of things that were not made while it was going on. And, secondly, there has been very little unemployment because the Americans and our own Dominions have lent or given us over £400,000,000 a year ever since the war stopped.

The Government calculate, and their leading members have declared, that but for the large subsidies which the United States have so generously supplied, but which the Socialists somewhat ungratefully do not even mention in their manifesto, there would have been between 1,500,000 and 2,000,000 unemployed in this island during these years. I am not prepared myself to challenge these calculations, though I think perhaps we could have done better than that. But that is what Mr Morrison and Mr Bevan say, and we must agree with our opponents on facts whenever we can.

Thus on the question of unemployment there is no real difference between the two political parties. Why then in this election should all kinds of wrongful charges and false claims of party achievements be bandied about, when we are all agreed that American aid has prevented the kind of unemployment which appeared after the last war and rose again to hideous heights under the Socialist Government of twenty years ago, and when we are also agreed on the kind of remedies we should use to cope with it should it occur? The Conservative and National Liberal Parties regard the prevention of mass unemployment as the most solemn duty of government. Great difficulties lie ahead when the consequences of devaluation come home to us and when American aid ends. If human brains and will-power can conquer these dangers, we shall, with God's blessing, succeed. It is not the first time we have been through a life and death struggle together.

Lastly our homes. It is the homes that I wish to end in tonight.

Three years ago we were promised that by the time of this election there would be no housing shortage as far as the mass of the British people were concerned. But the council waiting-lists are longer than ever. Before the war under a Conservative Government we were building by the normal process of supply and demand 1,000 houses a day. With all this need, and the same labour force, we are building only half as many now, and every house costs three times as much. Surely something must have gone wrong—and very wrong.

What then will you do about all these problems? Will you simply go on melting down the treasures of the past, and shrug your shoulders at the perils of the future? If so, a terrible awakening lies not so far ahead. It will not only be worldly fame and power which will pass from Britain, but the long treasured theme of British history and British greatness will be broken. I am sure it is not too late for our nation to lift itself above its troubles and resume, amid world-wide thanksgiving, its share in guiding the upward march of man. But if we should sink into mere materialism, and petty calculations of immediate personal advantage and fleeting gain, it will not be our reputation only which will perish, but our power to keep ourselves independent and even alive.

Class quarrels, endless party strife, on a background of apathy, indifference and bewilderment, will lead us all to ruin. Only a new surge of impulse can win us back the glorious ascendancy which we gained in the struggle for right and freedom, and for which our forbears had nerved our hearts down the long aisles of time. Let us make a supreme effort to surmount our dangers. Let faith, not appetite, guide our steps. There still remain forces in our island that can bring back all our true glories and range our people once again in the vanguard of Christian civilization to revive and save the world.

WOODFORD ADOPTION MEETING

A SPEECH AT THE WOODFORD COUNTY SCHOOL FOR GIRLS
28 JANUARY 1950

---

25 January—Conservative Party issues its Election Manifesto 'This is the Road'.

26 January—Formal proclamation of the Republic of India within the Commonwealth of Nations.

27 January—Anglo-American Mutual Defence Assistance Agreement under the North Atlantic Treaty signed in Washington.

[*28 January* 1950

I thank you sincerely for the honour you have done me in choosing me for the sixth time to be your candidate for Parliament. It is more than a quarter of a century since you first elected me, and it is indeed a pleasure to me and to my wife, the President of the Association, to feel that we still preserve your confidence and goodwill. Here in Woodford we have three opponents, Socialist, Liberal and Communist. On purely local grounds we are very content that they should all come and divide the hostile vote, among themselves. During the last fortnight the Liberal candidate has been changed. The one who has left us must have been a combative politician. He came out to fight me, but he has now gone to Lewisham to do his best to try to help Mr Morrison get in by fighting him. This somewhat curious procedure arises out of the decision of a very small and select group of Liberal leaders who conceive themselves the sole heirs of the principles and traditions of Liberalism, and believe themselves to have the exclusive copyright of the word 'Liberal'. I was very much amused to read a letter in the *Daily Telegraph* from the son of my old friend and colleague Mr George Lambert, who served with me at the Admiralty in Mr Asquith's Government before the First World War. Mr Lambert quoted some lines attributed to Dean Swift which he considered applicable to Mr Clement Davies and his associates.

> We are the chosen few
> All others will be damned
> There is no place in Heaven for you,
> We can't have Heaven crammed.

I have never read these lines before, but I think they deserve a wide circulation at the present time.

This super select attitude finds an example in the exclusion of Lady Violet Bonham-Carter and I may add of Sir Archibald Sinclair from the four broadcasts the Liberals are making between now and the poll. In Lady Violet Bonham-Carter we have not only a Liberal of unimpeachable loyalty to the party but one of the finest speakers in the country. Her speech against Socialism which was so widely read two months ago recalled the style of old and famous days. But her voice must not be heard on the air on this occasion. 'We can't have heaven crammed.' Perhaps there may be more room after the votes have been counted in this particular celestial parlour. It is fifteen years since we have had a Liberal opponent in Woodford and we certainly have had very good and agreeable relations with our Liberal friends and have worked together in many ways. I earnestly hope that they will set an example to Liberal voters throughout the country by voting according to their consciences and convictions, and according to the long established principles of their party and world Liberalism against the establishment of the Socialist State.

When Mr Attlee's Government came into power nearly five years ago we did not underrate the difficulties with which they would have to contend. These difficulties would have strained to the utmost all the resources of a National Government and a united nation. We did not grudge the new Ministers their offices, nor envy them their responsibilities. We have steadfastly supported them in every step they have taken sincerely in the public interest. I always felt that we should need American aid to enable us to get on our feet again. We therefore supported the Government policy of seeking an American loan, and used what influence we possessed in the United States for that purpose. We hoped this would tide us over the transition from war to peace and help us to re-equip our industries, our agriculture and our mines. We also supported the policy of Marshall Aid. Indeed, General Marshall directly connected this broadminded and generous American action with the speeches which I had made about the need for European unity. If such help, or anything like it, had been forthcoming from across the Atlantic after the First World War almost measureless advantages might have been reaped by both Europe and America, and our own fortunes here at home in those hard days would have been far brighter. But this time we had a real chance. The object of the American Loan and of Marshall Aid, and the only possible justification for this being given or accepted, was to enable us to get our industry and agriculture working with the fullest activity, and to bring in the necessary food and raw materials to keep us going till conditions of world trade were restored. It was thought that this would take between three and four years of good administration, strict economy and united effort by all parties and classes under conditions of growing freedom from wartime restrictions.

Alas, these hopes were falsified. The Socialist Government, instead of devoting themselves to the supreme national task which the pe '᠆ had confided to them, put their party politics and the advancement of the doctrines of Socialism above all other considerations. Owing to their follies and wrongful action, a great part of all the loans and gifts we have received from abroad has been spent not upon the re-equipment of our industry, nor upon the import of basic foodstuffs: instead much of this precious aid was lavishly frittered away in American films and tobacco and in large quantities of foods and fruits which, however desirable as indulgences, were not indispensable to our recovery. When you have to borrow money from another country for the sacred purpose of national rehabilitation it is wrong to squander it upon indulgences. It was also wrong to send vast sums in unrequited exports to India and Egypt, both of which countries owed their safety from Japanese or German conquest to the exertions of our fleets and armies. We had every right to demand from those we had saved fair consideration for the immense expense to which we had been put in shielding them from the horrors of foreign invasion. It was also most improvident for our Government to make loans, advances and gifts to foreign countries on a scale out of all proportion to our means. We could not afford this lavishness ourselves but had to pay for it all out of borrowed money. There is an old saying, 'Be just before you are generous.'

The truest service we could render other countries in these years after the war was won was to get Britain on her feet again erect, strong and self-supporting. Thus we should have become again a world safeguard not a world problem. But Mr Attlee's Government seemed to have no thought of the grim realities of our position. They embarked upon the most profuse expenditure in all directions. As you know, in their four and a half years they have spent nearly £17,000,000,000. They have raised our taxation until it is the highest in the world, and even stands higher today than in the worst years of the war. With the immense aid given us by the US and our Dominions from overseas and the unparalleled sacrifices exacted from the taxpayers here, there was no reason why we should not have got back by now to solvency, security and independence. This has been denied us not only by the incompetence and maladministration of the Socialist

Government and their wild extravagance, but even more by the
spirit of class hatred which they have spread throughout the land, and
by the costly and wasteful nationalization of a fifth part of our industries.

We now approach the crisis to which every spendthrift comes when
he has used up everything he can lay his hands on, and everything he
can beg or borrow and must face the hard reckoning of facts. That is
no doubt the reason why they have fixed the election now instead of
June, and hope to take advantage of the brief lull before the consequences of extravagance and devaluation come down upon us with
their full inexorable force.

Our national campaign has opened well. The Conservative statement of policy *This is the Road* not only gives the detailed answers to
many of the disputed and difficult questions of this momentous election,
but also constitutes a broad, humane and progressive policy in which all
Conservatives, Unionists and Liberal-minded men may find a wide
sphere of common action. I have never seen any declaration of this
character which has been received with so wide a measure of acclama-
tion and approval.

A few months ago the Socialists hoped to win the election on the
issue of unemployment. The Tories they said, would like to have unemployment which they could use as a spur to compel greater exertions
from the wage-earners. This was an outrageous charge. But although
the British Socialist Party profess great hostility to Communism,
they seem to have learned the Soviet doctrine, which was also Hitler's,
that if you repeat a falsehood often enough it counts just as much as
the truth. They claimed for themselves the credit of having provided
full employment, and drew contrasts with what happened after the
last war. Is it not surprising that in their official manifesto they should
not even mention the aid they have received from the United States?
There is not one word from the beginning to the end of this document,
either of thanks to a generous and friendly nation, for the help on which
they have lived politically or of recognition that, but for the American
subsidies, mass unemployment would have fallen upon us, with all its
sorrow and suffering. Yet Mr Morrison and Mr Bevan have both
declared in public that, but for American aid there would have been
between 1,500,000 and 2,000,000 unemployed during these years.
However, the truth has become so widely known and realized that
it is difficult for the Socialists either to make good their claims to have
cured unemployment since the war, or their unfair charge that the
Conservatives are not as resolute as they are to do everything in
human power to prevent it.

Let me repeat, however, that we regard the maintenance of full employment as the first aim and duty of a Conservative Government. We do not underrate the difficulties which will follow the stopping of American aid under the Marshall Plan. We realize the efforts that will be required from the whole nation—all classes, all parties—if we are to regain our economic and moral independence. We believe, however, that nothing will help us more than that revival of world confidence and credit which would attend the return to power of a Conservative and National-Liberal Government pledged to a sound administration of the finances, and the simultaneous dismissal from power of a Socialist administration whose aid and object is to destroy wealth by class warfare and to stifle enterprise by nationalization.

It is worth while looking further into the Socialist election manifesto. We are told that it is Mr Herbert Morrison's plan for catching the middle-class vote. The word 'Socialism' is only mentioned twice. It is called *Let Us Win Through Together*. Mr Aneurin Bevan, the most popular figure in the Socialist Party, their potential Prime Minister, has been kept off the air. As he has described millions of his fellow-countrymen as 'lower than vermin' it no doubt was felt that his appeals through the broadcast might not fit in with the theme, 'Let us win through together.' There might seem to be some incongruity. So he has been muzzled. Hitherto he has been neither muzzled nor led. The Prime Minister did not feel able to disavow his insults, but now—

> The Trumpet's silver voice is still
> The warder silent on the hill.

Nevertheless we should look searchingly at this latest Socialist manifesto. It must be remembered that if they were returned to office, even though upon only a minority vote, the Socialists would feel themselves entitled to carry into law, or by regulation or executive action enforce every point that is mentioned in their declaration, however modestly it is tucked away.

They will of course nationalize the steel industry. Quite apart from the injury to this magnificent feature in our domestic life and export trade, this will give them the power to dominate for their party interests a large group of other industries for whom steel in one or other of its thousand forms is the foundation. They will have immense political power over all these industries and can make or mar them by expediting or delaying vital supplies, about which a tangle of formalities will be created in triplicate. Here, in itself, would be a long step forward to the establishment of the Socialist State. All this is rendered possible by the harmless looking words, 'The steel industry will be responsible to the nation.' It has certainly rendered our country incomparable and irreplaceable service, under the system which has been in practice for so many years of free enterprise, subject to Government supervision on prices and development as in Conservative days.

All this is to be thrown into disorder not because the Government want more *steel* but because they want more *power*. Should we be sustained by the electorate we shall repeal the Steel Nationalization Act before it comes into operation. The House of Lords has secured you the opportunity of deciding this question by a direct vote. Let us not forget that if the steel industry falls into Socialist Party hands it can be used as an instrument and weapon of party warfare to create the full Socialist State. There is another paragraph which has a deep and formidable significance. 'The Government will be empowered,' says their manifesto, 'to start new competitive public enterprises in appropriate circumstances.' That means that a Socialist Government can use the resources of the taxpayer to compete in trade rivalry with any private business they dislike or which, apart from any law, does not obey their wishes. They would in fact have the power to ruin any private undertaking in the country. They would be the sole judges of how, when and where to strike at it, and if they waste public money in this form of trade warfare, they have only to send in the bill to the Exchequer. No more deadly or far-reaching threat at private business and companies of all kinds—and it is on these that we depend for four-fifths of our whole industry, including more than nine-tenths of our export trade—has ever been levelled at the free productive life of Britain.

Other prosperous and well-managed industries, like cement and sugar and chemicals, are to be nationalized so that the consumer will have to pay more for their products, as he does for coal and electricity and transport, and so that a new horde of officials can be set up over them with new vistas of patronage opening out to Socialist politicians. Having made a failure of everything they have so far touched, our Socialist planners now feel it necessary to get hold of a few at present prospering industries so as to improve the general picture and the general results. There appears to be no plan or principle in the selection of these industries, except caprice and appetite. It does not matter how well they are now managed, how well they are serving the public, how much they sustain our export trade, how good are the relations between employers and employed. The Socialists just like the look of them, and so they think they will have them. But here you have your vote and your responsibility.

There is one more organization which is mentioned, and because it is mentioned made liable to nationalization. I refer of course to the vast business of life insurance, for which we are renowned all over the world and by which we earn over £30,000,000 a year in foreign exchange. The only anxiety which the Socialists have about nationalizing life insurance is whether it will lose them support among the very large number of insurance agents who have done so much to popularize thrift in the homes of the people. They are most anxious to reassure these agents for the time being, and until they have got them properly in their grip. What they now seek is the control of the vast sum of money which represents the savings over many years of millions of people to provide by self-denial and forethought, for their widows, their orphans and their own old age or infirmity. The control over this great mass of investments would be another most powerful means of bringing the whole financial, economic and industrial life of Britain into Socialist hands.

I have no hesitation in saying that the new Socialist manifesto contains, under much smooth language, an effective design or plot— for that is a truer term—to obtain a power over their fellow-country-men such as no British Government has ever sought before, and that this would be fatal alike to their freedom and prosperity. Here I must point out that there is no dispute between parties on this important point. 'The important fact,' says the *Tribune* weekly newspaper which is the voice of Mr Aneurin Bevan, 'The important fact about the manifesto is that it will give a new Labour Government the mandate to go forward with the construction of a Socialist society in Britain.' This is indeed a clear case of 'You have been warned.' Before I leave the Socialist manifesto there is a point I noticed in the paragraph dealing with children's welfare. The admission is all the more revealing because it is unconscious. Here it is:

'The policy of putting the children at the head of the queue will be continued.'

We are all agreed that the children should come first in our thoughts and in our resources. But why should they be at the head of the queue? Why should queues become a permanent, continuous feature of our life? Here you see clearly what is in their minds. The Socialist dream is no longer *Utopia* but *Queuetopia*. And if they have the power this part of their dream will certainly come true. Our earnest hope is that it may be granted to us to proclaim not the continuance but the doom of the queues and restore the normal relations between the shop-keepers and the public.

But beware! For we may be at the parting of the ways. The wisdom of our forebears for more than 300 years has sought the division of power in the Constitution. Crown, Lords and Commons have been checks and restraints upon one another. The limitation of the power of absolute monarchy was the cause for which as Liberals used to say, 'Hampden died in the field and Sidney on the scaffold.' The concentration of all power over the daily lives of ordinary men and women in what is called 'the State', exercised by what is virtually single-chamber government, is a reactionary step contrary to the whole trend of British history and to the message we have given to the world. The British race have always abhorred arbitrary and absolute government in every form. The great men who founded the American Constitution expressed this same separation of authority in the strongest and most durable form. Not only did they divide executive, legislative and judicial functions, but also by instituting a federal system they preserved immense and sovereign rights to local communities and by all these means they have maintained—often at some inconvenience—a system of law and liberty under which they thrived and reached the physical and, at this moment, the moral leadership of the world. The Socialist conception of the all-powerful State entering into the smallest detail of the life and conduct of the individual and claiming to plan and shape his work and its rewards is odious and repellent to every friend of freedom. These absolute powers would make the group of politicians who obtained a majority of seats in Parliament, the masters and not the servants of the people and centralize all government in Whitehall.

So far we are only at the first stage in this evil journey. But already enterprise, daring and initiative are crippled. Property is destroyed by the heaviest taxation in the world. Regulations increasingly take the place of statutes passed by Parliament. These are contained in twenty-eight volumes, which can be purchased by all and sundry for £65. In these you may find that there are thousands of new crimes unknown before the war, now punishable by fine or imprisonment. The right is claimed in full peace by the executive Government to direct a man or woman to labour at any work or in any place a Minister or the officials under him may choose. Here are the words which Mr Isaacs, the Minister of Labour, used in the House of Commons on 3 December 1947, nearly three years after the war had stopped; when defending the Order giving him absolute power over the livelihood and employment of all men and women between the ages of 18-50 and 18-40 respectively:

'If any specific case is brought to our notice of a person claiming conscientious objection to a particular job we will give it our consideration; but we are not prepared to recognize that anyone has a right to conscientious öbjection to going to work unless that person is prepared at the same time to say that he will not eat.'

This is the old and shameful doctrine of 'Work or starve', which no Government in Britain has ever dared to utter in time of peace for more than a hundred years. It is the greatest affront offered in modern times to the dignity of labour which rests upon a man's right to choose or change his job. I made my protest at the time, but in vain. The Regulation was imposed. It is still imposed. The Socialists have not dared to use it on any large scale, as yet. They are waiting for a renewal of their mandate. Conservatives and National Liberals on the other hand are resolved to expunge this blot from our industrial life.

In the face of moral issues like these, cutting right down to the roots of civilized society, it astounds me that liberal-minded men of any party can doubt where their duty lies. Picture to yourselves upon this background the small group of Left-Wing Liberals gathered in London and planning to run four hundred candidates, of whom not one in fifty and perhaps not one in a hundred will be returned to Parliament, in the hopes that by splitting votes they may frustrate the will of the majority of the nation and so show how important they are. I am sure that British Liberalism will recoil from and rise superior to such sorry and wanton machinations.

The British nation now has to make one of the most momentous choices in its history. That choice is between two ways of life; between individual liberty and State domination; between concentration of ownership in the hands of the State and the extension of a property-owning democracy; between a policy of increasing restraint and a policy of liberating energy and ingenuity; between a policy of levelling down and a policy of finding opportunity for all to rise upwards from a basic standard. It is no exaggeration to say that what we do here on the day of electoral trial will not only determine the course of British history, but will profoundly influence the immediate future of the world. Grapple with your duties and your perils while you still have your ancient strength.

ELECTION ADDRESS

A SPEECH AT THE TOWN HALL, LEEDS

4 FEBRUARY 1950

---

30 *January—Agreement signed by Britain, Denmark, Norway and Sweden for closer co-operation under the objectives of the Organization for European Economic Co-operation.*

1 *February—Responsibility for valuation for rating purposes transferred from local authorities to Inland Revenue.*

3 *February—Proclamation dissolving Parliament signed by HM the King. Dr Fuchs arrested for betrayal of atomic research secrets.*

[4 *February* 1950

I must admit that my earlier political life was more concerned with Lancashire than Yorkshire, but I have learnt enough about Yorkshire folk to know that they despise flattery. So I will not waste any time upon it this afternoon. You know well enough your importance and responsibility in Britain, and through Britain, in world affairs. I trust indeed that Yorkshire may be rightly guided at this fateful hour and point the way to others. Whatever side you may take in the election battle which has now begun, no one who looks at things with a steady and truth-seeking eye can fail to take a serious view about the immediate future of our country. We have a population of 50,000,000 for whom we can grow here at home only half the food they need to keep them alive. Our finances are in sad disorder. During their $4\frac{1}{2}$ years of office the Government have spent every penny they could lay their hands on. Every asset they could realize has been spent in lavish profusion. Every reserve has been cut down below the safety level. We have been living upon the generous aid, loaned or given by the US or by our Dominions. The buying power of the British pound has been steadily dwindling. The Government have now been forced to devaluate our money so that we have to give a third more hours of labour to buy the same amount of what we need from dollar countries.

The election has been held at a date carefully chosen by Mr Attlee in the hopes of obtaining a new lease of office before the further inevitable rise in the cost of living comes down upon us. He has not dared to produce a Budget which, if it had been honest, would certainly have been unpopular. The trade unions have been persuaded to maintain the wage-freeze until after the votes have been counted. Supplementary estimates, even above the immense expenditure of £3,300,000,000 budgeted for last year, have been kept in the background. Probably £100,000,000 or more must be added to the bill. The Government have made no plan to fill the dollar gap. The American subsidies which, according to Mr Morrison and Mr Bevan, have alone saved us from having nearly 2,000,000 unemployed, will come to an end at the latest in 1952. German and Japanese competition in all the export markets on which we depend to make the wheels of British industry turn, has already begun and will grow more severe with every month that passes. Even if all our strength were united we should be confronted with the hardest task and problem we have ever faced in time of peace. But we are a deeply divided nation. Class warfare has rent the unities and comradeship which brought us through the war. Party politics dominate the scene. A great gulf of principle and doctrine is open in our midst. But even while this remains vital it is obscured by appeals to envious self-interest.

There is another element of instability in our British life which does not exist in most of the other free countries of the world. There is no written constitution. The safeguards provided by the Parliament Act have been almost entirely swept away. We have virtually single-chamber Government. If after this election the Socialists have a majority in the House of Commons, even though they only have a minority vote in the country, there is nothing they cannot carry into law. We see that they have taken power in their manifesto to make a very large increase of nationalization of industry and also to start up rival businesses with public money to knock out any existing firms whom they do not like or who do not comply with their wishes, apart altogether from any law. There is therefore no limit upon the action they may take to overturn and sweep away the entire structure of our society and industry as these now exist and by which we earn our daily bread. According to the interview which Mr Attlee is reported to have given to an American journalist, his own intentions are to set up an absolute Socialist State at the earliest moment. Let me read you what he is reported to have said, which he has not contradicted: When asked, 'When does Socialism stop in England?' he replied, 'It does not. It goes right on. Nothing can stand between a nation and its goal. No one has any cause to misunderstand. Twelve years ago, long before our party came to power, I gave a specific warning.' So here we are at a moment of extreme financial and economic instability also confronted with a declaration by the Prime Minister in favour of the most overwhelming changes in our slowly-built up British way of life which have ever been proposed. There is at this moment no foothold where anyone in Britain or those who watch us from outside can say, 'This is solid ground.'

Remember also that, as a Socialist Prime Minister working for the establishment of a Socialist State, Mr Attlee and his party are alone in the English-speaking world. The United States at the head of the world today vehemently repudiate the Socialist doctrine. Canada repudiates it. Australia and New Zealand, after a considerable trial of it in a very incomplete form, have just shaken themselves free. Remember also there is no Socialist Government in Europe outside the Iron Curtain and Scandinavia. It seems to me a very perilous path that we are asked to tread, and to tread alone among the free democracies of the West.

I rest my hopes on a new Parliament. It cannot be more unequal to the nation's needs nor more unworthy of its destiny than the one which has just been dissolved. I hope that the Government arising from the new Parliament will represent the will of the people as expressed by a majority of the votes cast. It will be an additional misfortune if another administration comes into power which only represents a minority of the electors. That section of the Liberal Party which is led by Mr Clement Davies has openly avowed its desire to bring about a deadlock or stalemate, so that the handful of members who follow his guidance may hold the balance and dominate the scene. As they cannot exceed seven or eight, this is a vain expectation, however gratifying to the self-importance of a few individuals. In order to realize it they are running 400 candidates, procured by dozens and scores, and insuring with Lloyd's against the forfeit of 250 deposits. In nearly every case the votes cast for these candidates will be thrown away; that is to say they will play no part in deciding the tremendous issues which are at stake. It is hoped, however, by the authors of this reckless demonstration that they may so queer the pitch that the result of the great electoral struggle may be meaningless. They take a great responsibility upon themselves for which they may afterwards be held accountable to public opinion. The return of a number of minority candidates through split votes cannot be of any help to the British nation in its present difficulties and dangers. Moreover, it is essentially undemocratic for a party or section of a party to work for the return of minority candidates, and thus frustrate or pervert the true expression of the national will.

I do not believe that these tactics will be successful. But I am very sorry that such a state of things should have come about. It certainly is not my fault. Nothing would have given me greater comfort two or three years ago than to have made an honourable and friendly arrangement with all who hold to the Liberal faith, which would have enabled all true Liberals and Conservatives to work together as separate and independent parties for the main interests of the nation and in resistance to the establishment of a Socialist State to which both are equally opposed. But when overtures were made they were repeatedly spurned, and we were mocked for our efforts. Thus the years passed. Conservative candidates came forward and every constituency was filled. It is not possible at the last minute to ask men who have built up their position in the different constituencies to stand down. Nor would the local associations agree to their doing so. Here and there a sensible arrangement may be made; but in the main the die is cast. We have therefore at this grave and critical moment in our history an element of confusion which, however understandable because of the hardships which the present electoral system inflicts upon minorities, is a serious aggravation of the public dangers.

A main cause of our present plight has been the waste, disorder and uncertainty arising from the Socialist policy of nationalization. Instead of bending all their strength to recovery after the war, and to carrying through our Four Years' Plan, which surely was enough for any Government, they have divided the nation by a series of ill thought-out measures to make the State the owner and employer in about one-fifth of our industries and services. In every case this has already been proved an injury to the common weal. All nationalized industries either show actual losses in their accounts which fall upon the Exchequer, or increased prices and reduced services to the public. This has done harm in many directions and in none more than to the trade unions concerned, who have ceased to be able to give whole-hearted service to their members because they owe policy and party allegiance to the Executive Government. The nationalized industries, which have been transferred from the credit to the debit side of our national balance-sheet, can only be sustained by the industries and enterprises which are still free and profitable, and on which the whole of our vital export trade is founded. So far as it has gone nationalization has been already proved a total failure.

But even more injurious to the national economy is the second dose of nationalization with which we are menaced. The prosperous and active steel industry will at once pass into the hands of State officials and Government favourites, and this Act is so framed that it will give Socialist Ministers the power to interfere with and hamper the great number of other trades which use steel in all sorts of ways. But for the service which the House of Lords has rendered under the Parliament

173

Act, the electors would have been denied the opportunity which was surely their right of pronouncing upon steel nationalization before it had become law.

There is also another series of prosperous key industries, rendering services of the highest efficiency to the public, upon all of which the clammy grip of Socialist politics is to be laid. Our cement, the cheapest in the world; sugar, water supplies, meat, perhaps chemicals, are to pass from the skilled and successful management by which they have been developed, into the dull and uncomprehending control of official boards. Over 60 per cent of the profits of these industries now go to the Revenue and provide for the social services. These profits will soon be converted into losses borne by the taxpayer, or higher prices paid by the consumer.

There is one more which is threatened, namely, industrial life insurance. But now, on the eve of the election, the Socialists have had second thoughts. Their doubts do not arise from any lack of zeal or appetite, but only because they are afraid they may lose votes by offending the numerous and influential bands of agents who have done so much to popularize thrift. This, and this alone, has led to a modification of the Socialist plan for industrial life insurance. Here is a good example of how British interests are handled by Socialist doctrinaires and fanatics. These matters are not dealt with on their merits, or even in accordance with Socialist theory. Conviction is lacking. Plan and design, even for a mistaken policy, do not rule once it is a question of votes. You can in no country, least of all our own, least of all at this moment, make a way forward under such principles of public conduct.

The insurance raid is not only a question of votes. It is a chance of getting more power. Upwards of £1,300,000,000 are held by industrial assurance and friendly societies, gathered by the thrift and forethought of a generation for the widows, the orphans, the old and the infirm. The Socialist object is to get hold of the investments in stocks and shares and rig the market with them so as to dominate the fortunes of what is left of free industry. This is part of the plan by which Mr Attlee and his minority of convinced Socialists hope to become effective masters of the whole field of our national life. This is an additional power which they mean to take if you do not stop them.

Here again Conservative policy is clear. We shall restore the safeguards of the Parliament Act and repeal the nationalization of steel before it can come into law, and we shall free all other industries from the cloud of oppression and uncertainty under which they lie at the present time by forbidding all further nationalization. No single broad decision will do more to prevent unemployment, to improve our credit, and to lighten and simplify our problems both at home and abroad than the stopping of nationalization.

During the war when every sacrifice had to be made to preserve the life of the nation all kinds of controls and taxes were imposed and everyone was proud to give life, liberty and worldly possessions in the cause of freedom. All the democracies of the Western world were equally desirous of getting rid of wartime controls when the peril had passed away. The United States led the way and in 1946 by a most daring decision of policy they swept away practically all the wartime controls, prices, rationing and regulations of all kinds which they regarded as a great evil likely to hamper their recovery.

As I said in Parliament more than two years ago, 'They threw the reins on the horse's neck and trusted him to pull their wagon up the hill.' Although a Presidential Election has taken place meanwhile, none of these controls have been reimposed. The strong horse still has the reins on his neck and is still pulling the wagon up the hill, and letting us hitch-hike behind him. Our Dominions have followed the same course, though step by step. Every country in Western Europe has moved in the same direction, including the nations who were actually defeated and marched through and occupied. Our friends in France, Belgium, Holland and Denmark have all freed themselves as fast as possible to the utmost extent, and all have made remarkable recoveries from the conditions of war. Rationing has been abolished in all these countries, which like ourselves depend on democratic institutions and universal suffrage. We see in all of them that controls are regarded as a wartime evil to be dispensed with at the earliest moment. Our former foes have done the same, as far as they could. In particular Germany, fortified by an appeal to the people on a democratic franchise, has shaken itself free in a manner remarkable in a people so often criticized for their love of regulations and discipline. Thus some peoples learn wisdom in defeat while others are led into folly by victory.

Of course conditions vary in different countries. With so little home-grown food we in Britain must move with more caution. We must first ensure that the prime necessities of life are within the reach of every family and each individual. But there is no doubt of the direction in which we ought to move as quickly and as strongly as we possibly can. The point to notice in all these examples I have given you is that rationing and price controls are everywhere in the world, outside the Soviet sphere, regarded as evils and an impediment to be got rid of at the earliest moment. But here in Britain the only Socialist Government now existing outside Scandinavia and the Iron Curtain saw in wartime controls not an evil to be got rid of but a means of getting everybody's daily life into the Socialist clutches. They saw the opportunity of creating 'Socialism in our own time', by prolonging the evils which were necessary in war. British Socialism is indeed a prolongation of wartime conditions in time of peace. In Soviet Russia and its satellite States the withdrawal of the ration book is the most normal and most lenient method of enforcing direction of labour or political discipline. By this mechanism British Socialists hope to get everyone into their power, and make them stand in queues for the favours which an all-wise and all-powerful governing machine chooses to bestow. To have power over their fellow-countrymen and be able to order them about is the natural characteristic of any Socialist. He loves controls for controls' sake—'Rationing is permanent,' says Mr Bottomley, the Parliamentary Secretary for Overseas Trade. 'We are the masters now,' says the Attorney-General. I must say this rouses indignation in my heart.

Mr Attlee's Socialist Government in time of peace decreed, though they have not yet ventured to enforce, the direction of all labour, demanding the right to take any man from his job and his home and move him under threats of imprisonment to any form of work in any part of the country they may choose. No greater affront to the dignity of British labour has ever been perpetrated. The right to choose or change his employment is one of the fundamental distinctions of a free Briton. British labour has now been deprived of this ancient right. A Conservative Government will immediately restore it.

I must now speak about conscription or national service. The Labour Party have enforced conscription in time of peace. Everyone must serve in the Armed Forces for eighteen months. While we cannot approve industrial conscription, we have felt it our duty to support the Socialist policy of compulsory national service in the Armed Forces. We think it is necessary in order to preserve peace. If Britain were to repudiate national service at this election, as the Liberals ask you to do, it would mean, in my opinion, the downfall of the whole great structure embodied in the Brussels Treaty, in the Atlantic Pact, in Western Union, in the whole idea of the English-speaking world, and of course of the united British Empire and Commonwealth of Nations. If Britain were to pull out now, all this vast defensive structure that has been raised by both the Labour and Conservative Parties in this country, might crash to the ground, and then you would be once again in danger of the most horrible of all fates—a third world war. That is what we are determined to avoid. Now nothing would have been more easy than for the Tory Party to gain votes at the expense of our political opponents by finding many good reasons to abandon conscription. If we had come out against compulsory service in the Armed Forces, we should have gained many votes in the General Election. But I and my colleagues would be ashamed to gain a party advantage on terms which would weaken the whole structure of the free democracies of Europe and America, through whose increasing cohesion world peace can alone become continually more secure.

But this does not mean that I do not think that great improvements cannot be made in our military system. It may well be that much better value in fighting power can be obtained for the money we are spending. The Conservative Party do not intend to take compulsory powers to lengthen the term of national service. On the contrary it is our view that too many men are being called up each year, either for the staff to train or for the units to absorb, and that the burden of national service can be sensibly reduced. I have a feeling, having handled these things before, that unless the foreign situation gets worse, which I do not think it will (but of course I may be wrong), a considerable reduction in the expense and burden of our defences might be combined with an actually stronger fighting power and better conditions for the troops. Let us leave it at that.

I do not join with those who suggest that our people are not working as they ought to. Most people do a good day's work in Britain, and after the intense effort of the war a sense of psychic and physical fatigue was natural. Sir Stafford Cripps has said that we have increased our output since 1939 by nearly a third—30 per cent. If this is confirmed it will be good. It may be good and yet it may not be good enough. The Americans in the same period have increased their output by 80 per cent. But our people have also put up with severe austerity. They have submitted to thousands of regulations. They have not had the houses they were promised, nor the meals which a free market could have brought. They have shown both fortitude and discipline. Properly handled by a National Government such as won the war, their ordeal need not have been so hard and its results would have been far more fruitful. The property of the rich has been largely confiscated by taxation; but every class has borne very heavy exactions in PAYE, purchase tax and in enormous taxation of tobacco, beer and skittles. More nourishing and stimulating food would mean better work. More eating would mean less drinking. Less spent outside the home would mean more spent inside it. It would all be good. I am not sure we cannot get it if we pull together in a sensible way.

Then there are incentives which can be given to all classes merely by taking off taxes, especially taxes which discourage overtime, high piece work, exceptional skill. We were told the other night by a

Government speaker that there were fewer bankruptcies now than before the war. That is because fewer people are running risks in business, and new people cannot start and supersede the old and inefficient by ceaseless competition for the benefit of the public. It is pretty hard for a young ex-serviceman with a good war record—not a conscientious objector or anything like that—to start a new business, and put his life into the show. But there is always politics. Socialism offers great prizes as a political career. The ideas of Socialism are contrary to human nature. To maintain a robust and lively progress all adventurous and enterprising spirits should have their chance to try, and if they fail to try again.

The commercial and industrial greatness of this island at the beginning of my lifetime was unrivalled in the world. All its businesses and firms and small employers, and careful obliging shopkeepers were the result of much wisdom and many virtues. All this was not built up as Socialist speakers would have you believe by sharks and rogues exploiting the masses. There was more in it than that. We should never have got our great population here but for these intense insatiable energies, or without the long patience of self-denial, for thrift and savings. We can never keep our population even at its present standards without foreign help, unless all these forces are working at their utmost compass underneath well-known laws, vigilantly strengthened wherever necessary to correct abuses. If difficulties have come upon us since our triumph in the war, it is not only because of our being temporarily wearied by our efforts, but because our activity has been hampered. Fancy adding 500,000 officials, since 1939, good, decent, honest men—but fancy adding them all to the burden borne by the producers, manual and skilled, in order to tell everybody what to do. If we find that at the end of a hard journey, in spite of enormous foreign aid we have a sombre, bleak patch in front of us, it is not the fault of our people, but because of the wrong-headed way they have been led and managed.

Let me look abroad. There is a lot of dispute about what is going on abroad. Those who come back tell opposite tales, many in accordance with what they think their parties wish. The Germans have rapidly built themselves up with Allied aid, rightly given, from almost nothing to a very active community, working like demons, and eating well amid ruins. When Socialists say there are 1,700,000 unemployed in Western Germany they ought not to forget that 8,000,000 people have fled as refugees from the old Eastern food-lands of Germany, and have had to be absorbed in the liberated part of the Reich. What would have happened here if 7,000,000 or 8,000,000 extra people of our own stock had suddenly been dumped on us? Do not underrate the recovery of Germany. I am glad of it. I want to work with them and the French. We three, together with our cherished friends in the 'Benelux' countries, Belgium, the Netherlands and Luxembourg, and several other countries outside the 'Iron Curtain', all constitute a vast and solid organization of free, civilized, democratic peoples which once forged and riveted together is not likely to be molested.

I spoke of France just now. I have worked in peace and war on the side of France for more than forty years. I rejoice in the undoubted growing recovery of France; but I want to warn you that the kind of political whirligig under which France lives, which is such great fun for the politicians and for all the little ardent parties into which they are divided, would be fatal to Britain. We cannot afford to have a period of French politics in Westminster. It is not in accordance with the British character, but still more it is not in accordance with the grim facts of our life. France is a self-supporting country. If the French woke up tomorrow morning and found that all the rest of the world had sunk under the sea, and that they were alone, they could make a pretty good living for themselves from their fertile soil. But if Britain woke up tomorrow morning and found nothing else but salt water on the rest of the globe, about one-third of our people would disappear.

What distresses me about our plight and our mood is that so many of our people take everything for granted and feel quite sure everything will work out all right whatever they do. Certainly I can give them the assurance that all the world outside Britain is not going to disappear under the waves of the sea. But they really must understand that we are not a self-supporting country, that we are an artificial country precariously poised at a splendid height. Above all things we must make sure that our foundations are not undermined. We cannot afford to play the pranks which French parties and French politicians play. We have not got, thank God, the cruel spur of defeat which animates the Germans. If ever there was a moment, when after all our victories and service to the cause of human freedom every patriotic man and woman ought to be thinking about the country and taking a long view, that moment is NOW.

Whatever happens at this General Election it will be a pretty rough show for those who win as well as for those who lose. There are some who say, 'Let the Socialist Government reap where they have sown.' A stronger dose is needed to put our people back on the right line. Nothing, they say, will convince the British people but suffering and disaster. They always insist on buying their experience over again each time. But I do not say this to you. I do not think we need plunge

179

into the pit of torment to rise again like the Phoenix from her ashes. I cannot feel sure that in this vast and swiftly-changing modern world that has grown up around us in the twentieth century, if we fell, we should ever emerge again as a great power, and we certainly cannot go on living on Dominion charity and American subsidies, even if they were going to continue. No—we have got to rise NOW to the occasion, and overcome all perils to our life and independence as we have always done before.

Mr Herbert Morrison said the other day, there must be no Coalition. There certainly seems no likelihood of that. I am quite sure that a Coalition between men and parties as the result of a lot of petty bargains and deals and compromises would be no use at all. There must be some great common bond of union, like we had in 1940, to lead to that melting of hearts where sacrifice seems to be an indulgence and pain becomes a joy, and when life rises to its highest level because death has no terrors.

If we got into that state of mind, which most of us have been through no doubt we could all come together, and then I do not doubt that Britain would rise again in her unconquerable strength. Do not fail in your effort. Do not despair of your native land. No one can tell what the future will bring forth. But I believe that if we act wisely and deal faithfully with one another and set our country, its history, glorious and inspiring, and its future, unlimited except by our own shortcomings, before our eyes, we should come through. Not only can the dangers of the present be overcome, and its problems solved, but, having saved the world in war, we should save ourselves in peace.

ELECTION ADDRESS

It gave me great pleasure to drive along the splendid road you have so kindly named after me. I greatly value this honour which you have conferred on me, and it will last long after party differences have passed away. Perhaps you will allow me to tell you about an incident which, though it happened long ago, was a cause of controversy when the naming of this road was under discussion. I am told that the Socialists and Communists continually spread the story that I used the troops to shoot down the Welsh miners and that the story of Tonypandy will never be forgotten. I am quite content that it should be remembered, provided that the truth is told.

When I was Home Secretary in 1910 I had a great horror and fear of having to become responsible for the military firing upon a crowd of rioters or strikers. Also I have had sympathy for the miners and think they are entitled to better treatment because they work far from the light of day. At that time there were many disputes and much violence in the Cambrian Coal Trust Collieries and the Rhondda Valley. Shops were looted and property destroyed. The Chief Constable of Glamorgan sent a request for the assistance of the military and troops were put in motion in the usual way. But here I made an unprecedented intervention. I stopped the movement of the troops and I sent instead 850 Metropolitan Police from London with the sole object of preventing bloodshed. I was much criticized for this so-called weakness in the House of Commons. But I carried my point. The troops were kept in the background and all contact with the rioters was made by our trusted and unarmed London police who charged, not with rifles and bayonets, but with their rolled-up mackintoshes. Thus all bloodshed, except perhaps some from the nose, was averted and all loss of life prevented. That is the true story of Tonypandy, and I hope it may replace in Welsh villages the cruel lie with which they have been fed all these long years.

Today we are facing a turning-point in our British way of life, and I come here to ask for your support. The Conservative Party of our day is the heir and apostle of those great traditions and principles of Tory democracy enunciated by Benjamin Disraeli and after him by my father, Lord Randolph Churchill. One of those principles, whose truth is borne out again and again upon the pages of history is Disraeli's oft-cited maxim, 'Centralization is the death-blow of public freedom.' The truth of these words was never more apparent than it is today, nor more relevant to the thought and resolve of those who would have men not only live, but live freely. Welsh traditions and culture go back to the dawn of our island history. The Education Act passed by the wartime Government of which I was the head safeguarded the position of the Welsh language with all its expression and poetic force.

Your great university, now deprived of its Parliamentary representation, and the National Museum here in Cardiff abide as monuments of Welsh fame and culture. Forty years ago as Home Secretary I read a Proclamation creating a Prince of Wales to an august assembly at Caernarvon Castle. It would be a shocking loss if all this pride of nationality were to be merged and engulfed in some centralized Socialist State where the rich variety of British life would be replaced by drab uniformity. How natural it is that the Welsh people should resent the increased control of their affairs from Whitehall which comes inevitably with Socialism. The Welsh people must be careful that the handcuffs of centralization are not slipped on them by a Socialist Government at Westminster.

The Liberal Party say that there ought to be a Parliament in Wales. It is easy, though not very dignified, to make promises when you are quite sure you will never be called upon to fulfil them. If I thought a Welsh Parliament at the present time would be in the best interests of the Welsh people I would not hesitate to recommend it to you. But Wales and England though two nations are a single, economic whole. A Welsh Parliament which could not consider the main economic issues, or could only consider them in isolation from England would not be good for you, or for us.

Should the Conservative Party be called upon to assume responsibility of government and I were connected with it I should at once assign to one member of the Cabinet the special responsibility for Welsh affairs. Advised and assisted by a Council of Wales, broadly representative of all aspects of Welsh life, he would ensure that Wales obtained steady and effective representation at the highest level in every aspect of national life, and that the machinery of government would work more speedily, more effectively and with full comprehension where Wales is concerned. The road would thus be open for the building up, not by the hands of Government, but with all the aid that Government can give of a strong, wide range of industries founded upon Welsh mining, and iron and steel. We shall do our utmost to assure to rural Wales a better provision of water and electricity and vigorous development of hill farming, and the strengthening of rural life which dominates her character. 'Freedom dwells in the mountains', but there is no reason why Wales should not have abundance, too. Freedom and abundance are our watchwords.

An extraordinary propaganda of falsehood has been spread in all directions by the Socialist Government about the lamentable conditions in Great Britain mainly under Conservative Parliaments between the wars, and a lot of young people are being taught to believe that this was a sad period of stagnation in our national and social life. In Mr Herbert Morrison's flowery language the period between the wars 'was paradise for the profiteers and hell for everyone else'. He seems to have got through it all right himself. But the Socialist Party hope that by creating this impression they will find some excuse for their own failure, which has brought such needless hardship on the masses of our people at the present time. In fact, however, the years between the two wars, although scarred by a general strike and a prolonged coal stoppage, which I did my best to avert, and although scarred by the economic and financial collapse of Mr Ramsay Mac-Donald's Second Socialist administration in 1931—these years were a period of almost unequalled expansion, and progress in the life of the wage-earning masses throughout this island.

Let me give you a few facts to support that statement. Between 1919 and 1939 4,000,000 new houses were built in England and Wales alone, or half as many houses as already existed before the First World War. Before the First Great War the average week in the majority of industries was 54 hours. But before the Second World War in 1939 under Parliaments resting on Conservative majorities the normal hours of work had come down to 47 or 48. The Socialists claim for themselves all the improvements which modern medical science has brought within our reach. They did it all themselves—so they did. To hear them talk one would think that no one had ever thought of children's welfare before that unlucky day when, much to their surprise, they found themselves in office four and a half years ago.

But you would like to know the truth. I will tell it to you. Immense improvements in the care of children were made in these terrible Tory days when Mr Morrison was what he calls 'in hell'. This I may remark is a somewhat disparaging description of the London County Council in which he was a prominent figure. I hope it will give him no additional twinge if I remind him that children's school meals and free milk were instituted by the pre-war Conservative Government and later extended by the wartime Government over which I presided.

In this period of 'hell for all except the profiteers' the expectation of life for all babies who had the courage to be born rose by nine years. That was an important fact to be borne in mind not only by the parents but by the baby. When these survivors of five years of hell went to the elementary schools in London it was found that they had gained an average of two inches in height and five pounds in weight compared with the standards before the First World War. How very surprising! The warm climate must have suited them. There was also a steady improvement in the food of the people, and a marked increase in the consumption of milk, cheese, butter and eggs, and of fruit and vegetables. But I do not wish to make your mouths water.

In the fifteen years from the formation of Mr Baldwin's Second Administration in 1924 in which I had the honour to be Chancellor of the Exchequer, down to the outbreak of war in 1939, in these fifteen years, a period during which for more than twelve years there were controlling Tory majorities in the House of Commons, wage rates increased by nearly 6 per cent and the cost of living fell by nineteen points. In this Tory 'hell' there was no wage freeze. I suppose it was too hot. And all the time the £ rose in value instead of falling, as it has done in the Socialist paradise, to 16s. 3d. So much for the Socialist planners and their boasting. So much for Mr Herbert Morrison and his sojourn in the infernal regions.

Both Nazis and Communists have held the common principle that if an untruth is told often enough and widely enough it becomes as good as the truth. Their doctrine is that the difference between truth and untruth is whether it is good for the party or not. Now of course the British Socialist Party are as much opposed as we are to these wicked totalitarians. But they sometimes take a leaf out of their book. And there is another example of this evil practice which I must bring to your notice. It is more serious because it has only just happened, and because the falsehood is not merely part of a whispering campaign but the official declaration of the Socialist Party, prepared with deliberation and in cold blood. I mean the 'empty bellies' story which appears in the Labour manifesto. This is their official statement: 'Empty bellies,' one Tory has said, 'are the one thing that will make Britons work.' Fancy a great party, governing the land and asking for a further lease of office, picking out the foolish remark of one unnamed irresponsible person among all the millions of Conservatives, and trying to defame the whole Conservative Party by fastening on them the monstrous charge that they wish to inflict empty bellies upon the people to make them work harder. We have, however, made inquiries. Apparently a Mr Higgs, formerly a Conservative member, made this statement three years ago when visiting New Zealand. He had no right whatever to speak for the Conservative Party. His words were, however, noted by our vigilant central office and they were promptly, at the time, officially repudiated. Here is what was said and published in the Conservative Weekly News Letter of 19 April 1947: 'Mr Higgs is not at all representative of the Conservative Party. He would never be adopted as a candidate on that sort of speech, for it is the most arrant nonsense.' They added the following comment, which I can't help reading: 'If Mr Higgs' theory were right our national output would be very high today, for thanks to Mr Strachey's efforts, our bellies are getting emptier and emptier.' I did not know that the Socialist Government were so hard-pressed, even at the outset of this campaign, that they have to sink to such methods. It gives you a measure of the kind of propaganda by which the Socialist Party hope to win the votes of the British nation. I invite Mr Attlee, or Mr Morrison, when they next address you either to maintain or repudiate this 'empty bellies' story, for which they are at present nominally and formally responsible.

The British people have worked hard since the war and the great qualities of perseverance and endurance which they showed in the struggle have not been found wanting in the years that followed its close. The Conservative Party has done its utmost to aid the Government and the people as a whole in every step which has been taken with a sincere desire to regain our prosperity and to re-establish our peacetime life. The post-war effort of the British nation has been made not through the help of the Government but to a very large extent in spite of it. The greatest burden which the people have had to carry has been the practical incompetence and misguided mentality of the Socialist Party. At a time when every scrap of our life and strength should have been devoted to reviving our prosperity they have added to our difficulties and burdens for the sake of their party doctrinal fads.

The greatest mismanagement has been in finance. Dr Dalton and Sir Stafford Cripps have each squandered the public treasure at a pace unknown before. It is a photo finish between them. Not only have they spent all the prodigious wartime taxes we imposed upon ourselves in the supreme hour of trial, but they have even added to them. Our taxation today is heavier than it was even in the most intense climax of the war. The Government of today is spending 40 per cent of the entire national income through the hands of its officials. The taxes in Britain are higher than in any other country in the civilized world. Waste and extravagance are presented on every hand. £18 5s. a night for every Government guest entertained at what is called the Cripps Austerity Arms off Park Lane. £16,000,000 for information services to blow the Government's trumpet when the Ministers get tired. £31,000,000 for Mr Strachey's groundnut excursion. £80,000,000 lost to date on nationalization. These are but instances which leap to the mind. The Socialists attempt to escape the public censure to the profusion in the following way: they tell their supporters 'Never mind, it is all taken from the rich'. This is a stupid error and one which is effectively exposing itself. If everything were taken from every man and woman whose income is above a thousand pounds a year, earned or unearned, it would not meet a quarter of the expenditure in which the Socialists are indulging. We are brought up against the hackneyed saying, 'Making the rich poor will not make the poor rich'. It is only in the first part of this policy in which the Socialists are having any success.

The Socialist housing policy has turned out even worse than we feared. Under the much abused Tory rule before the war, we were able to build 1,000 permanent houses a day in this island, two-thirds by private enterprise. In the last 4½ years of the Socialist new-world impulse and revelation, vast, profound State planning, we have built barely 400 permanent houses a day. The Minister of Health declared: 'I confidently expect that before the next election every family in Great Britain will have a separate house.' In this city of Cardiff alone there are no fewer than 15,000 families on the waiting list for houses. This tragic fiasco, causing severe and needless distress to hundreds of thousands of overcrowded people, is mainly due to the pedantic, irrational enforcement of Socialist prejudice. In a spiteful desire to wipe out the private builder by ordering that only one house in four should be built by private enterprise, the Minister responsible has thrust a burden upon the local authorities which in many cases they were quite unable to bear. The Socialist Government have failed in almost everything they have touched. Houses are built of bricks, mortar and good will, not of politics, prejudices and spite.

I always like to come to Wales. I was the friend and comrade of the most famous Welshman of our time, David Lloyd George. Most people are unconscious of how much their lives have been shaped by the laws for which Lloyd George was responsible. He it was who launched the Liberal forces of this country effectively into the broad stream of social betterment and social security along which all modern parties now steer. Nowadays this is called 'the Welfare State'. We did not christen it but it was our political child. I hope the Liberal Party whose aid we need so much will not forget all this now. When I first became his friend and active lieutenant nearly fifty years ago his deep love of the people, his profound knowledge of their lives and of the undue and needless pressures under which they lived made a deep impression on my mind. Nearly two generations have passed since those great days. I also served under his leadership in the First World War when he rendered lasting service to the British Empire and to the cause of freedom and brought world-wide honour upon the name of Wales. I must turn aside for a moment to make one observation. There can be no greater insult to his memory than to suggest that today Wales has a second Lloyd George. Oh, I think it much better not to mention names.

Mr Lloyd George was a democrat if ever there was one, but he recoiled, like all those who are ready to fight for freedom must recoil, from the fallacy and folly of Socialism. This is what he said about it almost a quarter of a century ago. His words are vivid: they are also prophetic:

'You cannot trust the battle of freedom to Socialism. Socialism has no interest in liberty. Socialism is the very negation of liberty. Socialism means the community in bonds. If you establish a Socialist community it means the most comprehensive universal and pervasive tyranny that this country has ever seen. It is like the sand of the desert. It gets into your food, your clothes, your machinery, the very air you breathe. They are all gritty with regulations, orders, decrees, rules. That is what Socialism means.'

These are the words of Lloyd George. See how they live and ring through the years. He might have said this yesterday. He knew what it would feel like long before it came upon us.

I hope you have all mastered the official Socialist jargon which our masters, as they call themselves, wish us to learn. You must not use the word 'poor'; they are described as the 'lower income group'. When it comes to a question of freezing a workman's wages the Chancellor of the Exchequer speaks of 'arresting increases in personal income'. The idea is that formerly income taxpayers used to be the well-to-do, and that therefore it will be popular and safe to hit at them. Sir Stafford Cripps does not like to mention the word 'wages', but that is what he means. There is a lovely one about houses and homes. They are in future to be called 'accommodation units'. I don't know how we are to sing our old song 'Home Sweet Home'. 'Accommodation Unit, Sweet Accommodation Unit, there's no place like our Accommodation Unit.' I hope to live to see the British democracy spit all this rubbish from their lips. Mr Herbert Morrison made a complaint the other day. 'Socialized industries,' he said, 'are the subject of the most persistent misrepresentation, whereas the difficulties and deficiencies of private industries are glossed over.' How does he mean, '*glossed over*'? If private enterprise fails the owners may find themselves in the bankruptcy court. Is that being glossed over?

It makes no material difference to the official bulk buyer or Government nominee on some Board of Control whether the business is solvent or sends in its bill to the Exchequer. So long as he does his duty in an honest way, attends punctually to his work and is respectful to the Socialist politicians who employ him, he is safe and secure. Whereas a private businessman may have everything to lose if his judgment is wrong or his administration wasteful. Thus you maintain the most searching process of natural selection, out of which the public gets increasingly good service and value for their money. Nationalized industries are monopolies in the worst sense of the word. If a private business should become a monopoly and abuse its position there is no difficulty in dealing with it. But a Government monopoly has behind it the whole strength of the Government and, under a Socialist Government, the Ministers themselves have a political interest in trying to bolster it up so as to justify their own policy and conduct. In this remark which I have quoted, Mr Herbert Morrison shows how little he realizes the actual facts and processes which are at work in modern life. We have seen lately the extraordinary case of Lord Pakenham repudiating the report on a terrible aeroplane accident by an impartial committee which he himself had picked and set up, thus weakening confidence in the safety of British landing grounds among all other countries.

I remember in Victorian days anxious talks about 'the submerged tenth' (that part of our people who had not shared in the progress of the age) and then later on in the old Liberal period (the grand old Liberal period) we spoke of going back to bring the rearguard in. The main army we said had reached the camping ground in all its strength and victory, and we should now, in duty and compassion, go back to pick up the stragglers and those who had fallen by the way and bring them in.

That was the Liberal solution then. It is the policy of the Conservative and National Liberal parties now. But now, under the Socialists, it is no longer a question of bringing the rearguard in, but of bringing the whole army back. It is no longer the plan of helping the submerged tenth, but of submerging the other nine-tenths down to their level. This is what in fact is taking place day by day, as you can see in your own lives and homes as you look around you.

Mr Morrison (I am so sorry to keep mentioning him. Perhaps we'll hear from Mr Attlee. He is the Prime Minister, you know) said at Leeds the other day, 'We are leading the world.' So far as social services are concerned we have always led it. But as for leading the world in any other sense what nation is following the British Socialist Party? The Russian Soviet Government and its satellites claim to be going on ahead. They claim to lead. They call upon Socialists to come quicker. The rest of the world has turned decisively away from the Socialist theory. As a Socialist Prime Minister working for the establishment of a Socialist State, Mr Attlee and his party are alone among the English-speaking peoples. The United States, at the head of the world today, vehemently repudiate the Socialist doctrine. Canada repudiates it. Australia and New Zealand, after a considerable trial of it in a very incomplete form, have just shaken themselves free. Remember also there is no Socialist Government in Europe outside the Iron Curtain and Scandinavia. It seems to me a very perilous path that we are asked to tread, and to tread alone among the free democracies of the West.

ELECTION ADDRESS

A SPEECH AT THE FORUM CINEMA, DEVONPORT
9 FEBRUARY 1950

I last visited Devonport when I was First Lord of the Admiralty to welcome home the *Exeter* after her glorious victory in the Battle of the Plate. Alas, the gallant *Exeter*, after all her victories, was to sink in action under the fire of overwhelming numbers of the Japanese fleet, but her name will live for ever, and the memory of those who died for their country and the cause of freedom will long be cherished in Britain and throughout the west country.

The next time I came to you was on the morrow of one of your worst bombing raids; my wife was with me when we drove through your streets, and I was inspired to see the high morale which everyone in the city and in the dockyards maintained. We went through a lot in those days together. Let us make sure we do not throw away, by the follies of peace, what we have gained in the agonies of war. Let us make sure that in the exhaustion which follows fighting for the freedom of others we do not cast away the freedom which has made us what we are.

I would like to say a word or two in favour of my son. Randolph is a mature, formidable and experienced politician. He has done his part in the struggles through which this country has passed, and I was glad— very glad—that he escaped from any terrors in the war, and I have a feeling he is going to come into his own. We have here also Mr J. J. Astor. I trust they may carry on the torch. We want them both. We want them both now. We rely on you by your exertions to gain two distinguished Members and send two valuable supporters to what, I trust, will be a Conservative Government.

I should like to make it clear, at the outset, not only here at home but to foreign countries, that at this General Election full political liberty is being maintained and that the voting will be conducted in a correct and fair manner. All votes may be freely recorded. All will be fairly counted; and let me add that the ballot is secret. No one living in council houses need have the slightest fear that their rents will be put up if they vote Conservative. It is necessary to make this statement as there is a good deal of anxiety about it in the new estates which are coming into being.

I wish I could say the same about the propaganda with which we are assailed. In this election we have had to face several grotesque untruths the kind of thing that could not be maintained in Parliament or before any fair-minded audience, but which can be mouthed from door to door by the Socialist canvassers.

The first colossal misrepresentation of facts—'terminological inexactitude', if you like the expression (there are shorter variants, but we have to be very careful now at this election, which we are told must be kept thoroughly genteel)—well, the first of these misrepresentations of fact was a statement that the Conservative Party meant to create unemployment in order that the need for finding a job should add a greater spur to labour. There is no truth in this. It is a monstrous suggestion. There was reference to this last night on the wireless by a Government spokesman (Mr James Griffiths).

The Socialist boast that they cured unemployment has been exploded out of their own mouths by the statements of Mr Morrison and Sir Stafford Cripps. All of them have said there would be anything up to 2,000,000 unemployed if it had not been for the American Loan. Fancy the Socialist Government in England keeping itself alive, economically and politically, by these large annual dollops of dollars from capitalist America! They seek the dollars; they beg the dollars; they bluster for the dollars; they gobble the dollars. But in the whole of their 8,000-word manifesto they cannot say 'Thank you' for the dollars.

It has also been proved that we had a joint plan in the days of the wartime Government for dealing with unemployment should it occur after the war. To this plan all the leading Socialist Ministers were party. That plan still holds good. So it is no longer a matter of dispute. We are all agreed upon it. They admit unemployment has been avoided by American dollars; and we are broadly agreed what we should do to prevent it or mitigate it should it recur. Everyone knows that any Government that comes into power as a result of this election will do its utmost to prevent unemployment. How far they will be successful will depend upon the methods they employ and the plight we are found to be in. I assure you there can be no greater safeguard against unemployment in the coming years than the return of a Government which will revive confidence in our country all over the world.

And now there is the tale of food subsidies. Sir Stafford Cripps told us on the broadcast that the Conservative Party had decided to abolish food subsidies. £406,000,000 is being spent in food subsidies, which is represented as a kindly gift by the kindly Government to the whole nation. It is not a gift. A great deal more is taken in tax by the kindly Government. Mr Morrison, evidently in collusion, repeated this

whatever-you-care-to-call-it on a separate night. It is utterly untrue.
We have no intention of abolishing food subsidies until and unless we
are absolutely sure that the basic necessaries of life are available at
prices all the people can pay down to the poorest in the land.

More than a fortnight ago Dr Edith Summerskill said at Kettering:
'The British Government could abolish rationing tomorrow if it were
prepared to let the lowest income groups do without while the
wealthiest bought up all available supplies. But it was not prepared to
do so.' This is a very good example of the cumbrous and costly working
of Socialist methods and machinery. The question immediately arises
whether there is not some better way of helping the lower income
groups to obtain their food at cheap prices than to keep in being for
their sake the whole vast, complex, costly apparatus of rationing.

In our view the strong should help the weak. In the Socialist view
the strong should be kept down to the level of the weak in order to
have equal shares for all. How small the share is does not matter so
much, in their opinion, so long as it is equal. They would much rather
that everyone should have half rations than that anybody should get a
second helping. What are called 'the lowest income groups' before
the war when there were no rations in fact consumed under the
'wicked Tories' one and a half times as much meat and more than
twice as much sugar as Dr Summerskill doles out to all of us today.

In the years before the war the dietary of London workhouses was
in every way superior in meat, fats, sugar and also in variety to that
which can be bought by a fully-employed wage-earner today. Yet to
hear the Socialists talk on the broadcast, especially Mr Herbert Morrison
and Sir Stafford Cripps, you would believe that we were living in a
perfect paradise of plenty and good management. To apply the
Socialist principle of equality at all costs is, in fact, to lay down the
law that the pace of our advancing social army must be the pace of
the slowest and the weakest man. Such a principle is, of course, destructive of all hopes of victory in social and philanthropic advance.
It would undoubtedly condemn our island, with its enormous population, to a lower and more restricted standard of living than prevails
anywhere else in the civilized world.

We are told: 'See what happened when sweets were derationed.'
I am not at all sure that that was not a put-up job done with the hope
of failure, so as to be an example. Certainly it was done in the most
clumsy manner by those who had every interest to prevent its being a
success. We certainly look forward to the day when we shall cease to be
the only country in the civilized and free world where wartime rationing prevails. But I pledge any Conservative Government with which

I am concerned not to take off rationing on any basic commodity until we are certain it will not only confer benefits upon the great mass of the people, but will protect the lower income groups from hardship.

You know, ladies and gentlemen, our Socialist masters think they know everything. They even try to teach the housewife how to buy her food. Mr Douglas Jay has said: 'Housewives as a whole cannot be trusted to buy all the right things, where nutrition and health are concerned. This is really no more than an extension of the principle according to which the housewife herself would not trust a child of four to select the week's purchases. For in the case of nutrition and health, just as in the case of education, the gentleman in Whitehall really does know better what is good for people than the people know themselves.'

That is what Mr Jay has said. Was there ever a period in the history of this island when such a piece of impertinence could have been spread about by a Minister? Let us call upon this Government to account for more of their own failures. Let us take them first on all the promises they made about housing. Before the war, under the 'wicked' Tory Government, with Mr Neville Chamberlain in charge, we were running to a thousand homes a day. There was no fuss about it. A certain amount of aid was given to local authorities, but no subsidizing of private industry. They just let things work naturally. A thousand houses a day!

Now what has happened? They cannot build half what the Tories under Mr Neville Chamberlain were building without mentioning it; without it being a political question at all. The 'wicked Tories'—a thousand; the 'noble Socialists'—five hundred, each of them costing three times as much as they did before the war. Here in Plymouth I am told you have a waiting list of 11,000 houses. Randolph tells me that there are in Devonport houses which were built by private enterprise before the war in 1938 for which people paid £685. These houses sell for £2,000 today. What a sign of Socialist efficiency. What a sign of getting value for money. What a sign in the fall of the purchasing power of money, on which depends for everyone the innumerable transactions we have to carry out between man and man in any community.

If the Government had been trying to give you houses instead of playing politics; if they had been thinking in terms of bricks and mortar instead of in spite and venom, many a family in this city and many a score of thousand families in this island would today have a roof and front door and a hearth of their own. I think the Socialists should be called to account by the electors after their sorry and discreditable performance. Boasts, promises, pledges on the one hand, and the shameful under-production on the other. No Government but this Socialist Government could have fallen so far short of public duty and of solemn obligation.

I should like to say a few words to the numerous owners of motor-cars and motor-bicycles in this country. People are not necessarily 'lower than vermin' because by their skill and thrift they have earned and saved enough money to buy a car or a motor-bicycle. We realize the deprivation and often hardship involved in the strict rationing of petrol which the Socialist Government have enforced, and we are determined to put an end to it at the earliest possible moment.

We cannot, and do not, make any definite promises at this stage. We have been kept in the dark to such an extent that it is impossible for us to measure the difficulties and repercussions which freeing the sale of petrol at this moment might involve. But when we remember the enormous amount of petrol produced in the sterling area, it does seem strange that this country should be almost the only one in which petrol is rationed. We believe that by skilful management and re-adjustment of exports of sterling petrol, even if it may not be possible to abolish petrol rationing altogether, it may soon be possible for a Government concerned with the interests of owners of motor-cars and motor-cycles at any rate to increase greatly the basic ration.

Sir Stafford Cripps is reported to have said: 'You must have controls so that people cannot do just as they like.' There speaks the true voice of the Socialist. People must not do what they like. They must do what their Socialist masters (to use the word of the Attorney-General) think is good for them and tell them what to do. Thus the Socialist Party and Dr Summerskill have other reasons for wishing to keep the whole business of food rationing in full operation, besides their sympathy for the lower income groups and ignorance of the best way to help them. Mr Bottomley, the Under-Secretary for Overseas Trade, said eighteen months ago in Copenhagen: 'As long as a Socialist Government remains in office in Britain it can be expected that a rationing system will be maintained.' Thus we have not only rationing for rationing's sake, but the Food Ministry for the Food Ministry's sake. And under Socialist administration these sorts of organizations grow in cost with every month that passes.

In wartime, rationing is the alternative to famine. In peace it may well become the alternative to abundance. There is now one Food Ministry official for every 250 families in the country. There are more than 42,000 officials in all. But Dr Summerskill and her chief (I will not say her superior), Mr Strachey, exult in the feeling that they have so large an army to command. Their difficult and anxious problem is to make sure that it has enough to do to justify its existence, and give them this great mass of patronage and innumerable opportunities of interfering with other people's lives.

In the crisis of the war in 1940, when Lord Woolton was Food Minister, when the U-boats were sinking our ships and the air raids destroying our ports, the salaries paid to the Ministry of Food officials were less than £4,500,000 and the total administrative costs of the whole department were less than £8,000,000. However, the costs of all these departments tend to grow. The Socialists try to make them grow because it is part of their policy to have this vast machinery in existence. Also, they like to have as many ordinary people as possible in their power and dependent upon them as often as possible every day. In 1949 the salaries paid by the Socialists to the Ministry of Food officials had gone up from £4,500,000 in 1940 to nearly £14,000,000. The total administrative cost of running the department and working the rationing scheme had gone up from £8,000,000 to £21,000,000. It has well been said, 'The costs go up, but not the rations.'

Who do you suppose pays for all these 42,000 officials and lavish administrative expense? Every family in the country pays for it on the food they get. The food they get comes to their table weighted with this heavy charge, for which you pay as well as for the food subsidies which are given regardless of expense to millions of well-to-do people who do not need them at all. In order to pay for this and similar Socialist institutions, oppressive taxes are exacted from all, and beer and tobacco are taxed as they have never been taxed before. The purchase tax inflicts real hardships on the housewife, and particularly on those who have households and families to keep.

Income tax levied upon overtime and the highest forms of skilled craftsmanship discourages the extra effort and superior skill without which our industries cannot hold their own and compete in the modern world. Socialists pretend they give the lower income groups, and all others in the country, cheaper food through their system of rationing and food subsidies. To do it they have to take the money from their pockets first and circulate it back to them after heavy charges for great numbers of officials administering the system of rationing—which Mr Strachey and Dr Edith Summerskill are determined to keep in being whether it is needed or not—have been deducted. Little gifts have been given and came in handy for the election. We are all expected to change our political convictions and give our votes to the Government because a little extra tea and sugar has been saved up and given out. It is an insult to the intelligence of the British nation.

Sir Stafford Cripps now boasts, having first denied it, that the Socialist Government had given away to countries abroad £1,500,000,000 since they came into power to help the reconstruction of the world. They had to borrow it first from the United States or be given it by them. It was only lent or given to help Britain get on her legs again. Now it is gone. One-hundredth part of this £1,500,000,000 would have been enough to give every private motorist a reasonable ration of petrol. Conservatives are as keen as the Socialists to help revive the other countries of the world; but we believe we should be just before we are generous. It will take very strong arguments to convince me that our people should be deprived of the use of their motor vehicles, while other countries enjoy abundant supplies of petrol, largely bought with the money which we have presented to them, and for a large part of which we still remain debtors to America.

Socialism is contrary to human nature. Commerce and trade have always been a great power in this country. If difficulties have come upon them these last four and a half years it is because they have been hampered. The black patch confronting us now is due to the men at the head of the Government who have led and managed us. We must plunge into this pit of torment to rise again and overcome all perils to our life and independence as we have always done before.

The reason I ask for a strong majority is not that one party might ride roughshod, or that special favours might be granted to one class, or to vested interests. I ask for a strong majority towards that broad national unity in which our salvation will be found. Do not fail in your effort. Do not despair of your native land. No one can tell what the future will bring forth, but I believe that if we act wisely and deal faithfully with one another, and set our country, its history, glorious and inspiring, and its future—unlimited except by our own short-comings—before our eyes, we should come through. Not only can the dangers of the present be overcome and its problems solved, but, having saved the world in war, we should save ourselves in peace.

ELECTION ADDRESS

A SPEECH AT THE USHER HALL, EDINBURGH
14 FEBRUARY 1950

---

14 *February—30-year Treaty of Friendship, Alliance and Mutual Assistance between Russia and China signed by Marshal Stalin and Mao Tse-tung in the Kremlin.*

[14 *February* 1950

I have spoken several times in the Usher Hall during this twentieth century so filled with tumult, but I am sure that there was no occasion, not even in the height of the war, when the issues which it was in our power to settle were so serious for the whole world, for Great Britain and for Scotland. The Prime Minister, Mr Attlee, has made it clear that his intention is to establish a Socialist State in this island at the earliest moment. He intends to create a society in which the State will control and own all the means of production, distribution and exchange. We have had one instalment of this during the last four and a half years, and now we are asked to vote whether we want to take a second plunge into this immense social and economic revolution. The Socialists have issued a manifesto which, in a vague and general manner, prescribes the limits within which they will feel themselves entitled to act in the Parliament about to be elected. They involve already a profound change in our national life and one which, having been adopted, will be irrevocable.

The Socialists propose at once to nationalize steel, for which the Bill is already passed, and in addition they mention cement, sugar, chemicals, meat and industrial life insurance. They also claim the right to set up with the taxpayers' money rival State businesses wherewith to knock out any private enterprises which they dislike or which do not, apart from the law of the land, obey their wishes. If they ruin those businesses it will be bad. If they fail in their ventures they have only to send in a bill for the loss to the Exchequer and you will pay it in your taxes. This is what they call their programme and what they would feel themselves entitled to do if they got a majority in the country, or even if they have a majority in Parliament resting upon a minority of votes in the country.

There is, however, no guarantee that they will keep themselves

197

within these limits. If the more violent element in their party get control there are no lengths to which they cannot go. The Minister who might well be Mr Attlee's successor in leading the Socialist Party has not hesitated to speak of revolution, civil war and a blood bath. You have every need to use your votes to protect our country from such hateful threats. This attempt to establish a Socialist State in Great Britain affects the relations of England and Scotland in a direct and serious manner. The principle of centralization of government in Whitehall and Westminster is emphasized in a manner not hitherto experienced or contemplated in the Act of Union. The supervision, interference and control in the ordinary details of Scottish life and business by the Parliament at Westminster has not hitherto been foreseen, and I frankly admit that it raises new issues between our two nations.

If England became an absolute Socialist State, owning all the means of production, distribution and exchange, ruled only by politicians and their officials in the London offices, I personally cannot feel that Scotland would be bound to accept such a dispensation. I do not therefore wonder that the question of Scottish home rule and all this movement of Scottish nationalism has gained in strength with the growth of Socialist authority and ambitions in England. I would never adopt the view that Scotland should be forced into the serfdom of Socialism as the result of a vote in the House of Commons. It is an alteration so fundamental in our way of life that it would require a searching review of our historical relations.

But here I speak to the Scottish Nationalists in words, as diplomatic language puts it, of great truth and respect, and I say this position has not yet been reached. If we act together with our united strength it may never arise. I do not believe that the British nation or the English people will accept the Socialist State. There is a deep fund of common sense in the English race and they have all sorts of ways, as has been shown in the past, of resisting and limiting the imposition of State autocracy. It would be a great mistake for Scotsmen to suppose that Mr Attlee's policy can be effectively imposed upon us at the present time. And here in this election, so momentous in its character and consequences, we all have the opportunity of inflicting a shattering defeat upon this menace to our individual liberties, and to the well understood and hitherto widely-admired British way of life. I most strongly urge all Scotsmen to fight one battle at a time. We have every hope that the Socialist schemes for netting us up and tying us down will be torn in pieces by the votes of the British people. We shall know more about it after February 23rd. It may indeed be a turning-point in our island story. Scotsmen would make a wrong decision if they tried to separate their fortunes from ours at a moment when together we may lift them all to a higher plane of freedom and security. It would indeed be foolish to cast splitting votes or support splitting candidates, the result of which might be to bring about that evil Whitehall tyranny and centralization, when by one broad heave of the British national shoulders the whole gimcrack structure of Socialist jargon and malice may be cast in splinters to the ground.

We of the Conservative and Unionist Party hold firmly to the principles of union and freedom, and we hold equally to those two principles. We have every reason to believe that we shall win, and that the strength of the Socialist forces will be so broken that they will not be able to impose their restrictive tyranny upon us. Let Scotsmen therefore take one step at a time, and not take extreme decisions carrying with them grievous misfortunes both to England and Scotland, before no other choice is open. Besides all this, as we know from many a hard fought fight, the Scots do not quit their comrades in the hour of peril.

The Socialist centralization menace has however advanced so far as to entitle Scotland to further guarantees of national security and internal independence. These can be provided effectively by new additional representation at the centre and at the summit which, if the Conservatives and Unionists are returned to power, will be accorded to Scotland by a Unionist Cabinet. Besides strengthening the establishment of Under-Secretaries of State, we shall advise the creation of a new office of Minister of State for Scotland. He would be a Minister of Cabinet rank and would be deputy to the Secretary of State. Such an appointment would enable a senior member of the Cabinet to be constantly in Scotland. Because of the large changes in economic and financial affairs which have come about in recent years, we shall appoint a Royal Commission to review the whole situation between Scotland and England, and we shall take good care that this does not become an instrument of delay upon practical action.

During the first fortnight of this election battle, we have had to combat a number of falsehoods launched upon us by our opponents. I can but mention them. First there was the unemployment falsehood. This took the form of party propaganda claiming that they had cured unemployment by their planning, whereas they had already repeatedly admitted that there would be 2,000,000 unemployed but for the subsidies from capitalist America, on which the British Socialist Government have lived financially and even more politically.

Even worse, there has been the vile and shameful charge that the

Conservative Party would deliberately create unemployment in order to make the rest of the people work harder. This has been refuted overwhelmingly by the White Paper presented to Parliament in 1944, for which all the leading Members on both Front Benches are responsible. This proclaimed our joint resolve to ward off unemployment and also prescribed the methods which should be adopted should it come upon us. Here was a policy to which all parties had pledged their faith, and it still remains the policy to which all Conservatives adhere. Therefore, the unemployment falsehood has been repelled from all forms of open and public discussion, though it may still be whispered in lies and slanders from doorstep to doorstep.

The next main falsehood by which we are assailed is found in the official manifesto of the Socialist Party. It charges the Conservative and Unionist Party with seeking to make people work harder by cutting down their food supplies. I must read you the actual phrase, 'empty bellies'. 'Empty bellies are the one thing that will make Britons work.' This was attributed to an unnamed person and used as a means of vilifying the whole of our great party, representing, as will presently be shown, the majority of the nation. The Socialist leaders have printed this irresponsible utterance without mentioning that it was repudiated at the time and described as 'arrant nonsense' by the official authority of the Conservative organization. I invited Mr Morrison and Mr Attlee to cleanse themselves from this unfair and untruthful behaviour. I am surprised that they have not chosen even to acknowledge the repudiation which we immediately gave to such a cruel and unworthy accusation.

Then there are the family allowances. Everywhere the Socialists have been spreading the double falsehood that they initiated the family allowances and that we, the Unionist Party, intend to cut them down. The reverse is the truth. It was the Conservative Caretaker Government over which I presided which established the family allowances and if, in the reform and reorganization of our finances which are so urgently needed, family allowances are altered in any way, it will be not to diminish them but to augment and improve them.

All these three sets of falsehoods have been voiced by the leading Socialist Ministers and all, I am glad to say, have been beaten down in public controversy before we are halfway through our election campaign. We are therefore entitled to turn over to counter-attack. The field is too broad for me to traverse tonight, but I will select for special censure the two grossest failures of the Socialist Government. Here they are:

The total failure of their housing policy and their wild financial extravagance which has brought our country to the very verge of bankruptcy. In May 1946, the Minister of Health, after he had had ample time to survey the whole prospect before him, said:

'I confidently expect that before the next election every family in Great Britain will have a separate house.'

Yet today the waiting lists in many large cities are higher than when he spoke. Hundreds of thousands of families are living in distressing conditions of overcrowding and discomfort made all the worse because the high hopes to which they were led by the Socialist Government no longer sustain them. Before the war, with the same labour force as now, but under Conservative Government, a thousand houses a day were built. Now under Socialist maladministration the record is only four hundred and the target for this year is only five hundred. But the need is far greater. How distant now seems the chance of resuming the attack on slums and overcrowding which pre-war Conservative Governments had begun so well. Yet that must continue to be our aim and we shall bend all our energies to the task. Bad as the conditions are in England today, they are far worse in Scotland. In 1944 the Scottish Housing Advisory Committee estimated that Scotland needed 500,000 houses. The need now is, of course, far greater. Towards it the Socialist Government has built less than 70,000 permanent houses. They promised that, when the programme of temporary houses came to an end, the increase of permanent houses of all kinds would make up for the loss. But they did not build more, they built less.

Mr Attlee, the Prime Minister, has been making play with the expression 'property-owning democracy', which constitutes an essential part of Conservative policy. He said:

'The nation was much more a property-owning democracy than when Labour came into power. They own the railways, the Bank of England and the coal mines, and there are a lot more things the nation will own presently.'

I doubt if it gives very much pleasure to the average Socialist when he wakes up in the morning to say to himself, 'Oho, I own the Bank of England, I own the railways, I own the coal mines.' But if it does give him any actual pleasure, he is certainly paying dearly for it. It may gratify his pride, but it makes a nasty hole in his pocket. In order that these Socialist enthusiasts may enjoy this little thrill in the morning, very large sums are being taken from them and their wives and families in taxes, or in prices, or in both.

His thrill of pride has cost him and the rest of us dear. I am quite sure that when the railwaymen, who have behaved in a public-spirited manner in not pressing their wage claims at this critical juncture, wake up in the morning they do not get much fun out of saying to themselves, 'We own the railways.' In fact there is a great deal of evidence to the contrary, as will be proved when the votes are counted. Railway workers had a far better bargaining position when they were dealing with the railway companies and could have had the full help of their trade unions than when they have to bargain with an all-powerful State monopoly whom the union leaders are in with and do not like to offend.

Mr Attlee's remark about a property-owning democracy reminds me of a story told me at one of the naval stations a few years ago. A portly gentleman demanded to go on board a battleship as she lay alongside the quay. 'Who are you?' said the sentry. 'I am one of the proprietors' was the reply. But he did not see much of the battleship. The truth is that Mr Attlee and his friends feel the force of our Conservative theme, a property-owning democracy, and are trying to avoid it by talking nonsense about it. They know perfectly well that what we mean is a *personal* property-owning democracy. Households which have possessions which they prize and cherish because they are their own, or even a house and garden of their own, the Savings Certificates that their thrift has bought, a little money put by for a rainy day, or an insurance policy, the result of forethought and self-denial which will be a help in old age or infirmity, or after their death for those they love and leave behind—that is what the Conservatives mean by a property-owning democracy. And the more widely it is distributed and the more millions there are to share in it, the more will the British democracy continue to have the spirit of individual independence, and the more they will turn their backs on the Socialist delusion that one ought to be proud of being totally dependent on the State.

Mr Attlee also referred to my statement about the need for increasing the petrol ration. He described it as 'window dressing', and said I had not given a minute's thought to it. I give a great deal of thought to what I say and to what I do. My task at this election has not been the dressing of windows so much as the undressing of humbugs. It is curious that almost at the very moment when Mr Attlee was deriding the idea of an increase in the basic patrol ration at Liverpool, his own Minister of Fuel, Mr Gaitskell, at Harrogate was saying that the prospects of an increased petrol ration were 'not bad'. Talks, he said, were now going on in Washington to see if we could get extra petrol without spending dollars. This is important news, and I am very glad to have extorted it from the Government by the demand which I made for a review of the petrol ration. I have never suggested we should use dollars to buy petrol. We have vast masses of petroleum in the sterling area, and if the Socialist Ministers had not shown their usual ineptitude and incompetence the refineries would be in existence and at work today which would secure us ample supplies.

Everything they touch turns to muddle, whether it be Mr Bevin's mismanagement and loss of influence in the Middle East, which has led to the closing of the Haifa refinery, or whether it be the Socialist departmental red tape and restrictions which have hitherto paralysed the construction of the great refinery at Southampton, the cause is the same; a thoroughly inefficient administration absorbed in playing party politics, and a Prime Minister who has failed to give the necessary guidance and leadership, which no one else but a Prime Minister can provide. Mr Attlee spoke of the importance of controls. He took as an example the lorry from which he was speaking. He said that without controls the lorry would run into the ditch. That is just what is happening to the Government, of whose lorry he was supposed to be the driver. What we need is fewer *controls* throughout the country and more *control* at the head of the Government.

The vote-catching election cry 'Fair shares for all' should not deceive keen-minded men and women. It is meaningless unless it is also stated who is to be the judge of what is fair. The Socialist appeal is to envy and hatred. These can be no foundation for a civilized or prosperous society. But what the average Socialist really means when he speaks of 'Fair shares for all' is *equal* shares for all. Equal shares for those who toil and those who shirk. Equal shares for those who save and those who squander. No reward offered to the skilled craftsman. No incentive to the industrious and experienced piece-worker. No extra payment for overtime that is not taken back from him in PAYE. No reward for enterprise, ingenuity, thrift and good-housekeeping. 'Equal shares for all', that is what the Socialist Government really mean.

Even in Soviet Russia such ideas are not applied. If carried into force they would bring the whole community down to a dead level with the weakest, the idlest and the most wasteful. But that is what they mean. It would bring ruin to any but the most primitive society. Yet these are the ideas which are put forward not only by the wilder members of the Socialist Party but by the Chancellor of the Exchequer himself. Sir Stafford Cripps has a brilliant intellect, but it is so precariously poised that his public life has been disfigured by lamentable and spasmodic utterances to which he falls a victim in moods of excitement or moments of strain. I can quite understand the stresses through which he is passing now when his clear mind sees so plainly the harm he has wrought his country and when his career and ambitions prompt

him to try to outbid Mr Aneurin Bevan. Nevertheless, I was astounded
to read what he said at Bristol on Saturday. I quote the report in the
London *Times*. These are his words:

'We are sharing out more fairly the national resources that exist.
We have not shared them out all equally *yet*. It takes a bit of time to
do these things.'

Here you have the gospel of equal shares for all proclaimed as the
aim and policy of the Chancellor of the Exchequer responsible for the
finances of this vast and complicated, but now seriously endangered,
British society. It is not 'Fair shares for all', whatever that may mean,
but a levelling down to a uniform standard governed by the contribution of the weakest elements in our national life. In the whole English-
speaking world, in the whole of Europe outside the Iron Curtain,
there is no government today that would tolerate such language from
its finance minister. In the whole world Great Britain is the country
which can least well afford to suffer the injury which such frantic out-
bursts will do.

In the first place the Chancellor obviously struck a mortal blow at
the Savings Movement, which all parties have been urged to support
and have supported, and in favour of which he himself has made so
many speeches. What right has he to appeal for thrift and saving, forethought and self-denial when at the same time in his heart he is aiming
at the confiscation of all property down to the level of equality for all
(except of course members of the Government and those who enjoy
their favour). Nothing could be more likely than this declaration to
weaken the impulse to production at home, or still further impair our
credit abroad. Nothing could be more likely to bring unemployment
upon our people. My hope is that the British electorate will by a
strong and ample majority repudiate these reckless and frenzied
exhibitions by the Chancellor of the Exchequer. We have an Administration intent upon the class war and hostile to every form of wealth
and property. Sweeping them out of power will do more to prevent
unemployment, revive the purchasing power of the money we earn,
and regain for us the confidence and credit of the civilized world than
any other step that could be taken. You have the opportunity of taking
that step on February 23rd.

I have waited till I reached this imperial and ancient capital of
Scotland to say a few words about world politics. We are all absorbed
naturally during the election in domestic disputes. But outside this
island a vast and formidable world has come into being dwarfing our
calm and Victorian days. It laps us about on every side, and we no
longer have controlling power or even it seems to me a sufficient

influence upon what happens. When the war stopped the United States, Great Britain and Russia were what was called 'The Big Three'. But with the decision taken by the British electorate in one day of voting in 1945, we lost for the time being our place and rank in world affairs which we had gained and held throughout the terrible days of struggle. We became a nation absorbed in its own class and party warfare. All the countries of the free and civilized world were conscious of a sense of loss. Then we fell into our economic difficulties which would in any case have been severe, and very soon instead of being one of the world leaders, our famous island became one of the world's problems.

I recognize fully that Mr Bevin, steadfastly sustained by Mr Attlee, has followed in main essentials the right course in foreign policy. The execution of that policy has been marred by many pitiful blunders. Mr Bevin has managed to make British foreign policy equally disliked by France and Germany, by Jew and Arab, and by Communist and by anti-Communist forces. He has done this through some great and many minor errors. Still, he has not failed to uphold the main principles on which our life and safety depends. He has followed with steadfastness the line I marked out at Fulton of fraternal association with the United States, and the closest unification of our military arrangements. In the Atlantic Pact we have a great instrument making for world peace. In the Brussels Treaty and the building up of Western European Union he has, albeit somewhat sheepishly, given effect to the theme of United Europe. But for his personal feelings it might all have been a great deal easier. Nevertheless he has come along more or less quietly, and Western Union has taken its place with the British Empire and the English-speaking fraternity in that vast amalgamation of free democracy upon whose unity and strength world peace depends. These supreme objectives have not been lost. We have given our Conservative support to the main principles of the Government's foreign policy while we have deplored the astonishing errors which have hampered its application. In the end it is the larger issues that will count.

While we are all so busy with our internal party controversies we must not forget the gravity of our position or indeed that of the whole world. Soviet Russia—the immensely powerful band of men gathered together in the Kremlin—has ranged itself against the Western democracies. They have added to their dominion the satellite States of Europe; the Baltic States, Poland, Czechoslovakia, Hungary, Bulgaria, Rumania. Tito of Yugoslavia has broken away. Greece has been rescued by the United States, carrying on the task which we began.

At the other side of the world the 500,000,000 of China have fallen into the Communist sphere. But Communism is novel and China is old. I do not regard China as having finally accepted Soviet servitude.

Still, when you look at the picture as a whole you see two worlds ranged against one another more profoundly and on a larger scale than history has ever seen before. The Soviet Communist world has by far the greatest military force, but the United States have the atom bomb; and now, we are told that they have a thousandfold more terrible manifestation of this awful power. When all is said and done it is my belief that the superiority in the atom bomb, if not indeed almost the monopoly of this frightful weapon, in American hands is the surest guarantee of world peace tonight. But for that we should not be talking about all these burning domestic questions that fill our minds, our mouths and our newspapers today. It is my earnest hope that we may find our way to some more exalted and august foundation for our safety than this grim and sombre balancing power of the bomb. We must not, however, cast away our only shield of safety unless we can find something better and surer and more likely to last. When I say 'we' I must not let you forget that 'we' means the United States and that it is their power which protects not only Britain but Europe. I really do not know why it is that when we were so far advanced into this new, mysterious region of atomic war, we should have fallen so completely behind in these last four years. When we are spending such enormous sums upon our army, navy and air force, it is very odd that we should not have been able to make the atomic bomb for ourselves by now. It seems to me one of the most extraordinary administrative lapses that have ever taken place. It is like the unwisdom of selling a hundred of our very few jet aircraft to the Argentine for a couple of million pounds or so. It would be incredible if it had not happened.

But I must not be drawn from the larger theme. I look back to 1945 when I was last in relation with Mr Stalin and his colleagues. I read to the House of Commons a year ago one of the telegrams I sent him then, and I am glad to repeat these words because they express what is in my heart today. Here is what I wrote in April 1945:

'There is not much comfort in looking into a future where you and the countries you dominate, plus the Communist parties in many other States are all drawn up on one side, and those who rally to the English-speaking nations and their associates or Dominions are on the other. It is quite obvious that their quarrel would tear the world to pieces and that all of us leading men on either side who had anything to do with that would be shamed before history. Even embarking on a long period of suspicions, of abuse and counter-abuse and of opposing policies would be a disaster hampering the great developments of world prosperity for the masses which are attainable only by our trinity.'

That was written nearly five years ago. Alas, it was only too true. All came to pass with horrible exactitude. But I do not blame Mr Bevin for that. All the talk at the 1945 General Election about Left speaking to Left has been proved to be foolish, but on the main issue he has done his best. I have not of course access to the secret information of the Government, nor am I fully informed about the attitude of the United States. Still I cannot help coming back to this idea of another talk with Soviet Russia upon the highest level. The idea appeals to me of a supreme effort to bridge the gulf between the two worlds, so that each can live their life, if not in friendship at least without the hatreds of the cold war. You must be careful to mark my words in these matters because I have not always been proved wrong. It is not easy to see how things could be worsened by a parley at the summit, if such a thing were possible. But that I cannot tell.

At least I feel that Christian men should not close the door upon any hope of finding a new foundation for the life of the self-tormented human race. What prizes lie before us; peace, food, happiness, leisure, wealth for the masses never known or dreamed of; the glorious advance into a period of rest and safety for all the hundreds of millions of homes where little children play by the fire and girls grow up in all their beauty, and young men march to fruitful labour in all their strength and valour. Let us not shut out the hope that the burden of fear and want may be lifted for a glorious era from the bruised and weary shoulders of mankind.

THE MOMENT OF DECISION

A PARTY POLITICAL BROADCAST
17 FEBRUARY 1950

Nearly three weeks have passed, my friends, since I last spoke to you all, and we now approach the end of this momentous election which all the world has watched with anxious eyes. The moment of decision draws near, and all can vote freely. They can vote with the certainty that the ballot is secret, and that if they live in council houses, or are on the long waiting-lists to get a house, or even if they are State employees, they cannot be called to account for the way in which they use their vote any more than they can by the landlord or private employer. This we owe to the respect still shown to our slowly built up British constitution and British way of life. Long may it be preserved.

All the same, everyone is accountable to his or her conscience, and everyone has an honourable responsibility to give their vote according to what they believe will be best for our country at this difficult moment in its history. We are in fact at a turning point in our fortunes, and the result of your action on Thursday may well shape the whole structure of our island life for long years to come. As Mr Gladstone said on a famous occasion: 'Think well, think wisely, think not for the moment, but for the years that are to come, before you make your choice.' Above all, do not abstain; do not stand out of the fight through indolence or hesitation or throw your votes away on candidates who have no chance of becoming Members of Parliament.

Since the election fight began, the issues at stake have become more serious. This is due to the statements about ultimate aims in Socialism by the Prime Minister and the Chancellor of the Exchequer, with all their high authority. Mr Attlee has made it clear that he does not regard the Socialist election manifesto—except, I presume, in the coming Parliament—as setting any limit to his aims. 'Socialism does not stop,' he said. 'It goes on. Nothing can stand between a nation and its goal—no one.' Here then is the proclamation by the Prime Minister of his resolve to create the complete Socialist State as soon as he can, by the nationalization of all the means of production, distribution and exchange—that is to say, the creation of a monster State monopoly, owning everything and employing everybody. Here is the goal towards which Mr Attlee seeks to lead the British nation. In fact, however, I doubt very much whether even a fifth part of our people are convinced Socialists, or that they realize the sacrifice of personal liberty, both economic and political, which must inexorably follow from the concentration of all industry and the direction of labour in the hands of the State.

The Chancellor of the Exchequer has not lagged behind his chief; for at Bristol on Saturday last he used words which reveal his mind and purpose. This is what he said, and when challenged he has not withdrawn, about sharing out the national resources: 'We have not shared them out equally yet. It takes a bit of time to do these things.' That is what he said. These are indeed grave words. They imply a levelling down of British society to a degree not hitherto presented by any responsible person. There would of course be the governmental and political and official class lifted, as in Soviet Russia, into a privileged position above the mass of the people whose lives they direct and plan. But on the basis of 'equal shares for all' there would it seems to me be little consideration for what Mr Arthur Deakin, the General Secretary of our largest trade union, has aptly called the 'differentials' in industry, and for all the infinite variations in the human contribution. This confession of the Chancellor of the Exchequer's inner purpose spells the death-blow, so long as he remains at the Treasury, to the great savings movement which at his request we have all supported. He is of course angry with me for giving world-wide publicity to his own imprudent and baleful words. His rival, Mr Aneurin Bevan, during this election has at least given us this reassurance: 'It is not part of our programme,' he said, 'this time that all private enterprise should be destroyed.' Thank you so much.

I do not mind what names they call me. The grave point for us all is what will happen to the credit and well-being of this country if men who hold the doctrines and pursue the aims of Mr Attlee and Sir Stafford Cripps and their associates were to be given a mandate at this critical juncture in our national affairs to carry Britain another long stage towards their disastrous goal. Nothing would be more likely to bring upon us the mass unemployment which all parties are pledged to do their utmost to avert, but which all parties know threatens us when Marshall Aid is withdrawn.

In taking another plunge into Socialism we should be absolutely alone in the free and civilized world. The United States, on whose bounty Mr Attlee's Government have been living, produces its vast wealth and high wages upon the capitalist, free enterprise system. Canada, that mighty land of the future, is anti-Socialist. New Zealand and Australia have at their recent elections cast Socialism off. Although they had only taken the dose in a modified form, they cast it off. In Europe there is not a single country outside the Iron Curtain, except in Scandinavia, where there is a Socialist government, and even in Scandinavia they have called a halt. The first declaration of the Socialist Prime Minister in Norway after winning the election was: 'No further nationalization for the next four years.' The British Socialist Government now ask us to go forward under their guidance alone. Alone we are to make this dire experiment. We are the only one to try it now. Mr Morrison says we are leading the world—but the world is not following. On the contrary, all free and civilized States are in recoil from Socialist rule and Socialist doctrines. One of the chief reasons which has turned the tide in Europe against Socialism is the utter failure of Socialist governments to make any effective resistance to Communist aggression and permeation.

Now you will have to say on Thursday whether we are to plunge deeper into the thickets and briars of Socialist regulations and controls, or whether, by a resolute effort, we shall rejoin our friends and comrade nations on the high-road of ordered freedom and progress. By one heave of her shoulders Britain can shake herself free. Do not miss this opportunity. It may not return. I am reminded of the tale of the prisoner in the Spanish dungeon. For years he longed to escape from his bondage. He tried this, he tried that—all in vain. One day he pushed the door of his cell—it was open. It had always been open. He walked out free into the broad light of day. You can do that now on this very Thursday, and what a throng there will be to welcome us back in the forefront of the nations who now regard us with bewilderment and pity, but for whom only a few years ago we kept the flag of freedom flying amid all the winds that blew.

The Socialists have tried to confuse the main issue by a number of false statements with which I must deal. The Conservatives, they say, would like there to be some unemployment because it would make men work harder. This is an unworthy accusation. Our policy is of course the exact reverse. Our aim is full employment and abundant food. We have no intention of abolishing food subsidies until and unless we are absolutely sure that the basic necessities of life are available at prices all the people can pay, down to the poorest in the land.

It is also said that the Conservative Government would cut the family allowances which the Labour Government has given you. But what is the truth? The Family Allowances Act was passed by the Conservative and National Liberal Government over which I had the honour to preside—the Caretakers, you remember, they were called—

I suppose because they took good care. The Family Allowances Act was passed in June 1945. We have no intention of altering family allowances except to improve them or extend them as part of some larger beneficial scheme.

All parties are equally desirous to maintain the social services and where necessary improve them. The question is whether Socialism or free enterprise would best be able to find the money to pay for them. This money has in the main to be found from the earnings of industry. If the Socialists go on nationalizing one great industry after another, turning their profits into losses or into rises in cost to the public, the revenue from taxation will shrink until the country can no longer pay and the social services will in consequence collapse. Only by liberating the creative forces in British industry can we earn the revenue to maintain that edifice of social security, of the building of which the Conservative and the Liberal Parties had the right to be proud before the Socialist Party ever figured in national affairs.

Our opponents are also telling old-age and ex-service pensioners, as they go from door to door: 'The Tories will cut your pensions.' But it is they who have already cut them by 3s. 9d. in the pound through the rise in prices, and the full results of devaluation, when they fall upon us, will cut them still more. We, on the other hand, by reviving national credit and the buying power of our money will restore to the pensioners and those who live on fixed incomes at least—I say, at least—what has been taken away. I have felt obliged to present to you these outstanding falsehoods because no matter how often they are contradicted the whispering campaign goes on.

The oppressive burden of taxation is the first problem to which a Conservative Government will turn its attention. Ours is the most over-taxed country in the world. Our people are prevented from putting forth their full effort. The initiative of industry is being stifled; the incentive of overtime and piece rates is diminished. Those who would like to save for marriage or old age are discouraged. We intend to revise and reduce the rates of both direct and indirect taxation, including especially PAYE and purchase tax. By reducing taxation we shall stimulate increased industrial activity, increased output, and in consequence we shall increase earnings. By this means we shall make good a large part of the revenue which would otherwise be lost by reducing taxation. The rest we shall save by purging lavish Government expenditure, by abolishing the wasteful system of bulk buying in food and materials, and by stopping the unbridled extravagance in Government departments and nationalized industries. During this election the Government have made it plain that they do not mean to make any reductions in taxation. In fact, Sir Stafford Cripps has threatened increases. He said in his broadcast that no substantial economies were possible. We are now spending at the rate of £3,300,000,000 a year and if the Labour Government cannot, or will not, even try to cut out waste, it is high time someone else comes in who will.

Another matter in which the Socialist Government have failed the British people is housing. The Minister of Health, after he had had a year to survey the situation, promised that every family in the land would have a separate home before this election. Everybody knows from the waiting-lists of their local councils that today we are further from that objective than we were five years ago. The Socialist Government are building at the rate of only 500 houses a day, whereas with the same building force under a Conservative Government before the war, 1,000 a day were built. We intend to use to the full all the resources of the building industry, building houses both to let and for sale, and make an intense effort to recover the leeway and all the time that has been lost, and all the energy that has been spent in bitter politics.

You must not blind yourselves to the fact that many grievous difficulties lie ahead. The election has been held in February instead of June in order to get it over before the consequences of devaluation came home to roost in higher prices, and before a Budget had to be produced which if it were honest would be unpopular. A new outlook, a more efficient administration and a new impulse with less faction, hate and spite will, I believe, be given to our people. And if so it may bring to them the power to realize many hopes and desires which are dear to their hearts.

I have now dealt with the great choice we have to make in our domestic affairs. I have once again contradicted the falsehoods by which we are assailed. But I cannot end my message and appeal to you (as you sit in your homes searching your hearts and minds, I hope, and wondering who is telling you the truth, I daresay, and what it is best to do for our dear land)—I cannot end my message without looking beyond our island coasts to the terrible and tremendous world that has grown up around us in this twentieth century of shock and strife. At Edinburgh the other night I said: 'I cannot help coming back to this idea of another talk with Soviet Russia upon the highest level. The idea appeals to me of a supreme effort to bridge the gulf between the two worlds so that each can live their lives, if not in friendship at least without the hatreds of the cold war. At least I feel,' I said, 'that Christian men and women should not close the door upon any hope of finding a new foundation for the life of the self-tormented human race.'

Mr Bevin, the Secretary of State for Foreign Affairs, dismissed all this by the scornful word 'stunt'. By this he only showed how far his mind dwells below the true level of events. Why should it be wrong for the British nation to think about these supreme questions of life and death, perhaps for the whole world, at a time when there is a general election? Is not that the one time of all others when they should think about them? What a reflection it would be upon our national dignity and moral elevation, and indeed upon the whole status of British democracy, if at this time of choice, this turning point in world history, we found nothing to talk about but material issues and nice calculations about personal gain or loss! What a humiliation it would be if proud Britain, in this fateful hour, were found completely absorbed in party and domestic strife! I am glad I put a stop to all that.

Even on the material basis a continuance of the present arms race can only cause increasing danger, increasing military expense and diminishing supplies to the homes. The only time when the people really have a chance to influence and in fact decide events is at a general election. Why should they be restricted to the vote-catching or vote-snatching game? Why should they be told that it is a 'stunt' or 'soap-box diplomacy' to speak to them of the great world issues upon which our survival and salvation may well depend?

Mr Bevin says that everything must be reserved to the United Nations. We all support the great ideal of world government; but the United Nations cannot function while it is rent asunder by the conflicting forces of the two worlds which are ranged against each other. It is only by the agreement of the greatest Powers that security can be given to ordinary folk against an annihilating war with atomic or hydrogen bombs or bacteriological horrors. I cannot find it in my heart and conscience to close the door upon that hope. By its fruition alone can the United Nations discharge their supreme function.

My friends, I ask for a strong majority, for one capable of giving both guidance and design and securing the necessary time to make great purposes effective. We do not seek the power to enable one party to ride rough-shod over the other, we do not seek the power in order that special interests or classes should have privileges or unearned increment and profit. This will be the supreme opportunity for the Conservative and National Liberal Parties to prove that they stand high above the level of mere sectional appetites. Should we become responsible we shall govern on behalf of the entire British people no matter to what party or class or part of the country they belong. We shall respect the sentiments of minorities in what is just and fair no matter whether they vote for or against us. This is the true essence of democracy. It is only by inspiring the nation with unity and common purpose and by taking without fear or favour the necessary measures to restore our solvency and independence that we shall overcome the dangers and solve the problems that confront us.

Of course, I am—as I am reminded—an old man. It is true that all the day-dreams of my youth have been accomplished. I have no personal advantage to gain by undertaking once more the hard and grim duty of leading Britain and her Empire through and out of her new and formidable crisis. But while God gives me the strength, and the people show me their good will, it is my duty to try, and try I will. I do not know tonight the full extent of the harm which has been done to our finances, to our defences and to our standing in the world. I am grieved at what I see and hear but it may well be there are worse facts, not made public, and perhaps not even understood by our present rulers. Therefore we are not going to promise you smooth and easy times. What we promise is, that, laying aside every impediment, we will faithfully and resolutely carry forward the policy we have proclaimed, we will do our best for all, and build on a sure foundation the structures of British greatness and world peace. Goodnight to you all. Think—and act!

DEBATE ON THE ADDRESS

A SPEECH TO THE HOUSE OF COMMONS
7 MARCH 1950

---

21 *February—Mr Edgar Sanders, together with other employees of the Standard Electric Company in Hungary, charged with espionage and sentenced to thirteen years' imprisonment.*
23 *February—General Election.*
   Results:

	Seats	Votes
Labour	315	13,331,682
Conservatives	296	12,415,806
Liberals	10	2,679,712
Irish Nationalists	2	65,211

 6 *March—New Parliament opens.*
   Government White Paper 'Statement on Defence for 1950' provides for defence budget of £786,820,000.

[*7 March* 1950

Order read for resuming Adjourned Debate on Question [6 *March*]:
   '*That an humble Address be presented to His Majesty, as follows*:
   Most Gracious Sovereign,
   We, Your Majesty's most dutiful and loyal subjects, the Commons of the United Kingdom of Great Britain and Northern Ireland, in Parliament assembled, beg leave to offer our humble thanks to Your Majesty for the Gracious Speech which Your Majesty has addressed to both Houses of Parliament.'—[*Mr Dye.*]
   Question again proposed.

I must frankly confess, as I look around, that I like the appearance of these Benches better than what we had to look at during the last 4½ years. It is certainly refreshing to feel, at any rate, that this is a Parliament where half the nation will not be able to ride rough-shod over the other half, or to sweep away in a Session what has been carefully and skilfully constructed by generations of thought, toil and thrift. I do not see the Attorney-General in his place, but no one will be able to boast 'We are the masters now'. On the contrary, if it be not presumptuous for me to say so, we are equals. So far as the Conservative and Socialist parties are concerned, we seem to have reached in the electoral field that position—if I may listen to the echoes of the election—of equal shares for both. I will not say equal shares for all, for we certainly have not achieved even fair shares for all.

Here, I must guard myself carefully against any suggestion of uttering what are called blandishments to the nine representatives of the Liberal Party, most of whom we see in their places under the guidance so generously provided by the Principality of Wales. I do not often quote from *The Times*, but I must say that I found myself in some agreement with their leading article of 27 February, that the Liberal leaders who are here, and others out of doors, have performed 'a national disservice'—these are not my words; I am only quoting, having read them with some relish in *The Times*—'by the irresponsible spattering of the electoral map with hundreds of candidatures for which there was never the remotest chance of substantial support, but which might just deprive the Members elected of certainty that they represented the majority of their constituents. The legislature, by requiring the £150 deposit, has expressed its disapproval of frivolous candidature; but it was never foreseen that a great and historic party would use its considerable financial resources to evade the spirit of the rule.' The object of the Liberal leaders was nakedly stated by Lord Samuel in his broadcast of 7 February, when he said:

'It may be that no party will have a working majority in the new House of Commons. In such an event the Liberals might be called upon to form a Government.'

It is quite true that one of the objectives mentioned by Lord Samuel has been gained. No party has a working majority. A stalemate or deadlock has undoubtedly been produced in the effective government of the country and there is the certainty of a prolonged electioneering atmosphere at a time when the situations both at home and abroad are grave and crucial.

Lord Samuel's second objective—the formation of a Liberal Government—still remains in a sphere so speculative as to be outside even the bounds of Lloyd's insurance. It has, perhaps, been too readily assumed that the nine gentlemen below the Gangway on this side will have in this Parliament a position of exceptional and undue influence. I hope that the House of Commons is not going to allow itself to be dominated or let its fate and future be decided by any small body of hon Members. We do not wish to emulate some foreign Parliaments where small parliamentary parties are able, by putting themselves and their favours in the balance, to sway the course of considerable events. Indeed, it seems to me that this would be an undignified attitude for the Mother of Parliaments, especially in a time so serious as this.

I have lived nearly all my life in the House of Commons and I believe it to be the enduring guarantee of British liberties and democratic progress. I do not think we ought to assume that this new House of Commons, elected by the greatest vote ever recorded in our history, and with earnestness and heart-searching by tens of millions of our people, should fall into petty bargaining almost before it had breathed. The House of Commons is founded on the party system, and, in the main, very much in preponderance upon the two-party system. But, personally, I have the feeling—as I ventured to say the other day when offering you, sir, my congratulations on your election as Speaker— that this assembly, fresh from contact with the people, is a more potent body than the mere numerical aggregate of its parties suggests, and I hope that this feeling will play its full part in our Debate, whether its life is destined to be long or short.

Whatever view we may take of particularist manoeuvres to frustrate the will of democracy as expressed through majorities, and thus creating the present grave embarrassment to the country, we must not be blind to the anomaly which has brought to this House of Commons 186 representatives who are returned only by a minority of those who voted in their constituencies. Nor can we, to whatever party we belong, overlook the constitutional injustice done to 2,600,000 voters who, voting upon a strong tradition, have been able to return only nine Members to Parliament. My experience of life, becoming a long one, has led me to the belief that ill-conduct often results from ill-treatment. I do not think this is a matter which we can brush aside or allow to lie unheeded.

I therefore make the following proposal to His Majesty's Government—namely, that we should set up a Select Committee to inquire into the whole question of electoral reform. A Select Committee of the House of Commons would not be likely to lose its way amid the endless arguments and details with which this question bristles. I am well aware that it has several times been examined before, but we have never examined it in the light of a practical situation of major importance such as has now been brought about. I believe a House of Commons Committee would take a practical view and give us advice which would be a guide to future Governments in this Parliament or in another Parliament. As to the composition of the Committee, I would suggest that it should be based not on the numbers of the Members here, but upon the numbers of votes recorded by the electorate for the three parties which are represented in the House, as, otherwise, I do not see how the Liberals would obtain any representation at all on a matter which is certainly of keen and special interest to them.

I ask the Government—I ask the right hon Gentleman the Lord President who, I understand, is going to follow me—in the course of this Debate to say whether they will allow such a Committee to be set up or not. We have certainly reached a parliamentary deadlock or stalemate differing in its character from any in living experience. It is not true that the Liberal Party here or, what is of far more importance, the Liberal Party in the country, can, by simply throwing its weight on to one side or the other determine the issue. Any step that was taken as a mere bargain or deal might not only be difficult to implement, but might well produce unfavourable reactions for those concerned. The nation might deeply resent the feeling that its fortunes had been bartered about without regard to principle by a handful of politicians, no matter what party they come from, and that its vital interests were but a piece in a jig-saw puzzle. In such a situation candour, sincerity, simplicity, firm adherence to well-known and publicly asserted principles, combined with a dominating regard for national rather than party interests, will be found to be the surest guides.

We have, of course, on this side of the House, to discharge our duties as a Parliamentary Opposition, and the period before us will be very difficult. Moreover, it is by no means certain that another election, held in a few months under conditions which no one can foresee and arising from occasions which perhaps no one can select, would remove the conditions of deadlock which now prevail. I am one of the very few who lived in high office through the year 1910. I was Home Secretary then—[*Interruption*]—well it is a very important office and very well discharged by its present occupant.

There was an election in January 1910, and another election in December. There was virtually no difference between the two results. The people remembered how they had voted last time and they meant to vote the same way again. Unless some entirely new facts can be found to place before the people there is no certainty that the electors will alter their opinion, however much we might plead with them in the interval covered by the compass of a year. There will, therefore, be an indefinite period of uncertainty, extremely detrimental to our country at this critical time. Every action of the Government will be taken, no doubt, in regard to the impending election. We all have to be careful of every word we say or fact we cite.

THE LORD PRESIDENT OF THE COUNCIL [MR HERBERT MORRISON]: You especially.

MR CHURCHILL: I thought the Chancellor of the Exchequer interrupted.

THE CHANCELLOR OF THE EXCHEQUER [SIR STAFFORD CRIPPS] *indicated dissent.*

MR CHURCHILL: I do not think I am the only one who needs to be careful.

Every word we say may be pounced upon and made the peg for some monstrous misrepresentations—[HON MEMBERS: 'Hear, hear.'] I am quite willing to carry the whole House with me on that. The reasoned Amendment which was moved to the Health and Insurance Bill which we originated in the Government over which I presided, and which I did my utmost to help forward, was recently misrepresented to the electors as Tory hostility to the principle of the Measure. Certainly it will be very difficult to find good solutions in the national interest for the grievous, dark and difficult problems which press upon us. Yet there never was a time when good solutions and drastic remedies in our financial and economic life were more needed and more overdue. We must do the best we can.

I am coming now to the text of the Gracious Speech to which we listened yesterday. A friend of mine has suggested that it might have been stated more shortly. This was his suggestion: 'My Lords and Members of the House of Commons: My Government will not introduce legislation in fulfilment of their election programme because the only Mandate they have received from the country is not to do it.' There is however one paragraph in the Gracious Speech about the need for a renewed effort to expand the production of food from our own soil, which will, I am sure, be welcomed on all sides. It conforms very closely to the statements contained in our Agricultural Charter and in the Conservative election manifesto. And I said myself, at Luton Hoo in June 1948:

'Anyone can see that the vigorous production of food on the largest possible scale in this island holds the first place. Let us be under no error in this matter. The prosperity of agriculture and food production depends on larger supplies of labour, and to have the labour we must have the rural houses in which they can dwell and rear their families. These the Socialists have refused. It also depends upon a full supply of the agricultural machinery which the Government has so recklessly exported to foreign countries. This was indeed devouring the seed-corn. In our Agricultural Charter, published this morning, we have declared that the proper level of agricultural production in this country must be half as much again as pre-war. This is our aim.'

I see I also said at Luton Hoo:

'The State is entitled to give guidance and, if necessary, to see this is enforced, to ensure that farmers and landowners do not flout the rules of good husbandry and good estate management.'

[HON MEMBERS: 'Hear, hear.'] I thought you would like that. This speech was at the time dismissed by the Prime Minister somewhat curtly as 'Luton Hooey'.

Well, we have a more helpful response in the Gracious Speech. I assume of course that it is not intended to use compulsory powers to nationalize marginal land, or to nationalize water supplies in rural areas, unless it is proved to the satisfaction of the House as a whole, that no other method is available in certain exceptional cases. If this be so, I see no reason why this important paragraph, which I admit was not contained in my abridged edition of the Gracious Speech, should not provide some common ground between us during these next few months. I cannot leave this agricultural topic without referring to the Bill announced in the Gracious Speech for the placing and maintaining of cattle grids on the highways. I see the Patronage Secretary is in his place. We are always glad to see him in his place. Surely he should study with special attention in times like these any measure to keep the herd from straying.

Much was said upon the hustings about mass unemployment. There is no real difference between the parties on this subject. All the leading men on both sides agreed to the White Paper laid before Parliament in 1944 by the Government over which I presided. We adhere to that Paper, though happily the conditions with which it was intended to deal have not yet arisen. Moreover, the principal Ministers concerned have frankly told us that there would have been between 1,500,000 and 2,000,000 unemployed but for the American aid which we have been receiving. That was an altogether unwonted slip on their part, I am sure, for which I must say they have had to endure a good deal of punishment in the discussions which have taken place. But we have not challenged them upon that point. There is, therefore, a broad measure of general agreement between us, although of course Socialist Ministers naturally claim all the credit, past, present and prospective, for everything good that has been done in this field.

There is, however, another aspect which the House should bear in mind, especially as it presents itself as an addition to the statements about the help of the American subsidies to which I have already referred. I state these points simply as facts, but serious facts. If we compare the present situation with that under the Chamberlain Government in 1939, the year before the war, there are four important differences on the point I am making. There are many other differences, but these four are relevant to this problem of employment or unemployment.

First, there are 750,000 more national and local government officials than existed then. Secondly, there are 250,000 more men in the Armed Forces—I do not say whether rightly or wrongly; I merely mention it. Thirdly, about 400,000 young people are withheld from the labour market by the extension of the school age. I am not arguing this afternoon whether that is good or bad, though personally I am not greatly attracted by overcrowded schools and underpaid teachers. However, that makes a total of 1,400,000. Fourthly, it has been estimated that there are 500,000 people employed in making unrequited exports, in the main to India and Egypt—that is to say, exports in return for which nothing comes back into this island from this heavy expenditure of our life energy expressed in sweat and skill. Again I do not attempt to argue this afternoon the merits of the so-called sterling balances or repayment of unfair British wartime debts as they are in fact, though I should be quite prepared to do so on a suitable occasion.

Nor do I say that the Government are wrong not to make a violent change in this method of preventing further unemployment in the circumstances that prevail. Nevertheless we should not shut our eyes to the realities. We should not go on without being conscious of the fact that we are getting nothing back in return. Trade is exchange, or, at the simplest, barter. It would be much better, for instance, if some of this work could find its reward in the spread of goods to the public convenience at home, or in their sale to other countries in the sterling area, which would repay us to some extent in nourishing imports for this immense outward stream of valuable commodities.

There are the four differences. Finally, there are the 350,000 persons who are actually unemployed at the moment, many of whom no doubt are changing from one job to another. This makes a total of 2,250,000 persons altogether not now employed in production industry, comparable with the 1,100,000 unemployed at the time of the Chamberlain Government in the year before the war. [*Laughter.*] The hon Member for Sparkbrook (Mr Shurmer) is not a new Member; he should not show himself so conspicuously needing Parliamentary education as he does this afternoon. This is, of course, without taking into consideration at all the fruits of the American subsidies. I am quite sure that there is now more real unemployment in the sense of people not being employed in requited or productive work than in the years immediately before the war—not that I in any way underrate the valuable services rendered by those very numerous categories which I have mentioned. I think the party opposite might address their minds to this topic because it plays an important part in the understanding of our affairs.

There is another whole series of difficult questions connected with the Ministry of Food. The discussions on food subsidies and rationing are, of course, hampered by the fact that an election cannot be far off, and we may, no doubt, be again exposed to the slander that the Conservative Party wish to make food dear so that the rich can live in luxury while the wage earners are impelled by 'empty bellies', to quote the official document of the party opposite, to work harder.

I see that experienced politician the Lord President of the Council opposite me; he is, I believe, the supreme author of the manifesto in which this incident was mentioned, and it does astonish me. He and his friends must have very strange opinions about their fellow countrymen if they think that 12,500,000 of them would support such a cruel and wicked policy as that. Where they go wrong is that they assume that the mass of the people are taken in by arguments of manifest unfairness and untruth. But for that there would not be this thoughtful, pensive air upon the Government Front Bench. No doubt, every word spoken in our Debates on food subsidies and other aspects of the food problems will be liable to be wrested from its context, carefully scanned and pulled out if there is anything worth having in it, in order to provide material for electioneering of this disreputable kind.

Our policy is, in fact, aimed at full and better meals for the nation and we are quite sure that the more food manual workers can get to eat the better will be our output. I do not think we should be deterred from discussing these grave problems by the peculiar and, I admit, unpleasant conditions which prevail in this precariously balanced Parliament. I do not hesitate to say that it is foolish to prevent production through oppressive taxation by paying food subsidies to enormous numbers of people who do not need them, and that it is our duty to search for more sensible solutions of the problem, while maintaining a basic standard for all. I was glad to read the statement of the new Minister of Food*—I do not think he is in his place—that he would think in terms of food and not of calories. This seemed to me the most helpful contribution we have had on this subject from the Minister of Food so far. We wish the right hon Gentleman success in the arduous office which he has undertaken.

The food question is, however, not one which can be judged apart from the state of our national finances. The need to reduce the heavy burden of taxation and arrest the continued fall in the purchasing power

* Mr Webb succeeded Mr Strachey as Food Minister immediately after the election.

of wages, pensions and allowances of all kinds is urgent and, as we believe, vital. The House was, I am sure, impressed with the figures given yesterday by my right hon Friend the Member for Warwick and Leamington (Mr Eden) about the ever-increasing drain of the sterling balances upon us. On the top of all this comes devaluation, and I would be most grateful to the Chancellor of the Exchequer if he could attend just to this one point; I know he has to prompt his colleague, for it would be lamentable if a different theme were developed; devaluation means that British labour has to work one-third longer hours to earn the same quantity of dollar imports as before. It is a terrible fact—one-third longer hours and what you get back is no more than it was before. You call yourselves the Labour Party, and yet it does not even rouse you and strike a note in your breasts. It is a shocking and odious thing that we should so handle our affairs as to have to work twelve hours instead of eight to obtain the same return.

There is also the danger that further devaluation may become necessary. From this crowded island our life blood is draining away in an ever more copious flow without compensating nourishment. That is my very deep fear. We are a hard-pressed blood-donor whose general health has already been weakened by his war service. This deadly process is to some extent, no doubt, veiled by the American subsidies under Marshall Aid, but they are coming to an end. Indeed, they may soon be offset by the obligation to repay the first £1,000,000,000 loan so blithely dispersed as soon as it was received.

The restoration of the £ sterling at home and abroad and the re-establishment of confidence and credit will not take place as long as there is a Government in office which, even though held in check in this Parliament by lack of voting strength, is known to be animated by bitter hostility to accumulated wealth and is the declared enemy of the capitalist system to which all the rest of the free democracies of the world outside Scandinavia, and with some exceptions there, constantly affirm their adherence on a basis of universal suffrage.

It would be vain to touch in the Debate upon the vast sphere of finance and economics. I ask that an opportunity for a full Debate upon it may be accorded to us in the next fortnight or so.

MR H. MORRISON *indicated dissent*.

MR CHURCHILL: It will take more than the oscillation of the Lord President's head in this Parliament necessarily to convince us that our desires must be put aside; I ask for a full Debate. So much has been concealed from us and distorted by the speeches of the Ministers concerned during and before the election that we really do not know where we are. [*Laughter.*] The hon Member opposite should not think it is funny or be delighted that half the House of Commons has not been properly informed. I am sure he is no better informed than we are.

I ask that the true facts should be laid before the House as soon as possible. If they are good we shall rejoice. If they are bad we must all face them, if not together at any rate at the same time. I find encouragement from the fact that the Government evidently wish to continue in office. There is something real about that. It gives one a certain assurance that the prospects in the next few months are not too bad. I trust my intuition has not misled me on this point. The Government would, I am sure, be well advised in the interests of the country as well as in their own interest, which they are not prone to overlook, to make a full and candid statement before we separate for Easter.

We have certain supply days at our disposal if no facilities are given. We shall expect a statement from the Chancellor of the Exchequer. If he refuses to give one we shall certainly not hesitate to draw any inference we choose, but we are quite sure that if he had a favourable statement to make he would be the first to put it out either in the House or over the broadcast. I see the Prime Minister arriving; he has been away on duty and I should like to put him in touch. I was asking for a Debate on the financial situation so that we may have a general statement made on the position before we separate for the Easter Recess. We shall try to press that by every means open to us, which are more numerous than they were.

We have thought it our duty, in accordance with our political convictions, and those of the constituents who returned us here, to place two Amendments to the Address upon the Order Paper.

[*But humbly regret that the Gracious Speech contains no reference to the future of the Iron and Steel Industry and that in a time of rising world competition this vital industry will be kept in a state of anxiety and suspense.*]

[*But humbly regret that the Gracious Speech makes no reference to the grievous and growing distress in town and country arising out of the continuing decline in the number of new houses built each year and contains no indication that the Government intend to take more effective measures to deal with the situation.*]

The first deals with the nationalization of iron and steel. Owing to the action of the House of Lords under the now mutilated Parliament Act, the people were given the right to say whether they wanted this Measure or not. The electors, by a large majority in votes, have pronounced against it, but it will come into action automatically, perhaps in the lifetime of this Parliament, unless parliamentary action is taken either to repeal the measure, or, at least, to alter the date, so that the electors will certainly have a further chance of affirming their repudiation of it.

It is obvious that the Government have not the power to nationalize cement, sugar, chemicals, or to mutualize industrial assurance. But steel is different. It happens unless it is stopped. Had we obtained a majority we should have repealed the Act; and that is, of course, our policy. Nevertheless, we should be willing not to press our Amendment to a Division if the Government will give the assurance that the position of the steel industry will not be worsened because of the present deadlock, or by its indefinite prolongation. We ask for a declaration that the vesting date shall be not less than nine months after the next General Election, and that all necessary measures shall be taken to that end.

I think it is a very modest demand. There was an enormous vote of the people against this measure, and with a Parliament which admittedly has no right to bring it into law—[HON MEMBERS: 'Oh.'] No right. I thought it was understood that that was not asserted. So I ask for something which would put us into exactly the same relation, after another Dissolution, to the time factor as we were on the last occasion. We could not make a more reasonable request than that.

This will have the double advantage of making sure that the people are duly consulted before their decision is reversed, and that the industry will be given a breathing space, of probably at least a year, to get on with their vital work. If we can receive those assurances today it would, I think, be convenient to the House as a whole. If not, we feel ourselves bound by our convictions, and by the mandate we have received from the electors, to vote for the Amendment in our full strength.

We also feel compelled to invite the House to express itself upon the lamentable state of our housing. No material issue affecting the daily lives of the people has stirred them more than the housing shortage, which strikes at the very root of family life. No one underrates the many difficulties which constitute the housing problem at the present moment, and we no doubt shall hear more about them in due course from the Minister who bears a direct and peculiar responsibility for the failure.

I will only venture to mention a suggestion—a constructive suggestion—which I made to my colleagues in our wartime Government, and which seems to me still to have relevance. It occured to me as a member of the bricklayers' trade union, of which I still hold a membership card signed by Mr George Hicks, whom we miss as the former Member for Woolwich, although he has had adequate replacement.

The bricklayer or builder's operative is always asking himself, 'What happens when this job is done?' He is really like a man on a raft in mid-ocean who has to burn a bit of his raft every day to cook his dinner. With all this vast mass of building that is needed, it ought to be possible to give the building operatives, bricklayers and others, effective security. It seemed to me that this was so in 1944, and I, therefore, made the following proposal to my colleagues in what was called a 'directive':

'The whole of the emergency housing scheme must be viewed in relation to a ten years' plan for the steady full-time employment of a considerably enlarged building trade for permanent houses. Instead of a fever for three or four years and then a falling off, the building trade should have a broad, steady flow giving all its members a good assurance of employment, and thus encouraging piece-work.'

I venture to keep that particular suggestion alive at the present time, although it is only one small contribution to a mass of improvements which could be made in the whole process of our winning houses for our people to live in.

The two sides of the House face each other deeply divided by ideological differences. I have lived through many of the fierce quarrels of the past, about Irish Home Rule, about church or chapel, about free trade and protection, which all seemed to be very important at the time. They were, however, none of them, fundamental to our whole system of life and society. Those who believe in the creation of a Socialist State controlling all the means of production, distribution and exchange, and are working towards such a goal, are separated from those who seek to exalt the individual and allow freedom of enterprise under well-known laws and safeguards—they are separated by a wider and deeper gulf than I have ever seen before in our island.

This was, in my view, the moral and intellectual issue which was at stake in the election, and which a substantial Socialist majority, if obtained, would in four or five years have carried, in all probability, to irrevocable depths. It is a significant and serious fact which should not escape the attention of thoughtful men that the differences which separate us have become more pronounced by the voting, because each of the main parties has very often increased its strength in those very parts of the country where it was already the stronger. We shall certainly not survive by splitting into two nations. Yet that is the road we are travelling now, and there is no sign of our reaching or even approaching our journey's end.

The basic fact before us is that the electors by a majority of

1,750,000 have voted against the advance to a Socialist State, and, in particular, against the nationalization of steel and other industries which were threatened. The Government, therefore, have no mandate, as is recognized in the Gracious Speech, to proceed in this Parliament with their main policy. The Prime Minister is the only Socialist Prime Minister in the English-speaking world—the only one; and he has behind him a majority of only seven—or it soon may be only six. Nevertheless, he continues not only to persevere upon his path, but to state the differences which separate him and his followers from the rest of us all over the world in the most extreme terms.

The right hon gentleman complained during the election that I quoted his interview with an American journalist, which he had not disavowed for some time after it was published and which was much commented on. In fact I saw only the comments and then searched for the actual text. I will meet the right hon Gentleman. I promise him that I will quote that interview no more. I do not need to quote it any more because in his letter to his candidate at Moss Side he has proclaimed his faith and policy beyond the slightest doubt and in the most sweeping terms. He wrote on 2 March:

'Labour stands for the policy of equal shares, and for the ordered and progressive realization of a society based on social justice.'

The last part covers both sides of the House. But this 'equal shares' declaration goes even further than the speeches of the Chancellor of the Exchequer in his election campaign at Bristol, when he spoke of 'fair shares for all' being only a preliminary step to 'equal shares for all'. It is at least an advantage that the differences between us should be stated so plainly, because there can be no excuse for anyone making a mistake about them afterwards.

The *Tribune*, which is believed to express the views of the Minister of Health, fully supports the Prime Minister's pronouncement. I quote from its latest issue of 3 March:

'It is the faith of Socialism carried across this land with a new crusading zeal which can win the second election in 1950. And once that fact is securely grasped, how futile becomes the talk of compromise and manoeuvre in the House of Commons, which must continue until the new appeal to the country takes place.'

The Prime Minister has accepted the burden of government in virtue of his majority of seven; and no one doubts that it was his right and his duty to do so. But we on this side feel that he, and those whom he leads or with whom he goes, have inflicted deep injury upon our country in years when our task of recovery was heavy enough, and we are sure that the course he now proclaims has only to be followed far enough to lead to our economic ruin, and to our inability to maintain 50,000,000 people in this island, still less to maintain them on their present standards of living, such as they are. We are therefore bound to confront him and those who follow him with our united and resolute resistance, and we believe that this is the first duty which we owe to our country, to the British Commonwealth of Nations, to Western Europe and to the English-speaking world.

DEFENCE

A SPEECH TO THE HOUSE OF COMMONS
16 MARCH 1950

---

9 March—Ministry of Labour discontinue Control of Engagements Order. The Australian Minister for External Affairs, Mr Spender, calls for closer co-operation between the countries of the British Commonwealth and proposes that frequent meetings should become a permanent feature between the Ministers of the countries concerned.

[16 March 1950

No one will accuse the Minister of Defence of plunging the House into vehement controversy by the speech he has just made. He seems to have been guided throughout by a strong spirit of self-restraint and of moderation of statement rendered even more remarkable by the regular forms of official verbiage in which it was so happily expressed. So far as adding to the knowledge of the House upon this vast and grave topic, I can only say that I found his remarks about the atomic bomb a model of non-informatory eloquence. This is what the Minister told us about the atomic bomb, which is after all, a topic of some lively interest: 'The chiefs of staff have given full weight to this new factor.' There we may leave it for the moment. Let us hope it will be content with that position.

As the House knows, I, and some of my colleagues, at the Government's invitation, have had several conferences with the Prime Minister and Service Ministers in the last Parliament at which disclosures of matters not known to the House, or not fully known, were made. In my published correspondence with the Prime Minister I made the following stipulation:

'In order that the Opposition should not be embarrassed in Defence Debates, I must ask you, as I did Mr Baldwin in 1936, that we should be free to use in public any information of which we are already possessed, with due regard to the national interest and safety.' The Prime Minister agreed to that. Last year, we moved a reasoned Amendment on defence and we had thought of repeating it in the same terms this year.

I was not myself particularly anxious to have a Division on this issue at this time, if it could be avoided. I found it, however, impossible to commit myself and my colleagues even tacitly to the word 'approve' which was announced to be a part of the Motion to approve the White Paper on Defence which is now before us. Such a step on our part might well be regarded hereafter, in view of the conferences that have taken place, as to some extent committing us to sharing, albeit in-directly, in the Government's responsibility. While recognizing the efforts which have been made we could not take any responsibility for the present state of affairs in the Armed Forces. I am, therefore, obliged to the Prime Minister for being willing to substitute for the word 'approve' the words 'take note of' in the Government's Motion. I am sure that, in all the circumstances that prevail, this is a right decision on his part. Therefore there is no need to divide the House tonight.

I must now refer briefly to the disagreeable topic of the recent Ministerial appointments in the military sphere. I do not wish to dwell upon them unduly, but they cannot be omitted from any review of our defence position. I said in December 1948 in this House:

'We all understand the difficulties of a party leader in these times when he has not only to conduct government but to preserve general good feeling among all his supporters. In these appointments I must say it seemed to me that the Prime Minister put party first, party second and party third. . . . I thought the appointment of the present Secretary of War was surprising. . . . I believe that the Army would be better entrusted to men who are not engaged in the most bitter strife of politics. Nor should the War Office be regarded as a receptacle for Ministerial failures.'

MR SHINWELL: Would the right hon Gentleman prefer to appoint his son-in-law to a post?

MR CHURCHILL: I was not aware that he had been appointed to a high military post.

THE PARLIAMENTARY SECRETARY TO THE ADMIRALTY [MR JAMES CALLAGHAN]: Anyway, the right hon Gentleman is the biggest party politician there is.

MR CHURCHILL: I am merely reading what I said a year and a quarter ago. No doubt it has stung the right hon Gentleman, but it is really not so much an attack upon him as a criticism of the method of these appointments. We now have a different situation. We have a new Parliament. We have other personalities, yet I cannot feel that my complaint of December 1948 is not as valid and true as when I uttered it. Indeed, it seems to have had renewed confirmation. Under the Atlantic Pact we have much military business to do with the United States and other Powers, and I cannot feel that that business, or other aspects of our military organization, will be facilitated by the Prime Minister's choice.

Coming to a more general question, it seems to me that more information should be given to the House about all the three Services. The guiding rule should be to tell Parliament everything that is certainly and obviously known to those foreign governments with whom we do not have confidential relationships in defence matters. That is a good working guide. It is not right, for instance, that the House of Commons should be so much worse informed about our defences than the Soviet Government. What is well known abroad should also, in most cases, be imparted to the House of Commons which, after all, has the responsibility of providing the money now required on an unprecedented scale in time of peace.

I am sure it would be a great advantage if we could have a Debate in secret session on defence. We might then go into the atomic bomb question and see whether more information can be elicited than that 'the chiefs of staff have given full weight to this new factor'. I do not mean that the Government should impart all their secret information to the House. Even if no further disclosure of military secrets were made, it would be much easier to discuss the whole question of defence without having every word reported and read all over the world.

It is sometimes one's duty to say things in public which give rise to anxiety and alarm. This may give satisfaction in some foreign countries and cause distress and want of confidence in us in others. I had to do this on several occasions before the late war when I was dealing with a Government and with Ministers at least as capable as those with whom we are now concerned.

MR SHINWELL: Does the right hon Gentleman's observation apply to the late Sir Thomas Inskip?

MR CHURCHILL: Yes, sir. I certainly think he had a far greater command of the large sphere of thought and action over which he presided as Minister for the Co-ordination of Defence than—since the right hon Gentleman puts the point—the right hon Gentleman himself is ever likely to acquire. I carefully refrain from pressing the points against the right hon Gentleman because, although he has many faults, I still believe his heart is in the right place. But he should not show himself so frightfully sensitive. We are only at the beginning of an ordeal which will be prolonged during this Parliament whatever duration it may be, and we earnestly trust the right hon Gentleman will reserve some of his retorts and indignation for later phases in the criticism he will have to undergo. I was on the question of the importance of having a Debate on defence in secret Session. I think it would be an advantage to have one in the next few months. I have never yet, in my experience, seen a secret Session from which the Government of the day did not derive advantages. I think there are a good many points which ought to be rammed home with more force than one would like to do on these topics in public hearing.

I therefore ask the Prime Minister to consider whether, in view of the balance of parties in the House and in view of the fact that the new House of Commons has been purged by the electors of certain untrustworthy elements, and that we are all united in our opposition to Communism, we should not have the advantage of the candour and freedom of speech together with any fuller information possible in a Session at which only the Members of both Houses can be present. If this request were refused one would have to consider whether more would not have to be said in public upon matters already known to foreign governments in order that our own people should be more truly informed. This afternoon, however, I shall say nothing that is not public knowledge to the newspapers in this or other countries, or that I do not derive from my own knowledge and do not mention on my own responsibility.

I will begin with the Army. In the forefront of Army policy comes the question of National Service. The Labour Government have enforced conscription in time of peace. Everyone is liable to serve in the Armed Forces for eighteen months. We could not approve industrial conscription in peacetime, and I am very glad that it has been withdrawn, but we have felt it our duty to support, and we still support, the Government in maintaining the principle of compulsory National Service. It would have been very easy for us to gain popularity and votes at the recent election by denouncing it, as did the Liberal Party, but we felt bound to help the Government carry this burden. We think National Service is necessary not only to maintain the structure of the Army but to preserve peace. If Britain were to repudiate National Service at this time, as the Liberals propose, it would mean, in my opinion, the downfall of the whole defensive structure embodied in the Brussels Treaty and in the Atlantic Pact, and now being very slowly brought into being. We therefore made our position clear during the last Parliament, and we adhere to it now.

I think we were somewhat ungratefully treated on this subject in the election. I was surprised to learn that an active whispering campaign was on foot, especially in garrisons abroad, in Germany and the Mediterranean fortresses, in Singapore and Hong Kong, that the length of compulsory service would be increased if the Conservatives were returned to power. [HON MEMBERS: 'We never heard of it.'] We received numerous communications of that character. The troops were upset by the suggestion that they would be kept abroad for a longer time. We contradicted this false rumour as best we could, but it only shows how difficult it is to develop a true and wise national policy in a period when prolonged and vicious electioneering is the order of the day.

I still adhere to what I said last year:

'I am strongly of the belief that if the great policy and decision of national military service had been used properly and a smaller number called up for a longer time, great economies might have been made and might still be made in the Military Services.'

The right hon Gentleman in one of his references did not challenge that. He said there were other considerations. Of course, that statement in no way affected men who were already serving, and I was much shocked to hear, for instance, that widespread rumour was being put about at Malta and everywhere that if the Conservatives were returned the men would all have their service increased.

THE PRIME MINISTER: The right hon Gentleman is constantly talking about whispering campaigns. There was the ridiculous one which he suggested had been put about that he was dead. No one has heard of these whispering campaigns except the right hon Gentleman. [HON MEMBERS: 'Oh.'] Perhaps the hon Members on the second Opposition bench will allow me to address their Leader. Unless the right hon Gentleman can give us some evidence of where these whispering campaigns came from, he should not make charges of this kind. No one here has heard of any of these reports. I am unaware that anyone out in Malta has. It is extraordinary to have these constant suggestions by the right hon Gentleman about these whispering campaigns being put about.

MR CHURCHILL: I certainly do not withdraw what I have said. Hundreds of messages and letters were received. Of course, I have not suggested that the Prime Minister himself went about whispering, but that and other statements——

MR PAGET (Northampton): On a point of Order. The right hon Gentleman has referred to certain documents. Ought not those documents to be available to the House?

MR CHURCHILL: The hon and learned Gentleman should learn a little more about our Rules of Order before he raises points of Order. All I can say is that I was very glad to be in a position myself to deny the rumour that I was dead, and I only regret it was not as easy to get upon the track of and kill a great many other falsehoods to which we were subjected. Personally I think it was very shabby for hon

Members and others, if they were engaged in the campaign at all—
[HON MEMBERS: 'If.']—considering the help that we have given them
in supporting National Service, to have taken every advantage that
that they could as occasion offered. Hon Members do not disturb me
at all by their indignation. I am only sorry that the topics I have to
deal with this afternoon are of a laborious and technical character and
do not enable me to stimulate them more vigorously than I shall be
able.

I am now coming to the question of the structure of the Regular
Army. Here I must say that I do not agree with the Government's
view, expressed in the last sentence of the White Paper on Defence,
which reads:

'The idea that the present principle of universality of national
service should be abandoned in favour of a scheme under which a
smaller number of men, selected by ballot or otherwise, would be
required to serve for a period of eighteen months or more is, in the
Government's view, impracticable.'

Nearly 300,000 men come within the scope of National Service
every year. Of these the intake for 1950-1 is to be 168,000. I am quoting
from the Paper. I do not suggest that this number should be increased.
On the contrary, I think that by wise administration it might well be
somewhat diminished. But I believe that the method of choosing
those who are required could be greatly improved, and I do not
exclude the principle of selective service by ballot from a proper
application of our National Service law. I think it is a matter which
should not be too lightly brushed aside.

I believe that if, by various inducements of a voluntary or optional
character, men called up could be persuaded to serve for a somewhat
long period, important economies, easements and improvements would
be possible in our whole military system. I am satisfied that conscription could be applied with less burden and with less expense, combined
with greater efficiency, having regard especially to our peculiar needs;
and I do not think the Minister of Defence disagrees with that. I do
not propose, however, to go into details, but I renew the assurance,
which I gave during the election, that the Conservative Party do not
intend to use compulsory powers to lengthen the terms of National
Service above the eighteen months which now prevail.

One aspect of the evils of the present application of the compulsory
Service Acts is shown in our lamentable inability to produce, even
with the present severe measures of compulsion, any adequate reinforcement or expeditionary force even for the minor contingencies
which arise in the world, and that for a nation whose responsibilities,

as the Minister of Defence reminded us, are still so widely spread as ours. We have, of course, the German garrisons to maintain and more troops are needed in the Far East; but to set against this there is the relief of what used to be our prime burden of maintaining a great long-service army in India.

Even with all the compulsory powers which the Government have taken, with 380,000 men in uniform, I do not believe there are a couple of well-formed brigade groups which could be sent abroad at short notice; I should be quite ready to be contradicted on that point and very glad. That would compare with the six divisions produced under the Haldane scheme, without compulsion, before the First World War, or with the four or five divisions which stood ready at the outbreak of the Second World War. Of course, things are not exactly on all fours, I quite agree. There have been many changes, but such great contrasts should not be ignored and, with facts like these staring us in the face, it is hard to believe that we are presented with a successful solution of the military problem by those who have had unprecedented control for the last $4\frac{1}{2}$ years. We have an enormous mass of men in uniform, and here we are reduced to this pitiful shortage of the means to send small reinforcements, modest reinforcements, abroad at short notice. It is not a thing to laugh at; it is a thing to puzzle at, and to try to find a way to do it. We shall not get through our difficulties by this attempt at geniality when under examination.

Time does not permit me this afternoon to recur to the extraordinary disappearance and dispersal of immense masses of war materials which were at our disposal when the present Government came into office. The right hon Gentleman said something about it, and of course some weapons become obsolete in a few years but others, properly taken care of, especially artillery and rifles, of which we had enormous masses, can be kept in good order for a whole generation. Now I return to the recruiting for the Regular Army and for the Territorial Forces. How seriously this has fallen off is shown by the figures on page six of the White Paper. There has been a fall in the Regular Army recruiting from 33,900 in 1948 to 23,800 in 1949—that is to say, a drop of nearly one-third. Yet it is on this Regular Army, so heavily burdened by the need of training the National Service recruits, and losing them as soon as they begin to be most useful, that there falls the task of providing not only our garrisons overseas with units of real fighting quality, but also the supply of effective reinforcements available at short notice, which all admit are needed.

I come to the wider aspects of our military affairs. The decision to form a front in Europe against a possible further invasion by Soviet Russia and its satellite States was at once grave for us and also imperative. There was a school of thought in the United States which held that Western Europe was indefensible and that the only lines where a Soviet-satellite advance could be held were the Channel and the Pyrenees. I am very glad that this view has been decisively rejected by the United States, by ourselves and by all the Powers concerned in the Brussels Treaty and the Atlantic Pact. I find it necessary to say, however, speaking personally, giving my own opinion, that this long front cannot be successfully defended without the active aid of Western Germany. For more than forty years—and what years!—I have worked with France. Britain and France must stand together primarily united in Europe. United they will be strong enough to extend their hands to Germany. Germany is at present disarmed and forbidden to keep any military force. Just beyond her eastern frontier lies the enormous military array of the Soviet and its satellite States, far exceeding in troops, in armour and in air power all that the other Allies have got. We are unable to offer any assurance to the Germans that they may not be overrun by a Soviet and satellite invasion.

Seven or eight millions of refugees from the East have already been received and succoured in Western Germany. In all the circumstances this is a marvellous feat. Another 250,000 are now being or about to be driven across the Polish and Czech frontiers. This mighty mass of the Russian armies and their satellites lie, like a fearful cloud, upon the German people. The Allies cannot give them any direct protection. Their homes, their villages, their cities might be overrun by an Eastern deluge and, no doubt, all Germans who have been prominent in resisting Communism or are working for reconciliation with the Western democracies would pay the final forfeit. We have no guarantee to give except to engage in a general war which, after wrecking what is left of European civilization, would no doubt end ultimately in the defeat of the Soviets, but which might begin by the Communist enslavement of Western Germany, and not only of Western Germany. If the Germans are to have neither a guarantee of defence nor to be allowed to make a contribution to the general framework of defence they must console themselves, as they are doing, by the fact that they have no military expense to bear—nothing like the £800,000,000 we are now voting or the contributions of the French and other treaty Powers, or the far greater sums provided by the United States. They are free from all that.

The Germans may also comfort themselves with the important advantages which this relief from taxation gives to German commercial competition in all the markets of the world, growing and spreading with every month that passes. I cannot feel that this is a good way to do things, or that we should let them drift on their course. I say without hesitation that the effective defence of the European frontiers cannot be achieved if the German contribution is excluded from the thoughts of those who are responsible.

The Minister of Defence does not attempt to deal with this issue, although it and others are the foundation of the responsibilities confided in him; but I hope that the Prime Minister will be able to speak to us about them tonight. The decision, of course, does not rest with this country alone, but we must have a policy, and the House ought to know what is our policy. To remain as we are now for a long period of time is certainly not the best way of preventing the measureless horrors of a third world war. It is painful to witness the present indecision, and also the petty annoyances, by which the reconciliation of France and Great Britain with the German people is hindered, by the belated dismantlement of a few remaining German factories and the still more belated trials of aged German generals. All this plays into the hands of the Communist fifth column in Western Germany and the reviving Nazism, or neo-Nazism, which is only another variant of the same evil. All this squanders the precious years that still remain in which war can be averted and peace established on a lasting foundation. I felt it my duty to raise this subject today, and I think it would be altogether wrong that these Debates should proceed upon a basis of guarded platitudes and the avoidance of any real statement of the issues upon which our lives and fortunes depend.

Now I come to the Navy. Estimates of £193,000,000 are put forward for the Navy, and a reduction is proposed in the manpower under Vote A from 144,000 at 1 April 1949 to 127,000 in April 1951. I do not quarrel with this. I have urged in successive years the combing of the tail and the numbers employed ashore in non-combatant jobs and in clerical duties at the Admiralty. I am glad to see that the Minister of Defence is a convert to this process. I am glad to see it has been going forward, albeit slowly and tardily. I was sorry, however, to read in the Admiralty paper that 'for reasons of economy there will be no increase in the strength of the Royal Fleet Reserve during 1950 to 1951'. The maintenance of the Royal Fleet Reserve is not expensive in proportion to the security which it gives and the service that it renders. I have also studied the tables given in the Admiralty paper of the strength of the Fleet, both active and reserve, and such information as is vouchsafed us about new construction, modernization and conversion. I do not propose to make any comments in detail upon this, but rather to deal generally with the great change that has come over the naval position, and to try to focus for the House, so far as is possible, the new Admiralty problem. This is not like the period before the First World War when all was thought to culminate in a decisive engagement betwen the battle fleets at sea, and we maintained the ratio of 16 to 10 over the German capital ships. There is no surface fleet potentially hostile to us in the world today. The only other surface fleet of consequence is that of the United States, nearly all of which—or a great part of which—has, with much wisdom, been placed in material reserve, protected from decay by costly but well worth while systems of preservation. In the Navy the war in the air and the war on the sea have become so closely interwoven as to be indistinguishable and inseparable.

It is obvious and imperative that the Navy should manage its own air service. Nevertheless, in the sea war of the future it is the air which will decide the fate and fortunes of ships of war. Therefore, the aircraft carrier with proper naval protection must increasingly replace the battleships of former times. But what kind of aircraft carrier, and how many of the large or small types? To decide this you must look at the actual problem which lies before us. The combat of gunfire between lines of battle is utterly extinct. What we have to face in the next few years is the Germanized Soviet U-boat. The nation does not seem to know much about this, and the right hon Gentleman did not mention it in his statement, but the salient facts are public property and govern the thoughts of all the staffs in many countries. I am not going to attempt to compute the Soviet U-boat force. According to Brassey's Naval Annual, the strength given out by Soviet propaganda is 250, and Brassey's Naval Annual regards this as a reliable figure. Between 75 and 100 of these, according to this authority, are of war-time or post-war construction.

It may not be wise to publish what we ourselves have in anti-U-boat craft and forces, but there really cannot be any reason for the Government not stating broadly what we might have to face. At the end of the war the Soviets became possessors of a great part of Germany and of several of its Eastern Baltic ports. They engaged, by persuasion or pressure, a large number of German scientific personnel. They have made a great U-boat fleet, in the designing and building and even handling of which a considerable proportion of Germans are involved, by seduction or duress. Certainly an immense advance has been made in the character and quality of the U-boat menace to the ocean life lines without whose maintenance we cannot live. An entirely new type of U-boat has been developed. Instead of a ship going eight or nine knots under the water and having to come up to breathe at comparatively short intervals, we have a type of U-boat which can manoeuvre below the surface at upwards of twenty knots or thereabouts. By the use of the breathing tube or Snorkel—or 'snort' as we call it—it can make passages of thousands of miles without appearing on the surface where it might be detected.

The flotillas and anti-U-boat vessels which, in enormous numbers, broke the U-boat peril and saved our lives in the last war are now largely obsolete for this purpose. In those days we used to employ 12-knot or 14-knot ships to hunt the U-boats, and it was comparatively easy to multiply those; but now, with U-boats capable of moving, for a short time at any rate, at 20 knots submerged, all this great anti-U-boat fleet which we created would be useless. We should have to have much faster vessels going at 30 knots or more merely to do the same hunting as we did in the last war.

Here also is a sphere in which numbers are imperative, but to create vessels of 30 knots in the numbers required involves impossible expense. We have to have many scores of them and each one costs four or five times as much as the old kind and takes two or three times as long to build or adapt. The problem of mastering the new German-designed and Soviet-owned U-boat cannot be solved along the lines of multiplying flotillas of larger and faster vessels. If the story stopped here, I should feel gloomy about it. Happily, however, as is often forgotten, all things are on the move together, and here the naval air and longer-range land-based aircraft come to the aid of the Navy.

The light type of aircraft carrier, if provided in sufficient numbers, can search immense areas of sea. There are also, no doubt, improvements in the methods of destroying U-boats. We have to find them, however, before we can destroy them, and only the air can do this. I submit to the House that the main emphasis of our naval effort at the present time should be to create the largest numbers of light fleet aircraft carriers and auxiliary carriers capable of carrying the necessary modern types of aircraft.

This is a time to concentrate upon essentials. It does not at all follow that this means a vast augmentation of expenditure. It is necessary to concentrate upon essentials and beware, of all things, of frittering strength away on remedies against dangers which have passed away in time. An intense effort should be made to improve the methods of detecting submerged U-boats from the air. Great advances have already been made. I heard no reference to this by the right hon Gentleman, but I have seldom seen a precise demand made upon science by the military which has not been met. Perhaps the solution has already been

found. At any rate, it may be possessed by others. On 23 February—
a date when some of us were preoccupied with other matters—the
United States authorities published an official statement on new
measures designed to combat the snorkel submarine. They said:

'The Navy has accepted delivery of a new model of the long-
range Neptune, which will be the first aircraft specifically designed
to meet the threat of snorkel type enemy submarines. This plane
holds the world's non-refuelling distance record of 11,236 miles.
Built by the Lockheed Aircraft Corporation, the twin-engined
Neptune carries the latest electronic and ordnance equipment. Its
sensitive search radar permits detection of smaller targets, such as a
snorkel tube, over a much greater distance than heretofore possible
with long-range patrol planes.'

That shows that the information that other countries find it possible
to give has all been made public; it is a contrast to the limits to which
the House of Commons is confined.

'To locate submerged submarines accurately, the P2V will
utilize magnetic detection gear and sonobuoys. These small radio
buoys are dropped in a specific pattern over the area where a
submarine is suspected. Floating on the surface the buoy lowers a
small hydrophone to the proper depth, where the noise of the
submarine's propellers is detected by the hydrophone and transmitted. Receivers in the aircraft permit the operators to plot the
submarine's position by interpreting the relative noise level transmitted by the sonobuoys.'

I have not read anything so encouraging or hopeful for many a
long day. I am bound to say I am astonished that more information
should not have been volunteered by the Minister of Defence in the
statement which he has made. If this should come true, the menace of
modern U-boats may be finally overcome under the attack of modern
aircraft launched from a sufficient number of small aircraft carriers.
I think that the House ought to know and reflect upon these important
facts in a debate of this character, and that they should play a real
part in our consideration of these questions of defence policy.

Now I come to the general air problem—not the one connected
with the Navy, but the general air problem. Here again, I shall only
mention to the House what is already well-known to those who study
such matters. In the forefront stands the enormous numerical strength
of the Soviet air force. There never has been an air force of the size
that the Soviet have built and are building in time of peace. In the air,
quantity is best defeated by quality. That is how we got through in
1940 when all hung in the balance. But now we have a far greater

disproportion of numbers to face, though happily of a lower relative quality. Still no one can say that a sufficient quantity cannot overwhelm superior quality. If we wish to have that strength which will deter war, or if the worst comes to the worst, enable us to win through, we require far larger numbers of the highest class aircraft than we now possess. Every sacrifice should be made on other branches of defence to make sure that that is not neglected. The highest priority should be accorded to it. Fortunately and providentially there is the American Air Force, far stronger than ours and of equal quality. We have allowed them to establish in East Anglia a base for their bombing aircraft, the significance of which cannot be lost on the Soviets.

We on this side supported His Majesty's Government in the steps they have taken. If any other party had taken such steps I do not know whether the Socialists in Opposition would have sustained them. Certainly they have not been put to that test. It was certainly a step which in any other period but this strange time in which we live might have led to war. What has distressed and disquieted me is that those who took it should appear not to be fully conscious of its importance. Our defensive forces in fighter aircraft should be raised and our radar precautions should be raised by our utmost exertions to the highest possible level.

We have the jet fighter. This is the product of British genius. There is nothing to surpass it in the world and it is continually improving. I was glad to read in the White Paper, page 5, paragraph 15, the plan for doubling the jet fighter strength of Fighter Command would be completed. I hope that means really 'doubling' and not merely filling up existing squadrons and bringing them up to strength. I was glad to read it for what it was worth. But I cannot understand why a British Government which has established an American base in East Anglia should have allowed anything to diminish the supply of jet fighter aircraft upon which our deterrent against war and our survival should it come might alike depend.

Here again I base myself only upon what has been made public in the newspapers and is common property. The right hon Gentleman made a reference to jet fighters. British jet fighters have hitherto been for many good but insufficient reasons—and a good reason if insufficient in a matter like this is a bad reason—dispersed and distributed in various quarters. I am content to deal only with those which have been sold to the Argentine, or written-off against what are called 'sterling balances' to Egypt. I do not know how many have been sent or given—for that is what it comes to—to Egypt; but it is already public knowledge that 100 jet fighter aircraft have been sold to the Argentine for little more than £2,000,000.

There is a sense of disproportion about an act like this which passes the frontiers of reason. The Air Force lays before us Estimates for £223,000,000, and yet to gain perhaps little more than £2,000,000 of foreign exchange—which the Liverpool Cotton Exchange could have earned for us in a year; a trifle compared to the vast scale of our expenditure—100 of these vital instruments have been sent away.

Even upon the basis of the facts known to the public I am prepared to argue this matter in a little further detail. A wise use of our jet aircraft would have enabled the whole of our Auxiliary Air Force squadrons to be at this moment effectively re-armed. I do not think that those who conduct the Government of the country, although animated I am sure by a sincere purpose, have comprehended this aspect of their problem. As far as I could understand him this after-noon, the Minister of Defence gave a most extraordinary reason. He said that the Air Force could not afford to buy them; and when I asked why they could not afford to, it was because apparently they had overrun the Estimate agreed with the Chancellor of the Exchequer. But all this is in the same sphere of ministerial responsibility, and money should be saved elsewhere rather than that a vital need of this kind should be denied to the Air Force.

I will try to put this problem in the simplest terms for the benefit of the right hon Gentleman. Here we have an Air Force at an overall cost of £223,000,000, and to get £2,000,000 of dollar exchange we deprive ourselves of this part of an element vital to our security. Let me take a really simple example derived from the days which some of us have lived in, in the early years of the century, of old-fashioned war. Suppose we had a regiment of Lancers 500 strong. It might have cost £100,000 a year. There were the overheads; there were the fine uniforms, there were the horses, the barracks, the band and all that. What would have been thought of an Administration which cut off the steel spear-points of 100 of the lances and sold them to the local ironmonger at half-a-crown apiece to reduce expense? I have put it simply to the right hon Gentleman, and I hope he has managed to take that in anyhow. But that is exactly what this particular transaction of selling 100 jet fighter aircraft to the Argentine, published in all the newspapers and common knowledge all over the world has amounted to.

We shall hear all sorts of excuses about the time it takes to lengthen runways on the airfields, the collection of skilled mechanics, the importance of building up, as the right hon Gentleman told us, a future clientele of customers abroad, and the like. We have only to think of the total cost of the Air Estimates of £223,000,000 to see what such arguments are worth. We have only to think of the time that has passed since we allowed the Americans to establish their bombing base in East Anglia to see how vain are these excuses for not having taken all the concomitant measures at the same time. If we had strictly safeguarded our jet fighter aircraft of the waste of which I have given only one example—and that because it is public—the whole of our Auxiliary Air Force could have been re-armed by now, and even further aircraft might have been made.

In putting this point before the House I must repeat that I am citing no fact which is not known to the world, or was not known to me apart from any information I have derived from discussions with the Government. I do not know how much of this sort of thing has been vitiating our enormous expenditure upon armaments, but I am sure that far greater value for the money we voted could have been achieved, and that far better use could now be made of our British resources. If we wish to prevent the fearful tensions which exist in the modern world we must not only be cool and patient, but also firm and strong. Here is one of the reasons why I could not possibly accept the word 'approve' when errors of this kind have been committed in the open light of day.

Do not, I beg the House, nurse foolish delusions that we have any other effective overall shield at the present time from mortal danger than the atomic bomb in the possession, thank God, of the United States. But for that there would be no hope that Europe could preserve its freedom, or that our island could escape an ordeal incomparably more severe than those we have already endured. Our whole position in this atomic sphere has been worsened since the war by the fact that the Russians, unexpectedly as the Minister admitted, have acquired the secrets of the atomic bomb, and are said to have begun its manufacture. Let us therefore labour for peace, not only by gathering our defensive strength, but also by making sure that no door is closed upon any hope of reaching a settlement which will end this tragic period when two worlds face one another in increasing strain and anxiety.

FOREIGN AFFAIRS

A SPEECH TO THE HOUSE OF COMMONS
28 MARCH 1950

---

21 *March—Chancellor of the Exchequer (Sir Stafford Cripps) states that the purchasing power of the £ sterling in January 1950 was about 16s. 2d. as compared with January 1945.*

24 *March—Treaty of Friendship between Italy and Turkey signed in Rome.*

[*28 March* 1950

I notice, Mr Speaker, that you looked to the other side of the House, and I certainly fully comprehend the motives which led you to look in that direction. I am sorry that the Foreign Secretary was not willing to open this Debate—[HON MEMBERS: 'Where is he?']—by making a general statement on foreign affairs to the new House of Commons. I should have thought that when a new Parliament assembled, the chief representatives of His Majesty's Government, either the Foreign Secretary or the Prime Minister, would welcome the opportunity of laying before us a full statement of their policy and theme. Nor can I recall any situation in which such guidance was more imperatively demanded, not only by the Opposition, but still more by the movement of events.

However, our request has been rejected. The object, I suppose, was a manoeuvre or tactics to draw whoever spoke for the Opposition into a statement of their views and then to pick out such odd points as emerged for debating purposes—and this on the subject of foreign affairs, which surely should be and can be lifted above the untimely and costly party struggles to which we are now condemned. In all the main issues of foreign policy the Opposition in the late Parliament supported, sustained and even pointed the course which the Foreign Secretary has pursued.

Then we were weak; now we are equals—almost. But our intention is to give the same help to His Majesty's Government in foreign affairs as we did in the years when we were helplessly outnumbered. In fact, it will be stronger help numerically. The Foreign Secretary need not, therefore—I trust that he is not in any way indisposed—[HON MEMBERS: 'Where is he?']—but it does seem to me that as he is going to reply to the Debate one would have had the opportunity of his attention at this moment.

The right hon Gentleman need not be afraid—perhaps someone will tell him when they see him—that any decision which he makes in the national interest will be obstructed or baffled by the votes of those over whom he has a majority numbered only by digits. On the contrary, he may feel assured that so long as he marches forward on the broad lines of policy on which we have been agreed, he has overwhelming Parliamentary support. The fact that the Government have a precarious existence need in no way hamper him. The fact that we lie between General Elections need not induce him, or whoever is to take his place, to take weak courses or play for small party gains. We do not intend that the national interest at a time so anxious and critical as this shall suffer from the equipoise of political parties. But let us make sure where our national interest lies and how our part in shaping world affairs can best be played.

I do not intend this afternoon to occupy too much time in the Debate in which so many Members wish to take part. I shall, therefore, not refer to a great many topics and episodes which are in our minds or attempt to deal myself with the Far Eastern problems, which, although they may be touched upon in this Debate, are so urgent and serious as to require a separate Debate as soon as opportunity can be found. I shall now only attempt to deal with the crucial and cardinal aspects of the Western scene. I select the key problems, namely, the relations between Britain and France, acting together, and Germany, and of the bearing of all this upon Western Europe, its life, its hopes and its self-defence. The whole of this discussion, of course, and the whole of my argument are sustained by the decisive strength of the United States as expressed by the Atlantic Pact. Thereafter it is my duty to refer to the relations of the Western democratic world with Soviet Russia. I am most anxious that the tremendous issues with which we are now confronted should be presented in a simple form.

The Prime Minister accused me last week of 'irresponsibility' in raising the question of Germany—by which I mean liberated Germany —taking any part in Western defence. My feeling is, and I hope, the Prime Minister will allow me to say so, that I am as good a judge of these matters as he is. Certainly I should not like to be responsible for not stating my true and faithful belief and counsel to the House, as I have done several times in the past when it was not particularly popular to do so. I remember that during the last Parliament, not to go too far back, I made a speech at Fulton which became the object of a Motion of Censure signed, I think, by more than 100 Members of the Socialist Party. But shortly afterwards, the policy I had advocated was adopted on both sides of the Atlantic and by all parties in this House. So I shall not feel myself utterly extinguished by the Prime Minister's censure.

The Prime Minister also complained that such a question as that of Germany aiding in Western defence should have been 'injected'—that is the word he used, 'injected'—into a Debate on defence, but that was surely its natural and obvious place in the first instance. Other hon Members, notably the hon Member for Coventry East (Mr Crossman), whom I see in his place, misquoted what I said and then criticized the distorted version. I picked my words very carefully and I do not wish to modify them in any way today. I said nothing about the rearmament of Germany or about recreating the German Army, but I see no reason why the Germans should not aid in the defence of their own country and of Western Europe, or why British, American, French and German soldiers should not stand in the line together on honourable terms of comradeship as part of a combined system of defence.

I try to pursue, as it seems to me, a steady theme and my thought as far as I can grasp it, is all of one piece. It is the building up of effective forces of resistance to tyranny and aggression in any form, or from any quarter. The House of Commons is the foe of tyrants, whatever uniform they wear, whatever formulas they use. We must discern their character in good time and labour to resist their force with all our strength. But I am not concerned today only, or even mainly, with the military aspect. We are nearly all of us now agreed in seeking the unity and restoration of Europe as a great hope for the future. We cannot do this without the aid of the Germans. The strong German race, which, during the last forty years, we and our Allies twice fought and defeated, have now the opportunity of rendering an immense service to mankind. Having submitted to internal tyranny and brought measureless suffering upon us all, and especially themselves, they now have a chance of redeeming the German name by helping to repair what has happened in the past and by playing their part—and it might be a great one—in lifting the civilization of Europe to a level where its old glories may revive and where the various forms of tolerant freedom and resulting happiness and culture may be restored. There can be no hope for a United Europe without Germany, and there is no hope for Germany except within a free and United Europe. How can these vital conditions be achieved? Here is a problem in which you may wander around all sorts of tangled labyrinths of thought, but you will come back to the overpowering fact that Europe cannot be restored without the active aid of Germany and that without a restored Europe world peace cannot be established on sure foundations.

When I spoke at Zurich nearly four years ago, I said it would be the proud duty of France to stretch forth her hand and lead Germany back into the European family. I said at the time that this statement would create astonishment, and it certainly did. But since then we have made great progress. The whole structure of Western Union has developed. We thank the Foreign Secretary for the part he has played in it. We are presently to have a meeting at Strasbourg of the Council of Europe and the Assembly where, we trust, in spite of all that has happened, French and German hands will be clasped in concord. I recommend to the House that we should do all in our power to encourage and promote Franco-German reconciliation as an approach to unity, or even perhaps some form, in some aspects, of union. Let anyone who can take a point on this beware how he mocks at such themes. But France, after her tribulations and in her present disturbed condition, may not be strong enough to accomplish single-handed her mission. That is why the intimate and inseparable relationship between Britain and France and between the British Empire and Commonwealth of Nations and France must be affirmed and asserted continually in the most effective manner. France and Britain, both sorely distressed, can combine together and, thus joined, have the superior power to raise Germany, even more shattered, to an equal rank and to lasting association with them.

Then these three countries, helping each other, conscious of their future united greatness, forgetting ancient feuds and the horrible deeds and tragedies of the past, can make the core or the nucleus upon which all the other civilized democracies of Europe, bond or free, can one day rally and combine. Woe be it to anyone in the free world, who, by lack of understanding, or by lack of goodwill, or by lack of world hope, or any more flagrant fault or blunder, obstructs or delays this essential combination. There was a time when men thought that the conception of a United States of Europe would be resented by the United States of America, but now we have the American people, with their own heavy burdens to bear, sacrificing themselves and using all their power and authority to bring about this very system. In this lies the hope of the Western world and its power to promote beneficial solutions, perhaps, of what happens in Asia.

I do not wish to fall into vague generalities. Let me, therefore, express our policy as I see it in a single sentence. Britain and France united should stretch forth hands of friendship to Germany, and thus, if successful, enable Europe to live again. I am distressed when I read in the newspapers, for I have no other information on these matters except my own knowledge, about petty obstructive vexations which hamper this grand design. We read of the belated blowing up of the tail-end of the German munition factories; and of the trial of aged and decrepit German field-marshals. We read on the other hand of an impudent Goebbels film improperly released in the American zone at which Germans cheer anti-British propaganda. How easy it is to mar large unities, how hard to make them. We in this House and in these islands must rise above these pettinesses. It may well be that our safety depends on our proving ourselves capable of doing so. Follies on one side lead to misbehaviour on the other. Europe, at this moment of resurgence, cannot afford to make silly mistakes, or, if they are made, allow them to darken her thought or divert her aim. We here have all been busy in a General Election, and over us hangs another with all its preoccupations for our divided and harassed land. But meanwhile many things are happening abroad which should not pass unnoticed or unmeasured.

Almost the same time that I spoke in the defence Debate a statement was being made by General de Gaulle on Franco-German relations. As the House knows, I have not always seen eye to eye with that patriotic Frenchman, who represented in the war more than any other man the will to live of France. Certainly there is no one in France who could have opposed with more vigour and injurious effect the reconciliation between the French and German people. He represents the most powerful forces which could have been arrayed on the wrong side. But what did he say? He spoke of the proposal which Dr Adenauer had just made for an economic union between France and Germany. I shall read his words. He said:

'I have followed for thirty years the ideas of the German Chancellor. In what this good German has said I have found the echo of the call of Europe.'

Relations between the two countries must be viewed against a European background. In short the Grand Design of Charlemagne must be readapted to modern conditions. General de Gaulle went on:

'Why should not the Rhine become a street where Europeans meet, rather than a ditch dividing hostile camps?'

I must say that when I read this statement in the newspapers I hoped that it might be received throughout Europe, as it has been here in the House, to quote the lines of Rupert Brooke, 'with the silence following great words of peace'.

It certainly was treated with the utmost respect throughout the

Continent. Some will call Dr Adenauer's proposal for an economic union between Germany and France premature, unsure, only partly thought out. Surely, however, it lies near the root of the matter. What we want is far more than that, but these two speeches by General de Gaulle and Dr Adenauer together constitute a memorable event.

Here is the forward path along which we must march if the thousand-year feud between Gaul and Teuton is to pass from its fierce destructive life into the fading romance of history. Here are two men who have fought and struggled on opposite sides through the utmost stresses of our times and both see clearly the guidance they should give. Do not let all this be cast away for small thoughts and wasteful recriminations and memories which, if they are not to be buried, may ruin the lives of our children and our children's children. It may be that this year, 1950, on which we have entered in so much perplexity and dispute, can be made the occasion for launching Europe on its voyage to peace with honour. Let us make sure that we play our part in turning thought into action and action into fame.

I am very glad to see the right hon Gentleman the Secretary of State for Foreign Affairs. I can assure him that he has a great fund of goodwill among all parties. We know what a burden he has had to bear. Some of us had to bear that burden for five years; he has borne it at the same tenseness for ten. We speak of him always with great feelings of personal regard although it is our duty to criticize errors in the conduct of foreign policy rather than in its inspiration which come to our notice. I hope to hear from the Foreign Secretary tonight that no British party will fall behind in its duty in the European cause. People say that all these are visionary and sentimental ideas which ignore the practical realities. They say they blot out the lessons of the past and the difficulties of the present and thus will have no real application for the future. But it is a great mistake to suppose that nations are not lead by sentiment. It takes too poor a view of man's mission here on earth to suppose that he is not capable of rising, to his material detriment far above his day-to-day surroundings. The dominant forces in human history have come from the perception of great truths and the faithful pursuance of great causes.

I have always held that the cause of united Europe would not be helped, and might well be injured, by attempts to draw up precise and rigid constitutions and agreements too soon or in a hurry. The first stage is to create a friendly atmosphere and feeling of mutual confidence and respect. Even a day's delay in working hard for this is a matter for regret. Once the foundation of common interest and solidarity of sentiment has been laid it may well be that formal agreements would take the form, not of hard bargains or weak compromises, but of setting down on paper the living basic truths and thoughts which were in all minds. Then difficulties at present insuperable might well become irrelevant.

In this field it is a practical and immediate step that can be taken, namely, the arrival at Strasbourg this summer of a German delegation to the European Assembly of the Council of Europe. More than two years have passed since the Germans came to The Hague on the invitation of our unofficial European movement. I had an agreeable and, to me, a memorable interview with them. It was there I met Dr Adenauer, little knowing how soon he would be the German Chancellor at the head of a German Government. Since then great forward steps have been taken. The Council of Europe and the European Assembly are institutions formally and permanently established; young, but august; sustained by many freely elected Parliaments. The presence of Germany in our midst will be an event from which nothing but good can come. It would be a great pity if doubts and further delays were caused by boggling and haggling, or the drawing up of conditions. I was sorry to see that the Germans had written out a number of conditions on which they would be prepared to join the Council of Europe. That is falling below the level of events.

Many voices are raised of provocation and false counsel on every side. I sincerely hope that Dr Adenauer will show that the new Germany can rise superior to such distractions, no matter how or whence they come. I am glad to see that there is better news about this today, but I would say to the Germans, 'Let it all happen naturally and easily, and you will find that very soon Germany will take her proper place, and that all questions of legalistic status will cease to be of any importance.'

I have one more observation to make about the European Assembly. Substantial results flowed from that Assembly at Strasbourg last year. But the contrast between the activities of the Assembly and the apparent inaction of the Committee of Ministers has created the impression that the Ministers are not whole-hearted in their intention to promote the Union of Europe. Whether this impression is correct or incorrect it is gaining ground, and I say to the right hon Gentleman, who is off on a journey there tonight, that only some positive unequivocal pronouncement by the Committee of Ministers when it meets next week can undo it. The situation is especially serious because our own position is called in question. It is widely thought on the Continent and in America that the British Government are lacking in zeal for the whole plan—'dragging their feet' is, I believe, the American expression. It is said that on the Committee of Ministers the Foreign Secretary is always amongst those who wish to advance less far and less fast. This is what is widely believed and it tends to weaken our general influence in Europe. I hope that the right hon Gentleman will clear away these misgivings when he speaks this afternoon.

It would certainly be ungracious on my part if I left the subject without acknowledging the services rendered by the recent Colombo Conference in proclaiming that there is no incompatibility or inconsistency between Britain's part in a United Europe and her position as the centre and pivot of the British Empire. Now I come to the last aspect of what I wish to say.

I come to our relations with Soviet Russia. I will begin by stating the reason why I do not believe that another war is imminent or inevitable, and why I believe that we have the time, if we use it wisely, and the hope of warding off that frightful catastrophe from our struggling, ill-informed and almost helpless human race. Here is the reason. There never was a time when the deterrents against war were so strong. If penalties of the most drastic kind can prevent in our civil life crime or folly, then we certainly have them here on a gigantic scale in the affairs of nations. It is extraordinary. The penalties have grown to an extent undreamed of; and at the same time many of the old incentives which were the cause of the beginnings of so many wars, or features in their beginning, have lost their significance. The desire for glory, booty, territory, dynastic or national aggrandisement; hopes of a speedy and splendid victory with all its excitement—and they are all temptations from which even those who only fight for righteous causes are not always exempt—are now superseded by a preliminary stage of measureless agony from which neither side could at present protect itself.

Another world war would begin by both sides suffering as the first step what they dread most. Western Europe would be overrun and Communized, with all that liquidation of the outstanding non-Communist personnel of all classes, of which I understand in respect of several countries elaborate lists have already been prepared—and which are, no doubt, kept up to date in those countries by the Communist groups and parties in their midst. That is one side. On the other hand, at the same time, Soviet cities, air-fields, oil-fields and railway junctions would be annihilated; with possible complete disruption of Kremlin control over the enormous populations who are ruled from Moscow. These fearful cataclysms would be simultaneous, and neither side could at present, or for several years to come, prevent them. Moralists may find it a melancholy thought that peace can find no nobler foundations than mutual terror. But for my part I shall be content if these foundations are solid, because they will give us the extra time and the new breathing space for the supreme effort which has to be made for a world settlement.

No one need delude himself by underrating the difficulties which stand in the way of a settlement or by closing his eyes to the gulf which yawns between the two worlds, now facing each other, armed and arming, reaching out for agencies which might eventually destroy the human race. As I said at Boston last year, I think it probable that the Soviet Government fear the friendship of the West even more than they do our hostility. The Soviet regime and the lives of its rulers might be imperilled by allowing free, easy and friendly intermingling with the outer world. An endless series of quarrels, a vehement and violent antagonism, the consciousness of an outside enemy in the minds of the masses, may be regarded by the Soviet as a necessary precautionary element in maintaining the existence of the Communist power. There indeed is a gloomy thought. There indeed is a reason for fear. But fear must never be allowed to cast out hope.

During the election I was most anxious that the return of a Conservative Government to power, which was a possibility, should not be taken as involving an exacerbation of the already tense situation that exists, and that we should make it clear above all things that we should strive faithfully for peace. I also felt, and feel, that we owe it to our consciences, all of us, that no door should be closed which may lead to better prospects. I do not, of course, take an over-sanguine view of the position whatever efforts are made, but it is our Christian duty to try our best. Moreover, the democracies of the West must be constantly convinced that those who lead them do not despair of peace if they are to take even the measures which self-preservation demands in case the worst should come to the worst.

Let me repeat what I said at Edinburgh—only a few lines:

'I cannot help coming back to this idea of another talk with Soviet Russia upon the highest level. The idea appeals to me of a supreme effort to bridge the gulf between the two worlds so that each can live their life, if not in friendship at least without the hatreds of the cold war.'

I was answered by the Foreign Secretary that all this was a 'stunt'. Whatever this American college slang, as I find it is described in the dictionary, may have implied, it did not seem to me completely to dispose of the subject which had been raised. He also said that through the United Nations must be found our only process and resource.

But three days later, on 17 February, at a Press conference at Lake Success, Mr Trygve Lie, the Secretary General of UNO, said he was in favour of great Power negotiations:

'all the time and on all levels—top level, middle level and lower level —inside and outside the United Nations. The world would be a lot better today if there had been more real negotiations among the great Powers during the past three years'.

He added, what we shall all agree:

'The only people who can rightly judge the timing and form of negotiations and meetings are those who are responsible for conducting the foreign affairs of the countries concerned.'

We are all agreed, but those who are responsible, as the right hon Gentleman and his principal colleagues are, must not fail to seize any opportunities. We cannot go on with a policy of hesitation and drift. Every day is precious if the chance occurs.

I have explained this afternoon the arguments on which I base my belief that a further spell of time will be granted to us. Even at the risk of afterwards being reproached for being wrong, I have not hesitated to state my view that it may well be that several years may pass before a war breaks out. I will take the chance of making that remark although I have no special information at my disposal. Certainly we must seek to negotiate from strength and not from weakness. We all agree on that. Certainly we must move hand in hand with our Allies, and above all with the United States, as the right hon Gentleman has so far done. We should do well to study the recent and most important announcements on foreign policy by the American Secretary of State, Mr Acheson, whose gifts and services are so widely recognized. And here let me say how warmly we welcome in this House the news that that great American statesman, Senator Vandenberg, has recovered from his grievous operation and is able to exert again his clarifying and elevating influence on world events. The American people are fortunate in finding so many outstanding figures at a time when they hold the leading place among the nations.

But if there is a breathing space, if there is more time, as I feel and do not hesitate to say, it would be a grave mistake of a different order, perhaps a fatal mistake, to suppose that, even if we have this interlude, it will last for ever, or even last more than a few years. Time and patience, those powerful though not infallible solvents of human difficulties, are not necessarily on our side. When the last Parliament met, I mentioned four years as the period before any other Power but the United States would possess the atomic bomb. That period has already gone by, and our position is definitely worse than it was in this matter both as regards our own safety and as to the conditions which are, I believe, effectively preserving the peace of the world.

There is no doubt now that the passage of time will place these fearful agencies of destruction effectively in Soviet hands, that is to say, where there is no customary, traditional, moral or religious restraint. Of course, there is an interlude between the discovery of the secret and the effective large-scale production of the article, and that also has to be borne in mind. Of course, the United States have their 'stockpile', as it is called, and it will be only by a gradual process that anything similar can be built up in Soviet Russia. The atomic bomb, though preponderating, is only one of the factors in the military situation before us, but it is the dominant factor. If, for instance, the United States had a 'stockpile' of 1,000 atomic bombs— I take the figure as an illustration merely; I have no knowledge of any sort or kind of what they have—and Russia had 50, and we got those 50, fearful experiences, far beyond anything we have ever endured, would be our lot. Therefore, while I believe there is time for a further effort for a lasting and peaceful settlement, I cannot feel that it is necessarily a long time or that its passage will progressively improve our own security. Above all things, we must not fritter it away. For every reason, therefore, I earnestly hope that we shall hear from the Foreign Secretary a clear exposition of the facts and policy of His Majesty's Government upon matters graver than anything which human history records.

Man in this moment of his history has emerged in greater supremacy over the forces of nature than has ever been dreamed of before. He has it in his power to solve quite easily the problems of material existence. He has conquered the wild beasts, and he has even conquered the insects and the microbes. There lies before him, as he wishes, a golden age of peace and progress. All is in his hand. He has only to conquer his last and worst enemy—himself. With vision, faith and courage, it may still be within our power to win a crowning victory for all.

THE BUDGET

A SPEECH TO THE HOUSE OF COMMONS
24 APRIL 1950

---

29 *March—Government defeat on a Conservative Motion for an ajournment on a Fuel and Power debate by 283 votes to 257.*

30 *March—Mr Attlee informs the House of Commons that despite its defeat the Government do not intend to resign as it was not a vote of censure.*

 1 *April—North Atlantic Treaty Organization meeting at The Hague approves plans for collective defence of the North Atlantic Region.*

 4 *April—Chancellor of the Exchequer announces a net gold and dollar surplus of $40,000,000 for the first quarter of 1950.*

14 *April—Lord Reading and Lord Rennell announce their resignation from the Liberal Party and apply for the Conservative Whip in the House of Lords.*

22 *April—Mr Dean Acheson outlines policy which the US will pursue in combating Soviet Communism.*

[24 *April* 1950

During the last five years the Socialist Government have spent or are spending more than £19,000,000,000. The Estimates for the year now before us amount to nearly £4,000,000,000. No one can say, therefore, that a 5 days' Debate and a 2½ hours' speech from the Chancellor of the Exchequer are disproportionate to these colossal figures which mark the most amazing dissipation of national resources on record in any civilized community of our size. Not only is our taxation the highest in the world, not only have we used up every available resource and asset on which the Government could lay their hands, not only has the future been mortgaged in every possible way, but we have enjoyed during this period of extravagance, upwards of £1,700,000,000 of financial aid from the United States and from our Dominions.

There is the first formidable set of facts which glare upon us today. However, I wish to state the case with sobriety and accuracy. We must not judge by the figures alone. The £4,000,000,000 we are to find this year are, owing to the depreciation of our money, really worth not much more than £3,000,000,000 compared with the goods and services they would have represented five years ago. The purchasing power of the £ sterling at home has fallen during this period by nearly

255

4s. We hear a lot of talk about the word 'inflation', with its refinements of 'disinflation', and so on, but that word carries little meaning to the average man. What is meant to him by the word 'inflation' is the fall in the buying power of the wages he earns or of the pension on which he lives. This is a serious and homely point both to himself and in many ways even more so to his wife. We see in our national Budget that Income Tax and Surtax provide 42 per cent of our tax revenue, but it must not be overlooked that the continued fall in the purchasing power of our money—of the £ sterling—is a tax on the wage earners of the utmost severity, and that it falls upon pensioners and those living on fixed incomes with cruel and devastating force. It finds no place in the balance of the Budget, but it ought to hang heavy on all our minds. If we take the wages earned and the pensions drawn in Britain in the last financial year and deduct 4s. in the £ from them—that is a little more than it actually is, but I take a simple figure—we shall see how much these five years of Socialist Government have taken from the wage earners.

I have had a calculation made on the basis of the official figures of wages, pensions and Government grants for social services which shows that all these classes and masses were deprived of £1,500,000,000 last year alone which they would have had in goods and services if only the money values of 1945 could have been preserved. And what right have the Socialist orators to talk to us of the exploitation of the toiling masses when the Socialist Government themselves have deprived the wage earners on a gigantic scale by this devaluation or depreciation of the money they work so hard to earn? Even more has the power of our money to buy goods across the dollar exchange been reduced. As the result of devaluation British industry and workers have now to do twelve hours' work to buy the same quantities of necessary goods and raw materials as nine hours would have produced before the devaluation of the £.

It is quite true that we have not spent all this money that I mentioned just now upon ourselves or upon the revival of British industry. The Chancellor boasted in the election that he had given away over £1,300,000,000 in loans or in repayment of so-called sterling balances—otherwise British debts incurred during the war from the countries we had defended from invasion. Indeed, he and his predecessor begged and borrowed immense sums from the United States with the one hand in order to transfer the treasure thus obtained to foreigners or overseas wartime creditors with the other.

It is common ground between all parties, and it was the main theme of the speech of the Chancellor, that we have now entered upon a period of the utmost difficulty and anxiety. The Chancellor made it clear that greater stresses lie ahead. Expenditure in his opinion will increase irresistibly; Marshall Aid will stop in the near future; German, Japanese and other competition will rapidly and steadily increase; taxation, direct and indirect, has reached its limit. At home the cupboard is bare. Here, then, is the background, the unchallengeable background, upon which the present Budget must be examined and judged.

What, then, is the upshot of the Budget speech? Let me quote from the *Economist*, a well-informed and independent organ which each side is always ready to quote when its observations are in harmony with their political views. This is what the *Economist* says of the Budget:

'It is a recipe for ever-increasing Government expenditure, and for a permanent structure of high taxes with no hope of relief—a guarantee, in sum, of ultimate economic decay.'

The speech of the Chancellor showed that there was no prospect for years to come of any improvement in the cost of living or in the rate of taxation. So, in a certain sense, we have reached finality. Utopia is no longer a dream of the future. This is it. Here we are. It is here now on top of us, and here to stay if only it does not get worse. The one thing, the Government say, is to know when you are well off and rejoice while good things last. What we are going through now is the result of five years' Socialist management and control with far more power and vastly larger financial resources than any other peacetime Government in history.

Now I come to some of the specific proposals of the Budget. None of them affects in any appreciable way the general depressing picture which the Chancellor has painted. We on this side of the House are naturally pleased that the Government have adopted the policy of lessening the discouragement of PAYE to overtime and highly efficient piecework. This is one of the points on which we fought the General Election, and we are very glad to have gained this limited concession for the most active and industrious class of wage earners. I was particularly gratified myself to hear the Chancellor announce the doubling of the petrol ration. As has been pointed out in this Debate, when I raised this matter during the election I was assailed with a storm of abuse for irresponsibility, for asking for the impossible in order to gain votes. How wicked, it was said, to squander the dollars needed to buy food and raw materials without which full employment cannot be maintained, in order to indulge the luxuries of pleasure motorists. The storm was severe but I survived it. Now, the Government are themselves forced to do the very thing that was urged upon them and which they sought to discredit by mockery and mis-statement. All this talk of dollar spending was, as I was advised at the time, and as the Government knew well at the time, quite unfounded. Only a few weeks later they have done themselves what they had so vehemently denounced. I gladly forgive them their abuse, the only result of which has been to deprive them of any claim upon the goodwill of the motoring community.

The continuing reductions of control and release of articles of food from 'points' are, of course, all welcomed by us. There is no reason why they should not have been done in still greater numbers two or three years ago, just as there is no reason why extravagances now detected and purged should not have been corrected three or four years ago and we had the advantage of the savings. We have suffered loss and inconvenience in the interval, for no good reason except that in those days the party opposite had more hope of carrying us irrevocably into Socialism than they have now.

We are also glad that the Amendment which we moved to the Address about the reduction of the housing target from 200,000 to 175,000, against which we voted, has been repaired and that 200,000 for this year has been restored. Why should we have to kick the party opposite into doing these things? It is not the need for giving houses to the people that has enforced this change in the last three weeks upon the Government, but only the fear that they might lose votes by refusing to alter their policy. Obviously, if it can be done now, it need never have been brought into question. Even so, we do not accept 200,000 as the target for three years to come.

I have nearly finished that passage of approbation and commendation which I felt it my duty to make upon the proposals contained in the Budget. I have nothing to say against the Chancellor's proposal to exempt the high-class motor cars from purchase tax. I remember five years ago pointing out how a thriving and fertile export trade could only maintain its continuous perennial quality by being based upon a strong domestic industry, and how I was rebuked by the Chancellor of the Exchequer, then President of the Board of Trade, for such reactionary ideas.

I am glad to see that the right hon and learned Gentleman's education in finance, for which we have to pay so much, is not wholly devoid of some signs of progress. He is not a star pupil but it would be too soon to say that he is completely unteachable. Of course, however, in this and some other aspects of finance he may have to encounter the criticism that he is, to use an American expression, 'taking the poor man's money away from the millionaire to give it to the plain rich'.

This brings me to the attitude of the Government towards wealth and large fortunes. Four years ago I travelled back from America with Lord Keynes, who had been on a Government mission and was working at the Treasury. I asked him why the then Chancellor of the Exchequer, when reducing the income tax by a shilling, should have made sure that the surtax on these largest incomes was retained at the confiscatory rate of 19s. 6d. in the £. I shall never forget the look of contempt which came over his expressive features, on which already lay the shadow of approaching death, when he replied in a single word 'Hate'. Hate is not a good guide in public or in private life. I am sure that class hatred and class warfare like national revenge, are the most costly luxuries in which anyone can indulge. The present Chancellor has boasted of the number of persons who have net incomes of £5,000 or over a year. He has boasted that it has been reduced from 11,000 before the war to 250 at the present time, and that the number of those over £6,000 has been reduced from 7,000 to 70. These are great achievements. However necessary this extreme taxation was in the war—I was responsible, as Prime Minister, for its imposition—it certainly is not a process which increases the long-term revenue of the nation or its savings.

I will take a simple illustration as I always find these financial matters better illustrated by simple illustrations. I will take that which occurred to me the other day when I was looking at a cow. Late in life I have begun to keep a herd of cows, and I find that quite a different principle prevails in dealing with cows to that which is so applauded below the Gangway opposite in dealing with rich men. It is a great advantage in a dairy to have cows with large udders because one gets more milk out of them than from the others. These exceptionally fertile milch cows are greatly valued in any well-conducted dairy, and anyone would be thought very foolish who boasted he had got rid of all the best milkers, just as he would be thought very foolish if he did not milk them to the utmost limit of capacity, compatible with the maintenance of their numbers.

I am quite sure that the Minister of Agriculture would look in a very different way upon the reduction of all these thousands of his best milkers from that in which the Chancellor of the Exchequer looks upon the destruction of the most fertile and the most profitable resources of taxation. I must say the cows do not feel the same way about it as do the Socialists. The cows have not got the same equalitarian notions and dairy farmers are so unimaginative that they think mainly of getting as much milk as possible; they want a lot of political education. The Lord President of the Council is turning his attention to the agricultural sphere and, no doubt, this will stimulate his fancy as to some suggestions he may make to the farmers.

I will pursue this point, I hope not unduly. Rich men, although valuable to the Revenue, are not vital to a healthy state of society, but a society in which rich men are got rid of from motives of jealousy is not in a healthy state. This brings me to the applause from his own side—a comparatively remarkable event—which the Chancellor gained last Tuesday when he announced that retroactive taxation would be imposed on two individuals who had received large gifts from the shareholders of the companies for which they worked. It is not a case of sympathizing with these gentlemen, or with the action of the firms concerned. Indeed, I shared the general feeling that such a transaction was unworthy of a time when the trade unions were loyally endeavouring in the national interest to prevent wage increases, justified by the ever-increasing cost of living.

I have no doubt that the promise that the Chancellor made to introduce retroactive legislation to hit these two men was worth many votes to him in the election, and it certainly gave him his loudest cheer when he opened his Budget. It is true also that there are precedents, especially in the war, for retroactive legislation in such matters. Nevertheless, I found myself in full agreement with the statement of the leader of the Liberal Party last week in condemnation of the principle of retroactive legislation and of the idea that a warning by a Minister which had no force of law should be accepted as a justification. After all, the law, as pronounced by the highest courts in the land, was clear. It was not new; the judgment was seven years old. The Government could easily, in their five years of office, have introduced into any of their Finance Bills the clause which they now propose to deal with this matter. The transaction was open—more than open, it was blatant. It was effected and made in full confidence of the validity of the law. It would have been more in accordance with the broad principles which guide our way of life to alter the law for the future than to use retroactive legislation, however popular it may be to penalize a couple of wealthy individuals.

The Chancellor's new proposals are on a comparatively miniature scale and affect only £80,000,000 or £90,000,000 of money one way or the other in the immense bill of nearly £4,000,000,000 we have to meet. They do not appreciably affect the finance of the year; 1 per cent, or 2 per cent, is the most involved in all of it. It cannot be said that they affect the life and effectiveness of the Budget which is before us. But the gravamen of the case against them is to be found in the new taxes which are now to be levied. The increase of the tax on petrol is a new burden to the travelling public and has already led to a rise in cab fares. Bus fares, I am told, will inevitably follow. The imposition of a heavy purchase tax on vans and lorries is a direct attack upon the economy and efficiency of our production and distribution, entirely out of harmony, indeed absolutely contrary, to the exhortations and lectures which we hear so often from the Chancellor's lips. Both the raising of the fares and the deterrent now placed on the sale and use of commercial vehicles and the tax on their fuel are, as everyone can see, designed to force the travelling public and our industry to use nationalized railways and thus offset by a countervailing evil the impending rise in railway freights and passenger fares. The Government bought the railways by compulsion, of their own free will, at a singularly odd moment in railway history and they feel they owe it to the cause of nationalization to make them into a paying proposition, no matter what that may cost.

Moreover, I submit that it is intolerable that any new taxes should be imposed at a time like this. Remissions are welcome, but they should be made by economies in Government expenditure and not by additions to taxation. We shall feel it our duty to vote against both these new taxes when the Resolutions concerning them are reported to the House on Wednesday next. Not to do so would be to abrogate the rights of Parliament out of fear of precipitating an appeal to the people. The Government have raised these provocative issues themselves, and we have no choice but to express our sincere conviction that both the new taxes are wrong in principle and will be harmful in practice.

I always try, especially in a new House of Commons, to study the opinions of those to whom I am opposed, their expressions and moods, so far as I can. I confess I am surprised that hon Members opposite who hold Socialist conceptions—there are, I believe, some of them— were not shocked at this rise in the bus and taxi fares. Is this not a case of rationing by the purse? Ought they not to ask themselves, on their theories, whether this is not allowing mere money to decide who can ride in a bus or taxi and who has to walk? And what about the pleasure motorist and so forth? Is it really fair that some poor man who voted Socialist at the last election, who spends his increased bus fare by lingering too long on the Chancellor's stronger beer in the public house, should have to walk home?

We on this side of the House stand for the policy of reducing both expenditure and taxation. I am repeatedly asked, 'How would you cut down expenditure?' The object of the question may indeed be to procure guidance, but it could also be used for election misrepresentations. We have not the detailed information which alone would allow a precise and detailed statement to be made. We do not know what we should find if we gained access to the secrets of Whitehall. I do not accept the statements of Ministers as giving a complete or even perhaps a correct picture. We are assured that they wish to hold on to office until after the next appeal to the country is made because they fear exposure at the hands of any incoming Administration.

Be that as it may, it is not possible for an Opposition to make a detailed plan without full knowledge of the true situation and the aid of the Government Departments. But I have no doubt, after a long experience of affairs, even longer than that of the Father of the House, if I may say so, that substantial economies could be made which could be passed on to the taxpayer in a manner which would be highly beneficial to production and to savings, and that they could be made in such a way as would effectually safeguard the weak and poor. [*Laughter.*] Do not laugh at the weak and poor. I know that in Socialist jargon they are described as 'lower income groups'. These concessions, secured by a reduction of taxes, might even restore to the weak and poor a portion of what they have lost through the depreciation of the wages they earn or the pensions they receive.

I will, however, say that our Defence Services, now costing nearly £800,000,000, require searching attention, and that I am sure there never was a time when we got less value in fighting power from the immense sums which Parliament has voted. Our foreign dangers, which seem to be sharpening, will not be warded off by the wasteful and ineffectual expenditure of money but rather by concentration upon the modern forms of war power in the light of our knowledge. The spending of vast sums of money in ill-conceived ways may salve people's consciences and make them feel that it is all right, but that in itself affords no guarantee for our safety although, of course, it may be described as a most full and generous provision for defence.

I turn to another point. If the National Health Service is to yield, over a long-term period, the results we hoped for when the policy was adopted by the National wartime Government, it will undoubtedly be necessary to purge abuses and waste and prevent the exploitation of State benefits by thoughtless or unworthy methods or habits.

In regard to food subsidies, now fixed at £410,000,000—the 'floor' and the 'ceiling' have come together—I say without hesitation that they should be recast in such a way as to concentrate the relief upon those who really need it, and not to squander enormous sums on the majority who could well afford to pay for their own food at prices which would soon be established in a free market, and which might easily fall to the level or below the level of the existing subsidized price. I am sure that a scheme can be rapidly evolved which would achieve a substantial reduction of Government expenditure without causing hardship to the lower income groups; and that this present time, when there is a glut of food in the markets of the world, affords the opportunity of regaining the economies, flexibility and conveniences of a free market such as has been successfully re-established in so many European countries, some of which were defeated in the war and long occupied by hostile garrisons.

There is also the general field of Government expenditure— travelling, advertising, wasteful State trading, mistaken investments in enterprises such as we have heard of before, enormous hosts of officials, never needed to manage our affairs before. All these provide a fertile field for additional economy. I was asked the other day: 'What would you do to economize?' I have, within the limits which are open to anyone who has not access to official information, offered a full and considerable statement of the field upon which I am bound to say I think we might hopefully advance with our blue pencils.

I have referred to the advantages of a free market, subject to proper safeguards, and provision for the lower income groups. We are all agreed that we are not going to make our great reforms and advances at the expense of the poorest of the poor. On this question of a free market, I am much interested in this experiment in regard to fish, which has been liberated after nine years of control. The Minister of Health—I do not think I see him in his place—said, in one of his more exalted moments, that we were an island of coal surrounded by fish. Perhaps it was later that he added that it was mainly populated by 'vermin'. I think it was a different occasion. But what about the fish? I believe that in this and in similar matters the higgling of the market will, under healthy and improving world conditions, after a month or two, give the people a far better diet than all the planning of all the planners. No doubt the markets would jump about, as we saw the fish market do, for a month or two, but in the end, and probably soon, they would come down to the true and natural level where the customer—not the 'gentlemen in Whitehall'—and the consumer, knows best. This is of course an old-fashioned idea, but it does not follow for that reason that it is necessarily wrong.

I have now surveyed the details of the Budget; those that I have felt it my duty to pay my tribute to, and those which I am bound to say it is equally our duty on this side of the House to resist by every means in our power. The Chancellor of the Exchequer stands before us at that Box when he speaks, uplifted, austere, almost ecclesiastical, pronouncing sombre judgments. A different aspect of his personality and outlook was presented to us at the General Election. At Bristol on 11 February he said:

'We are sharing out more fairly the national resources that exist. We have not shared them all out equally yet. It takes a bit of time to do these things.'

These were deplorable words. Never has a Chancellor of the Exchequer with all his influence upon domestic and international credit spoken in such a way. How the right hon and learned Gentleman could reconcile language of that kind with the appeals in which we are asked to join to save money and invest in Savings Certificates, it is difficult to explain. What he said, in the words I have quoted, is not even fair shares for all, whatever that may mean, and undoubtedly to have any meaning it depends on who is the judge of what is fair—it is equal shares for all, a condition which is contrary to nature and to every form of progress and civilization.

But in his Budget speech last Tuesday the right hon and learned Gentleman fell into heresies of the opposite character, and extremes of the opposite character. This is what he said: 'The real difficulty is that there are still'—he was explaining why he could do nothing for the lowest paid workers—'some cases of low earnings which are very difficult to correct without upsetting the relative wage levels that have been established within each industry for the different grades and classes of workpeople employed in it.' I fully agree that respect must be shown for what that robust trade union leader, Mr Arthur Deakin, has described as 'differentials' in industry. But to draw from this the principle that the lowest paid workers cannot have their position improved without all the classes above them receiving simultaneous and similar advances falls into an error which is anti-social. That error is to feel aggrieved because someone less fortunate than you gains an advantage which does you no harm. The principle of levelling up is right, and is free from the hate and envy which accompanies the process of levelling down.

I am astonished that the fine intellect of the Chancellor of the Exchequer, even if all else failed him, has not guarded him from self-contradiction and erroneous doctrines of the character I have described. I trust that the right hon and learned Gentleman will search his conscience in the matter, because, in my opinion, it is absolutely wrong to say that the lowest paid worker is not to have his wages brought up unless or until similar advances can be made to others. One of the very first Measures I had the honour to pass through this House was the 'sweated trades' Bill for the very purpose of 'bringing the rear-guard in', as we used to say in those old days; and I am not at all pre-pared to admit that there is any excuse for the exclusion of the poorest paid workers from all help and assistance in a Budget drawn up by a Chancellor who had a few weeks before given expression to the wildest levelling and equalitarian and totalitarian views upon equal shares for all.

I hope to detain the Committee very little longer. I have tried as well as I can to present the case as we feel it; an Opposition aggrieved at the maltreatment and mismanagement of our finances. But I think it also right to say that in my long life I have never seen the nation divided quite as it is today. It is not so much divided in enmity as in opinion. The question forces itself upon us—how long can we afford to be dominated by this ideological conflict which, as it paralyses our national judgment and action, must be deeply detrimental to an island like ours, with its 50,000,000 growing only half their food? I must confess that I cannot get these 50,000,000 out of my head. They keep recurring in one's mind—50,000,000 crowded in this small island, growing only half their food.

The floor which separates the two sides of the House, so evenly balanced now, is not a gulf of class; nor does it mark a breach in funda-mental brotherhood. It is one of theme and doctrine. The Conservative and Liberal Parties stand for a way of life which at every stage multiplies the choices open to the individual. The Socialist devotees—I will not say the party opposite, for many would repudiate it—stand for the multiplication of rules. There is planning on both sides, but the aim and emphasis are different. We plan for choices, they plan for rules, and in this lies one of the aspects of our melancholy domestic quarrel.

Let us look, if possible without party bias, at the effects of the present political tension as it governs our actions and our fortunes. Everyone knows that free elections, such as we have in this country, are the foundation of democracy. But no community like ours can thrive permanently in an electioneering atmosphere. It is not giving the people a fair chance, with all their hard work and other preoccupations, to ask them to live for prolonged periods under such conditions. Every word in this Debate, and others, which hon Members opposite or we on this side speak, will be considered by large party machines with regard to the forthcoming trials of strength in the constituencies.

I listened to several of the maiden speeches which were made and which have won approval from every part of the Committee. I sym-pathize particularly with these maiden speakers, because I felt that perhaps you, Major Milner, from the Chair might have said—this is not a criticism—'I have to warn you,' as the police formula runs, 'that anything you say may be used in evidence against you.' Here we are, in the supreme economic crisis of our whole history, watching each other like cat and mouse. And who shall say who is the cat and who is the mouse?

I was relieved when the Prime Minister announced in the beginning of the year that there would be an election in February. I thought that at any rate this would give us a solution one way or the other of our deep-seated domestic quarrels. The election was held, and I suppose everybody did his best according to his lights. But, far from ending the electioneering period, the results of the voting have been only to prolong it. We are split half and half as I have never seen this country split before, and the question arises: How long have we got to go on with neither one side nor the other having the power to do anything to grapple effectively on its merits with the national needs?

The fortunes of other countries are no guide in these matters. Party names do not mean the same things nor is their parliamentary government in any way the same as ours. In Belgium, for instance, which we rescued in the war, they are not worried apparently about material things and are entirely absorbed in a question affecting their monarchy. In France, whatever else happens, the fertile soil gives abundant food for all its people. In Germany, everyone has the natural resolve to recover from defeat. They want to have free petrol. They want to reduce their income tax below ours. Oh, how shocking! They even want to sing their national anthem. But none of these countries is in the same position as our island, with our 50,000,000 people, brought here in the great Victorian age by a vast expansion of manufactures and now left in a perilous plight.

I was thinking when I was preparing this speech about the whales who come ashore and are caught by the tide, but I remembered that I had used that before. However, when I woke up yesterday morning I found that the poor whales have come ashore again, and I must say it does seem to me that we run very great risks of finding ourselves stranded, with our immense population, on a shore which leaves very little hope of escape. To change the metaphor, suppose we were 50,000,000 of us on the fifth or sixth floor of one of these steel-structure buildings the foundations of which were being undermined and the major girders sawn through. Many societies have vanished in the past and found no recorded or recognizable place in history. But never has this hideous fate presented itself more brutally to so numerous, complex and powerful a community as we are, and never has it presented itself to a victorious nation on the morrow of its triumph in saving the freedom of the world.

Of course, there are politicians who say that it is only by suffering that the people learn, and that the English people, above all others, insist on buying their experience fresh and new every time. Things, we are told, must get worse before they are better. I am not comforted by this. We may easily get so far downhill that we have not strength left to climb back. In the modern world everything moves very quickly. Tendencies which 200 or 300 years ago worked out over several generations, may now reach definite decisions in a twelve-month. I hate to feel the lowered opinion of British strength, will-power and life-thrust, which now prevails alike in countries we have defeated and in those we have rescued. But, of course, if we go on year after year absorbed in our internal party and class fights, there may never be any chance for the might and glory of Britain to show itself again. Somehow or other we must reach firm ground again and have a Government that is not afraid or unable to do things if they are in the national interest.

I was pondering the other day upon what a difference it would have made to our fortunes if what happened in the 1950 election had happened in the election of 1945. Undoubtedly there would have been a national coalition. The old ties that had bound us together through the perils of the war had not been severed by the rough talk of the election as they have now been severed by all that has since occurred. The task before us was the completion of all we had worked for. We had won the war. We could have won the peace. An equipoise of parties would have been a national mandate for the continuance of the united action which had saved us from destruction. We had a common programme and a far-reaching four years' plan. But darker fortunes and more harassing ordeals were reserved for our exhausted people. The conditions of 1945 have passed away. It is 1950 now. Great disasters have come upon Britain, both in the economic sphere and in her standing among the nations. With them have grown antagonisms felt on each side by millions of men and women here at home. I do not believe in coalitions that are formed only as the result of party bargainings. It is vain to suppose that anything but a blinding emergency, internal or external, would revive the comradeship of the war-time years, or that an artificial arrangement between party leaders would meet our needs.

Therefore, it is with deep anxiety, into which my personal feelings do not enter at all, that I try to read the mysteries of our immediate future. How deep shall we have to descend the dark stairway which lies before us no one can tell. This should be an awe-striking thought for this new Parliament, so rich in earnestness and quality, so baffled and so bewildered, and so near, apparently, to its latter end. All the more should it be an awe-striking thought when we remember that we are responsible for all the millions of our people who fought so well, endured so much and try so hard.

UNVEILING OF A MEMORIAL TABLET TO LORD KEYES AND HIS SON

A SPEECH IN ST PAUL'S CATHEDRAL

27 APRIL 1950

Three years have passed since the Dean and Chapter of St Paul's Cathedral reserved a place for a memorial to Roger Keyes and his son, Geoffrey. And now we are gathered here today to unveil the tablet which preserves and proclaims the admiration of our war-worn generation for these two heroic Englishmen—the one a great naval commander, the other a young colonel awarded, after his death, with the Victoria Cross. The tablet also expresses the enduring affection with which their memory is cherished by their many friends and, most of all, by those who knew them best.

For more than thirty years I was one of the closest of the Admiral's friends. When I was at the Admiralty in 1911 he was already an officer of high distinction and in charge of our submarine flotillas at the time when this new and terrible weapon began to break upon the naval world and cast its menace upon the life and safety of Britain.

But we have to go back to the beginning of the century for the first occasion when the light of martial distinction shone upon the young lieutenant who, acting on his own initiative, stormed with thirty men the Chinese fort on the Pei Ho river, for which 4,000 Allied troops had been considered insufficient to attack, and thus opened the channel to the relief of the European garrisons besieged in Tientsin. From then, down to the last period of his life, Admiral Keyes sought glory in the face of danger, and his intense impulse for action was always armed with the highest degree of naval skill and technical efficiency.

He was always in the van of naval progress, and stimulated the tactical development of the destroyer flotillas, of our submarines and, most of all, of the Fleet Air Arm. His exploits afloat and ashore will always excite the enthusiasm of the youth of Britain, and are also full of guidance for the leaders of the Royal Navy.

The splendid feat of arms conceived and executed by him—that the canal entrance to the German submarine base of Zeebrugge, from which the U-boats sallied forth to attack our life-lines, was blocked and rendered useless—will long be famous. This outstanding example of audacity and organization is matched at every period in the sixty years of devoted service which Roger Keyes gave to the Navy and to the nation he loved so well.

In the late war, as Chief of Combined Operations, he lent a most important impulse to amphibious warfare. There radiated from him the Commando spirit to which we owe so many glorious episodes. He animated and impelled from his earliest days all the vast design and construction of landing-craft of all kinds, without the timely preparation of which the great victories of the West Allies could never have been gained. In many ways his spirit and example seemed to revive in our own stern and tragic age the vivid personality and unconquerable and dauntless soul of Nelson himself.

The tablet which I am to unveil adorns the walls of our famous cathedral. The light of honour and of duty which springs from it will, as the years go by, serve as an inspiration and beacon to our island race.

SCOTTISH UNIONIST MEETING

A SPEECH AT THE USHER HALL, EDINBURGH
18 MAY 1950

---

29 *April—Lord Woolton, Conservative Party Chairman, calls for co-operation between Conservatives and Liberals on a nine-point programme.*

1 *May—Casting vote of Deputy Speaker saves Government from defeat on a tie vote (278 for and against) on an Opposition Motion criticizing the Transport Commission's attitude to independent road hauliers.*

2 *May—In reply to Lord Woolton's call, the Liberal Party declare that they do not intend to compromise the independence of the Liberal Party.*

4 *May—On announcement by Tass Agency that all German prisoners of war in the Soviet Union have been repatriated, the Federal Ministry of Refugees in Western Germany state that 1,500,000 prisoners still remain unaccounted for.*

5 *May—Lord Cowdray and Lord Willingdon announce their resignation from the Liberal Party.*

7 *May—Mr Churchill issues statement that on every occasion when the Opposition has challenged the Government each case has been considered on its merits and that when it was felt necessary to force a division it was on matters which 'involved questions of policy and principle which could not be allowed to pass unopposed without dereliction of duty to the millions of electors who voted against the Socialists at the General Election'.*

9 *May—M. Schuman announces his plan for the integration of the coal and steel resources of Great Britain, France, Germany, Italy, Belgium, the Netherlands and Luxembourg.*

2 *May—Marshal Graziani found guilty of collaboration with the Germans after the Italian armistice and sentenced to nineteen years' imprisonment.*

15-18 *May—Meeting in London of the Foreign Ministers of the twelve North Atlantic Treaty Organization member-nations.*

[18 *May* 1950

Mr CHAIRMAN, My Lords, Ladies and Gentlemen:

I think I must regard this as a red-letter day. This afternoon I am victor in the Paradise Stakes, this evening I have the honour once again to address a great audience in the Usher Hall. When I was here last we had good hopes of bringing about an immediate and decisive change in the politics of our country and of establishing in effective power a Unionist and Conservative Government which would prove itself worthy of its trust and equal to these difficult and dangerous times. Now we see that in spite of the substantial advantages we gained, a second intense effort will be necessary. It is certain that another General Election must come soon. How soon we cannot tell. The initiative does not at present rest with us. It depends upon what the Socialist Government think will pay them best. Meanwhile we lie in the lull between two storms. The only Socialist Government in the English-speaking world and, apart from Scandinavia, the only Socialist Government in Europe outside the Iron Curtain, continues its control of our affairs, although in a minority of more than 1,500,000 votes in the country and with a majority of only seven in the House of Commons. In estimating this majority of seven it must be remembered that if the Speaker and the Deputy Chairman of Committees, who both sit for Conservative seats, were members of the Government party, as frequently happens, and if the Unionist seat held by Mr Macmanaway in Belfast were not temporarily disfranchized, the Government majority would be only two.

It is certainly satisfactory that such a Government with such credentials and with such a record is virtually deprived of all power of legislation. They have had to abandon for the time being their whole scheme for nationalizing another set of prosperous key industries, sugar, cement, insurance and the like, with which they threatened us at the General Election. Steel alone hangs in the balance, and it would indeed be an outrage if its nationalization were to be brought into force by the present Government, after its decisive rejection by the electorate. With this exception the Socialist plans for revolutionizing British industry have been brought to a full stop, and the Socialist Ministers and Members of Parliament have now to limit their immediate programme to the personal satisfaction of prolonged summer holidays on full pay. It must not be forgotten, however, that although the Government cannot pass any more mischievous laws, their power to squander our national resources remains unbridled. In their five years of office Socialism has consumed £19,000,000,000, and now in the new Budget they propose to spend nearly £4,000,000,000, and even to add to our taxation, already the highest in the world. Under devaluation, or or revaluation as they were so anxious to have it called, we are still forced to give twelve hours' work for goods purchased across the dollar exchange, for what nine hours would have sufficed before that disastrous measure. The rise in the cost of living, or in other words the fall in the purchasing power of the money we earn, continues steadily.

Hardly a day passes without some new increase in prices, in the cost of production, in fares and freights, in petrol, fuel and transport. Much of this adds to the burden upon every home and family, and to the difficulties of our country winning its livelihood in the increasing competition of the world. It is evident therefore that the longer this evil Socialist rule continues the worse our position will get, and the more grievous will be the problems we shall have to face. I need not appeal to you gathered here to make every exertion in your power in order to secure an effective majority for Unionism, at the impending election, because I know how earnest are your resolves and how tireless are your activities. But the need to secure a strong Government, opposed to the fallacies and frauds of Socialism, is not merely a party objective but a national aim.

We have every reason to be encouraged by the trend shown in the three by-elections that have taken place since this Parliament began, and still more with the decided victories which have been gained, especially in Scotland, during the municipal contests. But it seems to me that while we put forth every scrap of strength we can command, we should also endeavour to gather the support of all men and women of goodwill outside our own party limits. We should endeavour to unite in the common front against Socialism, not only Liberals, but the large floating vote, which played such a hesitating part last time in the trial of strength. For this purpose I should like to see an honourable understanding reached with the Liberals as a party, or where that is not possible, with individuals. This is a moment when we have a right to appeal to all patriotic and broadminded men and women who are in agreement on the main issues to do their utmost to secure the establishment of a strong, broadly-based, and stable Government capable of dealing in a courageous and progressive spirit with the ever-darkening problems that confront us. You read in the newspapers about negotiations. There are no negotiations. You read about party deals in seats. There are no party deals in seats. The Conservative and Unionist Parties have not the power to override and do not seek the power to override the decided will of constituency associations. Still, I feel this is the time when those who agree on fundamental issues should stand together. Let me mention to you some of the great issues on which Unionists and Liberals are agreed, and which constitute the elements of the common cause vital to our national welfare.

First, we proclaim that the State is the servant and not the master of the people. We reject altogether the Socialist conception of a division of society between officials and the common mass. We repudiate their policy of levelling down to a minimum uniformity, above which only politicians and their agents may rise. We stand for the increasingly higher expression of individual independence. We hold most strongly to the Declaration of Human Rights, as set forth by the United Nations at Geneva. It is worth noting that among all these United Nations we are the only great Power under Socialist rule. That is why Socialist policy has been in these past years increasingly out of step and out of harmony with, or lagging behind, the movement of thought among the democracies of the modern world.

Then we declare ourselves inveterately opposed to any further nationalization of industry, including, of course, and especially, the nationalization of steel. Further, we come to those large bodies of practical, domestic reforms set forth in *This is the Road*, and, from a very slightly different angle, and, with several interesting features, set forth in the Liberal manifesto. No doubt there are other points upon which Liberals and Unionists do not agree. But how small they are in scale and importance compared to the great body of fundamental principles and practical schemes of application on which both anti-Socialist Parties are in accord and which are supported by a large majority of electors all over the country.

There is a great overlap of agreement, both in doctrine and in action, between those who have hitherto been brought up to regard themselves as political opponents. But now the times are very grave, and it is the duty of every man and woman who agrees upon so large a proportion of the main principles and practical steps, to make sure that these are not overwhelmed by the ignorant and obsolete fallacy of Socialism, against which the British nation stands today in marked recoil. All I ask, and as your leader I have a right to ask, and it is a modest demand, is that those who agree upon the fundamentals shall, in our party conflicts, try to help each other as much as they can, and to harm each other as little as they must. Let that climate of opinion and theme of conduct prevail, and we shall have cleared the path of progress of many of its pitfalls and barriers, and perhaps gain the power to rescue our native land from some of the perils and forms of degeneration to which it is exposed.

There is no doubt that nationalization, so far as it has gone, has proved an utter failure financially, economically and morally. But there is now an argument against it which undoubtedly makes an impression upon the Socialist leaders—it is evidently politically unpopular. Therefore there is to be a conference this weekend at Dorking to see whether they can think of something else. They do not know whether to bury Socialism and nationalization, which they have been preaching for fifty years and practising for five, and look for some other method of carrying on the class war. In any case, we are confronted with a party which has lost its convictions and has no longer a theme and plan and which, instead of proclaiming an ideological design for the reconstruction of human society, is now hungrily looking around for a new election cry.

I see that some of the newspapers say the whole seventy of them at Dorking are to be *locked up* together. That I think would be going too far. After all we are still a free country. Besides Dorking is much too close to my home at Chartwell. I might have to go and feed them through the bars. If they ran short of coupons I might be put in among them. Then I should be told I was trying to form a coalition by backstage methods. It would never do.

Meanwhile we must do our duty in the new Parliament in such a way as to limit on every possible occasion the mismanagement of our affairs by the Socialist Government and so far as possible to mitigate the evils which it brings upon our people. I assert that from the beginning we have pursued the right policy, both during the election and since the session began. We have not pulled our punches, we have done the natural, honest, simple thing from day to day on serious issues in accordance with our mandate from the constituencies and with the principles and cause we all believe in. I do not know whether any of the violent squealings and squallings which this policy has aroused from the Socialists have reached you here in Scotland. It is natural that the Government do not like being opposed. Their argument is that the smaller their Parliamentary majority the less they should be opposed, and they even make the remarkable claim that the Opposition should never vote against them without being sure beforehand that there are enough Socialists in their places doing the work for which they are paid, to give the Government a majority. Any failure of their members to be in their places on a critical occasion they represent as a 'snap division'. This is a novel constitutional doctrine utterly inconsistent with British Parliamentary life, and it has that totalitarian flavour about it which we notice in some of the dummy parliaments which have been erected in the satellite countries of Europe. These Socialist complaints leave us unmoved. The course we have adopted has already procured several notable advantages for the country as a whole. We have forced the Socialist Government to make many concessions to the public interest which they harshly refused in the days when they had an automatic majority to vote down any opposition and ride roughshod over us all. The first of these has been the abolition of the compulsory conscription of labour in time of peace. That has been swept away. They have been forced to arrest all nationalization except steel. You will remember what an outcry they made when I said that the petrol ration should be increased, what a shocking thing, they cried, to cast away the precious dollars on which we depend for the food of our people, merely for the luxury of pleasurable motoring. How irresponsible to make such a suggestion, but now they have themselves doubled the petrol ration, proving, as I said, that it was always possible, or has been for a long time possible, and exposing the untruthful character of their electioneering arguments and propaganda. There have also been minor concessions in controls in the building industry. The private builder is to be given more scope in England and Wales at any rate, and it is to be easier for the citizen—fancy that, easier for him—to enlarge his house or his farm buildings. PAYE has been modified, as we urged in the *Right Road for Britain*, so as to be less penal in its discouragement of overtime and effort. We are even to be allowed stronger beer. I should certainly take Sir Stafford Cripps some of that. It might do him good. It could hardly do him any harm.

I must, however, draw your attention to the characteristic remark by Dr Dalton, the new Minister of Town and Country Planning. In announcing one of his minor concessions he said, 'This is an experiment in freedom. I hope it will not be abused.' Could you have anything more characteristic of the Socialist rulers' outlook towards the public? Freedom is a favour; it is an experiment which the governing class of Socialist politicians will immediately curtail if they are displeased with our behaviour. This is language which the head of a Borstal Institution might suitably use to the inmates when announcing some modification of the disciplinary system. What an example of smug and insolent conceit! What a way to talk to the British people! As a race we have been experimenting in freedom, not entirely without success, for several centuries, and have spread the ideas of freedom throughout the world. And yet, here is this Minister, who speaks to us as if it lay with him to dole out our liberties like giving biscuits to a dog who will sit up and beg prettily. This characteristic of the official Socialist temperament and attitude in office should not pass uncensured by the British people who expect Ministers of the Crown to behave as the servants and not as the masters of the nation.

Finally we have made them replace the 25,000 houses they had cut from the building programme, and raise the total from 175,000 back to 200,000 a year. I am very glad they have been forced to do this; of course it in no way meets the housing problem which continues to hold the first place in our domestic needs. Nevertheless all these concessions we have wrung and wrested from the Socialists show how right in fact, and how fruitful to the public has been the severe pressure which we have applied in the House of Commons and shall continue to apply. It would indeed be an ill day if an Opposition virtually as strong as the Government numerically were to be deterred from doing its duty in Parliament out of fear of causing an appeal to the electors. I must dwell for a moment on the housing problem—or on the housing scandal as it may be more justly described.

The Government now tell us that 200,000 houses a year is the most we are to expect for the next three years. Such a programme in no way meets the needs of the people or the capacity of the people to meet those needs; 200,000 houses a year is less than the number the Socialist Government themselves managed to produce in 1948. It is less than two-thirds of the number built each year under the Conservatives before the war, at less than half the price; 200,000 houses according to Mr Aneurin Bevan, was the number we needed merely to replace the houses which got worn out each year. It makes no attempt to reduce the melancholy and growing waiting lists kept at every Town Hall throughout the country. It offers no hope at all of resuming the slum clearance campaign, which was well on the move under the wicked Tories in the years before the war.

But if things are bad in England I assert that the Scottish housing programme is even worse. To tell the Scottish people, as the Socialist Government do, that it will take another three years to bring the Scottish building rate up to 27,500 houses a year, is a confession of administrative failure of the most shameful kind. Why, the waiting lists at Edinburgh and Glasgow alone amount to 110,000 families. Surely it is a time for a new deal, a new hand. Surely this is a time when the people of this country may say to the Socialist Government: 'We have had enough of you. Get out and let someone else have a go!'

The increased petrol tax, the new purchase tax on lorries, and the increases in rail charges, will place an additional burden of more than £100,000,000 a year on the cost of transport. In Scotland, where long distances often separate manufacturers and customers from their markets and sources of supply, the burden will be especially severe. In this as in so many other matters, Scottish needs and difficulties have received scant attention from Socialist-ridden Whitehall. The Unionist Party is pledged to give fresh consideration to the whole question of Scotland's place in our economic and political life, and to relieve her from the present over-centralization in Whitehall. In particular we have put forward proposals for the establishment of separate Scottish boards, in no way subordinate to the English boards, for the railways and other industries remaining under public ownership.

The increased railway charges are in effect a new tax of £27,000,000. Yet the Government were extremely reluctant to allow Parliament an opportunity of debating it. We insisted on a debate, but there was no opportunity of putting forward amendments. Increases in the price of nationalized coal, gas and electricity have never been laid before Parliament for approval. This in my view constitutes a marked abrogation of Parliamentary liberties and of the prime duty of the House of Commons to deal with taxation.

Control over taxation and the revenues of the State has always been the foundation on which Parliamentary Government has rested, and indeed there is no other foundation upon which it can rest. Once the State acquires sources of revenue independent of Parliament, then the power of Parliament to curb and check maladministration is seriously diminished. The whole system of controls rests on the Supplies and Services Act, 1945, which expires at the end of this year. Mr Morrison at the 1949 Socialist Conference announced that it would then be replaced by a permanent measure. I take this occasion of announcing that we shall oppose the permanent extension of the Act and insist on continuation only on a year-to-year basis, in order to retain full Parliamentary control. Well, after what I have said, they will not be able to call that division a snap division.

Our attitude as an Opposition today remains precisely what it has been ever since the Socialists took office in 1945. Every measure based on their party doctrine or prejudice meets with our resistance. Every measure conceived in the national interest, even if it is unpopular, receives our support. Thus we have supported conscription—in time of peace—when it would have been to our electoral advantage to have denounced it. We are entitled to justice and respect in these matters. We have supported every step Mr Bevin has taken in foreign policy, however belated or ill-combined. We have frequently sustained the Government against the attack of their own followers. What a contrast is all this to the behaviour of the pre-war Socialist Party, when they were in Opposition and when they opposed every defence estimate, did their best to hamper the recruiting campaign, and, led by Mr Attlee, voted against National Service only four months before war broke out.

I ask this great meeting of the Unionists of Scotland for a firm and decided endorsement of the work we have already done in this connection. Since we have been able to achieve these results while in a minority, it may well be that if the tables were turned the British nation could speedily be relieved of an immense network and oppression of needless controls by a new administration seeking the public welfare with whole-hearted sincerity.

It is with relief that I turn to wider fields. You will remember the last time I was here how I spoke of the world situation. There has just been a conference in London of the Foreign Ministers of all the countries associated with the Atlantic Pact and with Western Union, and above all with our common defence against aggression. As you know I have in Parliament formally disclaimed any responsibility for the actual military preparations nor can I be accused for the delays which have occurred, but naturally I am glad to see so much of what I and my friends have urged and worked for making progress, even if it is mainly in words and sentiments. Mr Eden pointed out at the beginning of the Parliament that although the Government had a small majority and were weak politically at home, there was no reason why they should not pursue a strong and imaginative foreign policy. In all these five years we have supported the Government on the broad lines of foreign policy. It was, and still is, easy for us to do so, because that policy has followed, although tardily, the path we have pointed and prescribed. For more than forty years I have worked with France. At Zurich I appealed to her to regain the leadership of Europe by extending her hand to bring Germany back into the European family. We have now the proposal which M. Schuman, the French Foreign Minister, has made for the integration of French and German coal and steel industries. This would be an important and effective step in preventing another war between France and Germany and lay at last to rest that quarrel of 1,000 years between Gaul and Teuton. Now France has taken the initiative in a manner beyond my hopes. But that by itself would not be enough. In order to make France able to deal on proper terms with Germany, we must be with France. The prime condition for the recovery of Europe is Britain and France standing together with all their strength and with all their wounds; and then these two nations offering their hands to Germany on honourable terms and with a great and merciful desire to look forward rather than back. For centuries France and England, and latterly Germany and France, have rent the world by their struggles. They have only to be united together to constitute the dominant force in the Old World and to become the centre of United Europe around which all other countries could rally. But added to this you have all the mighty approval of the great world power which has arisen across the Atlantic, and has shown itself in its hour of supremacy anxious only to make further sacrifices for the cause of freedom.

While therefore this Schuman proposal is right in principle we must consider with proper attention the way in which Great Britain can participate most effectively in such a larger grouping of European industry. We must be careful that it does not carry with it a lowering of British wages and standards of life and labour. We must I feel assert the principle of levelling up and not of levelling down. We are all surely proud of the British steel industry which plays so large a part in our export trade. The terms on which we could combine with Continental nations must be carefully and searchingly studied. If we were to destroy or even impair the efficiency of our steel industry by nationalization, we might find ourselves at a serious disadvantage compared to Continental countries which are free from Socialist abuses. We must be reassured on these and other points while welcoming cordially the whole principle and spirit of what is proposed. At present no detailed information has been published and the Government themselves were taken by surprise. I have therefore assented to Mr Attlee's request that the debate upon this matter should be postponed until after the Whitsuntide holidays, by which time we should all know more than we do now. Great events are happening. They happen from day to day, and headlines are never lacking. But we must not allow the ceaseless clack and clatter which is the characteristic of our age to turn our minds from these great events. I still hope that the unities now being established among all the Western democracies and Atlantic Powers will ward off from us the terrors and unspeakable miseries of a third world war. I wish also that every effort should be made on the highest level to bring home to the Russian Soviet Government the gravity of the facts which confront us all. I do not give up the hope which I expressed to you here on this very spot three months ago, of 'a supreme effort to bridge the gulf between the two worlds, if not in friendship, at least without the hatreds and manoeuvres of the cold war'. I have not abandoned that hope. But of this I am sure: that the best hopes will be founded upon the strength of the Western democracies and upon their unwavering willpower to defend the causes for which they stand. To work from weakness and fear is ruin. To work from wisdom and power may be salvation. These simple but tremendous facts are I feel being understood by the free nations better than they have ever been before.

I believe that the faithful discharge of our national duty by everyone of us laying aside all impediments, all prejudices, all temptation, will give the Unionist Party a chance of rendering true service to Britain, its Empire and the world.

UNVEILING OF A MEMORIAL TO LORD BALDWIN

A SPEECH AT ASTLEY, WORCESTERSHIRE
20 MAY 1950

---

19 *May—Points rationing abolished.*

[20 *May* 1950

I am honoured by being asked to perform the ceremony of handing over to the Trustees this Memorial to my old chief, Stanley Baldwin, under whom I served as Chancellor of the Exchequer for nearly five years.

I was very glad when his son, who is here today, asked me to do this, because although I had several deep political differences with his father, we were always good friends, and I never remember a time when I could not discuss with him any matter, public or private, frankly and freely, as man to man.

Here was a statesman who, over a long period of years, exercised a remarkable personal influence upon British politics and British fortunes. He was three times Prime Minister. He led the Conservative Party in five elections, in three of which he won the solid and considered support of the majority of his fellow countrymen. In domestic politics he was one of the most capable leaders you could have found for many generations. There was a strong sentiment of comradeship and kinship between him and the English people, and here near Bewdley, where he was born, and at Astley Hall, where he lived— here, in Worcestershire, which he cherished and revered, lay the centre of his strong patriotism. He loved England, and in every part of our country he found men and women who recognized in him moods and qualities which they admired.

He was the controlling power in two long and notable administrations. He was the most formidable politician I have ever known in our public life. He had profound knowledge of the workings of the mind of the average man, and a sincere desire to be helpful to them. If he shared some of their weaknesses he shared much of their calm, patient strength. He won and kept over nearly twenty years a steady measure of their confidence and good will. While pursuing by gradual and continuous steps his general theme of an ever-broadening democratic way of life, he was always ready to stand in the background

281

himself and let others have the publicity and spectacular prominence. In private life we must not forget how, after the First World War, he presented anonymously a fifth of his private fortune—£120,000—to the nation, seeking no thanks or political advantage.

In his administration from 1924 to 1929, in which I served as one of his most intimate colleagues, living in the house next door to No. 10, he achieved two enduring triumphs. The first was the Pact of Locarno, in the making of which he earnestly sustained Sir Austen Chamberlain. This marked the highest point reached in the peaceful settlement of Europe between the two world wars. The second was a five years' steady improvement, judged by every test, in the standards of life, labour and employment of the British people. There was nothing in our domestic life at the end of that period which, in spite of the harsh interruption of the General Strike, was not markedly better at the end than at the beginning.

I had parted political companionship with him before he began his second long term of power. My difference arose about India. I hold to the views I then expressed today, but I am content to leave history to judge as it unfolds over the years that are to come. But the British nation, all parties in the State, have endorsed Mr Baldwin's views and the consequences that follow from them. No one who accepted his guidance then has a right to reproach his memory now.

In his second administration, for the greater part of which he was not officially Prime Minister but actually wielded the controlling power, he undoubtedly presided over a great recovery from the financial and economic collapse of 1931, and brought us back into steady, stable and constantly improving conditions of national life. A whole series of foreign and military events with which he was not specially fitted to deal then broke in upon his conduct of home affairs. As I was his chief critic upon these issues, and my words are upon record, I have a right to declare here and now, by this sandstone memorial, that his courage and patriotism did not fail, although the tragic course of events belied his judgment.

When, at length, in 1937, oppressed by the infirmities of age, he retired from public office into private life, it was amid the almost universal plaudits and tributes of his fellow countrymen. Presently there broke upon us all those fearful catastrophes which have wrecked, though we are sure not irretrievably, the progress and prosperity of mankind. Not all who now claim superior wisdom foresaw what was approaching.

Here, then, there is erected this simple monument to the virtues and services of a good Englishman, who loved his country and faithfully sought the advance in the well-being of those whom it is now the fashion to call 'the common people', but who were always dear to his heart.

Of all parts of England, Worcestershire stood in his mind honoured and pre-eminent, and, of all parts of Worcestershire, the soil in which he lies and the ground on which we now stand was his most sacred spot. Let me now discharge my task by presenting this Memorial of Stanley Baldwin to the Trustees. As the years roll by and the perspective of history lengthens and reduces so many of our disputes to their due proportion, there will be few who will pass this place without giving their respectful salute.

FIELD-MARSHAL SMUTS'S EIGHTIETH BIRTHDAY

A MESSAGE RECORDED AT CHARTWELL, 8 MAY 1950, AND BROADCAST AT
THE BIRTHDAY DINNER IN JOHANNESBURG, 24 MAY 1950

---

22 *May—Steel rationing ended.*

23 *May—Great Britain, United States and France present Notes to the
Soviet Government protesting against the setting-up in the Eastern
Zone of Germany a militarized police force approximately 50,000
strong.*

[*24 May* 1950

YOUR WORSHIP THE MAYOR and Gentlemen:

It is with feelings not only of honour but of the keenest pleasure
that I propose on his eightieth birthday the health of Jan Smuts. It is
just over fifty years ago that I first met him. It was not an agreeable
occasion. I was a wet and weary prisoner-of-war, and he was questioning me on my status as a war correspondent and the part I had played
in the fighting for the armoured train in Natal. Since then our relationship has steadily improved, and tonight I can say that I have no more
respected and cherished friend in the world. Warrior, statesman,
strategist, philosopher, the illustrious Field-Marshal has indeed claims
to the admiration and gratitude of lovers of freedom and of civilization in every land.

Speaking to you as I do by the facilities of modern science, I can
almost feel myself among you all at your banquet in Johannesburg.
I have not seen your great city since I bicycled through its deserted
streets on the eve of its capture by Lord Roberts's Army, but I believe
you still dig for gold in the neighbourhood and sometimes find it—
or not, as the case may be. At any rate, Mr Mayor, I am with you in
spirit, and I know with what pride and satisfaction you preside over
this memorable celebration of the eightieth milestone in the life of the
greatest world figure South Africa has ever produced.

In my mind's eye, which is still ahead of modern science with all its
improvements, I can see your guest sitting alert, spick and span, wise,
competent and lively, listening with attention and, I trust, without
anxiety to what the voice from London is going to say; and, in a few
minutes, I and the millions in many lands to whom your festival is being
broadcast will hear his reply. This is at any rate an example of scientific
progress which is not likely to do anybody any harm.

284

The second time I met General Smuts was at the Colonial Office in 1906 when we were shaping the Transvaal constitution: that great act of generous statecraft which will always be associated in Britain with the name of Campbell-Bannerman, and in South Africa with the names of Botha and Smuts. No act of reconciliation after a fierce war which I can remember has ever produced so rich a harvest of happiness and goodwill or reigned so long as a living force in this age of shock and change. It led directly to the Union of South Africa and to the comradeship and brotherhood-in-arms between South Africa and the Old Country and between Boer and Briton, which was crowned with honour in the two terrible world wars. No event in which I have been even remotely concerned has ever been so richly rewarded over so long a time.

Our path is strewn with many disappointments and tragedies, but here, at least, was an outstanding example of the reward of magnanimity in victory. It was due to the fact that we in Britain had great men to deal with. In Louis Botha and in Jan Smuts we find those qualities of unswerving fidelity to honourable engagements, the power to see the other side's point of view, and, above all, that resolve not to be outdone in generosity, which ranks among the noblest impulses in the human breast. How I wish indeed such processes were at work in the world today, and how bright would be the future of Europe, and not of Europe only, if the spirit which animated the Peace Settlement between Britain and South Africa had been our motive power, and if men like Smuts had been our guide.

To be quite candid, there was one of his methods of enforcing cabinet discipline during his long years as Prime Minister of the Union which I did not follow. I have been told that when differences arose in the Union Cabinet, he was wont to take the ministers responsible for a walk up Table Mountain and, if full agreement was not achieved by the time they reached the top, he would walk them down again to the bottom. No temperamental divergence could withstand the double dose. I did not myself imitate this practice in spite of my comparative youth, and I do not do it even now in our Shadow Cabinet at home. The fact that we have no Table Mountain so handy to Westminster is not the only reason why I have chosen milder methods.

But, of course, my closest and most intimate contacts with our guest were in the last Great War from which the British Empire has emerged with so much honour and with so much injury. I cannot tell you how much I was helped by all the profound wisdom and strategic grasp, which will be revealed as our unceasing correspondence is published.

In all their largest decisions, in all their best thoughts, the British War Cabinet found themselves fortified by the spontaneous accord of the South African Prime Minister, thinking out the whole vast and mortal problem for himself—alone so many thousands of miles away. It was a comfort to all of us and, above all, a comfort to me, to feel that by this quite independent cross-check we were on the right course. I can hardly recall any occasion where we did not reach the same conclusions by simultaneous and separate travail of thought.

And now here we have him in our midst, an august octogenarian. Here is the man who raised the name of South Africa in peace and war to the highest rank of respect among the freedom-loving nations of the world. Let us pray that this may not be smirched or cast away in the demoralization which so often follows the greatest human triumphs.

Such a melancholy stroke will certainly not fall on South Africa if Smuts's life and strength are prolonged, and that is why we rejoice in his presence here tonight, and why I call upon this distinguished company to rise and drink his health, and wish him from the bottom of all our hearts many, many happy returns of the day.

THE SCHUMAN PLAN

A SPEECH TO THE HOUSE OF COMMONS
27 JUNE 1950

---

6 *June—UN Secretary-General, Mr Trygve Lie, issues a memorandum proposing a twenty-year peace agreement.*

7 *June—Mr Herbert Morrison (Lord President of the Council) at a Labour meeting at Perth gives a ten-point definition in a restatement of the case for Socialism.*

13 *June—National Executive Committee of the Labour Party issue a statement 'European Unity' setting out the party's attitude to Western European union, the 'Schuman Plan' and the Council of Europe.*

14-23 *June—Chinese People's Political Consultative Conference adopt Agrarian Reform Law for the redistribution of land under Communist control.*

25 *June—Forces of North Korean regime invade South Korea.*

26 *June—Security Council of United Nations, in absence of Soviet representatives, unanimously adopts Resolution which declares that the invasion of the Republic of Korea by the armed forces of North Korea constitutes a breach of the peace, calls for the immediate cessation of hostilities, and requests all Member States to 'render every assistance to the United Nations in the execution of this Resolution'.*

[*27 June* 1950

The hon Member for Nelson and Colne [Mr S. Silverman] said that he would recall the Debate from its more discursive aspects to the Motion and the Amendment which, after all, are matters which we have got to settle tonight, and I was very glad to hear him say so. When he strays into these biographical spheres, I will only venture to say that it appeared to me that he seemed to lay too much upon my burdened shoulders. I did hope that I might get away with nothing more serious than a charge of foresight; but apparently I actually set matters in train so that they occurred in accordance with my predictions. If it be so that I have in my words such mysterious and latent power, I hope he will pay the utmost attention to what I am about to say.

Those who accept responsibility for the Motion on the Order Paper represent, according to the figures of the recent General Election, a majority of 1,750,000 voters over those who support His Majesty's Government; and I might say that my feeling is that, on the whole, the balance of arguments have shown at least an equal superiority on our side. At the end of this Debate, I still retain the impression that the fundamental issues which have been raised have sprung largely from the mismanagement of our affairs, and that a competent administration would never have needed to thrust them upon us at this time.

The peculiar feature of this Debate is that it turns on a very small practical point, or a group of very small practical points, and at the same time raises in our minds many of the fundamental issues with which the future of a peaceful world is interwoven. When we study the White Paper of the Government's parleys with France, and consider it together with the apologia or explanation which our Ambassador at Washington has been instructed to tender to the American public, one really wonders why all this trouble has arisen between friendly Governments, and whether it could not have been avoided if there had been a Foreign Secretary fit to do his work or a Prime Minister able, amid graver preoccupations, to keep a grip on what was going on.

I did not like the attitude of the French Government in springing this large question upon us so suddenly, or in making pedantic stipulations before sitting in council with their wartime comrades. I admit I was nettled by it. I am quite sure that France would never have acted in this manner towards any British Government but the present one. But there is an explanation which I will give. It is an explanation, even if it is not an excuse, and it should be stated. As for the suddenness; the French Ministers no doubt felt that after we had upset the whole of their economy and finance by devaluation without even a word of warning, they were under no special obligations to study our convenience where other large issues were concerned. I do not say they were entitled to retaliate in this way. It is a feature of friendship to rise above and overlook such treatment on both sides.

There is also an explanation which the French may offer upon the merits of the question itself. They evidently wished the British Socialist Government to give a general affirmation in principle to the policy of a merger of the European heavy industries, and of British goodwill towards the ending of the quarrel of the centuries between France and Germany, which in our lifetime has cost us all so dear. Why did they do this? I will tell the House. It is because they suspected that the British Socialist Government was no friend to the process of the unification of Western Europe, or to what we call the European Movement, and they had good ground for their apprehensions. We have the record in our minds. We all remember, as my right hon Friend the Member for Warwick and Leamington [Mr Eden] reminded us yesterday, how the Socialist Executive and Government used all their influence to prevent any members of their party attending the Conference of the European Movement at The Hague in the summer of 1948, and how many of their pledge-bound supporters went there in spite of them. Everyone will recall the attitude of the Lord President of the Council and his colleague, the former Chancellor of the Exchequer [Dr Dalton], at Strasbourg last year. These matters are public.

What has not been made public, though it is well known and many of us have been continually informed upon it, has been the constant efforts to hamper, obstruct, restrict and diminish the powers and development of the European Assembly by the Foreign Secretary and his representatives in the meetings of the Council of Europe, which they had been forced by public opinion and their own party to accept. I have been told from time to time by some who were present at these meetings that the British were consistently using their influence to delay progress and to minimize decisions. Our Foreign Secretary was on almost every occasion regarded, rightly or wrongly, as the obstacle which must be overcome. I am not concerned today with his personal motives. We all regret his illness, but the prolonged illness of a Minister and his unfortunate absence from our Debates cannot arrest the march of events or relieve us from our duty to deal with them. I am sorry that this should be so, but none of us can help it. So I say, without hesitation, that the French Government had the feeling rooted in them by long or hard experience that the British Socialist Government and the British Socialist Foreign Secretary were hostile to the movement towards European unity and might, therefore, attend a meeting on the Schuman Plan only for the purpose of bringing it to naught. It was on these grounds that they were led to dwell, I think unduly and with a pedantic insistence, upon agreement in a broad and general expression of accord with the greater international objectives which were in view and are now before us. But this was no excuse for the British Government piling their own prejudices on the top of French pedantry. If we had had an effective Foreign Secretary able to get through his work and a reasonable measure of goodwill between friends, comrades and allies exposed to common and increasing dangers, this curious deadlock on matters not so much of principle as of procedure and etiquette would never have occurred, and if it had occurred could easily have been smoothed away.

When the House compares the words and the sentiments of the

Conservative and Liberal Motion with those of the Government Amendment, upon both of which we shall vote tonight—because we certainly cannot accept the terms of the Government Amendment even if we are not able to establish our own point of view—hon Members will find it hard to understand, when they compare these two, how the present breakdown and deadlock have occurred. We are, however, confronted with the situation as it now lies and with the larger issues which have now been raised. These have, of course, been carefully considered on both sides and the results are embodied in the Motion and the Amendment which, as I agree with the hon Member for Nelson and Colne, are the main direct topics before us. It is upon these that we have to pronounce this evening.

If the French needed proof that the British Socialist Party and Government are hostile to the idea of a united Europe and would try to restrict and retard any international conference of which they were members, they could not find more conclusive evidence than the extraordinary pamphlet—and I have it here—issued by the National Executive of the British Labour Party and timed in such a curious manner with, I can only call it, the soiled fingers of coincidence. In this document it is stated that the British Socialists are opposed to joining any European system which is not dominated by people of their own kidney, by other Socialists. This is what I may call the Dalton theme, plainly declared to the Labour Party Conference three years ago. The right hon Gentleman then said:

'If the United States of Europe is indeed to succeed and is to benefit its peoples, it can only fully succeed if all the countries of Western Europe commit themselves, as our electors committed themselves in 1945, to the belief that Socialism is the hope of us all.'

It is this idea which the document expresses and reiterates. It amounts to a declaration that if Europe is to unite and Britain is to play any part in such a union, it can only be on a one-party basis—and that party the Socialists.

This is a squalid attitude at a time of present stress and I should like to remind the House that this attitude is adopted at a time when Socialism is losing ground all over the free world outside the Iron Curtain, at a time when one cannot find any other Socialist Government in the British Commonwealth or in the English-speaking world or in Western Europe, apart from Scandinavia, which has a tale of its own to tell and is subject to many special factors. For instance, the first thing the Socialist Prime Minister of Norway did, on being returned to power with a majority—with an effective majority—was to say that there would be no more nationalization. We have had something like the same language used here, but there is a great difference that an effective majority does not lie behind the Government.

We are invited by the Government to bind ourselves to what the *Manchester Guardian* has well called 'insular Socialism' and to make a party distinction between us and the countries which do not take our view. There is, of course, one exception—the outstanding, mighty capitalist, free enterprise United States. That is the exception. But then, of course, they are paying us the heavy subsidies upon which the Socialists claim that they are able to maintain full employment is founded. But, apart from this important exception, it would be a lonely pilgrimage upon which we are to be led. The Socialist Party, which assumes this self-opinionated position—I might almost say this arrogant position—has just been shown to be in a minority in Great Britain. It has had to modify or suspend its whole policy of nationalization and is now looking about for a new version of the Socialist theme—I see the Lord President is out of the House, perhaps even engaged in this very task—upon which to found their class warfare. At home the Socialists are in full retreat. Abroad they claim to impose their ideology on nations and societies who, after bitter experience, have cast it off.

What plainer proof could the Government give of their hostility to European union than the appointment of the former Chancellor of the Exchequer—I like to keep the former Chancellor and the present both in view at once: both have rendered their contributions to the state of our national finances; both aspire now to lay their skilful hands upon our foreign affairs—but what plainer proof could the Government give than to appoint the right hon Gentleman to lead their half of the delegation to Strasbourg, in full view of the declaration which he has made, and to send him as their representative? I say that that is a grimace. I had thought of using the word 'outrage', but, on subsequent consideration, I thought that the more moderate word would cover the point in its correct proportions. I ask even now that this step should not be taken. If the Government persist, it is they who will suffer in the decline of their influence in Europe; but we shall all suffer, too.

In this Debate we have had the usual jargon about 'the infra-structure of a supra-national authority'. The original authorship is obscure; but it may well be that these words 'infra' and 'supra' have been introduced into our current political parlance by the band of intellectual highbrows who are naturally anxious to impress British labour with the fact that they learned Latin at Winchester. Although we may not relish the words, no one will wish to deny this old-school-

tie contingent their modest indulgence in class self-consciousness. As
I listened to the speech of the Chancellor of the Exchequer yesterday,
I could not help feeling very sorry that our relations with France have
been reduced to this long legalistic argument, taking point after point
with professional skill in order to reach and justify a deadlock. I reject
the Chancellor's claim that at no time in our history has the understanding between this country and France been greater than it is today. It
would hardly be possible to state that reverse of the truth with more
precision.

But what was really astonishing was the manner in which the right
hon and learned Gentleman based the breakdown upon the Documents
12, 13 and 14 of the White Paper, and omitted all similar mention of
Document 10. The brilliant rejoinder of the hon Member for Renfrew
West [Mr Maclay], exposed this glaring oversight—as we must hope
it was—for in their Memorandum of 30 May (that is, Document 10)
the French Government stated specifically the words which have
been read out to the House, but which are so important that I must
read them again.

'The special position,' say the French, 'in these negotiations which
the British Government wishes to preserve is justified in their
Memorandum by the intention, said to be held by the French
Government, of asking, as a prior condition, for full participation
in the discussions, for an undertaking to pool coal and steel resources,
and to set up an authority with certain sovereign powers.

'4. As their representatives have informed the British representatives orally, the French Government wish particularly to confirm
once more that these are not their intentions. As has already been
made clear, in the French Memorandum of 9 May, there will be
no commitment except by the signature of a treaty between the
States concerned and its parliamentary ratification.'

Here certainly was the point when the British Government might
have safely agreed to enter the conference.

The right hon and learned Gentleman the Chancellor has put to us
the question: What would you have done? We reply that once we
had the assurance conveyed in Document 10, that there would be
'no commitment except by the signature of a treaty between the
States concerned and its parliamentary ratification' we should not have
hesitated to attend the conference, and we should have replied in
the same sort of manner as the Dutch, and in terms similar to those
which are embodied in the Motion on which we are going to vote
tonight.

The right hon and learned Gentleman later proceeded to draw an alarming picture of what might happen to us if we accepted the principle of a supra-national high authority which '. . . could cause a whole coalfield or steel centre to go out of production without any social or political responsibility for their action. . . .' Surely, this is one of the points we could have raised at the conference in a decisive manner? To win the war we agreed to put our armies under SHAEF, a great Anglo-American organization that was for the tactical and limited purposes prescribed. No one would ever have suggested that General Eisenhower should have had the power to say what units of the British Army should be suppressed or disbanded, or how they should be raised or remodelled, or anything like it. All these remained questions within the control of the autonomous sovereign States which were willing to agree to a larger unity for certain well defined functional—I use the 'functional' because it is coming into use— functional purposes. Surely, this is one of the points we could have urged, and even have made conditional upon our agreement to any final scheme.

It is simply darkening counsel to pretend, as the right hon and learned Gentleman did, that by participating in the discussion, under the safe-guards and reservations I have read, we could have been committed against our will to anything of this nature. I would add, to make my answer quite clear to the right hon and learned Gentleman, that if he asked me, 'Would you agree to a supra-national authority which has the power to tell Great Britain not to cut any more coal or make any more steel, but to grow tomatoes instead?' I should say, without hesitation, the answer is 'No'. But why not be there to give the answer?

Nothing is said about the method of voting. We know nothing about the method by which voting power will be allotted to the different members of any supra-national authority which may be set up. But it is quite certain we should not agree to become members of it—and that we should have every right to disagree—if our great preponderance in coal and steel production did not receive full re-cognition. Then there is the question of the right to terminate such an agreement. That is surely a matter we could have looked at after discussion. Finally, there is the question of whether there could be two grades of members of such a body—full members and associate members. That is a matter also which should be borne in mind. I can-not conceive how such issues would not have benefited by any con-ference if we were there to shape and guide it. If they did not, if we did not succeed, our safeguards are overwhelming; we should not be bound in honour or good faith to accept adverse decisions on matters which we regarded as impracticable, but we would be the judges.

But that is not all. Even if the Ministers or representatives taking part in the conference were too weak or too facile to stand up for our vital interests and rights, even if they reached agreement round a conference table, nothing would be settled until Parliament had ratified the resultant conclusions. This is what the French say in their Document 10 of May 30th. By becoming a member of this conference on the conditions imposed by the French Government we should in no way abrogate the full rights of power of the House of Commons to judge the final result—to judge as a whole and not as a party or as supporters or opponents of a Government. The power of this House would be absolutely undiminished.

If we attend the conference we can use all our influence and all our arguments, and if these are not accepted we are not committed in any way to agreement, and there would be no agreement so far as we are concerned. If, however, our delegates agree, Parliament has still the full power to judge and to decide when the case is laid before it after it has all been thrashed out. There is the question: 'To be there or not to be there,' that is the question on which we shall vote tonight. It seems to me that we run no risk by being there, but let me examine some of the risks of our not being there.

The Prime Minister is soon to reply, when his own political creed and record are, if I may say so, in a sad plight. We all remember how before the war he said that national patriotism and national armaments were wrong. His words are upon record, but I will not trouble the House with them unless he wishes me to do so. In this faith, however misguided, in the years before the war the Prime Minister led the Socialist Party into the Lobby against every Estimate to strengthen, or even maintain our Armed Forces; and only four months before the explosion he urged his followers to oppose National Service. When in later years—a year ago in fact—the Prime Minister was taxed with this, he offered the defence that he would gladly have voted for armaments and conscription on an international basis, a collective basis, under the League of Nations, but he would not associate himself with any form of national armaments or rearmament in any way. This is what he said on March 16th last in this House:

'This party,' that is, his party, 'never opposed the proper rearmament of this country. No, my speeches are on record in this matter. We were always prepared to support a system of collective security.' But no system of collective security existed, as he knew well, and as we all learned only too soon.

This is the same leader of the Socialist Party who now, as Prime Minister, comes forward, or is persuaded to come forward, as the champion of the extreme insular view, which is inconsistent with the trend of what is going on, and also inconsistent with much that he himself has done. He seeks to win for himself and his party popular applause by strutting around as a Palmerstonian jingo. This diversity, in relation to the same story and the same issues, will not win for him or those who follow him any measure of public esteem.

Let me ask him a specific question, and I direct his attention to this document which I hold in my hand. He may have seen it. Has he read what may be called the 'Dalton Brown Paper'? It was issued before he made his first statement in the House on the Schuman Plan. Had he read it, or had he not? I quite understand his embarrassment. If he says he had read it, his first statement in Parliament was inconsistent with it. If he says he had not read it, he might well be accused of throwing an unfair burden upon his colleague. There is also a third aspect which I am sure he will not consider irrelevant, namely: What is the truth? What is the fact? It is no use for the right hon Gentleman to tell us that these are purely domestic party matters, and that the House of Commons has no right to ask questions about a declaration by the Labour Party Executive, or the Prime Minister's attitude towards it. So powerful a body as the Labour Party Executive, of which the Prime Minister and all his principal colleagues are active members, a body which has a recognized part in the constitution of the Labour Party, cannot be held to be outside the purview of the House of Commons; it is a living part of the way we are governed, and of the means by which we are governed. The Prime Minister cannot dissociate himself from it. We do not know now what his position is, but I ask him this simple question: Did he read this document before he made his statement on the Schuman Plan to the House of Commons, or did he not? If the right hon Gentleman does not answer, or dare not answer, then he will be the sufferer in reputation. Apart from being a Prime Minister he is a public man, and I doubt if there is any Member in this House who, if asked a question of this kind, would shrink from giving a plain and simple answer.

I venture, from long experience, to offer some advice to the House, which is naturally perturbed by the far-reaching issues which have been aroused in our minds, and which we have to discuss in the inevitably unpleasant atmosphere surrounding or between two fierce General Elections. It is not within our power, nor is it our task this evening, to settle all those vast questions of world destiny and Britain's part in it. We must keep them in our minds so far as we can perceive them, but we have not got to pronounce judgment upon them all.

We have to deal with the definite practical issues put before us in the Motion on the Order Paper. This can only be a step, and a carefully-guarded step, forward in what the great majority on both sides of the House believe to be the right direction.

We ought under all effective safeguards to take our part and use our influence in this forthcoming discussion, provided, first, that we wish it good success, and secondly, though no less important, that we reserve our full freedom to judge the final results. We cannot do that now. We do not know any of the details, or how they will emerge from a careful examination. We have only a general outline of what is proposed as a basis for discussion. Every Member should ask himself two simple practical questions: 'Do I wish to see the unity of Western Europe advanced?' and anyhow, apart, from that, 'Had we not better take part in the conference subject to the reservations which the Dutch have made?' These are the issues before us tonight.

More than a month ago when I addressed the Scottish Unionist Conference at Edinburgh we knew even less than we do now. Nevertheless, the course I should advise the Conservative Party to follow seemed clear. I will venture to read to the House what I said, because at that time I had no idea that this would become a controversial party issue. I hope that the House will forgive me reading this, but I think that it is relevant:

'While the Schuman proposal is right in principle, we must nevertheless consider carefully the way in which Great Britain can participate most effectively in such a larger grouping of European industry. We must be careful that it does not carry with it a lowering of British wages and standards of life and labour. We must, I feel, assert the principle of levelling up and not of levelling down. We are all surely proud of the British steel industry which plays so large a part in our export trade. The terms on which we could combine with Continental nations must be carefully studied. If we were to destroy or even impair the efficiency of our steel industry by nationalization, we might find ourselves at a serious disadvantage compared with Continental countries which are free from Socialist abuses. We must be reassured on these and other points while welcoming cordially the whole principle and spirit of what is proposed.'

That is what I said, and that is what, broadly speaking, I stand by now, and it is what I ask that we shall vote unitedly upon this evening.

We are asked: How can the Conservative Party reconcile its opposition to the nationalization of steel and yet give any countenance to the principle of internationalization in a European system? It is a fair question. The answer is that we oppose the nationalization of British steel because we wish to see it remain in the competent hands of those who under free enterprise have raised it to its present magnificent position among our industries. In our opposition to nationalization we have never objected to a proper degree of Government supervision; indeed we have always insisted upon it. What we have opposed, and shall continue to oppose, is State ownership and management— or mismanagement as it has proved so far—of the industry.

Under the Schuman proposals, ownership remains unaffected. We cannot see any objection in principle to a wider measure of international co-ordination if that proves practicable and in accordance with our essential interests. We see no reason why the problems of the British steel industry should not be discussed in common with the problems of the other European steel industries, and we have good hope that if this is done, an association mutually advantageous and acceptable may be created. But at any rate it will be far better for us to take part in the discussions than to stand outside and let events drift without us. That is the view of the present leaders of the British steel industry, and I am sure that it is a sensible and practical one.

The Socialist Government, as their Amendment sets forth, speak of their desire to follow closely the conversations from outside and they welcome the proposal which M. Schuman has made. The French Government have promised to keep us fully informed. But what is that compared with taking part in the discussions and influencing them in the powerful way which we could have done having regard to our preponderating individual stake? There is a great difference between being outside a conference and being perhaps a leading member of one. There may well be a certain resentment against the Government which is thought by the others to have wilfully refused under all safeguards even to sit at the table.

Here are the six Powers talking all these matters over among themselves with the United States beckoning encouragement to them from across the ocean. Nothing has done more harm in the United States than the publication in this country of this document—and Britain, although absolutely safe from being committed, finding excuses, elaborate excuses, to keep out of the conference altogether and thus perhaps spoil the hopes of a general settlement. The French have a saying: 'Les absents ont toujours tort.' I do not know whether they learn French at Winchester.

There is certainly a risk of all these matters of great consequence being discussed in our absence. We have no means of intervening from moment to moment. New difficulties may be springing up in our absence, as we sit here. All kinds of draft conclusions or draft proposals may be presented which would never have seen the light of day had we been able to use our influence on the spot beforehand. Perhaps resentment is too strong an expression. Let me call it 'a fellow feeling' among those who are there against the one who is out. Continental wages are lower than our own. If they were averaged out on the basis of those who were in, it might well increase in a marked degree the competitive undercutting power in the exports of all these countries. Whereas our influence at the table might well have been sufficient to turn the balance in favour of the British standard, it seems to me contrary to the interests of the British coal-miners and steel workers that they should never have been allowed to put their case for a levelling-up on the Continent instead of a levelling-down.

There is another reason why the boycotting of the conference is to be regretted. The absence of Britain deranges the balance of Europe. I am all for a reconciliation between France and Germany, and for receiving Germany back into the European family, but this implies, as I have always insisted, that Britain and France should in the main act together so as to be able to deal on even terms with Germany, which is so much stronger than France alone. Without Britain, the coal and steel pool in Western Europe must naturally tend to be dominated by Germany, who will be the most powerful member. This point was made by the hon Member for Coventry East [Mr Crossman] last night. I ask both sides of the House to consider whether it is really a wise policy for us to pursue at this particular moment of European recovery. It is difficult to imagine any course more inconsiderate to European interests in general, and to British interests in particular, than that into which the Government are forcing, not only the House as a whole, but their own party.

I have spoken of this document—this Brown Paper. There was, however, in the Socialist pamphlet one declaration with which I wholeheartedly agree. I mean the declaration against Europe becoming a Third Force between America and Russia and creating a 'neutral geographical block'. This was formerly the view of many of the Socialists in the days when they condemned my Fulton speech in 1946. I am glad to read this recantation. I trust the educational process may continue. I should myself regard the neutralization of Germany or Western Germany, still more of France and the rest of the six Powers now meeting together in Paris, as a disaster second only to actual war. It would simply mean that not only Western Germany but the European States in the neutral zone would be undermined and overcome one by one and bit by bit exactly as we have seen Czechoslovakia devoured before our eyes. The question which both the pamphleteers and we should ask ourselves tonight is whether British reluctance to assert herself within a movement towards European unity will not bring about just this very danger of a neutral geographical *bloc*, and whether we, by standing out, may not become responsible for bringing about the very situation the Socialist Executive in their pamphlet so rightly fear.

I was deeply moved by the decisive gesture which France made in the Schuman Plan for an effective reconciliation with Germany on the basis of such a measure of pooling heavy industries, which would, if developed, make impossible a renewal of war between these two nations. When I asked four years ago at Zurich that France should take Germany by the hand and lead her back into the European family, I could not hope that such an historic event would have come to pass so soon. It would be quite fair to ask me whether I should have welcomed this event even if there were no such thing as this Russian menace, or the Soviet Government or the Communist movement in many lands. I should say, 'Yes, certainly.' The unity of France and Germany, whether direct or in a larger Continental grouping, is a merciful and glorious forward step towards the revival of Europe and the peace of the world. The fact that there is a grave Soviet and Communist menace only adds to its value and urgency. Here surely we can find agreement on all sides of the House.

No one can say with justice that we are acting and feeling in this way in prejudice to the interests of the British Empire and Commonwealth. Everyone knows that that stands first in all our thoughts. First, there is the Empire and Commonwealth; secondly, the fraternal association of the English-speaking world; and thirdly, not in rank or status but in order, the revival of united Europe as a vast factor in the preserving of what is left of the civilization and culture of the free world. When one hears Socialist orators claim that they are the champions of the British Empire and Commonwealth of Nations and one remembers that they did not even take the trouble to tell the Commonwealth what was going on, it is impossible not to repress a feeling of scorn.

THE PRIME MINISTER [MR ATTLEE]: To what is the right hon Gentleman referring when he says we did not take the trouble to tell the Commonwealth what was going on?

MR CHURCHILL: I am talking about the Schuman Plan.

THE PRIME MINISTER: The right hon Gentleman is entirely wrong. The nations of the Commonwealth were kept fully informed.

MR CHURCHILL: Does the right hon Gentleman say that they were consulted upon the Government's refusal to accede to the Schuman invitation?

THE PRIME MINISTER: The right hon Gentleman said that they were right outside altogether, and that we have informed nobody. Anyone with experience of Commonwealth affairs knows that in all these matters the Commonwealth countries are kept fully informed, and any point which they wish to raise they do raise with the other members of the Commonwealth. In a matter which primarily concerns one member of the Commonwealth they are kept fully informed and they may raise points on that if they wish.

MR CHURCHILL: I must go into this a little bit, because I did not get the correct impression. I have only got in my mind what took place in the House. I understood that the Schuman Plan came as a surprise, and the right hon Gentleman the Prime Minister at short notice made a statement in this House, in which he spoke of it in welcoming terms. I do not know, but I have no doubt that the Dominions wished to raise some points. Before the Prime Minister took up the position he has taken up, I doubt very much if they had had any opportunity of expressing any opinion upon the course which events had taken. When I was asked at the Atlantic Conference in 1941 by Mr Roosevelt to agree that Imperial Preference should be eliminated, I said at once that we should never be able to take such a decision without consulting the Dominions themselves and this would take time. The argument was effective, among other reasons, because of the time factor in issuing a communiqué, about which the President was so eager. I cannot think of a better argument which the Government could have used to our French friends if they wished to have more time to consider their attitude than to say that they must consult on these matters with the Dominions by sending a telegram, affording them an opportunity to give a considered opinion. That it does not seem to have occurred to them is only another example of the extraordinary lack of efficiency with which our affairs are now conducted.

There are still one or two points which I must mention. The hon Member for Coventry East [Mr Crossman] last night asked the Tory Party whether they were in favour of the federal union of Western Europe. Such a tremendous step as the federal union of Europe as something like a United States of Europe is not a matter which rests with us to decide. It is primarily one for the peoples of Europe. In our European Movement we have worked with federalists, and we have always made it clear that, though they are moving along the same road, we are not committed to their conclusions. Personally, I have always deprecated in public our becoming involved at this stage in all the tangles and intricacies of rigid constitution-making, which appeals so strongly to a certain type of mind. I was sorry that the hon Member for Coventry East should have marred an able speech, as he so often does, by a gross misstatement when he says that European union 'is run and financed by federalists'. That is quite untrue, and I am very glad that my hon Friend the Member for Aberdeenshire East [Mr Boothby], who spoke earlier this afternoon, dealt effectively with that.

MR CROSSMAN (Coventry East): If that is untrue, then I wish to withdraw it.

MR CHURCHILL: Certainly, so far as the European Movement is concerned—and I took some trouble to make inquiries about it when I heard what the hon Gentleman had said about it—they rely upon voluntary contributions from England and America and they have not found any difficulty in finding the necessary funds. I am told that the difficulties of European federation are increasingly realized upon the Continent, and that it is one of the reasons why what I call 'functional' associations, like this proposed merger of the heavy industries, are being sought. But the question that we have to decide for ourselves—and there is certainly plenty of time for mature consideration of it—is, what association should Britain have with the Federal Union of Europe if such a thing should come to pass in the course of time?

It has not got to be decided today, but I shall give, with all humility, a plain answer. I cannot conceive that Britain would be an ordinary member of a Federal Union limited to Europe in any period which can at present be foreseen. We should in my opinion favour and help forward all developments on the Continent which arise naturally from a removal of barriers, from the process of reconciliation, and blessed oblivion of the terrible past, and also from our common dangers in the future and present. Although a hard-and-fast concrete federal constitution for Europe is not within the scope of practical affairs, we should help, sponsor and aid in every possible way the movement towards European unity. We should seek steadfastly for means to become intimately associated with it.

In this, we are supported by many of the leading statesmen in all parties in all the Commonwealth countries: Mr Menzies and Mr Evatt in Australia, Mr Fraser in New Zealand, General Smuts—for whose recovery we pray—and Mr Mackenzie King and Mr St Laurent in Canada. All have warmly advocated a forward movement towards European unity and have not, so far as I am aware, assigned any rigid or fixed limits to it. With our position as the centre of the British Empire and Commonwealth and with our fraternal association with the United States in the English-speaking world, we could not accept full membership of a federal system of Europe. We must find our path to world unity through the United Nations organization, which I hope will be re-founded one day upon three or four regional groups, of which a united Europe should certainly be one. By our unique position in the world, Great Britain has an opportunity, if she is worthy of it, to play an important and possibly a decisive part in all the three larger groupings of the Western democracies. Let us make sure that we are worthy of it.

The whole movement of the world is towards an inter-dependence of nations. We feel all around us the belief that it is our best hope. If independent, individual sovereignty is sacrosanct and inviolable, how is it that we are all wedded to a world organization? It is an ideal to which we must subscribe. How is it that we have undertaken this immense obligation for the defence of Western Europe, involving ourselves as we have never done before in the fortunes of countries not protected by the waves and tides of the Channel? How is it that we accepted, and under the present Government eagerly sought, to live upon the bounty of the United States, thus becoming financially dependent upon them? It can only be justified and even tolerated because on either side of the Atlantic it is felt that interdependence is part of our faith and the means of our salvation.

No one can contend that sovereignty will be affected by our participation in the discussions in Paris which are the subject of our Motion and the Amendment tonight. They are well protected by the cumulative safeguards which I mentioned earlier. Nevertheless, there is a great moral and idealistic issue which, though irrelevant to our immediate purpose, has been stirred by the discussions which have taken place. We are asked in a challenging way: 'Are you prepared to part with any degree of national sovereignty in any circumstances for the sake of a larger synthesis?' My right hon Friend the Member for Warwick and Leamington [Mr Eden], with his prolonged experience in foreign affairs, has faced the issue, hypothetical though it be, plainly and squarely. The Conservative and Liberal Parties say, without hesitation, that we are prepared to consider, and if convinced to accept, the abrogation of national sovereignty, provided that we are satisfied with the conditions and the safeguards.

Nay, I will go further and say that for the sake of world organization we would even run risks and make sacrifices. We fought alone against tyranny for a whole year, not purely from national motives. It is true that our lives depended upon our doing so, but we fought the better because we felt with conviction that it was not only our own cause but a world cause for which the Union Jack was kept flying in 1940 and 1941. The soldier who laid down his life, the mother who wept for her son, and the wife who lost her husband, got inspiration or comfort, and felt a sense of being linked with the universal and the eternal by the fact that we fought for what was precious not only for ourselves but for mankind. The Conservative and Liberal Parties declare that national sovereignty is not inviolable, and that it may be resolutely diminished for the sake of all the men in all the lands finding their way home together.

ROYAL UNITED SERVICES INSTITUTION

A SPEECH ON RECEIVING THE CHESNEY GOLD MEDAL
4 JULY 1950

---

28 *June—TUC abandons policy of wages restraint adopted in January.*
30 *June—Coal Board profits for the year* 1949 *amount to over* £9,000,000, *reducing the net deficit to* £12,000,000.

[4 *July* 1950

ADMIRAL MOORE, my Lords, Ladies and Gentlemen:

I regard it as a very great honour to be invited here today and see around me so many faces of so many friends and comrades of our late and former struggles, and to receive at your hands, Admiral, this medal, which I shall greatly treasure and value, and which will be preserved and handed down with my most precious possessions. I was reading the conditions which were laid down for the award, when it was instituted as a memorial to Sir George Chesney, that the recipient should be the author of an original literary work treating of naval or military science and literature which has a bearing on the welfare of the British Empire. Certainly I have been fully qualified so far as the writing of books about wars is concerned; in fact, already in 1900, which is a long time ago, I could boast to have written as many books as Moses, and I have not stopped writing them since, except when momentarily interrupted by war, in all the intervening period.

It gives me great pleasure to look along the list of those who have received this honour at your hands, and it stirs in my mind many recollections. With regard to your first recipient, Captain Mahan, he certainly qualifies in the highest manner for writing an original literary work treating of naval or military science, but I am not quite so sure that this had a directly favourable bearing upon the welfare of the British Empire. At that period, when Mahan was writing his memorable books, we had had for seventy or eighty years practically the only important navy in the world, and for the price of about £10,000,000 a year, or what a modern battleship, if you intended to build any of them, would cost today, or what a Brabazon aircraft has already cost, the Admiralty maintained the peace and the freedom of the seas; and our country never abused its trust or its greatness, though there was no other navy which could be a serious menace to it. But then there came along Captain Mahan, who pointed out a lot of things to a lot of people, of which they took a great deal of notice. He dwelt upon the immense advantages which Britain had reaped through sea power, and how our greatness had been founded entirely, or almost entirely, upon it; and this started up a wave of competitive warship building which led on from step to step, with very nice calculations of relative power, and new vessels completely wiping out all the old accumulations of quite valuable ships, until we entered on the more sombre chapters of the history of the twentieth century. Still, there is no more famous writer on naval affairs that I remember.

But I noticed other names that gave me great pleasure. Spenser Wilkinson rendered great services; and Vice-Admiral Richmond I had the pleasure of knowing and working with at many periods of my life. His ability and his contribution to naval and military thought were of the very highest order. I am delighted to see in this list General Sir James Edmonds—'Archimedes' as he was called in the little group of high military officers at the War Office, among whom Sir John French and Sir Henry Wilson were prominent and who thought intently about the conditions under which Great Britain could send an army—an idea which had been discarded for half a century—to fight at the side of France upon the European continent. They all had nicknames, and I well remember 'Archimedes'. He has been occupied ever since that war—the First World War, which certainly seems to most of us a long time ago—in writing the official history of it in one fine volume after another, all packed with facts and devoid of pre- judice of any kind. I understand that he has now finished his labours. Then there is General Maurice, who played a most important and distinguished part in our affairs, and at one time was held to have stepped somewhat beyond the bounds to which a serving officer should confine himself, but whose acquaintance and friendship I have always enjoyed, and who has rendered such invaluable services for many years to the British Legion.

Then there is General Swinton—I must tell you a story about him. I am so glad that he is the holder of this medal; no one could deserve it more. This was at the beginning of the 1914-18 war, about six weeks after the armies were engaged. In those days the Press were not given any look-in at all. They were told 'No, it is war; you get out of the way'. This position was not maintained indefinitely, and the war correspondent reappeared and has now built himself up a position in all military operations which, from what one can read in the news- papers, seems to have been in no way diminished or inroaded upon in the latest examples which are before us. But to return to my anecdote,

We had a Cabinet close by here, and the question was raised in September 1914 of proper representation of the Press, giving the public more information. A very strong discussion took place, and Lord Kitchener, on whose left I sat, was very much for holding the firm position which had been taken and for leaving the public to learn from the published dispatches of the Generals, which would reach them in due course and in proper time, what was actually happening at the front. I did not think that this attitude could be effectively maintained even in those far-off, happy days, and I said to Lord Kitchener: 'Why don't you have an official correspondent, a friend of the General, living in his entourage, who will give a continuous stream of information to the public, who are naturally rather interested in what is going on, and at the same time will neither commit indiscretions nor associate the Supreme Command with every word that is written?' His Lordship looked round and turned to me and said, 'It is easy to make such suggestions, but whom would you propose? Give me an example.' I said, 'Why not Major Swinton?' 'Major Swinton? Who is he? What has he ever written?' So I said, 'Have you read *The Defence of Duffer's Drift?*' 'What!' said Lord Kitchener, 'did he write that?' The subject dropped, but that afternoon Swinton went out to Sir John French's headquarters as an official correspondent.

I am most grateful to you for including me among these distinguished men. We have always to be very careful nowadays—we politicians, if we take an interest in military matters, or are held to have accumulated some knowledge and experience about them, lest we should be described for electioneering purposes as warmongers. Nevertheless, I cannot possibly escape some association with this military field, and I earnestly hope that all you members of this famous institution, so many of whom I see gathered in this beautiful hall, will make it your duty to keep alive in the thinking part of the British nation a keen and flexible volume of British thought upon the art of war, without a knowledge of which even now at the present time, after the wars to end wars are over, no nation can be sure that it will survive.

I earnestly hope that the thought of those who are capable of it and are concerned with it will be focused upon the new facts which are every day coming into being. You know the old joke about how the War Office is always preparing for the last war; and, of course, you cannot help men who have had experience and handled matters, after ten or fifteen years of peace from having rooted in their minds the strong impressions which they derived from the actual conduct of operations in the field. That is of the greatest value because, in the main, war consists of the same tunes, played through the ages, though sometimes only on a reed flute or a bagpipe and sometimes through a full modern orchestra. But it is of the utmost consequence that, besides cherishing the fruits of experience, everyone's mind should be open to the ceaseless and almost baffling rapidity of the changes which science is introducing into the whole field of war, into every aspect of it.

Above all, we have this intruder—the air, which has shoved its way in and continues to push forward in all directions, laying its hand now on this and now on that until a lot of people begin to think that it is the only pebble on the beach. That would be going too far: because I am quite sure of this, that when all modern science has been exploited and employed, and when all the worst that can be done has been done in some terrible encounter, which pray God may never occur, but, if that should be so, still the life of nations will depend upon the spirit, the courage of their race and of their men and women; and the bravery of fighting men, ready to continue whatever happens, will be the final decider of the life of nations, whether in a civilized or a barbaric world.

I thank you so much, Admiral. I remember our work in the war, when you were so great a help. We had those submarines sinking the ships, you remember, and tremendous difficulty in maintaining ourselves and developing our forces. It was natural that the Admiralty should at first measure their success by the reduction of our losses at sea; but presently a place had to be found for another idea, namely getting the largest quantity of cargoes in, or the minimum quota necessary of cargoes into our ports, and so we had to decide to run more risks and lose more ships and get still larger imports of the goods necessary for us and on which we lived. One of the factors was the enormous time wasted in the turn-round of ships. On that I think the Admiral worked for months, and I watched with the greatest anxiety his weekly results and reports. He was enabled to reduce the days spent in port by nearly one-third, or more than one-third, and this added to our available shipping a great mass of tonnage which we could never have built in the course of a whole year of the war. We owe him a great debt, and I am delighted to think that he is there at the Nore, watching out upon the Channel, which is, I am glad to say, no longer so dangerous as it was at one time; but I am sure that his Command, although unhappily stripped of the Royal Marines, will not fail to discharge its function, its invaluable function, with the same fidelity and precision which has characterized it so many times in the past.

I thank you very much, Admiral, for presenting me with this medal and for bringing me here and enabling me to see so many of my old friends and comrades. I thank them for their presence here, and I can assure you that I shall carry away sentiments of the utmost gratitude to you for all your kindness, and I shall carry away what will last longer than I shall, this beautiful medal, as a trophy and as a souvenir.

AMERICAN SOCIETY IN LONDON

A SPEECH AT THE INDEPENDENCE DAY DINNER HELD AT THE DORCHESTER
HOTEL

4 JULY 1950

YOUR EXCELLENCIES, My Lords, Ladies and Gentlemen:
I was glad when you asked me to join you tonight in celebrating
Independence Day. Among Englishmen I have a special qualification
for such an occasion, I am directly descended through my mother
from an officer who served in Washington's Army. And as such I have
been made a member of your strictly selected Society of the Cincinnati.
I have my pedigree supported by affidavits at every stage if it is challenged. So what? Well, Ladies and Gentlemen, it is a long time since
the War of Independence and quite a lot of things have happened, and
keep on happening. There is no doubt that I was on both sides then
and it gives me a comfortable feeling of simplification as the years
have passed to feel that we're all on the same side now. The drawing
together in fraternal association of the British and American peoples,
and of all the peoples of the English-speaking world may well be
regarded as the best of the few good things that have happened to us
and to the world in this century of tragedy and storm.

It was Bismarck who said in the closing years of his life that the
most potent factor in human society at the end of the nineteenth
century was the fact that the British and American peoples spoke the
same language. He might well have added, what was already then
apparent, that we had in common a very wide measure of purpose and
ideals arising from our institutions, our literature and our common
law. Since then, on the anvil of war, we have become so welded
together that what might have remained for generations an interesting
historical coincidence has become the living and vital force which
preserves Christian civilization and the rights and freedom of mankind.
Nearly two months have passed since the Ambassador talked over
with me the invitation with which you have honoured me. Mr Lew
Douglas is an intimate war comrade of mine, and one of the best
friends from across the Atlantic which our country had in the struggle;
and that is saying a lot. He is esteemed throughout this island and we
all have felt the utmost sympathy for him in his accident, and admiration for the courage with which he has surmounted so much physical
pain. No one I am sure can do more to prevent misunderstandings—

diplomatic or otherwise—between our two countries than His Excellency the American Ambassador.

When I accepted your invitation I could not foresee that when the date arrived we should once again be brothers in arms, engaged in fighting for exactly the same cause that we thought we had carried to victory five years ago. The British and Americans do not war with races or governments as such. Tyranny, external or internal, is our foe whatever trappings or disguises it wears, whatever language it speaks, or perverts. We must forever be on our guard, and always vigilant against it—in all this we march together. Not only, if need be, under the fire of the enemy but also in those realms of thought which are consecrated to the rights and the dignity of man, and which are so amazingly laid down in the Declaration of Independence, which has become a common creed on both sides of the Atlantic Ocean.

The inheritance of the English-speaking world, vast and majestic though it is in territory and resources, derives its glory as a moral unity from thought and vision widely spread in the minds of our people and cherished by all of those who understand our destiny. As you may have heard (I don't want to give away any secrets) we had a General Election here a few months ago by which a Parliament was returned very evenly balanced but still more sharply divided; but divided not by small matters but by issues which cut deep into our national life. We have not developed to any extent over here the bipartisan conduct of external policy by both great parties like that which has in these later years so greatly helped the United States. Nevertheless, once the deep gong of comradeship between kindred nations strikes, resounds and reverberates, and when our obligations to the United Nations are staring us in the face, we shall allow no domestic party quarrels—grievous though they may be—to mar the unity of our national or international action. You can count on Britain, and not only Britain. Four years ago, when President Truman, whom we salute tonight, took me to Westminster College at Fulton in Missouri I ventured to offer the American people my counsel, and I said, 'Let no man underrate the abiding power of the British Empire and Commonwealth. Do not suppose that we shall not come through these dark years of privation as we came through the glorious years of agony, or that half a century from now will not see 70,000,000 or 80,000,000 Britons spread throughout the world and united in defence of our traditions, our way of life, and the world causes which you and we espouse.' In the increasing unity of the Anglo-American thought and action resides the main foundation of the freedom and progress of all the men in all the lands. Let us not weary, let us not lose confidence in our mission, let us not fail in our duty in times of stress, let us not flinch if danger comes.

We must ask ourselves whether danger—I mean the danger of a third world war, has come nearer because of what has happened in the last week and is happening now. I do not think, myself, that the danger has grown greater. But then, I thought it very serious before. It all depends where you start thinking in these matters. I must say that we—Britons and Americans—and the many States and nations associated with us have had hard luck. The Russian Communists have built up an empire far beyond the dreams of the Tsars out of a war in which they might have been conquered or driven beyond the Ural mountains in spite of the bravery with which the Russian Army fought for its native soil. They would have been conquered or driven out but for the immense diversionary aid of Britain and the United States on land and sea and, above all, in the air. And also the vital supplies which had cost so much self-denial, and peril—and the Ambassador knows a lot about all that because the shipping on which everything depended was throughout influenced in the most effective manner by his personal care and courage. Not only do the Soviets hold at the present time all the famous capitals of Europe east of the line—which I call 'the Iron Curtain' drawn from Stettin to Trieste, not only are they endeavouring with great cruelties to compel these many States and countries to adopt the Communist system and become incorporated in the Soviet mass, but they have gained also vast populations in Asia, including practically the whole of China. And they are pressing forward in insatiable, imperialist ambition wherever any weakness on the part of the free world gives them an opportunity.

Thus, I say we have had hard luck, just when we thought we had finished with Hitler and Mussolini, with Nazism and Fascism, we have Stalin and Communism lumping up against us representing the former Hitler tyranny in barbaric form and Asiatic guise. We had hoped that the task of this hard-pressed generation was done. Your poet Walt Whitman said: 'Now understand me well it is provided in the essence of things that from any fruition of success, no matter what, shall come forth something to make a greater struggle necessary.' We pray this may not be so. These hard decrees may be the lot of the human race in its unending struggle for existence, but the question which we have to consider tonight, and in regard to which the Ambassador laid before you in a cogently related argument many essential facts, is whether our dangers have been increased by the Communist act of aggression in Korea. I agree with the British Government speakers that they have not been increased. How does this new menace differ in principle from the Berlin blockade, two years ago, which together we faced with composure and overcame by the Allied airlift, mainly carried by American planes but in which we bore an important share? It differs in one major fact. We are told that the Kremlin oligarchy now know how to make the atomic bomb. That is the one new fact. To that extent there is a change to our disadvantage. It certainly seems to me that there is a better hope of a general settlement with Soviet Russia following on the defeat of aggression in Korea on a localized scale, than that we should drift on while large quantities of these devastating weapons are accumulated. Indeed I feel that there is nothing more likely to bring on a third world war than drift.

It is always difficult for free democracies, governed in the main by public opinion from day to day, to cope with the designs of dictator States and totalitarian systems. But hitherto we have held our own, or we should not be here tonight. We have only to be morally united and fearless, to give mankind the best hope of avoiding another supreme catastrophe. But I must say one thing before I sit down. It is of vital consequence to these hopes of world peace that what the Communists have begun in Korea should not end in their triumph. If that were to happen a third world war, under conditions even more deadly than now exist, would certainly be forced upon us, or hurled upon us before long. It is fortunate that the path of duty, and of safety, is so plainly marked out before our eyes, and so widely recognized by both our nations and governments, and by the large majority, the overwhelming majority of the member States comprised in the United Nations Organization.

We owe it not only to ourselves, but to our faith in an institution, if not a world government at least a world protection from aggressive war, not to fail in our duty now. Thus we shall find the best hopes of peace and the surest proof of honour. The League of Nations failed not because of its noble conceptions, but because these were abandoned by its members. We must not ask to be taught this hard lesson twice. Looking around this obscure, tumultuous scene, with all its uncertainties as it presents itself to us tonight, I am sure we shall not be guilty of such incurable folly; we shall go forward; we shall do our duty; we shall save the world from a third world war. And should it come in spite of all our efforts, still we shall not be trampled down into serfdom and ruin.

KOREA

A SPEECH TO THE HOUSE OF COMMONS
5 JULY 1950

---

5 July—Sir Stafford Cripps (Chancellor of the Exchequer) announces in the House of Commons that the sterling area has earned a net gold and dollar surplus of $180,000,000.

[*5 July 1950*

On a Motion moved by the Prime Minister
  '*that this House fully supports the action taken by HM Government, in conformity with their obligations under the UN Charter, in helping to resist the unprovoked aggression against the Republic of Korea*'.

I feel that the whole House is indebted to the Prime Minister for the cogent and lucid account which he gave of the events in Korea leading up to the present situation, and also for the full disquisition which he gave on the legal aspects of the decision of the Security Council, on which some questions have been raised by the Soviet Government. I found myself in very general agreement with the Prime Minister in the closing part of his address, and am fully able to associate myself with him, for reasons which I will presently venture to dwell upon, in his broad conclusion that the action which has been taken by the United States and endorsed, supported and aided by His Majesty's Government gives, on the whole, the best chance of maintaining the peace of the world.

We consider that the Government were right to place a Motion on the Order Paper asking for approval in general terms of the course which they have adopted since the invasion of South Korea began. There are grave reasons, as we learned in the war, that false impressions may be created abroad by a Debate prominently occupied by a handful of dissentients. It is better to have a Division so that everyone can know how the House of Commons stands and in what proportion. Should such a Division occur, we on this side will vote with the Government. I do not propose to embark upon a detailed argument about the merits of questions which have been raised by events in Korea, nor upon the decision reached by the Security Council and the United Nations. They have been ventilated in the Press and have just now been clearly explained to us by the Prime Minister. I do not believe that Soviet and Communist propaganda, with its perverted facts and inverted terminology, has made the slightest impression upon the well-tried common sense of the British people. No one outside the small Communist circles in this island or their fellow-travellers believes for an instant that it is South Korea which is the aggressor and North Korea which is the victim of a well and deliberately-planned and organized attack. On the contrary, the very unpreparedness and inefficiency of South Korea is the proof of their innocence, though not, perhaps of their wisdom.

Few, I think, will believe that Seoul, Suwon and other places which have been captured by the North Korean armies have been liberated from tyranny by Communist rescuers. Even the charge that the United States has attempted to create a diversion in Europe by scattering Colorado beetles from their aircraft throughout Saxony and elsewhere —although it has actually formed the subject of a formal and official protest by the Soviet Government to the United States—has not, so far as I can gather, made any deep or permanent impression upon the British public. On this side of the House we hold, in full agreement with the Government, that President Truman's action in South Korea was right and that His Majesty's Government, accompanied as their action has been by the action of other members of the Commonwealth, were also right in acting as they have done under the mandate of the Security Council by giving armed support to the intervention of the United States. The Conservative Party give their full support to the Government in these matters. We understand that the Liberal Party take a similar view of their duty and that their position will presently be put before the House. [*Interruption.*] Do not despise help and friendship when it is offered. Neither of us see what else the Government could have done in the circumstances.

I must for a moment step aside from my general theme to express the hope that the action of the Government and their supporters will be upon this same level. I cannot overlook the fact that in giving our support we run some party and political risks. I was reading *Reynolds' Newspaper* at the weekend and in it there was an article called 'Tom Driberg's Column', though whether that has any direct relationship with the hon Member for Maldon [Mr Driberg]——

MR DRIBERG (Maldon) *indicated assent.*

MR CHURCHILL: 'Tories bay for war'—that is the headline, but— [*Interruption.*]

MR HAROLD MACMILLAN (Bromley): Did the hon Member for Ayrshire, South [Mr Emrys Hughes] say 'It is true'? That is shameful.

MR CHURCHILL: Perhaps the hon Member for Maldon will say that he is not responsible for the headlines but only for the text?

MR DRIBERG *indicated assent*.

MR CHURCHILL: I understand that the hon Member accepts the responsibility.

MR DRIBERG: Certainly, for both.

MR CHURCHILL: And also these words? Let me just read them, because the House ought to see how all this is working out:

'There is quite a substantial number of back-bench Tories who, true to their jungle philosophy, cannot help baying their delight at the smell of blood in the air.'

HON MEMBERS: Shame.

MR DRIBERG: I am grateful to the right hon Gentleman the Member for Woodford [Mr Churchill]——

MR OSBORNE (Louth): Judas.

MR DRIBERG: —for his courtesy in giving way. May I just say here and now that I consider that a perfectly accurate description of a scene in this House last week, and that I only wish that the right hon Gentleman could have seen it before the editor toned it down and modified it.

MR CHURCHILL: I know it is the hon Member's pride that he can be neither muzzled nor led, and no doubt what we have seen in the columns of *Reynolds' Newspaper* is only a bowdlerized version of the total and utter untruths which he was scattering to the world.

MR OSBORNE: Did the hon Member for Maldon [Mr Driberg] get thirty pieces of silver for it?

MR CHURCHILL: The cheers from the Conservative benches were for the Prime Minister when he made his declaration, while some of the benches behind him were curiously silent.

MR DRIBERG: That was not what I was describing.

MR CHURCHILL: We are also told that it is being put about in many constituencies that if the Tories had been in office there would have been war now. That is not true. If we had been in office when the news of President Truman's action arrived we should have acted in very much the same way as His Majesty's Government have done. I am not at all sure that we should have received from all the Members opposite and from all their followers the same measure of goodwill and support that we are giving them on this occasion. We shall not, however, allow our action to be deflected in great matters by behaviour of this kind. We believe that the electorate, in judging these matters for themselves, will be influenced by the ordinary British standards of fair play, and it is on that that we rest ourselves.

I must say one word here about the Secretary of State for War

[Mr Strachey], whose speech at the weekend was the subject of question and answer just now. As to the merits of his comments on the Schuman Plan, I shall not attempt to pronounce, except to say that they are very different from the formal Amendment placed on the Order Paper by the Government that they welcomed the French Plan, but I really wonder that the right hon Gentleman cannot a little cast his past behind him and rise to the occasion of the great responsibilities which he has the honour to bear as the head of a Fighting Service at this critical time. I really wonder that he should find it necessary to hamper his work in a great Service and reduce his influence in the country by plunging into these bitter political controversies. Surely he has enough responsibilities to bear and enough work to do, and surely he has been treated with a great deal of forbearance by the House of Commons?

I was commenting on the article of the hon Member for Maldon just now, but I must confess that in some ways I prefer his outspoken diatribes to the comments of the hon Member for Coventry who really has laid down a principle—[HON MEMBERS: 'Which one?'] The hon Member for Coventry East [Mr Crossman]. Certainly I would not like to saddle any other constituency with the responsibility of the hon Member. But this is to my mind one of those little sayings which should always be placed on record. This is what the hon Member wrote in the *Sunday Pictorial*:

'But there is one lesson we can and must learn from recent history —the time to start thinking about peace is the beginning and not the end of the fighting.'

All I can say is that it has usually been thought, and I hope will not be overlooked on the present occasion, that between the beginning of fighting and the end of fighting, between the beginning of a war or a military operation and peace, there is an intervening stage called victory. It seems that the hon Member for Coventry East in trying—curiously and even characteristically—to have it both ways has really excelled himself in this particular statement, which has only to be followed by any Government carrying on military operations to lead to certain military disaster. We naturally cannot accept the responsibility for creating the present situation, nor do I suggest that this falls primarily upon Great Britain. Still less, as I have already stated to the House, can we accept any responsibility for the military position of our country or of Europe, or for the use that has been made of the unprecedented sums of money which have been voted by the House for the Defence Services, or for the resources of manpower placed with our full support on this side at the disposal of His Majesty's Government.

Some time in May, before this crisis occurred, I asked the Prime

Minister for a Secret Session of Debate on our military position in order that this new Parliament might have some idea of where we stood in Europe and of the state of our own defences. The Prime Minister did not grant my request and we had therefore intended on this side of the House to have a public Debate on Defence before we separated for the Recess. Now that this crisis has arisen I do not feel that it would be helpful at this stage if we had a general Debate on Defence in public, even though all responsible Members taking part in it were to confine themselves strictly to facts which they were sure the Soviet Government already knew. But even within this limitation there is a vast amount of matter which is public knowledge, which has appeared in British newspapers, and, far more, which has appeared in the United States either in the Press or in the continuous proceedings of the Congress and its varied committees.

There never has been a period that I can remember covering the present century in which the British public and the British Parliament were so totally ignorant of the conditions which exist. I must, therefore, renew my request here and now across the Floor of the House for a Debate in Secret Session upon this matter before we separate. I do not ask that even in Secret Session we should be told any secrets of a special or technical character. On the contrary, I should be quite content if the Government limited themselves in their statements to what they are sure is already known abroad. I do not pretend myself to have anything like the detailed and precise information on which I based my warnings before the last war. Nevertheless, I am sure I could tell the House a lot of things which they ought to bear in mind, and these the Government could amplify or correct at their discretion, and other hon Members would make their fruitful contributions.

If a Secret Session is refused and we do not ourselves, even within the limits I have prescribed, have a public Debate, the House will go forward into this deepening crisis with less information about it than any previous Parliament at any similar time. It seems to me that the Prime Minister and his colleagues will be taking an invidious and unprecedented responsibility upon themselves if they refuse us the Secret Session for which we ask. It is a responsibility which we on this side can in no wise share. Our responsibility is limited to supporting them in what they are doing in the international sphere since last Tuesday week, and does not extend to the military field or to what has happened since 1945 or to the methods which have been adopted or to the Ministers chosen to deal with our defences.

I will, therefore, confine myself today to a few general observations which are necessary to justify the support we are giving to His Majesty's

Government. It might be asked of us: 'How can you judge without the fullest information whether the United Nations, the United States and Great Britain are strong enough to resist Communist aggression in the Far East when that resistance may conceivably bring about a major crisis in Europe? Might it not be that the rulers in the Kremlin are drawing us all into the Far East as a preliminary to striking in the West?' I answer these questions to myself, as one's mind asks questions at these times, as follows. The forces required for the defence of South Korea, or even its recapture should that become necessary, would not make any decisive or even appreciable difference to the situation in Europe. The immunity of Western Europe from attack depends overwhelmingly on the vastly superior stockpile of atomic bombs possessed by the United States. There is the deterrent, and the sole decisive deterrent, which exists or can be brought into being in the near future. Therefore I do not feel that a major issue of security is raised by the necessary measures which have to be taken in Korea.

Secondly, I have for a long time felt deeply concerned at the discovery by the Soviet Government of the secret of the atomic bomb, and the probability that it is already in production. I saw that General Omar Bradley, who occupies one of the most responsible executive positions in the United States defence system, said recently that in three or four years the Soviets will have a sufficient supply of these bombs to cause a major catastrophe at any time they so decided, or words to that effect. It is for this reason that I think it very much better that we should make a resolute effort to come to a settlement with them by peaceful means, but on the basis of strength and not of weakness, on the basis of success and not on fatuous incapacity of resistance to aggression. We should endeavour to come to a settlement with them before they become possessed of this devastating power in addition to all the military and air superiority and armour superiority which they undoubtedly possess at this present time in Europe and Asia.

I can quite understand the Communist propaganda about banning the atomic bomb, for such a decision would leave the civilization of the world entirely at their mercy even before they had accumulated the necessary stockpile themselves. Since this new aggression in Korea and the spirited reaction of the United States, I feel that we ought to bring the policy of drift to an end, and I believe that no better prelude to the opening of major discussions with the Soviet Government could be found than the successful repulse of the Communist forces that are now invading Korea. I believe that if this is achieved, conditions may be created less unfavourable to a general settlement than any others I can conceive before the Soviet power is freed from the deterrent of the immense American superiority in atomic resources. That hope may fail, but it is the best hope that now exists of averting from Europe and America perils and sufferings utterly beyond anything we have hitherto experienced. It is my belief that the American superiority in atomic warfare is, for the time being, an effective deterrent against a general Communist onslaught. Of course, I may be wrong—no one can tell; no one can give a guarantee.

Still, if it be true that there are at present no signs of exceptional preparations or concentrations behind the Iron Curtain in Europe, it would at least give a temporary indication that the supreme events of misfortune are not immediately imminent. Indeed, it may well be that the Soviet Government have been taken aback by the resolute action of President Truman, supported as it has been by His Majesty's Government and by so many other States and members of the United Nations. This is no time to despair of world peace being achieved upon tolerable foundations. Certainly, we must not despair. To do so is almost to despair of the life of the world. But one thing is essential now, and I cannot think that the Government will differ from me when I say that it is of vital consequence alike to our hopes of world peace and to our own safety here at home, namely, that what the Communists have begun in Korea should not end in their triumph. If that were to happen, as I said last night to an American gathering, a third world war under conditions more deadly than now exist might be forced upon us—would be forced upon us—before long.

There could be no more certain way of bringing about the destruction of civilization than that we should drift on helplessly until the Soviets are fully equipped with the atomic bomb. Neither, meanwhile, must we accept defeat and humiliations in one place after another wherever the Communists thrust and gnaw their way forward, and in this process of continued misfortune lose the faith in us of everyone else in the world, and lose our own confidence in ourselves. There could be no greater disaster than that; there could be no more certain road to what it is our first duty to avoid than that; and it is because of my confidence that those men in His Majesty's Government with whom I worked so long and with whom I have gone through so much are resolved to prevent by every means in their power anything like that, that I shall follow the Prime Minister tonight should the need come to give him a vote.

THE PLYMOUTH FAIR

A SPEECH AT SALTRAM PARK, PLYMOUTH
15 JULY 1950

6 *July—US State Department announces that all shipments of oil, as well as material with any war potential, are being discontinued to the Far East to prevent such supplies being utilized by countries sympathetic to North Korea.*

7 *July—Pandit Nehru outlines the Indian attitude to the Korean war, which, while supporting the United Nations, is of the opinion that 'the admission of the People's Republic of China in the Security Council, and the return of the USSR, are necessary conditions to enable the Security Council to discharge its functions adequately and to bring the Korean conflict to a prompt and peaceful conclusion'.*

11-12 *July—The Economic Affairs Committee of the Council of Europe adopt a resolution in support of the Schuman Plan.*

14 *July—Mr Fadden, Acting Australian Prime Minister, gives details of plan for national military training in Australia.*

[15 *July* 1950

Five months have passed since I came to Plymouth to address a West Country audience. Then we had good hopes of bringing about an immediate and decisive change in the politics of our country, and of establishing in effective power a broad-based Conservative Government which would prove itself worthy of its trust and equal to these difficult and dangerous times. Now we see that in spite of the substantial advantages we gained, a second intense effort will be necessary. It is certain that another General Election must come soon. How soon we cannot tell. The initiative does not at present rest with us. It depends upon what the Socialist Government think will pay them best. Meanwhile we lie in the lull between two storms. The only Socialist Government in the English-speaking world and, apart from Scandinavia the only Socialist Government in Europe outside the Iron Curtain, continues its control of our affairs, although in a minority of more than 1,500,000 votes in the country, and with a majority of only seven in the House of Commons. It is certainly satisfactory that such a Government is virtually deprived of all power of legislation. They have had to abandon, for the time being, their whole scheme for nationalizing another set of prosperous key industries, sugar, cement, insurance and the like, with which they threatened us at the General Election. Steel alone hangs in the balance, and it would indeed be an outrage if its nationalization were to be brought into force by the present Government after its decisive rejection by the electorate. With this exception, the Socialist plans for revolutionizing British Society have been brought to a full stop, and the Socialist Ministers and Members of Parliament have to limit their immediate programme to the personal satisfaction of prolonged summer holidays on full pay.

I need not appeal to you gathered here to make every exertion in your power in order to secure an effective majority for the Conservative Party at the impending election, because I know how earnest are your resolves and how tireless are your activities. The need to secure a strong Government, opposed to the fallacies and frauds of Socialism, is not merely a party objective but a national aim, on which the future of our country depends. But it seems to me that while we put forth every scrap of strength we can command, we should also endeavour to gather the support of all men and women of goodwill outside our own party limits, and unite in the common front against Socialism, not only Liberals, but that large floating vote, which played such a hesitating part last time in the trial of strength. This is a moment when we have a right to appeal to all patriotic and broadminded men and women who are in agreement on the main issues, to do their utmost to secure the establishment of a strong, broadly-based and stable Government, capable of dealing in a courageous and progressive spirit with the ever darkening problems that confront us.

I feel this is the time when those who agree on fundamental issues should stand together. Let me mention to you some of the great issues on which Unionists and Liberals are agreed, and which constitute the elements of the common cause vital to our national welfare. First, we proclaim that the State is the servant and not the master of the people, and that freedom under the law is not what Dr Dalton calls 'an experiment' but our *right*. We reject altogether the Socialist conception of a division of society between officials and the common mass. We repudiate their policy of levelling down to a minimum uniformity above which only politicians and their agents may rise. We stand for the increasingly higher expression of individual independence. We hold most strongly to the Declaration of Human Rights, as set forth by the United Nations at Geneva. While placing first in our thoughts the British Empire and Commonwealth of Nations, we welcome the growing movement towards European unity, and the ending of the old Continental feuds that have brought so much misery upon us all. We intend to help this movement forward all we can within the limits of our main obligations. We do not believe in the organization of Europe in the name of any single party. Socialist policy has been in these past years increasingly out of step and out of harmony with, or lagging behind, the movement of thought among the free democracies of the modern world and especially in Europe.

Far from being in the van of international progress, they have become a brake and an obstruction. We have seen a painful example of this in the abuse lavished on the Schuman Plan by a Minister and many of the rank and file in the last week. This is a plan to bring Germany and France together by a union of their basic industries, beginning with coal and steel. Every argument of prejudice and isolationism has been used against not only the plan but against our merely taking part in these discussions, while remaining effectively safeguarded from any commitments if in the end we do not feel the scheme is practical. Mr Strachey, so oddly Secretary of State for War in this critical period, has given his word of honour that he did not call the Schuman Plan a 'Plot'. If that is true it is almost the only term of abuse he did not apply to it. His views might have been taken almost verbatim from his old friend the *Daily Worker*, and are in this matter in full accord with the guidance given from Moscow to the Communist world. I trust they will not prevail against the decent and responsible elements in the Socialist Party.

Then we declare ourselves inveterately opposed to any further nationalization of industry, including, of course, and especially, the nationalization of steel. There is thus a large overlap of agreement, both in doctrine and in action, between those who have hitherto been brought up to regard themselves as political opponents. But now the times are very grave, and it is the duty of every man and woman who agrees upon so large a proportion of the main principles and practical steps, to make sure that these are not overwhelmed by the ignorant, partisan and obsolete fallacy of Socialism, against which the British nation stands today in marked recoil. All I ask, and it is a modest demand, is that those who agree upon the fundamentals shall, in our party conflicts, try to help each other as much as they can, and harm each other as little as they must. Let that theme of conduct prevail, and we shall have cleared the path of progress of many of its pitfalls and barriers, and perhaps have the power to rescue our native land from some of the perils and forms of degeneration by which it is oppressed. But I must make it clear that I do not contemplate merely the absorption of Liberals in the Conservative Party as individuals (that will certainly go on) but an honourable agreement and alliance between the Liberal and Conservative Parties as integral institutions. This will give the best chance of bringing into power a stable and progressive Government capable of dealing with our practical needs and in harmony with the movement of thought throughout the free world.

There is no doubt that nationalization, so far as it has gone, has proved an utter failure financially and economically and morally. But there is now an argument against it which undoubtedly makes an impression upon the Socialist leaders—it is politically unpopular. They do not know whether to bury Socialism and nationalization, which they have been preaching for fifty years and practising for five, and look for some other method of carrying on the class war. In any case, we are confronted with a party which has lost its convictions and has no longer a theme and plan and instead of proclaiming an ideological design for reconstructing human society is now hungrily looking around for a new election cry. Meanwhile we must do our duty in the new Parliament in such a way as to limit on every possible occasion mismanagement of our affairs by the Socialist Government and so far as possible to mitigate the evils which it brings upon our people. I assert that from the beginning we have pursued the right policy, both during the election and since the session began. We have done the natural, honest, simple thing from day to day, on serious issues, in accordance with our mandate from the constituencies and with the principles and cause we all believe in.

The course we have adopted has already procured several notable advantages for the country as a whole. We have forced from the Government many concessions to the public interest which they harshly refused in the days when they had an automatic majority to vote down any opposition and ride roughshod over us. The first of these has been the abolition of the compulsory conscription of labour in time of peace. That has been swept away. They have been forced to arrest all nationalization except steel. You will remember what an outcry they made when I said here in Plymouth that the petrol ration should be increased—'what a shocking thing', they cried, 'to cast away the precious dollars on which we depend for the food of our people, upon the mere luxury of pleasure motoring.' 'How irresponsible,' Mr Attlee cried, 'to make such a suggestion!' But now they have themselves not merely increased but abolished the petrol ration, proving what I said, and exposing the untruthful character of their electioneering propaganda.

There have also been minor concessions in controls in the building industry. The private builder is to be given more scope. It is to be easier for the citizen to enlarge his house or his farm buildings. PAYE has been modified, as we urged, so as to be less penal in its discouragement of overtime and effort. We are even to be allowed more soap and stronger beer. Finally, we have made them replace the 25,000 houses they had cut from the building programme, and raise the total from 175,000 houses to 200,000 for the next two years. I am very glad we have forced them to do this. Of course it in no way meets the housing problem, which continues to hold the first place in our domestic needs. Nevertheless, all these concessions we have wrung and wrested from the Socialists show how right in fact, and how fruitful to the public has been the severe pressure which we have applied, and shall continue to apply in the House of Commons.

Nowhere have the Socialists failed the hopes of the electorate more than in their gross failure to redeem their many promises to solve the housing problem. Four years ago Mr Bevan confidently predicted that when the next general election came every family in the land would have a separate home. Instead the waiting lists at every town hall grow longer. Fewer houses are being built today than in 1948. If it had not been for our constant pressure the figures would be even far worse. There is no prospect whatever of any early resumption of the slum clearance campaign, which was so vigorously sweeping away slum areas in the years of Tory Government before the war. In those years—which the Socialist propagandists falsely called 'years of neglect' —a thousand houses were built every day. The Socialist planners can manage to get only half that number built at three times the cost. Throughout the six years, 1933-9, 700 slum dwellers were rehoused every day. At that rate the last slum would have disappeared by about 1944 if war had not come. Since 1945, the whole of this great social reform has stopped. In these matters you do not stand still; you either advance or go back. Today we have more slum dwellings than for many years past. The housing shortage is also felt severely in the villages and hamlets, where it has hindered and handicapped our efforts to produce more food from our own soil. Mr Bevan, that marplot of Socialist progress, treated the housing needs of rural Britain with scant consideration. He refused to proceed with the Conservative Rural Housing Bill. He made no provision for reconditioning grants until 1949. Last week in Parliament he confessed that during the whole of the past year only one reconditioning grant had been made in the whole of the county of Devon.

Our general attitude as an Opposition today remains precisely what it has been ever since the Socialists took office in 1945. Every measure based on their party doctrine or prejudice meets our resistance. Every measure conceived in the national interest, even if unpopular, receives our support. Thus we have supported conscription when it would have been to our electoral advantage to have denounced it. We have hitherto supported every major step Mr Bevin has taken in foreign policy, however belated or ill-combined. We are sorry for his illness. We are also sorry that we have not had an effective Foreign Secretary during these critical months. We have frequently sustained the Government against the attack of their own followers. What a contrast is all this to the behaviour of the pre-war Socialist Party, when they were in Opposition and when they opposed every defence estimate—Navy, Army and Air, did their best to hamper the recruiting campaign, and, led by Mr Attlee, voted against National Service only four months before war broke out.

I ask from this great meeting, representing six constituencies in the West Country, a firm and decided endorsement of the work we have already done. Since we have been able to achieve these results while in a minority, it may well be that if the tables were turned the British nation could speedily be relieved of an immense network and oppression of needless controls, hardships and interferences with their daily lives by a new administration seeking the public welfare with wholehearted sincerity. It is our duty to fight hard as a party against Socialist wrong thinking and mismanagement. Everyone can see what a change has taken place in our position at home and in the eyes of other countries since that thoughtless vote of the electorate in 1945. When I laid down my commission the British nation, Empire and Commonwealth was victorious, respected and safe. There was perhaps no country in the world so much honoured, not only by friends, but even by vanquished enemies, as this island. It is painful to contrast our position and opportunities five years ago with what they are today. We had been united in our struggle to preserve the freedom of the world. Now when our dangers have revived and gathered again we lie in an unfortunate position. The indecisive vote of last February leaves us in the unpleasant atmosphere betwen two elections. Parliamentary democracy can only express itself by regular and not infrequent appeals to the electorate, but no one has ever suggested that prolonged electioneering is capable of settling our problems at home, or warding off our dangers from abroad. One can hardly imagine anything more unfortunate in Britain than that we should find ourselves at the present juncture split in half on domestic politics, with both parties gathering and arranging their forces for another trial of strength. That this should continue for many months without remedy can only be disastrous to our prosperity, and may well endanger both our life and even our survival as a great power.

Who is it that has brought about this deep gulf in our national life? No doubt each side will blame the other. Certainly many hard and bitter words are being spoken, by both sides. There are always words in partisan warfare, and the British people have always been free spoken in their party fights. But deeds are stronger than words, and it is the deeds, or misdeeds, of the Socialist Government, who alone wield executive power, which have brought about the present violent internal antagonism in the midst of renewed and increasing national peril.

Armed conflict has broken out between the United Nations, comprising almost all the free peoples of the world, and the Russian organized and well-equipped Communists of Northern Korea. The United States are bearing with courage and resolution in a noble way the burden of this clash which is in all essentials a renewal of our fight for human freedom against Hitler. I do not say that what has happened and is happening in Korea has made the dangers of a third world war greater. They were already grave. It has brought them nearer, and they are more apparent and I trust indeed that it has made the great masses of peoples throughout the free world more aware, awake and alive to where they stand.

I have myself for some time past believed that the worst chance for the life of the free world was to continue a policy of drift. At least three precious years of the United Nations have been wasted in floating along from day to day hoping, in spite of ceaseless disappointments and warnings, that all would come out right if we hoped for the best and let things take their course. But meanwhile the Communist menace and aggression continues to spread throughout the world. The fourteen men in the Kremlin are not drifting with events. They work on calculation and design. They have a policy the aim of which we can see; but the execution and timing of their ambition for Communist world government we cannot predict. They infiltrate in all countries with adepts and agents. Their adherents have no loyalty to any home. They care nothing for their native lands. They owe allegiance solely to Moscow. Communism is a religion with all its discipline and some of its fervour—a religion not only without God, but anti-God. It is a philosophy of base materialism in the name of which the world is to be reduced to the Soviet-Socialist pattern just as Hitler wanted it reduced to the Nazi-Socialist pattern. They have condemned Christian ethics and civilization, as we have known them, to a formidable struggle.

But behind all this doctrinal and ideological movement of thought which might well be defeated, and is indeed being defeated by the free play of Parliamentary democracy in countries where this is allowed, lies the mighty Russian armed power. The Communists pay lip-service to the doctrine of peace, but by peace they mean submission to their will and system. They preach the reduction of armaments, but they have more men organized and trained under arms than all the rest of the world put together. They urge the banning of the atomic bomb which in the hands of the United States is at this moment the only physical shield and protection of the free world, while they themselves have rejected any bona-fide international control and inspection, and are trying to make bombs as fast as they can. Meanwhile around all the vast frontiers of Soviet Russia and her satellite or conquered countries they maintain a policy of unending aggression or menace. Since the war nearly all China with its hundreds of millions of people has been incorporated in the Soviet system. They are massing troops against Tibet. They threaten Persia. They are seeking to over-awe and quell Yugoslavia. They cause deep fear in Finland and Sweden.

President Truman, under the full sanction and authority of the United Nations, and with the overwhelming support of the American people, and of the British Empire, and of its Commonwealth, has confronted aggression in Korea. I have not the knowledge to enable me to predict how this Korean fighting will end. But let me here express our admiration for the daring and skill with which the handful of American soldiers, three or four battalions at most, who have as yet been brought into action in Korea have fought their delaying action against overwhelming odds. I rejoice to learn that so far they have suffered only a few hundred casualties. Now, however, a more serious collision impends, or has begun. But whatever happens in Korea is only a part, and a small part of the pressures under which our free civilization lies, and which it must face or perish.

What is the position in Western Europe? Nearly half of Europe has already been subjugated by the Kremlin since the war. Large areas of Germany, occupied by the liberating armies of Britain and the United States, were handed over at the end of the war to the Russian rule, in virtue of wartime agreements which in so many other respects the Stalin domination had already completely broken in the case of Poland and Yugoslavia. I see that General de Gaulle declared a few days ago that Europe was in mortal peril. I have often disagreed with General de Gaulle, but I cannot feel that what he has said at this time is untrue. We are none of us free from peril even here in this island, where at least we have the waves, winds and tides of the Channel between us and the unhappy Continent. Even here in this beautiful and famous Devonshire so long and so valiantly defended in bygone generations we do not know what our fortunes will be. We live our ordinary lives, we go about our business and work hard as we must and ought to earn our livelihood and that of our country. But I tell you with the utmost earnestness that my own anxieties about the safety not only of the free world, but of our own hearths and homes, often remind me of the summer of 1940 ten tragic years ago. By this I do not mean that war is imminent. But I must not lead you to suppose that time is on our side; that we have only got to go on with our party quarrels and close our eyes and stop our ears to the facts of the situation to find that all will work out all right in the long run. This might be a fatal delusion. We have not been able ourselves since the war to make an atomic bomb. I don't know why.

We are dependent in this and in so much else upon the United States. But the oligarchy of the wicked men at the head of the Communist world have had the secret betrayed to them, and have found out also from other sources, how to make this fearful weapon for themselves. At present, so far as I have been able to learn, they have very few atomic bombs. But I do not see how the passage of two or three years, during which they will be building up a large stock of them, is going to make our problems simpler or our dangers less. It is time that the British people should know more about the facts upon which the causes they defended and championed, and their very lives, may well depend.

You may have noticed that I have formally asked for a Secret Session in order that Parliament may be given some fuller information on the state of our defences at home and in Europe, and that Mr Attlee has so far refused. But I hold that Members of the House of Commons are responsible to their constituencies for making themselves generally acquainted with matters which concern the lives and safety of those who sent them to Westminster. At present the Socialist majority are content to remain in ignorance even of the main facts, and are prepared to vote down any proposal to give more information. We may not even talk things over among ourselves in Parliament. I take a high view of the duties of the elected representatives of the people. They should be kept at least as well informed as their predecessors before the war about the main foundations of our national safety. This Parliament is more uninformed about these matters than any I have ever seen. We do not want to be told deadly technical secrets, but we ought to know broadly and truly where we are and how we stand. I should certainly not expect that even in Secret Session anything should be told us that the Soviet Government do not already know. But Members representing large masses of electors ought to have a sense of responsibility for their survival. It would be much better for Parliament to have a free discussion within the limits I have mentioned instead of going on blindfold like this.

It is argued that there would be leakage from a Secret Session. The disclosure of matters which pass in a Secret Session is a breach of privilege, and this has always proved a good check, even on indiscretion. Moreover, at the General Election we got rid of the Communist Members and the most noticeable of their fellow-travellers; and I cannot believe this present House could not be trusted with what His Majesty's Government would think fit to tell them, none of which would tell the Russians what they do not already know. Of course we have the right and the power to raise these matters in Public Debate, and if a Secret Session is refused this may be forced upon us by our duty to the country. It would indeed be wrong if the new Parliament were to disperse for a two-and-a-half months' holiday without its Members receiving from the Ministers of the Crown any assurance that the frontiers of Western Europe, and indeed our own national security, can be maintained in the face of a Russian Communist onslaught. I did not fail to give my warnings before the war although things were at least as dangerous as they are today.

I still hope that the unities now being established among all the Western Democracies and Atlantic Powers will ward off from us the terrors and unspeakable miseries of a third world war. I wish also that every effort could be made on the highest level to bring home to the Russian Soviet Government the gravity of the facts which confront us all, them as well as us. I do not give up the hope which I expressed to you five months ago, of a supreme effort to bridge the gulf between the two worlds, if not in friendship, at least without the hatreds and manoeuvres of the cold war. But of this I am sure: that the best hope will be founded upon the strength of the Western Democracies and upon their unwavering will-power to defend the causes for which they stand.

To work from weakness and fear is ruin. To work from wisdom and power may be salvation. These simple but tremendous facts are, I feel, being understood by the free nations better than they have ever been before. I believe, moreover, that the faithful discharge of our national duty by everyone of us laying aside all impediments will give the Conservative Party a chance of rendering true service to Britain, its Empire and the world. In this there lies before us an opportunity such as the centuries do not often bring.

DEFENCE

---

18 *July—Mr Younger, British Minister of State, in reply to a question in the House of Commons, confirms that since the commencement of hostilities in Korea no supplies have been sent to North China.*

20 *July—Mr Attlee makes a statement in the House of Commons on the recent conversation between Sir David Kelly and M. Gromyko on the Korean situation.*

21 *July—Due to failure to reach agreement on meat prices, the Argentine Government suspend all meat shipments to Great Britain.*

22 *July—Death of Mr Mackenzie King.*

24 *July—In reply to a question in the House of Commons, Mr Attlee replies that the only foreign armed forces now in Britain are American, comprising 1,500 Naval and about 10,000 Air Force personnel equipped with 180 aircraft.*

26-27 *July—Two-day debate in House of Commons on Defence.*

27 *July—Announced in Teheran that no foreign correspondents will be allowed to visit the Persian-Soviet border area or any part of Azerbaijan in order to 'avoid provocation to the Russians'.*

[26 July 1950

We gladly yielded our right to open this Debate to the Minister of Defence when he asked for this facility. It was certainly necessary that a statement should be made to the House before we separate. One of our reasons for asking for a Debate in public after a Secret Session, or a Debate in private, had been refused, was to give the Government an opportunity of explaining their position and, to some extent our position, and it was very fortunate, I think, that we did so. Otherwise, the House would have had no opportunity, according to the Government's plan, of debating the statement which has just been made to us. It is entirely due to our request that this difficulty has been surmounted. I do not intend myself to discuss in detail this afternoon the proposals which the Minister of Defence has announced, though they appeared few and far between, or the general tenor and character of his statement. I will reserve what I have to say for when we come to the Third Reading of this Bill tomorrow, either in public or in private session, as the House may decide.

330

Let me say at once that we shall give our support to any measures proposed by the Government which seem right or necessary in the public interest, whether they are popular or not. We may even feel it our duty to support measures which are not only belated but may be judged inadequate, while criticizing them in these respects. I could not help feeling, while I listened to the right hon Gentleman, that he gave no decided or clear answer on the question of lengthening the period of service, which clearly lies at the root of the economy of our Army. I ventured to say in the last Parliament that we should take fewer men for a longer period. I quite see the complications of that, but I can only say that should the Government decide to embark upon that course, in some way or other—undoubtedly one which would not be popular to the country or in any part of the House—we shall give them our support, as we have done throughout the whole story of national compulsory military service in time of peace.

I must say in passing that one would have thought, to hear the right hon Gentleman's speech about these great dangers, which were brought home to us by his candid statement of the vast strength of Russia in Europe, that he and his colleagues of the Socialist Government had only just come into power and that all this situation had developed overnight, as it were, whereas it has been building up for at least three years during which the Allied Forces were falling while the Russian power was steadily maintained and strengthened in every way. These are matters which we shall have to examine. But, sir, as we shall give the Government our support should it be needed at any time, they have no excuse for not asking for whatever they require, nor have they in the past had any difficulty because of the immense sums of money which Parliament has accorded them during these five years. During this period they have spent, I think, over £5,000,000,000 in maintaining the Armed Forces. It is remarkable that by far the vastest proportion of this was spent during the period when, according to the right hon Gentleman's argument, the danger was the least, and the amounts fell off steadily as the danger, by contrast, grew.

They also had the great advantage of starting with an enormous mass of munitions, much of which was quite new and some of which was even produced after the war had ended, because the factories were allowed to run to complete weapons on which they had begun— I do not say wrongly. Many of the rifles, which are the great foundation of the armaments of any nation, have been frittered away and squandered, but still there was a vast amount left. The artillery, in the main, is something which will last. A large portion of the munitions available at the end of the war could have been, if they had not been improvidently used, available for expanding the defensive forces that we had, and developing them. It seems to me that all this requires fairly careful detailed examination. After all, even weapons that were new five years ago are better than no weapons at all. This also touches the question of arming the forces of other countries, and I trust it will be looked into and examined.

I do not intend to be drawn into any personal controversy with the right hon Gentleman if I can help it. He stated at the weekend that I had no confidence in him. As I have said before, I have confidence that his heart is in the right place, and any reservations I might have to make would be in regard to other aspects of his suitability for discharging the tremendous tasks entrusted to him. There is, however, one point which occurred in the House last week to which I must refer. The right hon Gentleman, when speaking at Question Time about the possibilities of a Debate on defence said that he quite understood my 'natural curiosity'. If curiosity were my motive, I might easily have satisfied it, because the Prime Minister and the right hon Gentleman himself have several times, even since this new Parliament was formed, offered to give me and any colleagues I might bring with me the fullest information in their possession. I have not availed myself of this latest offer up to the present, for the following reasons. I did not find that the conversations we had last year, although conducted in a friendly manner on both sides, were fruitful in results. On the other hand, the fact that we had these conversations, which were in progress from June to October at intervals, undoubtedly made it difficult for the Opposition to examine in public the state of our defences and to make those criticisms which are usual every few months, or at any rate every year, in Parliament. In fact, the subject of our defence was not dealt with in a searching or controversial manner at all in the House last year by the Opposition.

The difficulty of the leaders of the Opposition parties receiving confidential information from the Government—the chief difficulty—is of course that their lips are thereby sealed in respect of everything they did not know before, and that these two fields of information— what they knew before and what they are told—overlap and affect one another in a manner which is certainly embarrassing to any public discussion which may follow. I therefore contented myself with saying, at the beginning of this new Parliament, that I accepted no responsibility for the present state of our defences, and, at my request, the Prime Minister altered the Government Motion on presenting the White Paper by substituting the words 'That this House takes note of' for the original words 'That this House approves'. Our position is therefore perfectly clear. We cannot take any course which may hamper us in the discharge of our duty as we conceive it, or prevent us giving any warnings to the House and also, in due course, to the country, which may be required as the situation develops.

I greatly regret that the Prime Minister and the Socialist Government persist in refusing a Debate in Secret or Private Session. It might, I think, have been quite natural and in the public interest that after hearing a public statement by the Minister of Defence and after some public discussion upon it, we should have gone into private Session and talked things over among ourselves as Members of the House of Commons. The point has been raised, that, if we were to hold a Secret Session, it would be resented by the United States Government, who would want to know what had happened, but could not be told. I can assure the House that there is no validity in this suggestion. The Americans are very familiar with the procedure of Secret Sessions. The Congressional Committees often hold them; they are called Executive Sessions. These Congressional Committees, especially those of the House of Representatives, have enormous powers of obtaining information for their members. They can summon generals, admirals, and other experts before them subject only to the veto of the Minister in charge of the Department, very rarely exercised, and can examine them to any extent, either in public or in secret. There is no doubt whatever that the American House of Representatives exercises its responsibilities towards its constituents in a far more vigilant and rigorous manner than anything we have adopted over here. We are a very ill-informed body on defence questions compared to them, and the idea that they would object to our having a Secret Session is utterly absurd, and indeed would constitute an interference with our domestic affairs of which, I am sure, the United States would never be guilty.

It was also said by the Lord President of the Council that there was no precedent for a Secret Session except in time of war, but we are now at war technically. As a mandatory of the United Nations, we are technically at war with the Republic of Northern Korea, so that that argument, for whatever it was ever worth, is effectively disposed of. I still hope that a Secret or Private Session will be claimed by the House tomorrow. I do not understand why the Government do not wish to take the House into their full confidence, so far as that may be possible without revealing secrets not already known to the Soviet Government and to the General Staffs of Europe and of the United States. The discussion can be easier and freer when every word we say is not carried immediately all over the world. I believe that such a

Debate might have the effect of bringing us more together and promoting a better understanding between us of the facts of our grave common danger. I feel that Members of Parliament have a deep obligation to seek the fullest information possible about matters which affect the lives and safety of their constituents, and that they might well be held accountable to those constituents if, by their votes tomorrow, they put their veto upon such a discussion.

Considering how evenly the parties are balanced in this Parliament, and that the Prime Minister's party is in a minority in the country of nearly 2,000,000 voters, it is much to be regretted that he should adopt such an authoritarian attitude. I cannot think that his decision will be helpful, either to his party, or, what is of far greater importance, to the welfare of the country.

With regard to the Debate tomorrow, I must make the reservation that I may have to make certain changes in what I think it is possible to say to the House, in accordance with the decision to which we have come. With regard to the Debate in public this afternoon, there is a great deal that can be said, especially on the administrative aspects, and much can be said on the general issue, without trenching on facts which are not already public property and well-known to those who follow these matters with attention in every country. I am sure that my hon and right hon Friends on this side of the House will be able to throw much light on our problems within the wide limits that are open to us.

DEFENCE

A SPEECH TO THE HOUSE OF COMMONS
27 JULY 1950

It has been decided by the House that our Debate must be in public,* and I shall confine myself to stating facts which are certainly well-known to the Soviet Government and to the General Staffs of Europe and the United States. The most important things that I shall say I have already said in public before. I shall base myself on matter which has already appeared in the newspapers or been disclosed by various authorities in Europe or the United States. I shall ask the Government a number of questions, but if they do not wish to answer them now that they have escaped into public Session, I shall not press them. I have little doubt that they could have been answered in private Session, as they are already within the limits I have prescribed of being certainly known to foreign Powers.

I had intended to open today with a statement of the strength of the Armed Forces of the Soviet Government. This would obviously give them no information which they do not already possess. But yesterday, in what seemed to me the most impressive part of his speech, the Minister of Defence gave us the figures on which the Government rely. There were, he said, 175 active divisions. This I presume is a part of the much larger number, nearly double, which could be produced in a few months. Even if only half of the 175 were used against us in Western Europe, they could, therefore, launch over 80 divisions upon us without any further mobilization. The Minister of Defence also stated that one-third of these 175 divisions are mechanized or armoured. Sir, that is a tremendous statement. I see that Mr Vinson, the Chairman of the Armed Services Committee of the House of Representatives at Washington, whom I mentioned yesterday, quoted the total Russian tank strength as 40,000, or seven times that of the United States. Our figure of 6,000 British, given yesterday by the Minister of Defence, is comparable, I take it, to this estimate of 40,000.

But even more important than the reserve or general stock of tanks is the number organized in formations. Could we be told, since so much has been disclosed, of the number of Soviet tanks now assembled

---

* On Mr Churchill's remark, 'I spy strangers', Mr Speaker had put the question to the House 'that strangers do withdraw'. The House divided: Ayes 295, Noes 296.

on or near the Western Front in formations? Would 4,000 or 5,000 tanks in organized formations be an excessive estimate? In Korea we have seen how formidable even a few score of tanks can be, and how tough the heavy Russian tanks are. Any development and improvement in the bazooka and other anti-tank weapons would be greatly welcomed. I do not know how well the Western Union Forces are equipped with the latest and largest patterns, but I cannot think that the threat of the enormous mass of the Soviet armour is in any way mastered, or that there is anything in use and service at the present time which could cope with the array of armoured avalanches we must expect on the outbreak of war, should war occur.

Now let us see what the Western Union could put against all this. The former war-time French Prime Minister, M. Reynaud, recently again a Minister, made some precise statements on this point last week, which have been published in the newspapers and which I do not think should escape the attention of the House. M. Reynaud said that we and our European Allies have in Western Germany two British Divisions, two American and three French. For the rest, he said the French have four divisions in Europe and, I think, the Belgians one, a total of twelve. I should think that M. Reynaud is tolerably well informed on these matters. The French and the Belgian divisions must inevitably be hampered in their tactical efficiency by having to train the annual intake of conscripts. The two British divisions are of course largely composed of men completing their eighteen months' service, and are almost entirely dependent upon a numerous German civilian contingent for their transport, without which of course they cannot move. One of the two American divisions, I believe, is armoured, but I ask if the British have one full armoured division.

On this assumption, Western Union would have twelve divisions, against more than eighty, and of which less than two are armoured, against anything from twenty-five to thirty. The Russians know their own strength, but it is certain that they also know with great precision the Allied weakness and condition. Apart from agents, there are Communists all over Germany who see the troops living among them day after day, and we here in the House of Commons are entitled to ask the Government—are these figures, which I have just quoted, and their proportions, broadly speaking, true? Are the odds in ground troops on the Western Front eight or nine to one against us, or are they four, five, or six, or seven to one? Or is there no truth in this figure at all and are things much better? I hope the Prime Minister, if he is going to reply—or is it the Minister of Defence?

THE MINISTER OF DEFENCE [MR SHINWELL] *indicated assent.*

MR CHURCHILL: I hope the Minister of Defence, when he replies, will tell us. There is really no reason why we should not know what the Soviets and all the General Staffs of Europe know, and what the Prime Minister and the Minister of Defence must themselves have known for a long time. In a Secret Session, there would I think, have been no difficulty in giving the broad facts.

When in March, in the Debate on the White Paper, I said in the House that it would be necessary and right to enable the Germans of Western Germany to take part in the defence of their hearths and homes from the hideous menace under which they lie, the Prime Minister dismissed my advice as irresponsible. However, it is the advice which I understand the military commanders of the United States, at any rate, would give. At present, we have followed the principle that the only Germans who may be rearmed are the Communist Germans in the Eastern zone, who have been formed by the Soviets into a highly effective police army with powerful weapons and numbering 45,000 or 50,000 men—it may be more—and with considerable off-shoots in the Communist cells and caches of arms known to exist in Western Germany. I do not wonder that something like panic prevails along the Eastern frontiers of Western Germany. Every true German friend of reconciliation with the Western democratic world, and of the redemption of their past by faithful service, knows that the lurking Communist in the neighbourhood has marked him down for early liquidation. How can there be any foundation for a helpful German policy under such conditions?

In all that I have said so far, I have only spoken of the Soviet forces with which we are confronted—eight or nine to one against us in infantry and artillery, and probably much more than that in tank formations. I have not mentioned the satellite powers. Poland, under strict Russian control, with a Russian marshal at the head of her forces, has a powerful party army. Czechoslovakia has another army, though less trustworthy, and the arsenals of Skoda, possibly the largest arms plant now in Europe, are steadily pouring out their weapons. If the facts that I have stated cannot be contradicted by His Majesty's Government, the preparations of the Western Union to defend itself certainly stand on a far lower level than those of the South Koreans. I notice that the right hon Gentleman said yesterday with candour:

'I will not conceal from the House that the Forces at present available, or in sight, fall a long way short of requirements estimated even on the most conservative basis. There is nothing to be gained by failing to recognize this fact.'

It is always, I think, true to say that one of the main foundations of the British sense of humour is understatement, and this appears to be a very excellent example of that fact.

We may, no doubt, throw much of the blame on France and the Benelux countries, weakened by the disasters of the war, but do not let us imagine that we are not in danger ourselves. If, as M. Reynaud says, and I have no reason to dispute him, the Soviet armies, with their armoured columns, could be at Calais and reach the Channel—or the Atlantic, that is to say—before any substantial reinforcements from the United States could arrive upon the scene—if that is true, then we ourselves, although protected from an immediate incursion by the anti-tank obstacle of the Channel, with its waves, tides and storms, will be subjected to a bombardment by rocket-propelled and guided missiles—I am not speaking of atomic bombs—incomparably more severe than anything we have endured or imagined. The Soviet Government picked up and developed all the Germans knew about this form of war. Peenemunde fell into their hands, and all the German secrets of this new phase of warfare, on which Hitler had set his final hopes, but the development of which was cut short by our advance—all this new phase of warfare has been developed in five years of intensive study and production.

The Russians do not need to come to the coast to plant their batteries. Very long ranges are within the compass of these weapons, and they can pick and choose their places. If we were alone, I might give some indication of the inconvenience which might be caused thereby. All this is true, and may be near—how near no one knows for certain, except the dictator oligarchy in the Kremlin, who accept no moral principles as known to us, but who are able to pursue, year after year, their calculated plans for world conquest without being concerned with public opinion or elections or any of the scruples which rule the Western and the Christian world.

Here I leave the first part of my subject—the relative strength of the armies and of the tanks upon the Western Front. Let us now look to the air. Immense figures have been published in America and in this country about the Soviet air forces—25,000 military aircraft produced yearly was one figure. The Minister of Defence said yesterday that the Russian forces—he was speaking of their total military forces—are backed by 19,000 military aircraft, including jet aircraft of the latest design, both bombers and fighters. But, on the Western front, which is the matter which I have most in point at the moment, in fighter and bomber aircraft, how many have they got in full commission? Would 4,000 or 5,000 or 6,000 be too large an estimate? I should be greatly relieved if the Government were able to answer this question in a reassuring manner. But, considering all we have been told of the Russian strength, I can see no reason why, even under the conditions of a public Session, it should not be answered. But, even if we take it as only 4,000, how many have we got? We and the Americans and the Western Allies, how many have we got on the Continent —I am not speaking of home forces—to sustain our Armies of perhaps twelve divisions, as stated by M. Reynaud, against eighty or ninety? Here, again, even if we were in Secret Session, I would not ask the Government to state the exact figure, but could they say, for instance, that we have a half, a third, a fourth, a fifth, a sixth, or a seventh of what we know we have to face? I do not press them for a reply unless they wish to give one.

Upon the question of quality, no doubt we may hope to have superiority in machines and pilots, but this is by no means certain. The right hon Gentleman has told us that a large proportion of the Russian aircraft are of the highest quality. They have certainly made great improvements on the jet aeroplanes in regard to which we so lightheartedly furnished them with our specimen engines a few years ago. There are other aspects of the Russian air menace not concerned with the mainland of Europe with which I must now deal. If the Russian Armies reached or approached the coast of France and held the airfields there from which we were attacked by the Germans ten years ago, they could, I fear, outnumber us in the air by a far larger number of machines than Hitler ever had. Anything that the Government choose to say upon the fighter forces available for the defence of London and our vital feeding seaports which would reassure the House would give the deepest satisfaction to us all.

But there is another aspect of the air defence of Britain which is even more grave and intense. Two years ago, the Government agreed that the Americans should establish a bombing base in East Anglia from which they could use the atom bomb upon the Russian cities and keypoints. The Americans have other bases, but this is one of the most important. We on this side of the House do not criticize the Government for taking this very serious step for which, in any case, they had the large Socialist majority of the last Parliament at their disposal.

MR SIDNEY SILVERMAN (Nelson and Colne): Would the right hon Gentleman give way for a moment?

MR CHURCHILL: Not at this point. All this has been in the newspapers for a long time. I would not have asked the Government, even in Secret Session, for the exact numbers of the American offensive forces for using the atomic bomb on Soviet Russia which are located here in this island. However, the Prime Minister stated them on Monday as 10,000 men and 180 planes in three bomber groups. To this, the Minister of Defence added last night that there were fighter squadrons also, so we may be sure that the Russians know the main facts pretty well. It is on this foundation that the Communists base their oft-repeated charge that Britain is an aircraft carrier moored to attack the Soviet Union. It is also, this base in East Anglia, our major defence against the consequences which would follow or accompany a Russian onslaught in Europe, and it is a vital part of the atomic bomb deterrent, which is what we are living on now.

More than two years have passed since this base was established and became public. It was obvious, whatever else was done or not done, that from that moment the utmost endeavours should have been used to make the base secure by every form of anti-aircraft artillery and by the most perfect and elaborate development of radar, and, above all, by the largest number of the latest fighter aircraft which we could produce ourselves or get from the United States. I hope this has been done. I naturally do not ask for a detailed reply, but one fact makes me anxious—it has been mentioned before, and I must refer to it now for it may be typical of much else in our present administrative policy. I simply cannot comprehend a policy which while, on the one hand, taking this extraordinary risk of establishing this base, can disperse or distribute so large a proportion of the jet aircraft in the production of which British genius has held the lead. We wonder how many jet aeroplane engines we have distributed to our friends or sold to foreign countries. I do not ask for a reply in detail; I will content myself with reminding the House, as my right hon Friend did yesterday, of what has been published in the newspapers and admitted by Ministers, namely, that 100 of these jets were sold to the Argentine, which lays its claims to the Falkland Islands and is at this moment in wrongful occupation of British territory in the Antarctic. It has also been stated, and not denied when raised in the House, that 110 were sold, traded or given to Egypt—written off against sterling balances, or the like— to Egypt of all countries at the present time, which was actually blocking the Canal in violation of the treaty, and no doubt given to them in order to enable them to face the new State of Israel. Here at any rate are 210 machines, only, of course, a proportion of what have been dispersed or disposed of, out of the total of these invaluable jets, and of these 210 we have been deprived by an act of improvidence beyond description or compare.

We have the Auxiliary Air Force, which is an important element in our home defence—about twenty squadrons—volunteers really worthy of the finest weapons which our factories can make. This Auxiliary Air Force could all have been rearmed by now with the jets we have distributed to these foreign countries. I simply cannot understand it. In the fifty years since I entered this House, I have never seen anything quite like it. I made my protests and appeals to the Prime Minister more than a year ago. Perhaps he or the Minister of Defence will tell us tonight that at least the sale of our jets to neutrals has now been stopped.

But this particular illustration of the manner in which the policy of the Government has been incoherent or unco-ordinated, ugly though it be, must not draw our minds from the general picture which I am presenting to the House. I have dealt with the relative strengths of the armies and the armoured forces on both sides in Europe. I have spoken of the Air Force, though I have not attempted to go into actual or relative strengths, except to state that we are, I believe, outnumbered as we have never been before.

Now I come, thirdly, to the naval sphere and the Soviet U-boats. Reliable naval reference books estimate the present Russian U-boat fleet at 360, divided, no doubt, between the Pacific and the West, of which between 100 and 200 are ocean-going and capable of high speeds. These seem to me very large figures, and I am not at all accepting them as final figures, but what is the truth about them? I do not see why the Minister of Defence should not give us his best estimate, considering the information which has been given about other portions of the Russian forces. Many of these boats, we are told, are of 20 knots. A modern 20-knot submerged U-boat would, it is calculated, be able to search five times the area of water as was covered by the last war U-boats with their maximum submerged speed of nine knots. What is the truth of this? There can be no harm in giving this information to the public. All German technical discoveries and, no doubt, some German technical aid have been at the command of the Soviets since the war.

Considering that we and the world have been told the deadly details of the American atomic force in East Anglia, surely the facts about the Russian U-boat construction can be given on the best estimate that is available? When I went to the Admiralty at the beginning of the last war the Germans had thirty ocean-going U-boats with a maximum underwater speed of nine knots. Only thirty! And now the figure of 300 is mentioned; but it may be much less and yet be most grave. I am not committing myself to any precise figure, but they only had thirty then. I hope it may be possible to reassure us on the present position.

I do not know, nor do I ask, what resources we have in up-to-date anti-U-boat craft, but I doubt very much whether they are in number equal actually, or still less proportionately, to what those who are called the 'guilty men' of the last war had prepared. I believe it is probably true to say that the Russian-Soviet U-boat menace to our trans-ocean Atlantic life-line and world communications, which also comprise all American reinforcements for Europe, would be far more severe than was the German U-boat force in their attacks of 1939 and 1940; and this seemed quite enough then.

We have, however, the Air Force Coastal Command, and in this and in multiplication of aircraft carriers and anti-submarine vessels lies our hope, and, I trust, our policy. But it was said yesterday that the Coastal Command is below its approved strength, both in aircraft and in their personnel. I hope this may be contradicted, and if it cannot be contradicted I trust it will be made good. I do not feel I should be exaggerating if I say that the Soviet attack by modernized German U-boats in Russian hands upon our ocean life-line would, for a year at least, perhaps for more, be far more severe than was the Hitler attack in 1939 and 1940. I ask specifically if the Minister of Defence will deal with this in his speech, because it is fundamental and vital.

Summing up the scene it looks as if there is at present no effective defence in Western Europe beyond the Channel, and that the Russian advance to the Channel or towards it will bring us under air bombardment, apart from the atomic bomb, far worse than we have ever endured. Secondly, it would be very bad for us if the Russians were to gain the command of the air over the Channel and over this island by an overpowering use of numbers. On the sea we are also at a serious disadvantage, as I have just described, compared with the last war. It is, perhaps, worth while for the House and the country to weigh these facts attentively. If they can be substantially corrected no one will be more fervently thankful than I.

If the comparison of British and Western Union forces ended at this point, with a survey of land, sea and air, our position might well be judged forlorn. We might feel the need of the striking phrase used the other night by my hon Friend the Member for Carlton [Mr Pickthorn] when he said: 'While there is death there is hope.' Fortunately, there is a fourth vast sphere of defence in which the United States have enormous and measureless superiority. Two years ago I said in the country, at Llandudno:

'If it were not for the stocks of atomic bombs now in the trusteeship of the United States, there would be no means of stopping the subjugation of Western Europe by Communist machinations backed by Russian armies and enforced by political police.'

Again, I said on the same occasion:

'Nothing stands between Europe today and complete subjugation to Communist tyranny but the atomic bomb in American possession.'

It is to this aspect that I must now recur. I understand that we have no atom bombs of our own. Considering how far we were forward in this matter during the war—we could not ourselves undertake it because we were under fire, that was the only reason why we did not —and that we earnestly pressed the Americans into it, as my conversations with President Roosevelt in 1942, which are on record, will show, it is remarkable, considering all this, how quickly we were denied the confidence of the United States after the war was over, and how we have never been able in five years with all our own gathered knowledge to make the atom bomb ourselves.

I also said in 1948:

'What will happen when the Russians get the atomic bomb themselves and have accumulated a large store? You can judge for yourselves what will happen then by what is happening now. If these things are done in the green wood, what will be done in the dry? If they can continue month after month disturbing and tormenting the world, trusting to our Christian and altruistic inhibitions against using this strange new power against them, what will they do when they themselves have large quantities of atomic bombs?'

And further:

'The Western nations will be far more likely to reach a lasting settlement, without bloodshed, if they formulate their just demands while they have the atomic power and before the Russian Communists have got it, too.'

No attention was paid to this. I fully realize the difficulties and the dangers of such a policy and that it did not rest entirely with us.

But now things have definitely worsened. It is painful in every respect to be told, as we were officially told some months ago, that the Russians have been able to gain the secret of the atom bomb through Communist traitors in the American and also notably in the British service. But between having the secret and making any large number of bombs, there is undoubtedly a considerable interval. It is this interval which we must not waste. We must endeavour to make up the melancholy leeway in military preparations which oppresses us today, and we must never abandon the hope that a peaceful settlement may be reached with the Soviet Government if a resolute effort is made on the basis not of our present weakness but of American atomic strength. This is the policy which gives the best chance of preventing a fearful war and of securing our survival should it break upon us.

I do not expect that any of the Allies know how many atomic bombs the Soviet Government have yet been able to make, but—here I am only stating my personal opinion—I do not think that they have made many yet, or that their rate of production is at present rapid. As I say, I only candidly state my own personal view to the House. It would be very wrong that the House should attach any undue importance to it, but it is one of the stepping-stones upon which my thought advances. I see, however, that I said to the House earlier in this Session, two months ago, that if the Americans had a stockpile of, say, 1,000, and the Russians had only 50, and we got those 50, it would not be pleasant. I was surprised that this crude remark did not affect opinion. But then, only two months ago there was a different atmosphere. All these matters, quite wrongly, seemed outside the range of ordinary politics and daily life. Now they dominate the minds of all thinking and patriotic men, and will increasingly do so as the months pass by.

It was stated officially at some Lobby conference with, I think, the Home Office, according to the *Daily Telegraph* of Tuesday, that each bomb costs as much as a battleship. This, of course, is ludicrous nonsense. It might be that the first two or three would cost that amount or more if they were saddled with the whole expense of research and production up to date, but once they were in production the cost would certainly be less than one-twentieth or even one-fiftieth of a modern battleship. Nevertheless I still adhere to my feeling—I am quite ready to be instructed by those who have the advantages of official information—that so far very few have been produced, and the extraordinary efforts which the Soviet Government are making to obtain even small quantities of uranium seem—I only say 'seem'—to justify a hopeful view.

If this should happily be true, there can be no doubt that the United States possesses at this moment a superiority so vast that a major act of Russian aggression is still subject to an effective and even perhaps decisive deterrent. It is for this reason I have ventured on several occasions to express the opinion that a third world war is not imminent, and I cherish the hope that it may still be averted. I noticed in the Debate on Civil Defence on Monday, at which I regret I was not present, that there was a considerable tendency, not confined to any one part of the House, to minimize the effects of the atomic bomb, and the Government have issued a carefully thought out booklet on this subject. No doubt, it is right nearly always to take a robust and cheerful view, but I expect this booklet, from what I have been able to learn of it, looking through it—I have not had time to read it with the attention it deserves—will be more cheering to the Russians than to us, because the atomic bomb is the only weapon on land, sea and air in which the Americans—that is to say the Allies—can possibly have overwhelming superiority during the next two or three years.

I should have thought, therefore, that it was a mistake in propaganda to weaken or discount the deterrents upon those who are already so much stronger in every other sphere except this. We shall need the whole weight of these deterrents to gain us the time which remains while this great advantage of ours endures. We are, of course, dependent upon the United States both for the supply of the bomb and largely for the means of using it. Without it, we are more defenceless than we have ever been. I find this a terrible thought. In 1940 I had good hopes that we should win the battle in the air even at heavy odds and that if we won, the Navy could stave off and repel invasion until eventually vast air power was developed here which would bring us out of our troubles, even if left alone. But now I cannot feel the same sense of concrete assurance.

We must never despair. We must never give in. We have over 5,000,000 men and women who had service in the Armed Forces in the last war. We have 750,000 who have been trained since, and there are nearly 700,000 now in the Armed Forces, and many thousands in our Volunteer and Auxiliary Forces. Our industrial capacity and that of the free world is gigantic. Our scientific and technical ability is unsurpassed. We may well have time to reorganize and develop the mighty latent strength of Britain surrounded by her Commonwealth. But I warn the House that we have as great dangers to face in 1950 and 1951 as we had ten years ago. Here we are with deep and continuing differences between us in our whole domestic sphere, and faced with dangers and problems which all our united strength can scarcely overcome. It was this that led me to hope that in Private Session the sense of the corporate life of the House of Commons might have asserted itself. But that has been forbidden by the Prime Minister. [HON MEMBERS: 'By the House.'] It has been forbidden by the Prime Minister, and at his request the House has prevented our meeting together and talking things over among ourselves in secret.

It is with deep grief that I have to say these things to the House, and to reflect that it is only five years ago almost to a month when we were victorious, respected and safe. The whole burden does not rest upon this country, nor upon the Government of this country. They have done several important things, like establishing compulsory National Service and the East Anglian American base. They have fostered the closest relations with the United States and our European friends, and they have maintained active resistance to Communism in its various forms. Nevertheless, I say they bear a fearful accountability. The Prime Minister and his party have had power, men and money never enjoyed before by any Government in time of peace. If they had asked for more Parliament would have granted it to them and we would have given it our full support. It was with a sense of relief that I felt entitled to say in March that we could accept no responsibility for the present state of our defences. That does not mean that we will not strive to help the Government, in spite of their total lack of consideration for our wishes and point of view, in every measure, however unpopular, which they may propose and which we recognize is aimed solely at securing national survival.

CONSULTATIVE ASSEMBLY OF THE COUNCIL OF EUROPE

A SPEECH AT STRASBOURG
11 AUGUST 1950

---

27 *July—After a boycott of seven months, M. Malik (Soviet representative at Lake Success) informs Mr Trygve Lie of his intention of taking the Presidency of the Security Council during August under the system of rotating chairmanship.*

1 *August—King Leopold of Belgium relinquishes his powers in favour of his son, Prince Baudouin.*

3 *August—The publication of the text of a British memorandum to Washington reveals a defence plan covering a period of three years and involving a sum of £3,400,000,000.*

4 *August—Mr Raymond Blackburn (MP for Northfield) announces his resignation from the Labour Party and his intention to sit in the House as an Independent. He gives as the reason his feeling that the country is in danger of 'very near war' and that in the circumstances a Coalition Government should be formed under the leadership of Mr Winston Churchill.*

The terms of a French memorandum to Washington indicate that France has prepared a three-year defence plan at a total cost of over £2,000,000,000.

M. Malik introduces to the Security Council of the United Nations a resolution calling on the Council to invite a Chinese Communist Government representative to take part in the deliberations on Korea; to grant the North Koreans a hearing; to suspend military action in Korea; and to withdraw all foreign troops in that country.

[11 *August* 1950

I am sure we can all agree with the Committee of Ministers that definite progress has been made in the last year in building up the European conception represented by this Assembly. There are, however, several important points which lie open between us. We regret that these should have been somewhat inconsiderately set aside by the Committee of Ministers until October. I think the Assembly should press its points and its opinion on the questions at issue. There really is, for instance, no reason why a Resolution passed here by a two-thirds majority should not be formally made known to and laid before our respective Parliaments, it being, of course, obvious that nothing can prevent either the Government or the Parliament concerned from taking its own decision upon the questions raised after whatever debate they may think desirable.

It is important to the future of this Assembly that it should be brought continually into closer contact not only with the executive Governments but with all the representative institutions upon which, in all true democracies, executive Governments can alone be founded. For Great Britain I can, however, guarantee that all Resolutions of the Assembly will be brought before the House of Commons for discussion on their merits, whether we agree with them or not. For this purpose we shall use the facilities at the disposal of the British official Opposition, and I do not doubt that the House of Lords will take corresponding action. I suggest to my colleagues of other countries here that they use the liberties of procedure which their own Parliaments possess in abundance for the same purpose, and that this become our general practice unless or until the obstructive influences on the Committee of Ministers have been overcome or have disappeared.

There are other points of difference which may well be readjusted as a result of our discussions. I have always thought that the process of building up a European Parliament must be gradual, and that it should roll forward on a tide of facts, events and impulses rather than by elaborate constitution-making. Either we shall prove our worth and weight and value to Europe or we shall fail. We are not making a machine. We are growing a living plant. It certainly is a forward step that Mr MacBride, the representative of the Committee of Ministers, should be here among us to express their collective mind—if they have one—directly to the Assembly, and to deal by word of mouth with matters which we may raise. Indeed, when we look back over the past twelve months—and not only over the past twelve months but to The Hague two years ago—it is marvellous to see how great is the progress which has been made in this time. From an unofficial gathering of enthusiasts, pleading the cause of reconciliation and revival of this shattered Continent, we have reached the scene today when we sit as a body, with ever-growing influence and respect, in our own House of Europe, under the flags of fifteen historic States and nations. In all that we do and say here, we must not belie the hopes and faith of millions and scores of millions of men and women not only in the free countries of Europe but in those which still lie in bondage.

The message which we have received from the 'composite throne', if such I may term it, has directed our attention to the Schuman Plan of associating in an effective manner the basic industries of the Western nations, and has invited us to express our opinion upon it. Sir, we as an Assembly are very ready to do so and it may well be that it is in our power to smooth away some of the misunderstandings which have arisen or the prejudices which have been stirred. We may handle this large and hopeful scheme in a manner which will be favourable to the general principles which it embodies.

Some of my British colleagues have offered a constructive contribution on this subject to the Debates of the Assembly, and I trust their views will receive careful and friendly consideration not only from other Governments and Parliaments but from their own. It will be a memorable achievement if this Assembly is able to offer practical guidance to uncertain Governments and competing parties in regard to a scheme which seeks to build around the tomb of Franco-German wars and quarrels the structure of a more productive, a more stable industrial life for the vast numbers of our peoples who are concerned. We express our thanks to M. Schuman for his bold initiative and also for his courtesy in coming here to tell us all about it.

But, sir, the message we have received from the Committee of Ministers directs our attention in its final paragraphs to the gravest matters which now impend upon world affairs. We are invited to approve the action of the United Nations in Korea and to proclaim our 'complete solidarity' with the resistance to aggression the burden of which is now being borne by the United States, but which involves us all. No one can doubt what our answer will be or that the European Assembly will do its utmost to sustain the cause of freedom and the rule of law in the face of a most grievous and violent challenge. But what is our position here in these smiling lands and war-scarred cities, their peoples so rich in tradition, virtue and glory, striving to rise again from the consequences of the tragedies of the past?

Sir, the Committee of Ministers has, by its message, virtually invited us to consider in their broader aspects the military aspects of our position. Certainly it would be futile and absurd to attempt to discuss the future of Europe and its relation to world affairs and to the United Nations Organization if this dominating military aspect were arbitrarily excluded. Nearly all the speakers who have addressed us, including our two British Socialist colleagues, have trespassed upon this hitherto forbidden territory, and its effective occupation by the Assembly has now become a *fait accompli*.

I am very glad that the Germans, amid their own problems, have come here to share our perils and augment our strength. They ought to have been here a year ago. A year has been wasted, but still it is not too late. There is no revival of Europe, no safety or freedom for any of us, except in standing together, united and unflinching. I ask this Assembly to assure our German friends that, if they throw in their lot with us, we shall hold their safety and freedom as sacred as our own.

I have heard it said that if any Germans—I think the argument was raised yesterday—except Communists were to be armed, this might be the pretext for a preventive war by Russia. Believe me, Mr President, the long calculated designs of the Soviet Government will not be timed or deflected by events of this order. There is no doubt that we are all of us in great danger. The freedom and civilization of Western Europe lie under the shadow of Russian Communist aggression, supported by enormous armaments. The Soviet forces in Europe, measured in active divisions, in Air Force and in armoured vehicles, outnumber the forces of Western Union by at least six or seven to one. These are terrible facts, and it is a wonder that we are sitting here in our new House of Europe, calmly discussing our plans for the future happiness and concord of our peoples and their moral and cultural ideals. It is a wonder, but at least it is better than getting into a panic. The danger is, of course, not new. It was inherent in the fact that the free democracies of the West disarmed and dissolved their forces after the war, while the dictatorship in the Kremlin maintained gigantic armies and laboured tirelessly by every means to re-equip them.

Two years ago the Western Union Pact was signed and a number of committees were set up which, as M. Reynaud and others say, have been talking ever since. Imposing conferences have been held between military chiefs and experts, assisted by statesmen, and the pretentious facade of a Western front has been displayed by the Governments responsible for our safety. In fact, however, apart from the establishment of the American bomber base in England, nothing has been done to give any effective protection to our peoples from being subjugated or destroyed by the Russian Communist armies with their masses of armour and aircraft. I and others have given what warnings we could, but, as in the past, they fell on unheeding ears or were used to sustain the false accusation of 'warmongering'.

Now, however, suddenly the lightning-flash in Korea, and the spreading conflagration which has followed it, has roused the whole of the free world to a keen and vehement realization of its dangers, and many measures are now proposed which, if they had been taken two years ago, would at least have yielded fruit by now. Indeed, what is now proposed and on the move, if inaugurated two years ago, might well have gone half-way to meet our needs.

I do not doubt that, as the realization of our mortal danger deepens, it will awaken that sense of self-preservation which is the foundation of human existence, and this process is now going forward. Our British Socialist colleague, Mr Edelman, reminded us of the immense superiority in steel, in oil, in aluminium and other materials on which the defence potential of the free nations rests. But much of this might be the prize of the aggressors if we were struck down. M. André Philip said on Tuesday that France did not wish to be liberated again. After a period of Russian Communist occupation there would not, as M. Reynaud pointed out, be much to liberate. The systematic liquidation of all elements hostile to Communism would leave little which would be recognized by the rescuers of the survivors.

We in this Assembly have no responsibility or executive power, but we are bound to give our warning and our counsel. There must be created, and in the shortest possible time, a real defensive front in Europe. Great Britain and the United States must send large forces to the Continent. France must again revive her famous army. We welcome our Italian comrades. All—Greece, Turkey, Holland, Belgium, Luxembourg, the Scandinavian States—must bear their share and do their best. Courage and unity must inspire us and direct the mighty energies at the disposal of our Governments to solid and adequate measures of defence. Those who serve supreme causes must not consider what they can get but what they can give. Let that be our rivalry in these years that lie before us.

The question which challenges us is: Shall we have the time? No one can answer that question for certain, but to assume that we were too late would be the very madness of despair. We are still under the shield of the atomic bomb, possessed in formidable quantities by the United States alone. The use of this weapon would shake the foundations of the Soviet regime throughout the vast areas of Russia, and the breakdown of all communications and centralized control might well enable the brave Russian peoples to free themselves from a tyranny far worse than that of the Czars. It seems very likely that such possibilities will constitute an effective deterrent upon Soviet aggression, at least until they have by a lengthy process built up an adequate supply of atomic bombs of their own.

There is another reason why the general armed assault by Communism against the Western democracies may be delayed. The Soviet dictators have no reason to be discontented with the way things have gone so far, and are going. Since the world war stopped in 1945, they have obtained control of half Europe and of all China without losing a single Russian soldier, thus adding upwards of 500,000,000 people to their own immense population. They have a wealth of opportunities for creating trouble and tempting us to disperse our forces unduly through the action of their satellites. It seems that Tibet is to be the next victim. Engaged in these diversions they are able to preach peace while planning aggressive war and improving their atomic stockpile. But in my judgment, which I present with all diffidence, we have a breathing space, and if we use this wisely and well, and do not waste it as we have already wasted so much, we may still greatly increase the deterrents against a major Russian Communist aggression. It is by closing the yawning gap in the defences of the Western Powers in Europe that we shall find the surest means, not only of saving our lives and liberties, but of preventing a third world war.

If in the next two years or so we can create a trustworthy system of defence against Communist invasion, we shall at least have removed the most obvious temptation to those who seek to impose their will by force upon the free democracies. This system of defence in the West will alone give the best chance of a final settlement by negotiation with the Soviets on the basis of our strength and not of our weakness. But there is not a day to be lost nor a scrap of available strength to be denied.

As I have already said, this Assembly has no power to act, nor do we seek to relieve the responsible executive Governments of their duties. We ought, however, to make our united convictions known. We should now send a message of confidence and courage from the House of Europe to the whole world. Not only should we reaffirm, as we have been asked to do, our allegiance to the United Nations, but we should make a gesture of practical and constructive guidance by declaring ourselves in favour of the immediate creation of a European Army under a unified command, and in which we should all bear a worthy and honourable part.

Therefore, Mr President, I propose to you a Motion which, after some previous consultation in various quarters, I have ventured to place upon the Order Paper. I trust that this Motion will, by an open and formal vote, receive the overwhelming, if not indeed the unanimous, support of this Assembly. This would be the greatest contribution that it is in our power to make to the safety and peace of the world. We can thus go forward together sure at least that we have done our duty. I beg to move that:

'The Assembly, in order to express its devotion to the maintenance of peace and its resolve to sustain the action of the Security Council of the United Nations in defence of peaceful peoples against aggression, calls for the immediate creation of a unified European Army subject to proper European democratic control and acting in full co-operation with the United States and Canada.'

THE PERIL IN EUROPE

A PARTY POLITICAL BROADCAST
26 AUGUST 1950

---

15 *August—HRH Princess Elizabeth gives birth to a daughter.*

[26 *August* 1950

When Parliament separated a month ago, the Government had just placed before us their £100,000,000 plan for strengthening our defences. Five days later the Prime Minister asked me to go to see him at Downing Street and there read to me the announcement of an entirely new and much larger plan, costing £300,000,000 or £400,000,000 a year for three years, and requiring far-reaching changes in our whole national industry and economy. Obviously, this was a matter on which the House of Commons should be consulted at the earliest moment. Indeed, we are all entitled to be told why there should have been this immense change between the policy of 26 July and that of 2 August.

After our talk I wrote to Mr Attlee that we should give our support to all measures proposed by the Government which were necessary for national defence. 'It is certain,' I said, 'that we are in a condition of great danger and that surprisingly little practical results have followed from the immense outlay of money and control of man-power used by the Government during recent years.' I added that our urgent need is to form efficient combatant units, of which we have hardly any at the present time, and that if the Government could bring forward well-conceived plans of this kind, even if they involved increasing the length of compulsory service, I should recommend the Conservative Party to support such measures both in Parliament and the country. We hold that national safety should rise above party differences, deep and wide as they have become in recent years.

I thought this offer was fair and friendly, and I hoped it would be treated in the same spirit. There was not, however, even the usual consultation with the official Opposition before the summoning of Parliament for 12 September was announced. A month's interval for an emergency recall of Parliament seemed much too long. I thought either the date should be earlier or its announcement have been put off. Mr Eden and I, with the Liberal Leader, Mr Clement Davies, were invited by Mr Attlee to visit him at Downing Street, and after a lengthy, and none too pleasant, discussion, he arbitrarily refused our request for an earlier recall. I do not think it is a wise or right course for a Prime Minister in a minority of nearly 2,000,000 votes at the recent election, and with a majority of only one in the House of Commons at the last crucial division—I do not think it is a wise course for him to treat with so little consideration the views of those political opponents who offer to support him on all the things that matter most and on whose help he is counting to carry through the measures necessary for public security. It is a bad thing that His Majesty's Prime Minister should show himself so sullenly resolved to lead only one-half of the nation.

We see from day to day many instances of the improvidence and want of foresight with which our affairs are conducted. Take this case of sending the expeditionary force to Korea: on 27 June, the United Nations called upon their members to defend South Korea against violent aggression from the north. It took the Socialist Government a month to make up their minds whether or not to send an expeditionary force to comply with this request of the United Nations Organization. There was no new fact in the interval. Another month has passed since the decision to send the small force from here was announced, and more than a third month will pass before it can embark on its six weeks' voyage. I should myself have thought it better to have sent even a smaller force in good time from Hong Kong and to replace it from home later on. I was told this was impossible, but now it has been done.

There are graver cases of lack of prevision, of hesitancy and changes of plan which are at work throughout our whole system of defence, adding to its heavy cost and diminishing its already inadequate strength. Some of these are more suited to a Secret Session of Parliament than to a public broadcast. I have already mentioned in Parliament the astonishing episode of selling hundreds of our jet fighters to Egypt and the Argentine, and actually sending some to Russia at an earlier period when all the time our own Auxiliary Air Force so urgently needed them, and this at the moment when, by establishing the American bomber base in East Anglia—a policy which the Opposition supported on national grounds—we have placed ourselves in the front line of targets in the event of war.

I heard a few days ago of a case which shows the same kind of infirmity and disconnection of thought and action, though in a different sphere. The head of the Craven Brothers machine tools works at Stockport—the largest but one for producing these vital and very slowly made instruments—informed me that he had for more than two years been asking the Ministry of Supply whether he should fulfil his contracts for making machine tools for Soviet Russia, particularly tools of the class required for the manufacture and repair of tanks, whether he should go on doing this when so many of our own Royal Ordnance factories are in sore need of renovation for this very purpose. He could not get any clear guidance. He told me that his highly skilled craftsmen were seriously disturbed at doing work of this kind for Soviet Russia and for her satellite Poland. They feared it would weaken our country and strengthen our most likely assailant. They also did not like the presence of Russian Government inspectors, under present conditions, inside their workshops, where a lot of confidential production is also being done for His Majesty's Government. Surely, orders should be given now to stop the export by any firm of machine tools, diesel engines and the like to Soviet Russia and other countries behind the Iron Curtain, and thus release these firms from the contracts, by which they are otherwise bound. I understand the Prime Minister is going to speak on this subject next week; I trust that he will be able to tell us that this, at any rate, has been done.

But fancy going on in this sort of way, and from day to day, with this lack of control and management of great matters, while everything is getting worse, and when we are literally begging the United States for aid in every form. It is a glaring example of the lack of grip, conception and design by our present ministerial planners. What is the use of appealing to the country for unity, exertions and further sacrifices when such feebleness of purpose vitiates our action? The question we must ask ourselves is how much more of this is going on all over the place? Another example of the Government's lack of foresight is shown in their treatment of the question of inviting German aid for the defence of Western Europe and of their own hearths and homes. Five months have passed since I raised this matter in Parliament, and Mr Attlee then described what I said as 'irresponsible' (this was the same word that I think he used about abolishing petrol rationing). Now his Government are making plans with the representatives of America and Europe for doing this very thing, for bringing Germany into the system of defence. Perhaps it is better to be irresponsible and right than to be responsible and wrong. I am certainly thankful not to be responsible for what has happened to our country and its empire during the last five years. At Strasbourg, where we had the meeting the other day of the Council of Europe, two very remarkable things happened. The Germans declared that they did not want to create a

German national army, but were willing to serve in a European defence force; and, secondly, France, by a noble gesture, welcomed the idea of French and German soldiers standing side by side in defence of freedom. This is a great event in the history of Europe, and I am proud to have had something to do with it.

Alas, it also marks the sense of common peril which oppresses us all. Dr Adenauer, the German Prime Minister, points to the very large, heavily armed Communist German forces which have been raised in the Russian zone which, he says, may amount to several hundred thousand men. They are disguised as police, but they are really an army. Is this not exactly the same technique which the Kremlin oligarchy carried out in Northern Korea before the recent attack? Except, of course, that the danger in Europe is nearer and on an incomparably larger scale. Mr Shinwell has made public what those who study these matters had long known, namely that the Brussels Treaty and Atlantic Pact Powers in Western Europe are already outnumbered six, seven or eight to one—it may be more—by the Russian armies, to say nothing of their satellites and Communist pawns. That is a terrible fact.

We have not been able ourselves to make an atomic bomb, although we played so great a part in its discovery during the war. But the Russian Soviets have had the secret betrayed to them by their spies and fanatics and we have been officially informed by our own Government that they have begun to make it. It is indeed a melancholy thought that nothing preserves Europe from an overwhelming military attack except the devastating resources of the United States in this awful weapon. That is at the present time the sole deterrent against an aggressive Communist invasion. No wonder the Communists would like to ban it in the name of peace. They would then have Europe naked and at their mercy.

European and British weakness endangers peace, for which we must all patiently strive. We are in grave danger. It is not a new danger. I have warned you about it for several years, but it is only since the war broke out in Korea that people have begun to realize how we all stand. I have several times said that I do not believe that a major war is imminent. No one can be sure, but I believe myself we still have a breathing space, and that if we use it wisely we may still ward off this horror from the world. I am sorry that an effort was not made to have a personal talk on the highest level with the leaders of the Soviet Government. I urged this at Edinburgh in February last, but nothing was done and all sorts of things have happened since.

My eyes are not fixed upon Korea, though I admire the American action there, and am glad our men are going to help. There may soon be Communist attacks upon Tibet and Persia. But the supreme peril is in Europe. We must try to close the hideous gap on the European front. If, in two or three years—should that be granted us—we can make a reasonable defence for the free countries outside the Iron Curtain, while at the same time the United States maintains and increases its superiority in the atomic bomb, the best hope will be given for reaching a final peace settlement. The only way to deal with Communist Russia is by having superior strength in one form or another, and then acting with reason and fairness. This is the plan for the battle of peace and the only plan which has a chance of success. Here at home the Socialist policy since the war has divided our own people in a needless and painful manner. We lie between two general elections. We have to make our case against each other. But we must never forget that, whatever our party differences may be, we all share the same dangers, and we all, when we wake up, mean to defend the same great causes. I pray we may wake up in time.

I have used the few minutes in which I may speak to you—I wish I had an hour—but now I can only say: let us not cast away the remaining chances, or the chances of all the free democracies, of averting a new world war, and of not being wiped out in it if it comes. If the Ministers—many of them at heart well-meaning and patriotic men—who have had all this power and control for the last five years are proved to be incapable of meeting our dire need, it is for Parliament and, above all, for the nation to say whether they should not be replaced by others before it is too late.

DEFENCE (GOVERNMENT PROPOSALS)

A SPEECH TO THE HOUSE OF COMMONS

12 SEPTEMBER 1950

---

30 *August—In a broadcast speech Mr Attlee announces increases in pay for all ranks of Regular forces.*

31 *August—The Foreign Office announce its intention to discontinue the publication of 'British Ally' due to drop in sales in Soviet Russia.*

1 *September—In a 'fireside chat' broadcast, Mr Truman outlines America's 8-point policy in the Far East.*

Publication of British Overseas Airways' and British European Airways Corporations' reports and accounts show a combined loss of £9,155,481 for the year ended 31 March 1950.

10 *September—Soap rationing in the United Kingdom ends.*

12 *September—The Foreign Ministers of Britain, France and the USA meet in New York to discuss the international situation.*

12-14 *September—The Prime Minister, opening the three-day debate on Defence in the House of Commons, announces that the Government's defence plan will cost £3,600,000,000 for the three-year period, and gives details of the proposed increases in the number of Regular Army divisions and the measures for strengthening the Royal Navy and the RAF.*

[12 *September* 1950

On a Motion moved by the Prime Minister

'that this House approves the proposals contained in the White Papers Command No. 8026 and 8027, designed by HM Government to meet the growing dangers to world peace of which the war in Korea is an example; and is of opinion that the necessary legislation to amend the National Service Acts should be brought in forthwith'.

We shall on this side, of course, support the Motion which you have just read, sir. We shall vote for it and we shall help to resist any Amendment which may be moved to it. We shall also support the Bill to extend the length of military service which is to be introduced. Several points may well arise upon that Bill for discussion in Committee, but I should hope that it can be passed through this House, certainly without any hindrance if not, indeed, in a single day.

I shall not on this occasion ask that any of our Debates should be in Secret Session. I just mention this to relieve any anxiety that may prevail on the benches opposite. Looking around, I cannot on this occasion spy any strangers participating in our debates. I must, however, make it clear that our approval of the Prime Minister's Motion is not a vote of confidence in the Government. We could not, on this side of the House, give a vote of confidence in the present Administration, least of all in its handling of military affairs. Although in all questions where the safety of the country is concerned we continue to give our support to His Majesty's Government, it must not be supposed that we are in any way ready to share their responsibility, such as it is, for the present condition of our affairs. We recognize that Ministers are by no means wholly responsible for the situation in which we all now lie. They have made many needless mistakes, but much that has happened has been outside their control.

Both Governments and Oppositions have responsibilities to discharge, but they are of a different order. The Government, with their whole control over our executive power, have the burden and the duty—and we can all see that it is a very heavy one—to make sure that the safety of the country is provided for; the shape, formation and direction of policy is in their hands alone. The responsibilities of the Opposition are limited to aiding the Government in the measures which are required, which we agree are required, for national safety and also to criticizing and correcting, so far as they can, any errors and shortcomings which may be apparent; but the Opposition are not responsible for proposing integrated and complicated measures of policy. Sometimes we do, but it is not our obligation. In voting for what the Government propose, which we are going to do on this occasion, we in no way limit our right and duty to comment with the fullest freedom upon their policy and the course of events.

The Prime Minister has appealed to us for national unity on Defence. That does not mean national unity on mismanagement of Defence. In our view, which I shall endeavour to sustain, the present Government, although right-minded on essentials, have shown themselves conspicuously lacking in forethought, conviction and design. It was never in their power, as I have most frankly declared, to prevent the sombre deterioration of our affairs which has resulted from the Russian-Communist aggression upon so many countries and the poisoning or infection of so many more. We are in full accord with the Labour Party, as I call them on occasions when I am in a good humour with them, in their resistance to Communism in all its manifestations. We can hardly compete with the Prime Minister in the language he uses on this subject, but we rejoice with them that the

Trades Union Congress should have so decisively ranged itself, as was only to be expected by those who understand the solid qualities of British trade unionism, with the unaltering and unflinching defence of the free way of life of the Western parliamentary democracies. A vote was given last week at Brighton—I think the Prime Minister referred to it—which ranges the overwhelming mass of the British trade unionists with His Majesty's Government and also with the Conservative and Liberal Parties—[*Interruption*]—these last two, for all the jeers and mockery of hon Members, comprising a majority of nearly 2,000,000 of our people, according to the recent election. In giving faithful and fearless support to the United Nations Organization in confronting totalitarian tyranny, whether it wears the garb of Communism, Nazism, Fascism, or Russian Imperialism—on these supreme issues Britain can indeed present a united front, not only for this island but for our sister nations throughout the British Empire and Commonwealth. However grave our differences are in domestic matters or however sharp must be our criticisms of ministerial handling of affairs, that is the message of unity which we are resolved to send at this juncture from the House of Commons to the world.

Having made this clear, I will give the House a short narrative of what has happened, so far as I am aware, since we separated six weeks ago. We had then received from the Minister of Defence a most serious statement of the immense preponderance—seven or eight to one—of the Soviet Forces in active divisions, in organized armour and in air power over the Western allies in Europe. The Government proposed that we should spend £100,000,000 on additional preparations for defence and this was, of course, accepted, so far as it went. However, five days after we parted, the Prime Minister asked me to come and see him and read to me the text of the statement which was to be published the next morning of an entirely new and greatly enlarged defence policy, namely, the three years' plan involving an additional expenditure of £1,100,000,000. Quick work, it seemed to me.

After this interview I wrote him a letter dated 6 August—before I had to go to Strasbourg—thanking him for informing me of the measures which he was now taking in concert with the United States, and saying:

'We shall give our support to all measures proposed by the Government which we ourselves deem necessary for national defence. This cannot, however, limit in any way the right and duty of the Opposition to criticize, either in public or secret Debate, the existing state of our defences, or the rate and methods with which the necessary increases are to be effected. However, we do not, of course, know anything about the Government's new plan, except what has now been published. It is certain that we are in a condition of great danger, and that surprisingly little practical results have followed from the immense outlay of money and control of man-power used by the Government during recent years. It seems to me and to those of my colleagues I have been able to consult that Parliament should be called together if possible before the end of August. I propose to hold a meeting of my colleagues on or about 15 August, and it is probable that we shall then make a formal request for the recall of Parliament.'

We were impelled to think of the steps made possible by the very full assurances given by the Lord President of the Council before we separated.

In the note which I enclosed to the Prime Minister on the military position—and it is that military aspect with which we are dealing today—I said:

'I do not myself see how the British contribution can be achieved without holding existing men with the Colours and increasing the length of service. The urgent need is to form efficient combatant units, of which we have hardly any at the present time. Should the Government bring forward well-conceived measures of this kind, I should recommend the Opposition to support them both in Parliament and in the country.'

That is what I wrote before I knew of the decision that the length of service was to be extended. That is what we now propose to do, and I hope the assurance given was of assistance to the Government in the extremely difficult problems which they are called upon now to face, and about which, of course, they have to agree among themselves.

I must say that it looks as if a meeting of Parliament in the last week of August would have given the Prime Minister a very appropriate and convenient opportunity for presenting not only his new proposals for the increase of our military expenditure to £1,100,000,000 under the three years' plan but also for telling Parliament of the Govern-ment's decision to prolong compulsory National Service from eighteen months to two years, as well as the welcome statement, so long pressed for on this side of the House, of the increase in the pay of the Regular Forces. However, the Prime Minister, without any further contact, even through the usual channels, announced the recall of Parliament for today, 12 September. So here we are.

This was an emergency recall, and it seemed odd to announce it nearly a month before, and with such timing as to make it necessary that the important declaration of the lengthening of the period of National Service should be given over a broadcast rather than presented, according to normal constitutional practice, to the House of Commons. But these are not large matters. [*Interruption.*] Still, after all, Parliamentary usage is something which is quite important to consider. I repeat, these are not large matters compared with the vast and glowering facts by which we are encircled. I put them to the House only to illustrate the sudden and inconsequent changes in Government policy which are now before us.

Why was it that, when we were last gathered here, we were offered the £100,000,000 plan whereas a few days later this was superseded by the three years' £1,100,000,000 plan? What happened in the interval to make such a sweeping change desirable? I gather from the Prime Minister's speech that the Americans appealed to us to take some further action. But surely all these matters should have been well known and familiar to a Government that have been for over five years in office? Surely we do not need the prompting of a foreign country, however friendly, to show us where our duty lies? What happened, I say? Why was it that only, perhaps, a fortnight elapsed after Parliament rose before the new, formidable decision was taken, namely, to prolong the period of National Service?

When we were last together the Minister of Defence told how completely undecided the Government were, when he said:

'In present circumstances, we are not satisfied that an increase in the period of whole-time National Service would solve our problem. But this is a matter we intend to keep under constant review.'

That was only a fortnight before this tremendous change was proposed and put forward and given to the nation. All we were told at that time was that we must keep the matter under continuous review. I may refer to that phrase about keeping things 'under continuous review' a little later. What happened, I ask, to make so complete a change of plan in the military structure of our country necessary?

This is the kind of quick, impulsive change in the dominating issues of our Defence policy which makes it difficult to have confidence that our vital affairs are being conducted in accordance with any clear and persistent theme. What new facts, I ask again, had arisen between our separation for the Recess and the £1,100,000,000 plan? All right: it is said America appealed to us. What new facts had arisen between the declaration of this plan and the declaration of the lengthened service and the other proposals which form the subject of the Prime Minister's Motion today? Surely, these are fair and, indeed, unavoidable questions? I do not feel that the Prime Minister has given any adequate answer to them in his speech today.

But this is not merely a matter of the last few weeks. I do not know of any great change in the balance of world power or the imminence of world danger that has occurred since the dark day when the Government informed us that the Russian Communist Government had gained possession of the secret of the atomic bomb and led us to believe they had produced it. But this was a year ago. It is quite true that the Soviet-impelled aggression in Korea, and the vehement and valiant action of the United States, in pursuance of the United Nations mandate, and the fierce and enlarging war now proceeding in Korea, had made everyone realize and pay attention to dangers which were quite well known to those who follow these matters, and were certainly well known to His Majesty's Government.

The dread balance has not been changed. It is only that the flare of actual war in one distant theatre—out of several that may be opened—has broken upon the public. But the Government must have had the whole picture before them for two years past or three years past. As I have said, it is for five years they have been studying all these matters—with responsibility and power. If the Motion before us this afternoon had been made two years ago how much better off we should be at this moment. The facts disclosed by the Minister of Defence, before we adjourned, about the position in Europe did not spring into existence overnight; they must have been known to the Prime Minister and his principal colleagues long ago. The war in Korea has only made the ordinary people in many lands understand what must have been plainly visible, nay, obvious, to those who were entrusted with the sacred duty of guarding their safety and who had all the knowledge that was available.

Why, then, were the necessary measures not proposed in good time? That is another question to which I cannot feel that the Prime Minister has given us any answer this afternoon or in his broadcast; but then, no doubt, he was occupied with more important topics. It is quite true that, unhappily, in this country we are deeply divided about internal politics and that first-class issues affecting the whole character of our country and its economic life are raised thereby. But the Socialist Government have been in a position of great advantage compared with other British Governments we have experienced. Compare their position, for instance, to that of the Baldwin and Chamberlain Governments before the war—[*Interruption.*] Hon Members opposite had better listen to what I have to say, then they will know which side to cheer.

The present Socialist Government have known that they could rely upon the whole-hearted support of His Majesty's Opposition, comprising both the other parties in the State, in any steps they might think it necessary to take for national defence, and international duty. At any time they could propose, with the certainty of our support, unpopular steps. They knew quite well that the Conservative Party in the last Parliament, as in this, would vote with them if, for instance, they demanded a prolongation of National Service, and would not vote against them, as the Prime Minister led the Socialist Party into doing on the same issue four months before the outbreak of the Second World War. I hope they will not indulge further in that propaganda of 'Guilty men' which has played so large a part in their platform talks in recent years. Such discrepancies of conduct—I can hardly use a milder term—will not affect our action or the course we are bound now to take in the national interest. But they cannot be, and ought not to be, excluded from our minds in judging the record and character of the present Administration. This indecision and these sudden changes, without any new material facts, in what ought to be long-term policies and, shall I say, 'supra-party issues'—I am always willing to endeavour to throw myself into the mood of those who, at any rate, we shall be supporting on this question—this indecision and these sudden changes have aggravated the inevitable perils and burdens of the position to which, with the nation's eyes at last opened, we have now come. That is why, in supporting the Motion now before us, we do not in any way absolve the Government from the just censure which lies upon them for their conduct of affairs.

Let me turn to another and more precise aspect of this indecision and hesitancy in regard to fateful but also simple issues. On 27 June, the United Nations organization declared the Soviet-impelled invasion of South Korea to be an act of aggression and called upon all its members to render support to the United States in resisting it. Accordingly, British warships and some local air squadrons were very rightly ordered to participate. But when, after nearly a month, the Government made up their minds to send a military force from this country to stand in line with the Americans, the question arises: Why have they not been able to send it out before? It certainly was what is called an 'eye-opener' to the vast majority of our people that, after all the money and control of manpower and control of administrative arrangements that the Government have enjoyed for five years, it should take months to organize even a strong brigade group from this country. It is not ready yet.

I thought myself that a token force should have been provided much earlier from Hong Kong and replaced by reinforcements of troops from this country, who need not be capable of going immediately into battle, but who would rapidly mature and fill the gap in the Hong Kong garrison. But the Government decided otherwise. Let me ask the Prime Minister a question: What was the date when he changed his mind and decided to send a force from Hong Kong to Korea? What was the date?

THE PRIME MINISTER: I am afraid that I have not that date with me. I did explain in a broadcast that the original request was that we should send a balanced force, and stress was not laid on sending them immediately; but, subsequently, we had an urgent request to which we at once responded by sending a force from Hong Kong.

MR CHURCHILL: It certainly was a great surprise to me, and I am sure also to my right hon Friend the Member for Warwick and Leamington [Mr Eden] and to the Leader of the Liberal Party. [Interruption.] I hope that members of the Liberal Party all over the country will take note of that cry of derision. No one counts at all except those who are managed by the Labour caucus; no one else counts at all. Yet they come forward appealing for national support and unity. It was a great surprise to us after our interview with the Prime Minister on 16 August to learn on 20 August that a force was to be sent from Hong Kong. The Prime Minister does not remember what was the date of the decision, but, at any rate, I have given him fairly limited brackets in which he will be able to make his further investigations.

THE PRIME MINISTER: I cannot quite make out what is the right hon Gentleman's special point about this date. What is he hanging on the date that is so important? I have told him the facts.

MR CHURCHILL: I am hanging on the fact that these great matters which are continually before us and before the nation appear to swing about between one day and another, almost upon caprice, at the hands of the Government.

THE PRIME MINISTER: The right hon Gentleman has more experience in conducting military affairs than anyone in this House. He has been accustomed, no doubt, to receiving advice from those who are responsible for running a campaign. The campaign in Korea is being run by the Americans. We respond to their requests, and if the request changes from what it was before it is not the fault of His Majesty's Government. We have responded to the request made to us.

MR CHURCHILL: No, sir. I do not feel that that is so. [HON MEMBERS: 'Oh.'] I think the Americans are bitterly disappointed. [Interruption.] Why is the Prime Minister's colleague shouting? He does not know anything about it. That is my personal view. I do not mind noise in the least. Please go on, although we gave the Prime Minister a very silent and patient hearing.

It is my personal view that the Government and their military advisers, having rejected this project for many weeks, suddenly made a right-about turn and did what they had hitherto declared to be impossible. There was really nothing new in the situation, except perhaps the growing disappointment of the United States that we were so long in sending them anything from anywhere. [Hon Members: 'Shame.'] The tangled story of sending and delaying sending, and changing of plans in the method of sending, what could only be a token force, and rightly could only be a token force, to Korea, is a culminating example of the incapacity to take decisions and of living from day to day, which casts its shadow on all our military affairs at a time when small-scale issues are sharp and urgent, and when potentially mortal perils gather their clouds around.

Now let me speak of another aspect. I do not think it will be any more agreeable to hon Members opposite. Let me speak of another aspect, not so much of indecision as of disconnection in policy—I mean the continued exportation of machine tools and other appliances to Soviet Russia and Poland. Our British industries are very short of machine tools. Diesel engines, electrical plant and many other kindred high-grade manufactures have been pumped out of this country in the last few years although they are greatly needed at home. This was done in the name of dollar balances or in unrequited exports. The sending away of machine tools which are needed here at a time like this is like selling the seed corn in the lean years, which in bygone days was regarded as an unwise thing to do.

We see the same kind of want of foresight, the same defective sense of values and proportion, which I have already mentioned in the military sphere, the same system and habit of indecision in this question of the export of machine tools as we have seen in the military sphere. Of course, the crowning example is the sale of hundreds of jet aeroplanes which were needed so imperatively for our own self-defence and security. The Prime Minister has referred to it today, and perhaps the party opposite will allow me to comment on his remarks. He said out of doors, that this is an 'old story'. But there has never been a satisfactory answer to it. One hundred and ten jet aeroplanes were sold or given to Egypt, and what we read in the papers seems to show that it has not at all improved their good feeling towards us. Fancy sending them away. Then, 100 to the Argentine. These are sent away at a time when our auxiliary air forces are hopelessly lacking and eagerly longing for these machines. The right hon Gentleman said that it would have upset all our financial and economic arrangements, or words to that effect. What nonsense! The aeroplanes that were sold to the Argentine were, I believe, credited for about £2,000,000 or £3,000,000. We are dealing with a Budget for which we voted £700,000,000 or £800,000,000, and now we come forward into these colossal figures. This £2,000,000 or £3,000,000, for an absolutely vital asset which we require, is brought up as a reason for this very gross neglect.

The Government have now, according to the broadcast of the Prime Minister, definitely decided that any machine tools, no matter how vital their war potential, which have been ordered by Soviet Russia or its satellites before the British restrictive regulations of eighteen months ago, must, when made, be delivered to Soviet Russia. I have heard a lot of vague language from the Prime Minister, but I could not see anything which countered or contradicted that quite definite assertion he made in his broadcast.

THE PRIME MINISTER: The right hon Gentleman has not got it quite right.

MR CHURCHILL: No doubt what I have said is quite true.

THE PRIME MINISTER: What I said was that the machinery and tools were being delivered in respect of contracts already entered into, and the statement made in 1949—I think in February—by the President of the Board of Trade to this House was that that was the practice we were following. I did not say that if at the present time we required these we should not step in and take them over. I was referring to what the practice was then. As a matter of fact, a whole lot of trading goes on which is outside the control of the Government.

MR CHURCHILL: It is very extraordinary that the right hon Gentleman should take the tremendous step of proposing a £1,100,000,000 three-year plan, announcing to the country the lengthening of service from eighteen months to two years, and no one in the Government should have seen that at some time a stoppage should have been put on vital military materials leaving this country. No, sir, what I gathered from what the right hon Gentleman said led me to preserve this particular phrase: 'The matter is to be kept under continuous review.'

Surely, if the Government's view is maintained this altogether ignores the position. These tools take a long time to make, and the British machine tool industry has for years been pressed with orders which it can only fulfil in sequence. There is an endless queue of orders for machine tools, and only comparatively few firms and craftsmen can make them. We have now reached the point where vital war-making materials are to be sent in an increasing flow for some time from this country to Soviet Russia. We think that is wrong and ought to be stopped. It is surprising that the Government, in other directions so prone to retrospective legislation, should find themselves puristically and pedantically hampered in the matter of war materials when an entirely new situation has arisen and become acute.

The right hon Gentleman said that he was endeavouring to stop certain materials being actually sent to North Korea which would help the North Koreans to shoot down our soldiers. We should all approve of a step of that character. The Prime Minister can commit himself to it without any fear that he would be severely criticized in the House. It is intolerable to think that our troops today should be sent into action at one end of the world while we are supplying, or are about to supply, if not actual weapons of war, the means to make weapons of war to those who are trying to kill them or get them killed. I was astonished when I was told what was going on. I was astounded by the attitude that the Prime Minister has taken. I should think that the feeling of the great majority of those in this House would be that no more machine tools of a war-making character and no more machines or engines which could be used for war-making purposes should be sent from this country to Soviet Russia or the Soviet satellite nations while the present tension continues. I do not intend to go into details this afternoon, though they are all available and can be produced if there is any challenge. I do not suggest that this is done out of any ill-will on the part of the Government, but is only another example of the disconnection between the various Departments arising from lack of grip and control.

I will return to the purely military aspect of this Motion, for which we intend to vote. The arguments for it are very strong. The imposition in time of peace of eighteen months' compulsory service was a severe departure from our past customs, and a heavy burden on our people. The Government deserve credit for having discharged their duty in this respect. However, as has now been realized on both sides of the House, a period of eighteen months was singularly awkward for our affairs. It gave us a very heavy burden for a very small result in combatant units. It is true that a great reserve of well-trained men for the Territorial Army is being built up, and I wonder that the Prime Minister did not emphasize that a little more, because certainly, it will be a very different kind of Territorial Army filled with men who have served eighteen months in the ranks. It is being built up, and if the other elements are provided this gives a strong foundation for military defensive power after a considerable interval.

But the need of producing a number of effective combat units speedily, and maintaining them abroad or on the continent of Europe—not quite the same thing in my opinion—is most unhandily met by a period of eighteen months' service. Our Regular formations are drained and also burdened by the need of training the large flow of recruits coming in throughout the year. I presume the Minister of Defence will look into the question of whether they are called fortnightly throughout the year or at longer intervals. I am not sufficiently informed to make up my mind. We lose our men just at the period when they really are useful for foreign service and for fighting formations. Our considerable sacrifice has given us the worst of both worlds. Clear thinking and clear policy on this question has, no doubt, been hampered by the harsh conditions of political and party strife which, however regrettable, now exists between us. There is no doubt that the proposal of this Motion for two years' compulsory service and a well-paid Regular Army will, if properly applied, bring a swift, solid and substantial increase in our defensive power. It ought to be possible under this system rapidly to build up a very good army if the weapons are found for them.

There will be a marked improvement even in the next six months if, instead of reaching a discord at a great cost, we reach a harmony for a somewhat heavier period. There can be no doubt that this is a wise measure, and also that in spite of all its difficulties it ought to have been taken before. All of us hate the idea of another war. Is there anyone in this island who can think of any country that we wish to attack or invade? But we must make ourselves capable of serving the great cause to which we have pledged our faith, and in which our own survival is also directly involved. There can, therefore, be no question, so far as we here on this side of the House are concerned, that this measure should go through, and if the Government gain credit for it—however belated it may be—so much the better for them. We need not at this time grudge anybody the credit of doing anything, anywhere, anyhow for anyone. That is the position to which we have got today. The military chiefs should in my opinion be held strictly responsible for making the best use of the extraordinary, unprecedented measures of State which are being taken to help them in their task.

The Prime Minister has spoken, not today but out-of-doors, scornfully about a European army—apparently, it would have been all right if I had said 'a European defence force'—and about the Germans being included in our Western defence system. Are they being discussed? No, they are being kept under continuous review. Where does he stand about these matters? Is he still opposed to Germans being armed as a part of the Western defence forces or as part of an armed German police force; or does he still think the only Germans to be armed are the Communist Germans, whom the Soviets have formed into a powerful army in the Russian zone? Again, I think the right hon Gentleman was very guarded and very obscure when he said he was keeping the matter under review, and what he said about the Germans was so very vague that one could hardly understand it. Still I must say that I was encouraged on both these points, and I feel that the normal process of belated conversion to the obvious is still steadily going forward.

Let me here say, again, that the fact that the liberated German representatives voted at Strasbourg for sending a quota to a European army, while not seeking to raise a national army of their own is a most helpful fact, and has been so regarded throughout Europe and the United States. This has rendered it far easier for the French to welcome them and for the closing of a thousand-year quarrel in the historic gesture of French and German soldiers standing in the line together against the Russian-Communist aggression and menace. I feel sure that all this process of bringing the Germans back into the family of united Europe and enabling them to take a part in a European army or European defence force for the defence of freedom and civilization—for which some of us on this side of the House have worked so hard for several years—has been helpful not only to the free world but even to the British Socialist Government. The Prime Minister should welcome it instead of discouraging or even disparaging it. But whatever his feelings may be he would be wise to accept it, because a European army with a strong German quota is going to be formed quite quickly—that is to say, if we are given the time. That is a fact that none can challenge or deny.

I have never seen an occasion when what is going on in Europe generally is more uncertain and what we ought to do is more clear. Never was the future more inscrutable and never was our policy and duty more plain. We have to form, as fast as possible, a European army of at least sixty or seventy divisions to make some sort of front in Europe to close what I have called 'the hideous gap' in the protection of Western Europe from a Russian-Communist onrush to the sea. For this purpose every nation still enjoying freedom from totalitarian tyranny should make extreme exertions. Each of the countries ruled by parliamentary democracies must dedicate their quota of divisions. Since these matters were last debated in this House, in March, the French have resolved to contribute twenty divisions, I understand, but it may be fifteen divisions. I rejoice to see the famous French Army lift itself again into the vanguard of freedom.

There should certainly be ten divisions from the United States, two or three from Canada and six or eight from this island. I must say that the suggestion of three from Germany and one and a half or two available here does not seem to me to be a proportionate contribution, even making allowance for the fact that although we have got rid of India we have still important obligations to meet in tropical countries. I do not think that that should be accepted as a full and complete contribution on our part. Germany and Italy should also contribute eight or ten divisions apiece and the Benelux countries, comprising ancient and characteristic States, at least four more. Then there is Scandinavia. So here are sixty or seventy divisions which can be produced and organized.

If such an army can be deployed on our gaping Eastern front, the greatest danger of a third world war in the next three or four years will be substantially diminished, if not indeed removed. We shall become free from the present horrible plight in which the American possession of measureless superiority in the atomic bomb is our only safeguard against what might well be the ruin of the world. This will undoubtedly give the Western democracies the best chance of securing the return to the normal relationships of States and nations. Whether we shall have time or not no one can tell. There are two factors which we cannot measure, let alone control, either of which may prove decisive. They are the following: first, the calculations and designs of the Soviet autocracy in the Kremlin, and, secondly, the anger of the people in the United States at the treatment they are receiving and the burden they have to bear. Neither of these is within our control.

It is my firm conviction that while there is a real, solid hope of building up an effective European army the United States will forbear, and that while American superiority in atomic warfare casts its strange but merciful shield over the free peoples the Soviet oligarchy will be deterred from launching out upon the most frightful of world wars yet waged in this unhappy and distraught world. It may well be that the vast masses of human beings, who ask for so little, but only to be let alone to enjoy the fruits of peaceful toil and raise their children in the hope of a decent and improving future, can still be rescued from the melancholy and frightful fate which has seemed to be, and now seems to be, closing in upon them. We cannot control, and no one nation can control, the march of destiny, but we can at least do our part. It is because the Motion now before us offers a minor but none the less considerable make-weight to the peaceful settlement of world affairs that we on this side of the House, Conservatives and Liberals alike, will give it our united and resolute support.

FIELD-MARSHAL SMUTS

A SPEECH TO THE HOUSE OF COMMONS
13 SEPTEMBER 1950

---

11 *September—Death of Field-Marshal Smuts.*

[*13 September* 1950

I earnestly join with the Prime Minister in the tribute he has paid to the life and work of Jan Smuts; and also in the sympathy he has expressed with that gracious and remarkable woman who has sustained his long march through life, and with his son who carries on an honoured name. Personally I mourn the loss of a cherished friend with whom I had worked intimately in many kinds of anxious and stirring events. It is just over fifty years since I first met him in somewhat unpropitious circumstances. I was a cold and tired-out prisoner of war and he was questioning me as to my status as a war correspondent and the part I had been said to have played in the fighting. I always followed with great interest after that the accounts of his long and dauntless fight as a guerilla leader for the independence of the Transvaal Republic, of which he had already been State Attorney.

My memories of him are, however, most enriched by the two main periods of our work together. The first was the framing and bringing into force of the Transvaal Constitution. It is only a few months since I referred to this on the occasion of his eightieth birthday. The Transvaal Constitution was an act of generous statecraft which will always be associated in Great Britain with the name of Campbell-Bannerman, and in South Africa with the names of Botha and Smuts. It led directly to the Union of South Africa, and to the comradeship and brotherhood in arms between South Africa and the old country and between Boer and Briton which stood the hardest strains which lay before us and which was crowned in the end with so much honour.

No act of reconciliation after a bitter struggle has ever produced so rich a harvest in goodwill or effects that lasted so long upon affairs. Magnanimity in victory is rare, and this is an instance and almost unique example of its reward, because rare though it be it is by no means always rewarded. This was because we in Britain found great South Africans to deal with. In Louis Botha and Jan Smuts we found those qualities of unswerving fidelity to honourable engagements, the power to see each other's point of view and, above all—and this was the point I made on his eightieth birthday—that resolve not to be outdone in generosity which ranks among the noblest and most helpful impulses in the human breast.

But it was, of course, during the last five years of the recent war that we came most closely together. Here I speak not only for myself but for my colleagues in the then War Cabinet, whom I think I shall carry with me when I say that in all our largest decisions and our best thoughts we found ourselves fortified by the spontaneous accord of the South African Prime Minister. In his farm near Pretoria or at Groote Schuur, no doubt receiving all the telegrams but without any of the whole process of consultation which we went through among ourselves and with the Chiefs of Staff, thousands of miles away, dealing with these matters practically alone, again and again he sent us conclusions and advice at which we had arrived here simultaneously by a much more elaborate and entirely separate process of thought. It was a comfort to all of us, and above all to me, to feel by this quite independent cross-check that we might have confidence in what we were going to do and that we were on the right course. I must say that I can hardly recall any occasion where we did not reach the same conclusions by these entirely different roads of mental travail.

Jan Smuts was a shining example of the Latin saying: *Mens sana in corpore sano*. His mental and physical efficiency seemed to undergo no change with the passage of years. Up to his eightieth birthday he could not only concentrate his mind for many hours a day, but could march with a brisk and alert step to the top of Table Mountain, and if he chose back again down the descent. Perhaps he did it once too often. This prolonged harmony of mind and body was the foundation of a luminous, normal, healthy, practical common sense, which guided him in daily action but in no way limited the depth of his vision or his far-ranging outlook over the world scene.

I agree with the Prime Minister in enumerating all the various fields in which he shone. Warrior, statesman, philosopher, philanthropist, Jan Smuts commands in his majestic career the admiration of us all. There is no personal tragedy in the close of so long, full and complete a life. But those of his friends who are left behind to face the unending problems and perils of human existence feel an overpowering sense of impoverishment and of irreparable loss. This is in itself also the measure of the gratitude with which we and lovers of freedom and civilization in every land salute his memory.

IRON AND STEEL

A SPEECH TO THE HOUSE OF COMMONS
19 SEPTEMBER 1950

---

14 *September—Mr Strauss, Minister of Supply, announces in the House of Commons the Government's intention to continue its plans for the nationalization of iron and steel and gives details of the membership of the board.*

15 *September—Speaking of the unofficial bus strike, Mr Isaacs, the Minister of Labour, states that the Government are keeping a close watch for subversive activities in industry and that all necessary action will be taken to combat them.*

18 *September—In reply to an Opposition motion to suspend exports of machine tools and strategic raw materials to Russia, the President of the Board of Trade announces the Government's decision to review all outstanding orders for Eastern European countries.*

19 *September—The Minister of Defence announces that the Government have agreed to establish a Courts-martial Appeal Court for all three Services.*

[*19 September* 1950

I beg to move:

That this House regrets the decision of His Majesty's Government to bring the Steel Nationalization Act into immediate operation during this period of tension and danger thus needlessly dividing the nation on party political issues and disturbing the smooth and efficient working of an industry vital to our defence programme.

Last week, the Conservative and Liberal Parties gave their support in all the measures which were deemed necessary for national defence. In spite of the very serious criticisms that could be made of the mismanagement of our defence problems and the inadequacy of the remedies, the Government Motion was passed without Division or Amendment. Furthermore, the Bill prolonging the period of compulsory service from eighteen to twenty-four months, imposing a very heavy sacrifice on British homes and families, was carried through the House of Commons in a single day, and has now received the Royal Assent.

This was done because everyone realized the grave and growing

374

danger in which we stand, and we have all agreed that an immediate strengthening of our Forces, in conjunction with those of our Allies, gives the best hope of averting a third world war and of escaping ruin should it break upon us. The speed and unanimity with which these far-reaching decisions were taken by Parliament sent a message forth to the world of British national unity, rising above internal quarrels, and in spite of the virtual equipoise in this House between parties, grievously divided as they are. Only the magnitude and imminence of possible mortal dangers could have enabled us to present this encouraging example to the friends of peace and law all over the world.

While, however, this beneficial process was going forward in Parliament, the Government were secretly preparing a new and deadly blow at national unity and co-operation by an act of party aggression which was bound to plunge us, and evidently has plunged us and all our affairs into violent controversy. The action of the Prime Minister in taking such a step at such a time and in such circumstances will, I believe, be sternly judged by the nation and by history. [*Laughter.*] Laughter will not carry it off. Objection is always taken on the other side of the House to the argument that, judged by the votes cast at the recent election, here is a Government resting on a minority of 1,800,000 votes, and that this applies particularly to the nationalization of iron and steel, which was a definite, direct and leading issue at the polls. The Prime Minister argues, if I understand him aright, that seats alone must count, and that the adverse votes of the people, however numerous, are irrelevant and should not influence Government policy. This theme does not do justice to the spirit of democratic institutions, nor is it at all in accordance with the way in which things have long been done in British public life.

The theory that a mandate has been granted by the election for any change, however sweeping, which has been mentioned only as an afterthought in the party manifesto, goes far beyond the bounds of reason. To claim that a majority of two, three, four, five or whatever it is, gives the Government a title to impose on the other half of the nation, and in this case the larger half, any law they may choose to propose is carrying meticulous logic to dangerous extremes. It is liable to make the fortunes and fate of any country that is so circumstanced dependent entirely upon accident and hazard. Very few democratic and parliamentary constitutions in the world are so devoid of safeguards as our own. Half of the nation ought not, in such circumstances, to claim the right on so slender a margin to knock the other half about and ride roughshod over it.

His Majesty's Government, in making far-reaching changes, should strive to act in harmony with a substantial preponderance of the mass of the people, and to interpret their general wish. Parliament can, of course, only decide by voting, but Ministers of the Crown who force the House to take decisions which rend the nation upon the vote of an individual Member or a handful of Members one way or the other, are abusing their trusteeship. I am quite sure that the underlying common sense of British democracy will endorse these general propositions. If all this be true in tranquil times, how much more is it true in these days of common peril and common action in so many spheres?

The British steel industry is a prime feature in our exports and the foundation for a thousand secondary trades and productive processes. It has served us well in the dollar struggle, which was certainly serious enough, but now in addition we are urged by the Government to support and aid in a rearmament effort, which is almost unanimously regarded in this House to be urgent and vital. This armament effort cannot possibly proceed except with the smooth, efficient working of the steel industry at its highest. To disturb and damage the steel industry at this juncture is to disturb and damage the whole effort which occupied our attention last week. The record of the steel industry in recent years has been magnificent. The output of the industry has expanded from its low point of 5,000,000 tons a year in 1931, when hon Gentlemen opposite were largely in office—I mean their party was largely in office. As I say, it has expanded from 5,000,000 tons a year in 1931 to 16,000,000 tons at the present time. [An HON MEMBER: 'Under a Labour Government.'] Yes, certainly, and why spoil it now? Each year when the present Government have set a production target, now vital to our rearmament, the steel industry has surpassed the target. Steel prices have risen by considerably less than the general rise in industrial prices, and are below the general level both in Europe and the United States. The Government are, in fact, picking out for fundamental disturbance the one great basic industry which, of all others, deserves the prize for its efficiency and its smooth working expansion.

Nothing is more remarkable in the history of the British steel industry than the good relations that have prevailed between the employers, management and the employees. I have known in my time a succession of leaders in the iron and steel trade union. I served in the Government in the First World War with Mr John Hodge, who became an important Minister. Then there was Arthur Pugh, who fought a splendid fight on my behalf for a 12½ per cent increase which, as Minister of Munitions in 1917, I wished to give to what I may call the non-commissioned officers of war-time production, the men who teach the dilutees and have taught them. I am sure that on both sides of the House there is a general respect for Mr Pugh. I did not know Mr John Brown, and I have only once, some time ago, met Mr Lincoln Evans, the present General Secretary of the Iron and Steel Trades Confederation. These remarkable men have played their part over the last half century in the Labour movement, and in the relations of ownership and labour in the key and basic industry of iron and steel. It is a fact that, apart from the General Strike of 1926, there has never been for more than fifty years a dispute in the steel industry which was not settled by the well-known machinery without a major stoppage of work. Why this industry of all others should be selected for the malevolence of Socialist politicians is impossible to understand.

There was the argument that industries which were failures and could not give good service to the public should be nationalized, but here, especially since the war, there has been the finest service. There was the argument that better service would be given by the employees if they were under the direct control of the State. But there is really not much margin now for further effort on the part of the steel workers. They have outstripped all demands made upon them. There is the argument that monopolies should not be in private hands and that so great an organization as the steel trade should not be free from public control. But this is all met, and more than met, by the excellent arrangements which have been in force under the Iron and Steel Board, and which have proved and vindicated themselves by results.

This new stroke of party faction by a Government already confronted with a vast superiority of potentially hostile forces in Europe, and also by the challenge of the Communist fifth column here at home—this new stroke, I say, took all of us and our friends by surprise. There was no need for the Prime Minister to take this hazardous course at the present moment. [*Interruption.*] I am sorry that the facts that I am unfolding give so much pain and cause so much confusion, but it only shows the guilty consciences and lack of conviction which prevail on the benches opposite. The Iron and Steel Act gives twelve months' latitude for fixing the vesting date. The reason given by the Minister of Supply on 28 April last year, nearly eighteen months ago, for taking this flexibility was plainly stated by him:

'There may be industrial or political developments which would make it harmful for the iron and steel industry to be transferred on that date.'

The date he was then speaking of was May 1950. But all his reasons for safeguarding flexibility are stronger than ever today, and the provision which he made in the Act leaves the whole of 1951 open.

377

Now, however, the Government have decided to appoint a Corporation on 2 October in order to facilitate vesting at the earliest possible date at the beginning of 1951. Surely there have been both 'industrial and political developments which would make it harmful for the iron and steel industry to be transferred' now, and which would fully have justified using this provision of the Act to see whether, in the face of common danger and on the basis of common action in defence, this Parliament might not have had a better chance of life and honour.

Let us look at the industrial developments to which the Minister referred. There has been one which is of the first importance. A new proposal has been put forward by the economic committee of the Trades Union Congress, in their report to their Brighton Congress, as an alternative to more nationalization. The report, which was approved by the Congress without any dissenting vote, states in paragraph 14 that 'if further extensions of nationalization are to be justified and acceptable to the community the existing schemes must be shown to be successful'. Some judgment is then attempted in the report upon the existing schemes, which are specifically referred to as 'coal, transport, electricity, gas and aviation'.

The report leads to the conclusion that it is only when these existing schemes can be shown to be generally successful that further schemes should be undertaken. The Trades Union Congress report says that no clear judgment can yet be reached on this. There is a significant paragraph in the report which reads:

'It may further be that in important cases a more practicable means of public control, alternative to both public ownership and development councils, would be the Statutory Board of Control on the lines of the tripartite body described in paragraphs 38 and 39.'

That is to say, on the lines of the Iron and Steel Board. In order that there may be no mistake I will read the bulk of paragraphs 38 and 39, the relevant parts of which are as follows. First, paragraph 38:

'Development councils are not an appropriate form of organization for all private industries, and particularly for those which are already high integrated. Consequently, an alternative method of public control over private industry which deserves further consideration is the statutory Board of Control. This method has already been used by the Government, for a short period, in the iron and steel industry with the intention of securing a measure of control pending the transfer of the industry to public ownership.'

[*Laughter.*] I am not quoting unfairly. Here is paragraph 39:

'The Iron and Steel Board was composed of representatives of employers and workpeople with independent members, one of whom was chairman. Its functions were to review and supervise the industry's development schemes; to supervise the industry generally and to administer such direct controls over production, distribution and imports as were needed; and to advise on price policy. What the Board lacked, however, was power to compel private firms to undertake schemes when and where they were considered necessary in the public interest, and it had no authority to undertake such schemes on its own initiative. If this form of control were to be used in appropriate cases it might be possible to extend the functions of such Boards to include the power to set up their own undertakings, either to promote development which would otherwise not take place or to act as a yardstick of efficiency for the rest of the industry.'

This report was presented to the Congress by Mr Lincoln Evans, the general secretary of the Iron and Steel Trades Confederation, in a speech which contained a significant sentence. I did wish to quote a great part of the speech because I admired its thought and structure so much, but this particular sentence is a relevant one:

'If the community can exercise sufficient control over industry without accepting the risks and liabilities of ownership, that is a matter which should have the serious concern of everybody.'

We on this side of the House are opposed to a general application of the principle of competitive public ownership which might, if clumsily or malevolently applied, lead to the ruin of slowly built-up private businesses, or which, if unsuccessful, would only cause a further burden on the taxpayer. I stated the objections to this method in the strongest terms in the election, and I do not in any way recede from them.

I am informed that the Iron and Steel Federation do not by any means close the door upon such an extension of the powers of the late Iron and Steel Board, within the limits of their own industry, and that they would welcome a discussion of the subject. If that were so, and an agreement were reached, the steel question would be settled, at any rate for the present years of crisis—matters could always be renewed and revived—in a manner agreeable to both sides in the industry. It would be a serious matter for Parliament to reject such a solution in a strictly limited sphere on the single ground of objecting in principle to competitive public ownership. Certainly both the grave and thoughtful report, which represents responsible conclusions of the Trades Union Congress, and the speech in which it was presented, are in refreshing contrast to the partisanship of His Majesty's Government. The Trades Union Congress report seems to seek practical solutions by agreement and goodwill. The Government are athirst with campaigning zeal and long for party triumph.

These pronouncements by the responsible trade union leaders, taken in conjunction with the dangers that surround us and draw near, might well have been made the subject of careful consideration not only by the Government but by the House. The flexibility of the Act gives the necessary time, and the general situation the natural impulse. I am told that the Iron and Steel Federation are agreed, not only in principle but in a great measure of detail, with the recommendations of the trade union report. Why, then, should the Government not take advantage of this wide area of agreement in the interval provided by the Act, in order to see if a better solution might not be offered to us than can be made by party warfare?

The decision of the Government to precipitate this internal crisis by immediately bringing the Iron and Steel Act into operation, setting up their Corporation, and fixing the vesting date at the earliest moment, has prevented a settlement which might well have led us into a very different atmosphere than is now, I fear, to be our fate. It might have given this House of Commons not only a longer life but an opportunity of rendering memorable service to the nation as a whole; but all that has been brushed aside by the Prime Minister, acting for the party doctrinaires on the political side of the Socialist movement. Instead of our being led into fairer fields, the Prime Minister has chosen to aggravate and inflame political and party strife, not by words only—we all use words in party politics—but by deeds. Actions speak louder than words and they cut deeper.

The initiative throughout has rested with the Government. The power of action is in their hands only. The choice was theirs, and the the responsibility for what is going to happen falls on them and on them alone. The Opposition have neither the power to act nor the choice of methods which are open to the Government. It is our duty on grounds far wider than party to protest to the utmost of our strength against this sudden and untimely decision, arrived at in the midst of our perils and common action. Why then should the Prime Minister, in the same week in which he had asked for and received the support of the whole House on the hard measures which he thought it his duty to propose for national safety, strike a blow at this vast and complicated sphere of our productive activities at the very moment when their smooth-working efficiency is more imperative than it ever was before? He is not only fomenting national discord for party purposes but, by disturbing the whole steel organization, he is placing an obstacle, which may be very serious, in the swift re-equipment of our

Defence Services. This will, I am sure, be condemned all over the country and all over the free and friendly world as both reckless and unworthy.

The right hon Gentleman the other day accused me of being party-minded. Everyone would naturally be shocked if a party leader were party-minded! But we are all party-minded in the baffling and unhappy period between election decisions and between parties so sharply divided and evenly balanced. However, the nation may be assured that, whatever the conduct of the present Government and dominant party may be, the Conservative and, I believe,. the Liberal Oppositions will not withdraw in any way the aid they have offered and given to all measures for the national defence. We shall do our utmost to encourage recruiting, and we shall be prepared to accept additional burdens wherever they are shown to be unavoidable. I trust that all Conservatives and Liberals throughout the country will not be deterred by this vicious by-blow from doing their utmost to stimulate production in all its spheres. After all, there are millions of Conservative and Liberal trade unionists throughout the land, and I say to them from here—and my voice carries some distance—that they must not let themselves be discouraged in their national efforts by the political and party manoeuvres of a fanatical intelligentsia—the Home Secretary is laughing; I did not mean to include him in the intelligentsia.

THE SECRETARY OF STATE FOR THE HOME DEPARTMENT [MR EDE]: I was quite sure the right hon Gentleman did not. That was why I laughed.

MR CHURCHILL: The right hon Gentleman could surely find other things in life to laugh at besides those which do not include himself. Otherwise life might be rather gloomy for him. I was saying—a fanatical intelligentsia obsessed by economic fallacies. Let us look for a moment at the new Corporation which has been set up to be the agent and instrument of the Government in nationalizing a curiously hand-picked but none the less dominant portion of the iron and steel industry, with far-reaching reactions throughout a far wider field. At its head is a millionaire Socialist, a recent recruit, who, I am informed, enjoys the reputation of being one of the strictest and sternest monopolists in the country. Hardly any of the Corporation members have the slightest knowledge of the steel industry. One has already resigned.

How can this Corporation compare with the tripartite Iron and Steel Board which commends itself to the Trades Union Congress and is even held up as an alternative model and has proved itself in every respect by its notable success? This change can only mean an immense impoverishment of the brain-power and experience which we never required more than we do now and profound disturbance of the life of the whole industry and of its innumerable ramifications. Leaders of the steel industry, both employers' and workers' representatives, have declined to become members of the new Corporation. Can we blame them for refusing to identify themselves with a policy which they consider—and I think rightly—prejudicial to the work to which they have given their lives and with a policy which they claim was disapproved by the nation at the General Election? They will, I am sure, continue to manage their particular firms, in so far as they are allowed to, in a faithful and loyal effort to limit the harm which is being so wantonly done, but no man can be blamed for refusing to take personal responsibility for an experiment of which he wholly disapproves and which he is sure will be harmful and for which, in his opinion, no decisive mandate has been given by the electors.

No doubt in the conflict so gratuitously forced upon us these men will be covered with abuse and slime by the party opposite. If they are attacked, let me read what the Minister of Supply said in the House of Commons on 16 November 1949. It has been quoted before, but it is very necessary that it should receive the widest publicity at this moment. He said:

'In an atmosphere of political tension and uncertainty it would plainly be unwise to proceed now with the selection of individuals to serve on the Corporation. Men who may well be best suited for this responsible task might understandably be reluctant to commit themselves to accepting such a position, and throw up their present jobs, as long as they think there is a possibility, however remote, that the Corporation may not, after all, be established . . . I think that right hon and hon Members on both sides of the House will agree that the success of the nationalized industry will depend to a considerable extent on the calibre of the men serving on the Corporation, and that it would be folly'—a word we have heard in other quarters—'to rush our selection of these people unnecessarily.'

I have a long past of speeches to look back upon, but it always refreshes me to look back on something which I said a year or two or even ten years ago and find out that it exactly fits the circumstances of the moment. I therefore offer my congratulations to the Minister of Supply who, nearly a year before the event, forecast this picture of the situation with astonishing accuracy and not entirely without happy colouring.

The word 'folly' is mentioned. I take that word and also the mood from *The Times* and the *Manchester Guardian*—those eminent symbols of wise, measured, superior judgment and responsibility. We are bound to proclaim the 'folly' of the proposals for immediate action which are now thrust upon us. We believe that the Iron and Steel Act now to be brought into immediate force will seriously damage the efficiency of production through the centralization of responsibility which the new Corporation will involve. We believe that added risks and burdens will be thrown on to the taxpayer. We believe that the position of consumers who are also manufacturers in relation to prices and other matters will be further weakened by vesting control in a public ownership Corporation in the place of an impartial non-ownership public board.

We believe that the position of labour in the industries affected will be weakened by concentrating control in a Corporation identified with ownership in the place of an impartial public board on which an active and responsible labour interest was jointly represented together with the management. We believe that the trade unions in their report, and the iron and steel industry in particular, have offered a solution which, from every angle, offers superior advantage both to the employees and to the safety and progress of our country.

The Government supporters place some hopes upon being able to darken counsel by spreading the allegation that the Conservative and Liberal Parties were willing, under the Schuman Plan—get ready to cheer now; a long breath—to hand over British iron and steel to the control of a supra-national European cartel which would have the power to close any mine or factory in Britain by a majority vote. I do not think hon Gentlemen—and I gather that from their rather quiescent mood today—will get very far with this falsehood in any prolonged national discussion. [An HON MEMBER: 'Wait and see.'] We thought, and we still think, that the representatives of the Government could perfectly well have gone to Paris and taken part in the discussions, it being clearly understood by all parties that they could break them off at any moment. [Laughter.] I have often gone to discussions which I could break off at any moment. [Laughter.] Do not be too sure that there may not be other discussions which can be broken off at any moment. There may be discussions in this House which the House may decide to break off at a suitable moment. As I have just said, the representatives of the Government could perfectly well have gone to Paris and taken part in the discussions, it being clearly understood that they could be broken off, and that in any case all the results were to be submitted for ratification to the House of Commons and all the other national Parliaments concerned.

It would have been an advantage not only to Europe but to our own steel industry for British representatives to have been present at meetings upon a project which carried with it many hopes for the ending of the Franco-German quarrels which have wrecked Europe in our lifetime and, by removing them, thus to strengthen the foundations of peace. We might have helped ourselves, and we should have run no risk of being committed to anything in the slightest degree— [HON MEMBERS: 'Oh.']—which affected the full control of the House of Commons.

We may, indeed, be encouraged by the adoption of this argument as an electioneering tactic, because it shows how weak is the Government case upon the main issues that lie before us.

MR HARRISON (Nottingham, East): This is one of your weakest efforts.

MR CHURCHILL: The hon Member may set himself up as a judge, but I must ask him to take his place in the general assembly of the House and not to assume that his will be the casting vote upon a decision of such moment.

There is another point I must mention before I close. On Friday last, the Minister of Labour made a serious statement to us about the Communist conspiracy to disturb and cripple our industrial life. He told us of the steps which were being taken, and of the possibility that legislation would be required. We are entirely at one with the Government in grappling with the Communist menace in our midst, and we shall no doubt support any legislation brought before the House, provided that the normal foundations of British liberty are not affected and that the right to strike, upon which British trade unionism is founded, is not in any way impaired when it is used by responsible official trade unionists. We must also preserve our sense of proportion. It seems difficult to believe that the activities of the small number of Communists in our midst could at the present time inflict upon our defensive effort, or upon our national unity, anything like the injury that will be done to us all by this Act of party sabotage.

Now let me say what would be the policy of the Conservative Party—[Laughter.] Why should hon Members opposite laugh? I have never seen that side of the House behave so disreputably. It does not affect me with fifty years' experience. I have seen many awkward situations. Hon Members opposite only reveal the deep, internal, mental and moral malaise which distresses and disturbs their consciences. Now let me say what is the policy of the Conservative Party, and, judging from the public declarations, of the Liberal Party also, on iron and steel. [Laughter.] I like hon Members to laugh. It may be undeserved but it may not be unrequited. What is now, and what will be the policy of the Conservative Party should the burden of public affairs be entrusted to us? We shall, if we should obtain the responsibility and the power in any future which is possible to foresee, repeal the existing Iron and Steel Act, irrespective of whether the vesting date has occurred or not. We shall then proceed to revive the solution which has been set forth in the Trades Union Congress Report and which is accepted by the Iron and Steel Federation, and we shall set up again the tripartite Board, which has been proved to have worked so well. This would be the policy if we had the power, either before or after another General Election.

The Prime Minister seemed vexed the other day because I had described him as 'sullenly resolved to lead only half the nation'. Certainly he has provided us with an illustration of my words this afternoon. It is, however, a compliment to anyone that they should be considered to have a chance of leading the nation. It is that hope which lends the highest honour to public life. Is he not, I ask him, throwing away a golden opportunity of serving the whole nation at a crisis in its fate? Take the famous words of Mr Gladstone:

'Think well, think wisely, think not for the moment but for the days which are to come.'

Let me, however, state the position in clear and unmistakable terms. If the Government were even now, even at this moment, to allow an effort to be made to settle the steel question on the lines suggested by the Trades Union Congress Report, which are accepted by the employers, and to agree to use the latitude they have fortunately reserved to postpone the operation of the Act, we might well reach an all-party agreement within the lifetime of the present House of Commons. If the right hon Gentleman says now that he will postpone the operation of the Act within its approved compass with a view to pursuing with common sense and goodwill a settlement on lines that apparently have the approval of the trade unions and the Steel Federation, I will, of course, at once withdraw this Motion. On the other hand, if he remains set upon his wrongful course, we have no choice but to resist him to the utmost of our strength. And let there be no doubt that the responsibility rests upon him for consequences which no one can foretell.

COPENHAGEN UNIVERSITY

A SPEECH ON RECEIVING THE HONORARY DEGREE OF DOCTOR OF PHILOSOPHY
10 OCTOBER 1950

21 *September—Publication of the second annual report of the British Transport Commission for the year 1949 shows a deficit of £20,761,000.*

29-30 *September—Mr Clement Davies, speaking at the Liberal Party Assembly at Scarborough, emphasizes the Liberal Party's intention of remaining 'a sovereign and independent party'.*

26 *September—The North Atlantic Council of NATO announces its intention to create an integrated North Atlantic Defence Force under a centralized command.*

2 *October—Death of King Gustav of Sweden at age of 92.*

2-6 *October—A resolution criticizing the Government's foreign policy is moved at the Labour Party's Conference at Margate. Mr Shinwell (Minister of Defence) and Mr Ernest Bevin (Foreign Secretary) uphold the principles on which the foreign policy is based.*

Figures published of steel production for the first nine months of 1950 show an all-time record production of 12,117,000 tons (530,000 tons more than in the corresponding period of 1949).

4 *October—The eight-nation resolution on Korea for the establishment of a 'unified, independent and democratic Government' for the whole country adopted by the Political Committee of the United Nations.*

9 *October—The Ministry of Supply announces 15 February 1951 as the date on which the transfer to public ownership of the steel industry will take place.*

[10 *October* 1950

YOUR MAJESTIES, Your Royal Highnesses, Your Excellencies, Mr Rector, Professors, Ladies and Gentlemen:

I must express my thanks to the Rector and to the Prorector for what they have said in their far too complimentary speeches—much that no man should hear till dead. I am most grateful for what Professor Hansen has said about England, or Britain. I was only the servant of my country and had I, at any moment, failed to express her unflinching resolve to fight and conquer, I should at once have been rightly cast aside.

Here I may mention a debt which Britain owes to the ancient

Danes. We did not regard it as such at the time. The Danish sailors from the 'long ships' who fought ashore as soldiers brought with them into England a new principle represented by a class, the peasant-yeoman-proprietor. The sailors became soldiers. The soldiers became farmers. The whole of the East of England thus received a class of cultivators who, except for the purposes of common defence, owed allegiance to none. Particularly in East Anglia did this sturdy, upstanding stock take root. As time passed they forgot the sea; they forgot the army; and thought only of the land—their own land, as it became. They merged with the English.

The Danish settlement differed entirely from the Saxon settlement 400 years earlier. There was no idea of exterminating the older population. The gulf between the Danes and Saxons in no way resembled that which divided the Saxons from the Britons. Human and natural relations were established. The bloodstream of these vigorous individualists, proud and successful men of the sword, mingled henceforward in our island race. A vivifying, potent, lasting and resurgent quality was added to the breed. As modern steel is hardened by the alloy of special metals in comparatively small quantities, this strong strain of individualism, based upon land ownership, was afterwards to play a persistent part, not only in the blood but in the politics of England. The centuries did not destroy their original firmness of character nor their deep attachment to the soil. All through English history this strain continued to play its part, and to this day the peculiar esteem in which law and freedom are held by the English-speaking peoples in every quarter of the globe may be shrewdly and justly referred to a Viking source.

I am very proud and very grateful to receive a Degree of Philosophy from the famous University of Copenhagen. As life unfolds I have been astonished to find how many more degrees I have received than I have passed examinations. I was never very good at those. But now I am treated as if I were quite a learned man. This is a good argument for not being discouraged by the failures or shortcomings of youth but to persevere and go on trying to learn all your life.

I never had the advantage of a university education. But it is a great privilege and the more widely extended, the better for any country. It should not be looked upon as something to end with youth but as a key to open many doors of thought and knowledge. A university education ought to be a guide to the reading of a lifetime. We should impress upon those who have its advantages the importance of reading the great books of the world and the literature of one's own country. One who has profited from university education has a wide choice. He need never be idle or bored. He is free from that vice of the modern age which requires something new not only every day but every two or three hours of the day. There is a good saying, which you may have heard before, that when a new book comes out you should read an old one, though I perhaps should not recommend too rigid an application!

The University of Copenhagen is justly renowned for its advance in the scientific sphere. I feel sure also that the humanities play their living and vital part in your curriculum. The first duty of a university is to teach wisdom, not a trade; character, not technicalities. We want a lot of engineers in the modern world, but we do not want a world of engineers. We want some scientists, but we must make sure that science is our servant and not our master. It may well be that the human race has already found out more than its imperfect and incomplete stature will enable it to bear. My old venerable friend, Lord Hugh Cecil as he was (Lord Quickswood), described science recently as 'organized curiosity'.

Take all these improvements in locomotion; what do they do but make the world grow smaller, making the heritage of man a far more restricted sphere. It is very convenient, of course, to flash about but, after all, the life of man does not depend upon the external conditions to which he is subjected, provided, of course, that they are compatible with the maintenance of his existence. No amount of technical knowledge can replace the comprehension of the humanities or the study of history and philosophy. The advantages of the nineteenth century, the literary age, have been largely put aside by this terrible twentieth century with all its confusion and exhaustion of mankind.

This is a time when a firm grip on all the essential verities and values of humanity and civilization should be the central care of the universities of Europe. The Greek and Latin philosophers seemed quite unconscious that their society was based on slavery. They propounded all the finest theories of freedom, but they were not conscious of the false foundations on which they all lived.

At least nowadays we cherish freedom, freedom for all. The light of Christian ethics remains the most precious guide. Their revival and application is a practical need, whether spiritual or secular in nature; whether to those who find comfort and solace in revealed religion or those who have to face the mystery of human destiny alone. And on this foundation only will come the grace of life and that reconciliation of the right of the individual with the needs of society from which the happiness, the safety and the glory of mankind may spring.

CONSERVATIVE ANNUAL CONFERENCE

A SPEECH TO A MASS MEETING AT BLACKPOOL
14 OCTOBER 1950

12-14 October—Conservative Party Conference at Blackpool at which a resolution is passed pledging the Conservative Party to a building target of 300,000 houses a year, against the Government's figure of 200,000.

[14 *October* 1950

I thank you all for your kindness which constitutes the bright flash in the serious times in which we live. We may all rejoice at the favourable turn the war has taken in Korea. The United States under Mr Truman's leadership, and with the formal and moral sanction and support of the United Nations Organization, acted with courage and promptness in resisting aggression by Communists inspired by Moscow. We are glad that British forces have been represented with those of other Commonwealth countries, and several other members of the world instrument, to preserve peace. We admire the skilful conduct of the campaign by that great soldier, General MacArthur, and we all hope that it may be brought to a speedy conclusion so that the people of Korea may be liberated and, if I may quote Mr Stalin's message on the subject, free to shape the future life of their country in accordance with democratic institutions.

We must also hope that the forces of the free peoples of the world will not become too deeply involved in the Far East, because the dangers there are upon a very small scale compared to those which, as the Government have told us, tower up against us on the Continent of Europe. The Soviet onslaught upon South Korea has made many people realize the perils which menace us, and all that is left of European civilization. The success which has been gained by firm action in Korea must not lull us into a sense of false security. None the less I believe that what has happened in Korea has set world peace for the time being on stronger foundations, and that there may be time—though no one can guarantee it—to build up a European Army, with strong aid from Britain, the United States and Canada, for the defence of the famous and ancient States and races who have no thought or aim but to dwell in peace, and who at present are protected from Soviet Communist ambitions only by the vast American superiority in the atomic bomb. I do not believe that war is inevitable. On the contrary, I believe that the hopes of reaching a peaceful settlement with Russia have been improved by what has happened in Korea. I need scarcely say, speaking in the name of the Conservative Party, that we shall continue to give our help to the Government in any wise measures, either of defence or diplomacy, which they may ask or take to establish that peace and freedom arising from moral and material strength, which is our heart's desire.

It is a year to a day since it was my duty to address the Conference of the National Union. At that time we lay under the burden of uncertainty in our political life. A Socialist Government held the levers of power. At any moment selected by them they could advise a dissolution of Parliament, and all that that brings with it in more than 600 constituencies. We had no means of knowing what their intentions were, and everyone felt that the marshalling-up of the two sides of the nation, if prolonged for an indefinite period, would be harmful to our common interests at home and abroad.

Well, a year has passed and I could describe the situation in more accurate terms than those I have used. There can be no doubt that it is bad for our country, I dare say for any country, to dwell for a long time in an electioneering atmosphere. His Majesty's Government should be thinking all the time for all the people, and for the long-term welfare and safety of our country over whose fortunes they have the honour, and it is a great honour, to preside. Any party Government has, every four or five years, to think about winning an election by gaining a party majority. Even His Majesty's Opposition cannot shut its eyes to that aspect. This is one of the ways, part of the process by which we make sure that the people own the Government and not the Government the people. But it is not good for our society, or for our survival as a leading power, that we should continue for long periods to be dominated by party politics, and that the two halves of the nation, who have to sink or swim together, whatever they may say or do, should have to face each other all the time like pugilists in the boxing ring.

Therefore I thought when we last met that the undue prolongation of a period of partisan conflict would hurt us all and weaken our influence in the world. But now when everyone can see that everything has become far more grave, we find ourselves in the same condition of party strife, impending elections and uncertainty as to when polling day will be fixed, as we did a year ago. Nothing could put a greater strain upon our island or hamper it more in making its gift of long-experienced guidance to the counsels and actions of the civilized world. We are a nation vehemently divided on domestic issues, but profoundly united as an island race, who have so long given guidance to the world on the progress of democracy, and who, in the greatest crisis of human affairs, kept the flag flying of British freedom, and not of British freedom only. How can Britain do herself justice or play her rightful part whilst this suspense continues? Yet it is Mr Attlee's policy to aggravate the uncertainty and prolong the strain. That is a responsibility which is a grave one for him and one which he bears in a personal sense.

Great harm was done to national interests at the General Election by the policy of the Liberal Party in running hopeless or vote-splitting candidatures in hundreds of constituencies. Nevertheless when the new Parliament met I thought it right to look forward and not to look back, and to do my best to help come together in the House of Commons and the country all those forces which are united in opposition to Socialism, and to the nationalization of the means of production, distribution and exchange. This process of union, of merging, has been making progress in many ways and in many constituencies.

The Liberals themselves have, of course, declared at their Party Conference that they are very strongly opposed to agreements or pacts to limit or in any way reduce the number of candidates at Parliamentary Elections. No offer has been made by us to them. Still it is my hope that in view of the great body of doctrine and principle which the opponents of Socialism hold in common an increasingly friendly mood will result in spite of minor provocations and churlishness, and that we shall, as I put it at Edinburgh in May, so conduct our affairs at the next election as to help each other as much as we can, and harm as little as we must.

It is also the duty of constituency associations to think not only of their own local position but also of the part which they have to play in our national struggle against the aggressive and unscrupulous forces which endanger the future greatness of Britain, and I trust that the constituencies will also consider carefully—especially those who can make the return of a candidate to Parliament almost a certainty—the selection of genuine active trade unionists and others representing the views of our brothers and sisters in the working classes of the nation with whom Tory democracy is for ever profoundly associated. I hope they will consider facilitating the return of such representatives to Parliament when the opportunities occur.

I invite you to compliment our party representatives upon their work in the House. We have already forced the Government to adopt five measures which we urged and they derided at the election. We have made them abolish the whole system of direction of labour in time of peace. We have made them abandon Mr Morrison's slimy plan of making permanent the Supplies and Services Act. This was the foundation of the means of interfering with our normal peacetime lives and will require to be sanctioned by Parliament only from year to year instead of being made permanent as the Socialists would have wished. We have made them abolish petrol rationing, which they said was impossible. They have raised the pay of the Services, as we had advocated for three years past. They have restored the cut of 25,000 houses which they had inflicted upon the housing programme. These are all proofs that our members in the House of Commons are able to make their efforts felt and that what we told the country at the last election, although we have not had the direction of affairs, has in many ways already been fulfilled.

Party Government naturally brings with it a degree of partisanship. But I cannot remember any government which placed partisanship so far above national interests as the one under which we now lie. Votes are their only thought. They do not want unity, they want partisan dominance. 'There will be no coalition in time of peace,' declares Mr Attlee, no one having asked him for one. 'We are the masters now,' blurted out the Attorney-General some years ago. 'The General Election,' said the Prime Minister at Margate, 'will come at the right time,' obviously meaning at the right time for his party. Mr Bevin speaking on foreign affairs said, 'My policy has not lost you any vote.'

What a strange and unworthy test to apply to this vast and anxious sphere in which, above all others, the Government should strive to act for the nation as a whole. Never mind whether the policy is right or wrong; whether or not it has brought war nearer; whether it has delayed and hampered the reconstruction of Europe; whether it has gained us the hatred of both Jews and Arabs in Palestine; the one test that matters is 'has it lost us any votes?' Then there is the nationalization of industry which the Socialists proclaim as the main theme of their party thought. 'We do not think it wise,' said Mr Herbert Morrison at Margate, 'at any rate at this stage, to commit the party to a time-table of socialization.'

But of course socialization remains their policy and their programme. It is their convictions only that are weakened, and the point on which they have weakened is whether it will bring them votes or not. What Mr Morrison in fact says to the electorate is: 'Don't be afraid of voting for Socialism because you do not like nationalization. There will be no more nationalization unless we can deceive enough people to give us a comfortable majority.' It must be dreadful to have a mind that works like that.

Every tendency of Socialist government is towards the centralization of power. It is inherent in their conception of State control. But, as history shows, the division of ruling power has always been for more than 500 years the aim of the British people. The division of power is the keynote of our Parliamentary system and of the constitutions we have spread all over the world. The idea of checks and counter-checks; the resistance to the theory that one man, or group of men, can by sweeping gestures and decisions reduce all the rest of us to subservience; these have always been the war cries of the British nation and the division of power has always been one of the war cries of the British people. And from here the principle was carried to America. The scheme of the American Constitution was framed to prevent *any one man or any one lot*, getting arbitrary control of the whole nation. Of course in America there are forty-eight States in the Union, all of which by their power to lead their own life in their own way within their wide limits, and to argue it out among themselves, are defended and protected against anything in the nature of a one man or one caucus autocracy.

But here in England all goes on the turn of whether the Socialists can get a caucus-ridden majority of four or five members to vote for any change, however sweeping, for any act of expropriation or of confiscation, however gross. The Socialists are moving steadily towards the concentration of power in the hands of their caucus. They are hostile to the distribution of responsibility to local authorities. Transport House is the centre of their policy, and Whitehall the summit of their administration. The Socialists claim to be the great champions and the bulwark against the Communists. But this is all rubbish. They have in Europe been found always the weakest of all the bulwarks against Communism. They lead people up the garden path or down the garden path to the brink of the precipice, then turn around and say as they tumble over: 'We are very sorry; we never meant to go so far.'

At this coming election the Communists have decided to support the Socialist Party. All their votes will be given to Mr Attlee's administration, not out of love, I admit, but on the broad grounds that 'we all go the same way home'. I am not going to pay any more compliments to the Socialist Party for resisting Communism now that they have definitely been given Communist support. At the next election the Communists will fight side by side with the Socialists. As a matter of fact they are very good helpers to them. Whenever any labour dispute or trouble occurs all they have to say is 'the Communists did it'. Communism is a great menace to the world. It is a great menace in France and in other countries of Europe, but it is not a major menace in this island. The danger here is more complicated, the danger here is Socialism clearing the way for a Communist advance, while pretending that the cause of all their mistakes and difficulties is Communist intrigues.

We Conservatives want the future planning to take place primarily in the individual home and family. If they do not plan for the future, no State organization can. It is only on their motive power that the larger progress can be made. There are the long-established laws and customs of our island. The State organization must go ahead and foresee developments in science and industry. Why do we elect these eminent men to power unless they are able to show us the way? But after all, it is the people who have to move forward from generation to generation, and it is their impulse and self-restraint which constitutes the life of our country. If the impulse of the people fails, no kind of planning of the road ahead will be any substitute. Socialism operating through bureaucracy destroys the individual impulse of millions of homes. The orthodox conclusion which many members of the Socialist Party draw from whatever happens is that they have only to vote Socialist and the State will look after the rest. But how little this has to do with the facts of the situation, when we have to struggle to earn our living at home and in the world, and when we have to defend our life against the challenge of armed and aggressive Communism as it presents itself in Soviet Russia. Believe me, the mainspring of British life and power is the home and the family. But in these you have had a free chance. Let the people use their good common sense, multiply the choices which are open to them at every difficult phase in their lives. Make freedom spring from its source in their hearts and then indeed you will have a country which with wise government may be made to play a great part in the world; but stifle the spring, hamper and restrict and fetter the necessary operations of thought and consultations that go on inside the home and all your fine Utopias will come crashing to the ground and this island itself will be faced only with the grimmest and most primitive issues of how to get enough to keep body and soul together. This is the hard plight to which our country is still condemned.

What then is the true duty of a faithful, patriotic, progressive-minded British citizen at this juncture? Although the Socialist Government have only a majority of, say, half-a-dozen in the House of Commons and are in a minority of nearly 2,000,000 votes in the country, they have all the power, initiative and prime responsibility. Now in everything that they do for national purposes and in the national in-interest, as we conceive it, we feel bound to support them. When the other day they thought it right to demand two years' compulsory military service, we gave them our full support in spite of the astonishing weakness of our defences after all the unprecedented sums of money and control over manpower which they have used and wasted.

Of course, as an Opposition it is our duty to criticize maladministration, the frittering away of British life energies, and other glaring examples which are presented, of the lack of any central grip or control. You will remember how six weeks ago I pointed out on the broadcast the unwisdom of selling and sending vital machine tools to the Soviet Communist Government of Russia and its satellites at the same time that we were actually, under the mandate of the United Nations Organization, sending our soldiers and sailors to fight in Korea. I was much abused for that but that has now, after the usual prevarication, been put right. But it is only an instance of the extraordinary lack of integration of Government policy in fairly simple matters.

Again there was the establishment of the American bomber base in East Anglia. This was indeed a formidable step. I wonder what they would have said about it if we had done that? Fancy coupling it with the sale to Egypt and to the Argentine of the jet-fighter aeroplanes which were vital to its defence and to our home defence. When we think of all the power the Government have wielded and all the money they have spent on our defences, it is impossible to understand why they could not even find in three months a brigade group to go as a token symbolic force—more than that it would not have been wise to send—in the valiant American effort to protect Southern Korea against the Russian aggression.

But in spite of all these and many other lamentable failures, now when fresh demands are made upon the country, and when fresh sacrifices are called for from its people, we, the Conservative Opposition, were ready to vote with the Government upon their new plans for rearmament, tardy and inadequate though they be. The necessary law was passed through the House of Commons in a single day, without a division, and it immediately received the endorsement of the House of Lords and the Royal Assent. One would have thought that a Government with so small a majority and so much latent disagreement, however carefully concealed within its own ranks, receiving from the Opposition this full and generous aid, would have shown themselves able to rise—for this moment at least—above the level of partisan strife. Even in this prolonged unhappy period of election suspense, for which they, not we, are responsible, they might have done that. But what happened?

On the very same day that we and the Liberals were carrying the Government's measures through Parliament, Mr Attlee plunged into an extreme act of partisanship by proclaiming his intention to force the nationalization of iron and steel into immediate action. It is said that he needed it to square his tail. But that is no excuse. That is the way that things are done. Anything that is necessary for the country that we support has to be balanced by some blow or stroke at the Conservative Party in order to placate and keep sweet this disreputable tail. There you will find the secret which animates the legislative and financial policy of His Majesty's Government.

Mr Attlee claims to have a mandate from the nation at two general elections for the nationalization of iron and steel. But this is quite untrue. They never dared to feature it at the election in February. On the contrary, nine-tenths of them left it out of their addresses. But we and the Liberal Party presented it as a definite issue to the electors, and a very large majority consciously and resolutely voted against it. One hundred Socialists who voted for it were cast out of the House. But then Mr Attlee argued that it does not matter how the electors vote, but whether the Government can gain a majority, be it only a handful of invalids, upon a division in the House of Commons. That, they say, is their democratic mandate to enforce upon the nation at this critical time a measure which will of course hamper the efficiency of the steel industry when it is most needed, and far more gravely exacerbate party differences. This bitter mechanical party fighting is an ugly feature in our present political life. I do not agree with the idea that the Government of this country should act only in the name of a single party. It should earnestly desire and strive for the broad assent and agreement of our whole people. But it is a feature of Socialist parties, not only here but elsewhere, to use the smallest Parliamentary majority maintained by the strictest caucus discipline to assert the right of one half, if they have that half, of the nation to ride roughshod over and maltreat the other, and in our case the larger half.

But even the six votes of their majority would not be theirs—on the contrary there would be six the other way—if Mr Herbert Morrison had not thought of destroying the university representation in breach of the agreement reached between all parties at the Speaker's Conference in 1944. What a cameo of gerrymandering and chicane!

It would have been possible to reach a good and friendly agreement about steel—an arrangement good not only for the steel industry as a whole, on which so much depends, but also in the moral sphere helpful to national unity. The Conservatives and Liberals would have been willing to support the Government in the policy recommended by the Trades Union Congress. This would revive the Tripartite control of the iron and steel industry by the really competent and responsible figures of ownership and labour with the necessary representation of the State. Complete agreement could certainly be reached by both sides of the industry at any moment on this. And if this agreement had been combined with the unanimity with which the national defence measures were supported, a far greater effective harmony and unity in our country might have been created. Here was Mr Attlee's great opportunity to rise above the narrow, bitter, partisan feelings which limit his outlook. He missed it and by this he has marked and defined the position which he will hold in British history. And now we have a situation where the steel trade, at the moment it is most needed for rearmament, is to be disturbed and hampered by the ignorance and incompetent rule of Government nominees. 15 February has been fixed as the vesting date. It is my duty to confirm what Mr Butler told you yesterday, that should we obtain a majority at the next election, whether before or after the vesting date, we shall immediately repeal this wrongful and mischievous Act and return to the plan advocated alike by the employers and the trade unions.

Now I come to the rise in the cost of living, or as I prefer to call it 'the money cheat'. When you are paid a sovereign do not forget you have been defrauded of 4s. by the Socialist Government as the result of their financial mismanagement or as the rake-off of their bureaucracy. The Socialist Government are now after their five years of office giving everyone a £1 note when they know perfectly well it is only worth 16s. compared to the end of the war. This disaster represents the consequences of five years of vast and reckless expenditure and extravagance. It is the result of economic policies which have changed like the changing tints of autumn, and of promises as thick as falling leaves. £20,000,000,000 in five years has been spent by the Socialists at a rate of £11,000,000 a day. £4,080,000,000 is being spent this year. How could anyone imagine a jaunt and jubilee of this kind, on the morrow of an exhausting war, could lead anywhere but to a grave misfortune in the community concerned? In spite of all the gifts and loans which the United States and Dominions have poured in here, and of all the capital assets which have been sold over the counter, our money has become false money.

The planners of our daily life, when they are boasting of their foresight, wisdom and generosity, do not tell us how they take away with one hand what they have given with the other, nor do they tell us that they have taken in taxation beforehand far more than they give back in the form of benefits. This depreciation of the £ sterling has imposed a cut of one-fifth on the spending power of the people. It has been felt in the value of wages, and still more severely in every home which relies on a fixed income from pension or from invested savings. I think I shall be expressing the opinion of all of you when I say our thoughts go out to the old age pensioners who at the end of a long life have only the interest on the savings that they have been able to make. Now that the real effects of the Cripps' Devaluation are beginning to be felt the rise in prices is becoming steeper and more marked. Clothes, shoe-leather, bacon, butter, rice, fuel and fares all go up. The Government pretend that the cost of living figure has lately gone down. No one believes that that represents the truth. Mrs Poynter has stood up here and told us that £2 10s. before the war meant a better living in her house and home—and there are many who have not even got a house and home today—than she can get now on a wage of £4 17s. 2d.

We shall of course be asked what will you do to remedy the evil? It is easier to cause evils than to cure them. I am sure that had a Conservative or National administration been in office since the war it could have controlled State spending so as to lighten substantially the burden of taxation now the heaviest in the world, heavier even than in the crisis of the war. Thus there would have been a strong increase in the incentives to effort and thrift. I believe this could have been done without impairing the efficiency of the great social services, to the development of which the Socialists are only belated contributors. Indeed by maintaining the purchasing power of money many cash benefits received under these schemes would have been safeguarded, instead of becoming a sham and a mockery as prices continue to rise. But all this lies in the past, and now we have a new heavy Bill, which the Government will present us, for reviving and restoring our national defences. It is certain that a careful pruning of the whole field of public expenditure, national and local, must be made. We must try to live within our means and not try to do everything at once. Savings which a few years ago would have lightened taxation are now imperative merely to avoid further increases. A few years of peace and of steady capable administration of the finances ought to see an improvement in the buying power of our money, or in other words, a decline in the cost of living. But I must tell you quite frankly that after the rake's progress of the last five years, with its aggressive attacks on industry and the class warfare with which ministers have tried to pay their way at every stage with their own more disreputable supporters, the resulting evils which have fallen upon us cannot be cured by a Parliamentary vote or a stroke of the administrative pen. To call a halt in the rising cost of living is the policy of the Conservative Party.

The salient feature of this conference has been the growing association of Tory democracy with the trade unions. After all it was Lord Beaconsfield and the Tory Party who gave British trade unionism its charter, and collective bargaining coupled with the right to strike. I have urged that every Tory craftsman or wage-earner should of his own free-will be a trade unionist, but I also think he should attend the meetings of the trade union and stand up for his ideas instead of letting only Socialists and Communists get control of what is after all an essentially British institution.

Nationalization of industry is the doom of trade unionism. The trade union leaders in the nationalized industries, for many of whom I have much respect, are increasingly embarrassed by a dual and in some respects divergent loyalty. The trade unions are being attacked from both sides. The Communists intrigue and infiltrate from the bottom, and the Socialist Government nationalizes and takes over the industries from the top. We no longer have the owners and the trade union leaders discussing matters together, with the State as an impartial arbitrator. We have the State in the nationalized industries as the owner and supreme power, and the trade union leaders more in the position of influential officials of the Government or party associates, than as the single-minded servants of the members of the union. That is a very serious state of affairs. So far only a fifth of the industries in this country have been taken over by the Government. As Mr Bevan has pointed out they have—the industries that have been nationalized—suffered from being surrounded by an 80 per cent miasma of free competition and free enterprise. It must be very tiresome to have your own follies and mistakes and failures paraded in front of so effective a background. In the past two years two-thirds of the time lost in industrial disputes has been in the field covered by the public corporations—docks, mines, railways, road transport and the gas industry. Two-thirds of the disputes in the country have been in this nationalized area which comprises one-fifth of its total labour force. Thus disputes are ten times more numerous in the Socialist sector of our life than they are in the wide area of free enterprise. We hear much about unofficial strikes and many of them are most wrongful and irresponsible and some at least are Communist inspired, but if the normal work of responsible trade union leaders is to some extent in abeyance because the industry has been nationalized, and the wage earners do not any longer have champions who are single-minded in their service, unofficial strikes are certain to recur.

If I were a craftsman or manual labourer, and I still hold my trade union certificate as a bricklayer, I would far rather work for a private employer who would go broke if he could not get on with his workmen over any long period of time, and in dealing with whom I should have the help of trusted union leaders, than deal with an all-powerful State, of whom many trade union leaders were becoming agents, and who if they lose money from the strike send in the bill to the taxpayer, and which also had the power to lock me up if I went on strike. Once you deal with nationalized industries the worker loses the protection of his own chosen representatives. He is confronted with the mighty State, of whom those representatives are the agents as in Russia they are already the tools. And if there is a strike from which the State-owned industry loses money, they do not go to the bankruptcy court, as I have just mentioned to you, they only send another bill to the Chancellor of the Exchequer, and everybody has to take their share of paying it.

This is a tremendous change in the structure of our social life. And the trade unionists of the nation have to make up their minds whether they will accept the corporate State, as in Russia, with its totalitarian consequences, or whether they would prefer to deal with individual employers or firms through the medium of trade unions as we have long known them. This is one of those questions which can only be solved by those concerned. Let the Conservative wage-earners join their unions, and attend their meetings. The more the better. Let them realize that they can make far better bargains for themselves, and keep the industries by which they live alive far more surely by dealing with a private employer than with an all-powerful State.

I have no doubt that in the next ten years, it may be the next five, it may be in the next one, the trade unionists of this country will see that in the advance of nationalization lies the death of their great movement, which over several generations has now become a root and necessary element in British industrial and economic life.

I have been impressed and encouraged by what I was told of the gust of passion which swept through our body yesterday about the shameful failure of the Socialist housing policy. Without the struggles imposed by extreme need, without the spur of seeing bomb-shattered sites, the Tory Government before the war was building 350,000 houses a year. We were doing this mainly by private enterprise and with comparatively few subsidies. Moreover, under the slum clearance campaign begun in 1933, 1,500,000 slum dwellers have been re-housed in England and Wales. In the last year before the war slum dwellers were moving into better houses at a rate of 1,000 people a day. If the war had not brought the Conservatives' programme to a stop, England would today be free from slumdom. The Socialist Government have been found utterly incapable of resuming slum clearance. Now the Minister, who has called us all 'vermin', you can remember his name for yourself and the name he called you after five years of power in time of peace, can only build us 200,000 houses at triple the expense and with enormous subsidies. I do not wonder at your anger. We share it with you. I agree with you that housing comes first in the whole field of social progress.

Well was it said of old: 'The foxes have holes; the birds of the air have nests, but the Son of Man hath nowhere to lay His head.' It is strange that this task of housing should have been deemed and found insuperable by those who have the handling of our affairs. For there is no object except self-preservation which could enlist behind it a greater drive of British ingenuity and effort.

You have demanded that the target that we should put in our pro-gramme should be 300,000 a year. I accept it as our first priority in time of peace. I and the Government of which I was head are the authors of all that is real and effective in the Health Act. We took all the decisions and had the plans worked out in great detail, but it seems to me that houses and homes come even before the reform of the health system, etc. Houses and homes come before health, because overcrowding and slum dwellings are fatal to the family life and breed more illnesses than the doctors can cure. It may well be that hard times lie before us, and that the opportunities for making a better Britain, which these foolish Ministers have squandered for party purposes, will not be open to those who take their places when the nation records its final verdict. No one can tell how the rearmament burden may strike our industry and finances, but this I am sure, that homes for people to live in and rear their families in in decent in-dependence come ever in front of wigs, spectacles and false teeth, however desirable all these may be and however urgent it is to press forward with meeting the public requirements in every respect. However our fortunes may go and from whatever angle the pressures of life may come, the Tory Party puts homes for the people in the very forefront of all schemes for our development.

We are ready for an election whenever it may come. Thanks to Lord Woolton's energy and inspiration, we now have a national organization second to none. It has achieved results far above the expectations which any of us had when the National Union last met in conference at Blackpool four years ago. Also I have the aid of colleagues whose ability has been proved in war and peace. In Mr Eden I have a friend and helper upon whom any office of the State, however great, could be devolved with the assurance that he has both given the proof and acquired the experience to do full justice to it.

In February's election we added nearly 3,000,000 to our poll, and 100 members to our Parliamentary representation. Now we need just one more heave. If all of us make the best use of whatever time and strength we may have, we may well fling this Socialist Government out of power and replace it by a broad, progressive and tolerant administration, the slave neither of class nor of dogma but putting national need first and determined to make Britain and the British Empire once again both great and free.

FIFTH ALAMEIN REUNION

A SPEECH AT THE EMPRESS HALL, EARLS COURT, LONDON
20 OCTOBER 1950

---

18 *October—Home Secretary announces that aliens who have entered Britain during and since the war will be 'screened' for security reasons.*
19 *October—Sir Stafford Cripps resigns from the post of Chancellor of the Exchequer.*

[20 *October* 1950

FIELD-MARSHAL MONTGOMERY, Minister of Defence, my Lords, Ladies and Gentlemen:

I always regard it as a great compliment and as a real pleasure to be invited to your Alamein reunions. May they long continue. I feel that comrades and veterans by this kind of meeting, year after year, realize the treasures of memory which they have acquired during rough and hard times in the field, but afterwards there's always something for a few pals to talk together about, and certainly they have managed to get a few pals here tonight.

General Montgomery has now great and important functions to discharge. But when all his toil and labour of life is over, and when he has finished entertaining any persons who nourish evil designs upon our country as they should be entertained, I earnestly hope that his great gifts of organizing public entertainment will be at the service of the English-speaking peoples all over the world. For certainly he puts as much thought and taste and skill and quality into an annual show like this as might easily have gained a great battle.

Ladies and gentlemen, Alamein was indeed a milestone and more than that, a turning-point in the war. You know I write books nowadays. I'm calling my fourth volume *The Hinge of Fate*. Certainly Alamein was where the hinge turned. Till then we'd survived; after that, we conquered. Till then we had nothing but misfortune to record, but also we were alive and kicking. But after Alamein, the long months of strife lay before us, but we never suffered—or hardly ever suffered—any failure in the field. And thus we came to our triumphant end of that terrible war. How hard it is that destiny compels us after all our victories, to face new, strange, gathering dangers. But I agree with the Field-Marshal, that we face them united; we face them united

403

in spite of certain difficulties which I should not attempt to dwell upon here.

Well, it is impossible, as I said to you last year, that we should not remain deeply divided at a time when a General Election is approaching. It is only in countries where tyrants rule and from which freedom is banished, that a sham uniformity is imposed, and that strong, sharp differences are concealed or forbidden expression. If they were not, if there were not to be full and free discussion here, then voting would be a mere pretence as in Soviet Russia or in the other Communist satellite countries.

My own hope—and this is what I said a year ago—is that this period of unavoidable party strife will be as short as possible. A year has passed, and still these evil conditions afflict us. But in all matters affecting national safety and honour we must act together. We have done so. The House of Commons passed in a single day the new National Service Act and thus sent a message to the world that Britain on the greatest issues is still a united nation. She kept the flag of freedom flying in the war and for a long time—or it seemed a long time— she kept it flying alone. She could never have done that had she not been united. We are united now; more than that, we are not alone. All the might of the United States and all the authority of the United Nations is with us, and I agree with the Field-Marshal that here is the true hope of peace.

The danger in Europe is serious. Montgomery—Monty, as we are allowed to call him, at any rate tonight—Monty has a great office and great responsibilities to bear. There must be created a European Army with the aid of the Atlantic Powers which can make a front in Europe, and thus enable the nations on both sides of the Iron Curtain to return to normal relations instead of war being held off only by the terrible, sinister weapon of the atomic bomb in which the United States, thank God, have overwhelming superiority.

How to build this Western Front, this front towards the East, how to build it is now a main preoccupation not of this country alone but of all those who are working with us. For more than forty years I have been the friend of France in peace and in war, in all the ups and downs of fortune, and never lost my faith in the French people and the French spirit. But where is the French Army today? Alas, it has still to be re-created. There are no means of making a defensive front for the West without the aid of the German nation in defending at least the soil they live on from Russian Communist aggression and sub-jugation. I trust that France will not become an obstacle to this idea of common defence. I feel sure that she will rise to the occasion, and

I do not believe that the United States would make the great efforts and sacrifices which are required from her in Europe if narrow and unwise views prevailed.

I say now, these words of serious import to you. We wish the Field-Marshal all good fortune in his work; in its success lies one of our surest hopes in averting the horrors of another war. We must all try our utmost to sustain the authority of the United Nations and thus lay broad and solid foundations for a world where law and freedom reign.

THE NEW COMMONS CHAMBER

A SPEECH TO THE HOUSE OF COMMONS
24 OCTOBER 1950

---

24 *October—M. Pleven, Prime Minister of France, presents to the National
Assembly his Cabinet's proposals for the constructive creation of a
European Army under a European Defence Minister which will solve
the problem of Germany's contribution to European defence.*

*President Truman addresses the United Nations General Assembly
(United Nations Day).*

[24 *October* 1950

On an Address moved by the Prime Minister in reply to a Message
from the King.

We are all indebted to the Prime Minister for his speech. We join
with him in all that he has said. His speech was full of memories
and showed how comprehending he is of the background to our daily
political life. We associate ourselves with the tributes he has paid to
the work of the Select Committee and my right hon Friend the
Member for Horsham [Earl Winterton], to the designers, architects
and engineers, and also to the craftsmen to whom the rebuilding of
the House of Commons was, I am sure, a labour of love. Also we
support him in expressing our thanks to the Governments of the
British Empire and Commonwealth of Nations, whose representatives we welcome and whose gifts we cherish.

I must thank the Prime Minister for his personal references to me.
I am a child of the House of Commons and have been here I believe
longer than anyone. I was much upset when I was violently thrown
out of my collective cradle. I certainly wanted to get back to it as
soon as possible. Now the day has dawned, the hour almost come, and
I am grateful to His Majesty's Government for the persistence and
vigour and efficiency which they have shown in the task of rebuilding
in so short a time and amidst many other competitive preoccupations.

It excites world wonder in the Parliamentary countries that we
should build a Chamber, starting afresh, which can only seat two-
thirds of its Members. It is difficult to explain this to those who do
not know our ways. They cannot easily be made to understand why

we consider that the intensity, passion, intimacy, informality and spontaneity of our Debates constitute the personality of the House of Commons and endow it at once with its focus and its strength.

It is likely, Mr Speaker—I must warn you of this beforehand—that there will be differences of opinion even among ourselves when we meet again in our old Chamber with so many Members who have only known this spacious abode. However, I believe that in ten or twenty years everyone will be thoroughly used to it. Anyhow, even if they do not, I do not see what they are going to do about it. For good or for ill the old gangs of all parties are united. They are a pretty tough lot when they stand together like that. That is not to say that minor changes may not be necessary, and we can quite easily, without raising structural issues, work our way into the most convenient arrangements for our lighting, heating, hearing, overhearing and ventilation technicalities.

I have been astonished to look what lies behind what I may call the presentation of Government policy in this matter. I trust that all their subterranean designs are not of such a highly elaborate and, on the whole, effective character. An hon Member who was wounded by being deprived of the pomp and perquisite of a special seat and special desk for himself in the Chamber might find himself fully consoled by the material comforts and conveniences which he can derive from his life underground.

The Prime Minister said—and said quite truly—that the House of Commons was the workshop of democracy. But it has other claims, too. It is the champion of the people against executive oppression. I am not making a party point; that is quite unfitting on such an occasion. But the House of Commons has ever been the controller and, if need be, the changer of the rulers of the day and of the Ministers appointed by the Crown. It stands forever against oligarchy and one-man power. All these traditions, which have brought us into being over hundreds of years, carrying a large proportion of the commanding thought of the human race with us, all these traditions received new draughts of life as the franchise was extended until it became universal. The House of Commons stands for freedom and law, and this is the message which the Mother of Parliament has proved herself capable of proclaiming to the world at large.

I have the honour to second the Motion.

THE NEW COMMONS CHAMBER

A SPEECH OF WELCOME TO COMMONWEALTH SPEAKERS
26 OCTOBER 1950

---

25 October—*Mr Herbert Morrison, Lord President of the Council, speaking in the House of Commons, proposes that nationalized industries should be subject to reviews by Parliament at periods of seven years.*

26 October—*Official opening of the new Commons Chamber attended by HM the King and Speakers or presiding officers of twenty-eight Legislatures of the British Commonwealth and Empire.*

The French National Assembly approve its Government's proposals for the creation of a European army, but expresses its intention 'not to permit the re-creation of a German army or General Staff'.

[*26 October 1950*

On a Motion moved by the Prime Minister
'*that this House welcomes the Speakers, Presiding Officers and other representatives of the countries of the British Commonwealth and Empire who have come from overseas to join in the ceremonies on the occasion of the opening of the new Chamber; expresses its thanks to their Legislatures and peoples for the generous gifts with which the Chamber is adorned; and assures them that their presence on this day will be a source of inspiration in the years to come*'.

In rising today at a somewhat mature time in my life to make my maiden speech in this House, I feel, Mr Speaker, that I ought not to conceal from you that I have a past. I have many memories of the air space in which we sit, now enclosed afresh in its traditional garments; in fact, I think I was the last person to speak here until today, and I have a lively recollection of the support and stern enthusiasm with which my remarks were then received.

There has, no doubt, been some change in the seating arrangements, for, so far as my recollection serves, I sat on the other side of the House. The Prime Minister and his principal colleagues sat beside me there. It seemed to me a very good and satisfactory way of carrying on our affairs. But then came a loud explosion, or perhaps that explosion was later on. So many things happened at the time that it was a little difficult to keep track of them, and my recollection may well be at fault. Anyhow, here we all are again, and, if everything is not entirely to our liking, we have, at any rate, much to be thankful for. The Prime Minister spoke of the Parliamentary systems shared in common by so many of us represented here, and how they combine the effective Government of the majority with full respect for the views of the minority. That certainly is a high ideal towards which we should all perseveringly strive.

I can also congratulate His Majesty's Government upon many features of the new Chamber which they have erected. When I think of all that lies above us, around us and beneath us, it seems to me that, so far as accommodation is concerned, His Majesty's Ministers have managed to combine in a singularly harmonious manner the greatest need of the greatest number with a reasonable preservation of the privileges of the deserving few.

It gives me great pleasure to support the Motion which the Prime Minister has commended to us in his admirable and eloquent speech. We are proud today to have with us the Speakers and representatives of so many famous States and Governments of the British Empire and Commonwealth of Nations. We rejoice that they are with us to see our phoenix rising again from its ashes, and we wish them all the same good luck should they at any time be exposed to similar vicissitudes.

There is no doubt that the assembly of the Speakers of so many free and fairly elected Parliaments on this historic occasion shows a new link of unity and mutual comprehension which has sprung into being in our world-wide society and family. It is our hope, sir, which perhaps we may be pardoned for expressing upon an occasion for rejoicing such as this, that the tolerant, flexible, yet enduring relationship which binds us all together by ties which none could put on paper but are dear to all, may some day be expanded to cover all the peoples and races of the world in a sensible, friendly and unbreakable association, and so give mankind, for the first time, their chance of enjoying the personal freedom which is their right and the material well-being which science and peace can so easily place at their disposal.

DEBATE ON THE ADDRESS

A SPEECH TO THE HOUSE OF COMMONS
31 OCTOBER 1950

Question proposed:
    '*That an humble Address be presented to His Majesty, as follows*:
Most Gracious Sovereign,
    *We, Your Majesty's most dutiful and loyal subjects, the Commons
of the United Kingdom of Great Britain and Northern Ireland, in
Parliament assembled, beg leave to offer our humble thanks to Your
Majesty for the Gracious Speech which Your Majesty has addressed
to both Houses of Parliament.'*—[*Mr Kenyon.*]
    Motion seconded by Mr James Johnson.

The Prime Minister has informed me that when he takes his place in
the Debate he will make reference to the lamented death of King
Gustav of Sweden. I am very glad to learn that that is his intention,
and I am quite sure that the words in which he will express our sentiments in the matter will be such as to command the universal assent
and agreement of the House.

It is customary to begin these speeches—and this is a period, an age,
in which traditions and customs are rated very high, I am glad to say,
after the electoral changes which have taken place—by paying compliments to the mover and the seconder of the Address. I certainly
find no difficulty whatever in recording what, I think, was the general
opinion, that they made excellent speeches, that they ranged over wide
and varied fields, that they never at any moment fell into sharp political
controversy, that where their point of view was indicated it was
outlined with great restraint, and, generally speaking, that they have
acquitted themselves in a manner which is certainly not likely to be
any detriment to them should events occur in the future where the
seats held on small margins or by minority votes will be in jeopardy.

I thank them both for what they have said and for the strong
support which they both gave to the measure against salmon poaching.
There may be a difference of opinion in the House as to whether there
ought to be salmon—at any rate privately-owned salmon—but we
can probably all agree that, pending any measure for the nationalization of the salmon industry, poaching should be sternly and severely
prohibited.

The hon Member for Rugby [Mr J. Johnson] spoke to us about the

Empire and Commonwealth, and I was very glad indeed to hear him use the word 'Empire'. I am quite prepared to use the word 'Commonwealth', although if we look into the historical foundations of the word 'Commonwealth', we will find a good many things which jar with the conception of a Constitutional Monarchy or a free House of Commons. But words alter their meaning as the years pass by, and there always was that sense attaching to 'Commonwealth', that everything you have is owned in common, which is, at any rate, a point of view deserving to be considered.

Both hon Members referred also to the Festival of Britain. We are going to have our Festival of Britain next year, and it is a matter in which both parties will take part. We shall do our best to help the Government make the Festival a success——

MR SHURMER (Birmingham, Sparkbrook): Let the right hon Gentleman talk to those behind him.

MR CHURCHILL: I may surely address myself to whatever quarter of the House I like. However, we shall do our best to help the Government make the Festival a success, although there is one feature in any true Festival of Britain which would commend itself above all others to me, and that is one in which I can hardly expect the support of the party opposite.

I congratulate the Government upon the way they managed and organized the celebrations for the opening of the new House of Commons. I like to see this reverence and respect for the past and all we owe to those who have gone before, and to see Ministers of State shake themselves clear from the obsessions into which they fall from time to time—that the only good things ever done in Britain occurred after the General Election of 1945. The celebrations which we embarked upon certainly had the effect of making us feel how much we had in common in the past, and how much, I hope, we shall find in common in the future. Personally, I welcome the Socialist Party conversion to Parliamentary government, instead of the direct action which was their mood twenty years ago, when there was a very strong feeling that Parliament was nothing but an impediment to the progress of democracy and that it would not be inside the walls of Parliament that any real advance could be made. Now there is a great reconciliation, and the House of Commons is accepted as a thoroughly democratic institution—there is even an ugly rush for the House of Lords. The Mother of Parliaments has a tough digestion, and very great improvements have, no doubt, been effected upon the character, substance and structure of the party opposite by contact with Parliamentary institutions, although I shall have a little later to indicate what may perhaps be thought to be a reversion to the bad habits of former days.

I am very glad, however, that we have found ourselves all agreed about foreign policy. I find it very difficult myself to avoid from time to time feeling in a kindly mood, especially towards those with whom I worked for so many years, although when we come to discuss public affairs in our present difficult situation I have no difficulty in finding barriers which exist between us. We seem to have followed, though with somewhat halting steps, the course which I outlined at Fulton, Missouri, in March 1946, and at Zurich in September of that same year. We have given the Government whole-hearted support on their measures for national defence, which they have asked us to approve, while, of course, reserving the fullest freedom to criticize the tardiness, inefficiency, insufficiency and failure to give value for the vast sums of money which the House has voted.

Naturally, I am glad that the Prime Minister and others are at length converted to the principle of a European Army or an Atlantic Defence Force—we will not quarrel about the terminology when the principle is the same—of an army of this character, for the defence of Europe, to which Germany will be invited to contribute divisional formations. In September, when we discussed this matter, I see that I said eight or ten German divisions. American opinion, I believe, inclines towards ten, and I gather that the Government are in general agreement with the United States. There is nothing like progressing on what I think are right and sound lines, and I congratulate the Government on not being hampered at all by anything they have said about these matters in the past but on addressing themselves boldly and with a free mind to the problems as they present themselves day by day.

The successful intervention of the United Nations in Korea and General MacArthur's brilliant conduct and measurement of military events are all, of course, things for general rejoicing. I should like to point to what appears to be the masterly character of his handling of the situation in Korea. First of all, there was the question of selling ground for time, very difficult and terrible to settle from day to day. Then there was the question of the size of the minimum perimeter that must be held. Obviously, it was desirable to hold as wide a perimeter as possible in order to detain as many of the enemy without being perpetually broken through because of being thin on the ground. Finally, there was the counter-stroke, the cat claw, the amphibious descent, which revolutionized the entire situation. I hope we shall find that the Americans in getting ashore opposite Seoul, were not so hampered by great quantities of vehicles as was the expeditionary force which the United States organized in conjunction with our forces to get ashore at Anzio in 1943. It looks to me as if the lessons of the last war have been well appreciated and understood, and that this great commander in the military field—I entirely agree that the civil authority has supreme authority over the military man—has rendered services from which we should not now withhold our hearty approbation and applause.

I was surprised not to find in the Gracious Speech any mention of the United States, not merely from the fact that the British Socialist Government have lived for five years very largely on their bounty, and without which, as the Lord President of the Council and the Minister of Health reminded us a little while ago, there would have been 2,000,000 unemployed at that time. Apart from that, it seems to me that tribute should have been paid to the Americans for their action in Korea. It was President Truman's prompt initiative in June which enabled unprovoked aggression to be resisted. I am glad that we had naval forces on the spot, though at the moment I do not know how big they were.

MR JOHN HYND (Sheffield, Attercliffe): The right hon Gentleman might give his own country some credit.

MR CHURCHILL: I have never been at all backward in defending the claims and considerations of this country, but I do not think that those claims are well sustained if they are based on a failure to recognize the overwhelming contribution which another country, the United States, have made. I have not got the actual figures of our contribution at the present time, but when we see what they are I think it will be found that an enormous proportion of the whole burden has been borne by the United States, and that the least we can do would be to accord that country some consideration. We have quite enough real achievements in our record without endeavouring to minimize the legitimate and rightful contributions of great allies towards the common cause which we support. Some recognition of the United States' efforts should have been contained in the Gracious Speech.

The local importance of events in Korea is far outweighed by the effects on the world situation. These events have definitely increased the prospects of averting a third world war. We are all agreed that the only hope for the future of mankind lies in the creation of a strong, effective world instrument, capable, at least, of maintaining peace and resisting aggression. I hope we shall pursue—I was very glad to see that it was being pursued—this idea of a United Nations armed force. I see that I said in the speech at Fulton to which I referred:

'I have, however, a definite and practical proposal to make for action. . . . The United Nations Organization must immediately begin to be equipped with an international armed force. In such a matter we can only go step by step, but we must begin now. I propose that each of the Powers and States should be invited to delegate a certain number of air squadrons to the service of the world organization. These squadrons would be trained and prepared in their own countries, but would move around in rotation from one country to another. They would wear the uniform of their own countries, but with different badges. They would not be required to act against their own nation, but in other respects they would be directed by the world organization. . . . I wished to see this done after the first world war and I devoutly trust that it may be done forthwith.'

I am glad to see there is progress in that direction.

Foreign policy and national defence can, of course, be discussed in the general Debate which is now open, but in view of the great measure of agreement prevailing on principle, they are obviously not suited to be the subjects of Amendments to the Address. We shall, however, ask for a Debate on Defence before we separate for Christmas. We consider that that Debate should preferably take place in Secret Session. I am sure that there are many questions of detail which it would be much better to discuss in Secret Session. On the general topics with which I dealt at the end of the last Session, and with which I could have dealt more in detail in Secret Session, much is now becoming public to the world. The strength of the forces in Europe is now well known, for example. The matters into which we ought to go now are all kinds of questions connected with the equipment of the troops, the details of our air forces, technical matters connected with our anti-submarine defence and so forth. It would be very much better that we talked these matters over among ourselves, and that the House should take responsibility for them on hearing for itself the facts. Therefore, we shall ask that the Debate shall be in secret. We may notice that in this House there are all kinds of things knocking about. I should not wish to take any unfair advantage of the Government in any way, but I must impress upon the Prime Minister that we shall ask that the Debate shall be in secret. There will also have to be a Debate on foreign policy before we separate. Although these matters can be discussed now, a full statement is required from the Foreign Secretary, whose recovery we hope is complete. All those matters must be dealt with.

Besides this, I undertook, with the representatives of other European countries at Strasbourg, to bring the resolutions passed by the Consultative Assembly to the notice of Parliament. We all promised to bring them before our Parliaments. I hope that the Government will find a day for this matter—I am really addressing myself to the Lord President of the Council. I hope that he will be able to find a day before the meeting of the Assembly on 17 November. Of course, if His Majesty's Government decline the honour of deferring to the wishes of this great international body which has grown up under their patronage, as they would say, other facilities are at our disposal. I should have thought that, on the whole, it would be a very reasonable thing that those resolutions should be laid before the House and that some discussion should take place upon them. I think it is all right, and I am very glad. I gather that the Prime Minister is going to assent to this proposal—unless I say something before I sit down which ruffles him up the wrong way.

I have now dealt in broad measure with matters on which there is agreement between us, although here and there I may have struck a note which did not obtain universal accord. I must now come to the Prime Minister's difficulties. His need is to find grounds for domestic quarrel and acts of partisanship and political spite to placate his tail, which may be feeling that there is too much of this goodwill all around, too much general agreement going on about foreign policy and defence, because there may be the danger of a Coalition, or something like that. The right hon Gentleman has been looking about— and I have no doubt that his faithful spaniel, if I may apply that term to the Lord President of the Council, has been looking industriously around—to find causes of quarrel and dispute. 'After all,' they may say, 'we must have some. We cannot be doing everything the Tories wish us to do.' Many years ago I sat in a Government which had presented to it problems in that guise.

It seems to me that the right hon Gentleman has been looking for causes of dispute between us when he proposes this extraordinary measure—[HON MEMBERS: 'On salmon poaching?'] That is not the only problem that unites the Government and the Opposition today. Happily we are hooked together. Whoever says: 'We are not picking a quarrel or trying to make bad feeling between the parties,' must look at the paragraph on the last page of the King's Speech about the Supplies and Services Act. I will not read the paragraph again, because it has been read several times already, but it seems to me that this vague language for giving all kinds of tremendous powers to the Executive to 'regulate production, distribution and consumption and to control prices', goes further than anything I have seen before. This is not planned economy. This is a blank cheque. The Prime Minister is sailing back upon his course, to the position which he adopted some seventeen or eighteen years ago. He is going back on the reform that we thought had been achieved in his character and conduct, and which seems to have slipped off him now. In using this language, he has gone back to the days when he wrote, in 1933—[*Interruption.*] All right, hon Members can quote me up to twenty years ago, but there is a Statute of Limitations—

'The important thing is not to do things with scrupulous regard to the theories of democracy or exact constitutional propriety, but to get on with the job. . . . It may be said that this is rather like the Russian plan of commissars and Communist Party members. I am not afraid of the comparison. We have to take the strong points of the Russian system and apply them to this country.'

The Lord President, too, speaking at Southport in 1934, said:

'I would sooner the State, through a Labour Government, got into its control key industries, service after service, until, within a reasonable time, we are substantially masters of the economic fabric of the community and the means of production and distribution. . . . Then is the time to take the big decision. . . . Then we can make a fair, clean and equitable sweep.'

How easy to make it!

These are the previous convictions of the right hon Gentleman opposite, and it seems very dangerous that the vain language used in this paragraph should be put into the mouth of the King by a party which in its root and origin is absolutely ready to go to the extremes of which the Prime Minister and the Lord President of the Council spoke. [*Interruption.*] Are hon Gentlemen opposite ashamed of what they said then? I welcome it if they are. Are the right hon Gentlemen ashamed of it? I think that they would rather have bitten off their tongues than have used such words. The fact that such statements are in their minds and records should be borne in mind in relation to the vain words of this paragraph about regulating production, distribution and consumption and controlling prices.

I thought we had reached a working arrangement about this last week. I thought we had had the answer that the Government would have an annual review. The Lord President of the Council said that the Supplies and Services Act should be permanent. We asked that it should be annual and he then said that it would be annual. Yet within a few days he has turned round with a rapidity which would excite the envy of the nimblest squirrel and comes here and says: 'We must have a Bill to make these wartime regulations permanent.'

Many regulations are made in wartime, and Socialism, as I understand it, is a continuance in time of peace of the wartime regulations, with others added thereto from time to time. Nevertheless, it astonishes me that this proposal should be put forward now. I do not know when notice will be given of the Bill. That will depend on when we shall be able to discuss it. It seems without any doubt whatever that this measure will give the Executive powers utterly beyond anything which is compatible with a decent and reasonable Parliamentary system.

I want to ask the Prime Minister this question. Does the measure for regulating supplies and services on a permanent basis include the direction of labour directly or indirectly? It would, of course, be quite easy, without actually mentioning it in those words, to arrive at the result, and I should like to know about that, because it was only the other day that, at our request, the measure for the direction of labour was abolished in time of peace. I really cannot understand why this measure is necessary after last week's arrangement. It seems to be at once full of vague menace and at the same time very silly, because it is unlikely that this Parliament will last long enough to make it effective and it is certain that any anti-Socialist majority would be opposed to controls for controls' sake and would labour to reduce them to a minimum, and, anyhow, would keep them, if need be, on an annual basis subject to annual review by Parliament. I really cannot understand what this was for. I do not know whether there was some vague idea of forcing a General Election or something of that kind. It is an extraordinary position. The Prime Minister should deal with these five lines of blatant and impudent demagogy.

Then there is the proposal about beet sugar, which is no doubt intended to keep alive the nationalization issue, but somehow or other the Government seem, while letting off both barrels, not to have hit Tate and Lyle. Perhaps that is what they were aiming at, but they seem to have shot at a pigeon and hit a crow. I will not venture to go further into the technical details of this measure until I am a little more acquainted with it. How could I be better acquainted with it when the Gracious Speech has only just been read this morning by His Majesty? It is true that I had an advance copy, but that told me very little more than what has appeared in the newspapers during the last three or four days. We shall await further details, but at first sight this looks to me as if it were an attempt to feed the fires of party controversy by which our country is already sufficiently disturbed. I should have thought that the enforcement of iron and steel nationalization would have been sufficient to achieve that evil purpose. Here, at any rate, is a fundamental division on a practical issue. The present position of the iron and steel industry seems to require immediate Parliamentary attention and we must see what is the best way by which it can be brought directly before the House.

On top of these acts of faction for faction's sake, I come to the evils from which we all suffer—I mean, both parties. This is the ever-rising cost of living. We have to pay 25s. for what £1 would have bought at the end of the war in 1945. These are terrible facts. No doubt world causes are at work. Do not laugh, Mr Chancellor of the Exchequer. You will find lots in this which will excite other emotions than those which excite your risible inclinations. Next door to you sits one of the prime architects of our financial misfortunes. Do not imitate his methods but learn from his fate what to avoid. We now pay 25s. for what we could have got for 20s. after the devastating struggles of the war and before matters were handed over to Socialist control. Hampering controls, bulk buying, the inefficiency and cost of nationalization, and wasteful and extravagant finance have accentuated and aggravated the movement of world causes, which, I fully admit, has played its part in bringing about this state of affairs. All this rise is in spite of the vast sums which have been given or lent to this country by the United States and by our Dominions. Enormous assets have been liquidated.

The precise Amendment to which we shall give precedence is, of course, housing. The utter failure of the housing policy of the Government must be brought home to the nation. The Minister of Health—[HON MEMBERS: 'Where is he?']—I should have thought that we were getting sufficiently controversial for the right hon Gentleman to have shown up. The Minister of Health has stood between the people and the homes they so bitterly need. We have said that the target should be raised—[HON MEMBERS: 'Target?']—from 200,000 to 300,000. The Lord President of the Council said that I introduced this word 'target'. Really, in the responsible position he has, with, I presume, people to keep him straight, on matters of fact, at any rate, I wonder that he does not look up a few of the facts and try to state true facts.

This is what my hon and gallant Friend the Member for Pollok [Commander Galbraith] said in moving the Motion—let me have the attention of the Lord President because, when one is found out to be utterly wrong, one may as well try to learn from it. I did not originate the word 'target' at all. This is what he said in moving the Motion:

'We have to set ourselves a target.'

Then he said:

'My submission is that the target should never be set lower than 300,000 houses a year.'

Mr Shurmer: Who moved the Motion?

Mr Churchill: This is the speech of a member of our party.

The Lord President of the Council [Mr Herbert Morrison]: Will the right hon Gentleman forgive me for interrupting? The comparison I made in the observations I ventured to utter was between the resolution of the conference, forced down the throats of the platform by the hysterical rank and file, which declared for a minimum production of 300,000 houses a year, and that two days afterwards the right hon Gentleman welcomed the decision but at once turned the minimum production of 300,000 into a target.

Mr Churchill: And two days before, the hon and gallant Gentleman who speaks for the Opposition Front Bench used this very same expression 'target'. There can be no doubt whatever that it is perfectly practicable and possible to build at the rate of 300,000 houses. All this outcry when I ask a thing like this is exactly what the Prime Minister and others did when we said: 'Reduce petrol rationing'—how irresponsible, how impossible. Do not hon Members imagine that the people of this country know perfectly well that building at the rate of 300,000 houses a year is a perfectly practicable measure, and one which should be taken as a direct and immediate aim?

This is the point I wish to make. It is treated as a most extraordinary thing that we should ask that the rate of building should be raised from 200,000 to 300,000 houses a year. That is the view. We are denounced for having suggested it. It seems to show a great lack of proportion. It shows the want of a sense of proportion to suppose that such a measure as building at the rate of 100,000 houses a year more is an impossible task for this powerful, well-equipped country. Why should it be thought to be impossible? 100,000 houses at £1,500 apiece would cost £150,000,000 a year. That ought not to be beyond our capacity if the priorities are properly arranged [Hon Members: 'Ah!'] I repeat, if the priorities are properly arranged and a reasonable time is given to collect the materials. [Hon Members: 'Ah!'] Certainly, it should not be impossible for a country to find this rearrangement of the expenditure of £150,000,000. It should not be impossible to find a method of doing that when we consider that our national income is around £10,000,000,000 a year. It is a very small readjustment and re-arrangement of priorities that is required. Do not let the House be put off by all this, what I should have thought was to hon Members opposite, most injurious outcry and clamour that to try to get 300,000 houses a year built for the people was a wrong and shameful thing for anyone to advocate. We shall ask the House next week to inflict its censure upon the Government for this grave mismanagement of the housing problem.

I have only one word more to say, because interruptions have rather lengthened what I had thought of saying. Uncertainty—I address myself very much to the Prime Minister—about the election date is harmful. Prolongation of the electioneering atmosphere is not good for the country. A year has passed already in which we have lived in that atmosphere, which can be felt here; even already it has infected our new House. The House is not at its best when parties are so evenly balanced and on the verge of another appeal. The increasing rigidity of party discipline deprives debate of much of its value as a means of influencing opinion except out of doors. All kinds of uncertainties are created in every direction; all kinds of animosities and rancours are fed and worked up, on both sides, I fully admit—[HON MEMBERS: 'Oh.'] Certainly; and I cannot think it good for the country that this should continue. The Prime Minister deliberately tries to increase and prolong this uncertainty. He says: 'The election will come at the moment when I judge fit.'

MRS BRADDOCK (Liverpool, Exchange): What did the right hon Gentleman do in 1945?

MR SHURMER: What would the right hon Gentleman do?

MR CHURCHILL: The hon Gentleman asked what I would do. I say deliberately that I think that if I were with the responsibilities of the Prime Minister at this juncture, having regard to all that is going on, I would try to limit the uncertainty as much as possible. I would carefully consider whether I could not say, provided we had the control of events, that we should not have an election until a certain date. I think it is well worthy of consideration whether that might not be of general interest. [Interruption.] I have finished. I have given the hon Member more than he deserves. Of course, it is very natural that anyone should like to feel that he can keep the rest of his countrymen on tenterhooks and that we are always awaiting the moment when he shall give the signal. All I can say is that I am quite satisfied that the right hon Gentleman is indulging his personal power in these matters in a manner most costly to the community and harmful to all large enduring interests of the State.

DEBATE ON THE ADDRESS (HOUSING AMENDMENT)

A SPEECH TO THE HOUSE OF COMMONS
6 NOVEMBER 1950

---

1 *November—Attempted assassination of President Truman by two members of the Puerto Rican Nationalist party.*

Mr Attlee, in a speech to the Foreign Press Association, denounces the sponsors of the 'Peace Congress' as Communists and describes the proposed meeting in Sheffield as 'bogus'.

6 *November—Security Council at Lake Success study a report from General MacArthur confirming twelve instances of Chinese Communist forces intervention in Korea.*

The Opposition move an amendment to the Address regretting that the Speech from the Throne shows 'no resolve to ensure a steady increase in the rate of building houses up to at least 300,000 *a year'.*

[6 *November* 1950

The hon Member for Blackley [Mr Diamond] seemed, so far as I was able to follow his argument, to be somewhat diverging from the party line in addressing himself to the merits of the subject. I am bound to say that it seemed to me that he raised many interesting points in the course of his speech. Of course, one quite realized the strength of feeling behind his condemnation of vote-catching in any form. That is certainly greatly to be deplored. On the other hand, we must not forget what votes are. Votes are the means by which the poorest people in the country and all people in the country can make sure that they get their vital needs attended to. [HON MEMBERS: 'Hear, hear.'] I am very glad to begin upon a note which receives such universal approbation because I had, after all, been led to expect that I was to undergo very unpleasant ordeals on this day. The Prime Minister—he is not here at the moment—expressed his confidence that the Minister of Health would 'wipe the floor' with me. As I have only just taken the floor and he has already exhausted his right of speaking, I naturally feel a sensation of liberation and relief. But I cannot feel that this prospect, or the language of the Prime Minister, did justice to the grave issue open between the two parties and still less to the housing problem.

The suffering caused to millions of people by the want of houses throughout the island is a tragedy, and this is on quite a different level

421

to any clashes that may occur across the table, or across the floor, between individual Members of the House. I think this Debate should end, as it has largely been maintained, upon a serious note, and I was very glad that my hon Friends on this side of the House did not allow themselves to be provoked by taunts or abuse from an embarrassed party or a guilty Minister. During the whole of the last Parliament the need for houses and the failure to supply them was constantly debated, and the outlines of the controversy are familiar to us all. It is necessary, however, to restate the salient points on the verge of an important division. They may be summed up as follows: First, the expectations aroused by the Government's assurances and pledges in 1945; secondly, the extraordinary shortfall in their fulfilment; thirdly, the gravity of the position and prospects now before us; and, finally, the need and the hope of a new constructive effort. It is on these points I shall venture to dwell tonight.

The House knows only too well the catalogue of pledges and promises which were made to the people by the Socialist Party during the election of 1945. All were renewed on many occasions by the responsible Ministers after they had obtained power and were fully acquainted with official facts and figures. A few examples will suffice— I do not wish to burden the House with them. The former Minister, Mr Charles Key, said on 12 October 1946:

'Six million houses are needed in the next ten years. To get that figure we shall have to build 600,000 a year, but I believe that by temporary prefabs and things of that sort we shall be able to do it.'

The present Minister of Health said on 24 May 1946:

'I confidently expect that before the next election every family in Great Britain will have a separate house.'

Again, two years later, on 24 April 1948, he said:

'By the next General Election the back of the housing programme will have been broken.'

Contrast all this—and it could be multiplied to any extent; whole budgets of quotations are available—with the actual performances of the Socialist Government. In 1948 they had reached a total of 227,000 permanent houses. Since then, instead of getting better, things have got worse, and in 1949 the total of permanent houses was only 198,000. These results are indeed deplorable when we consider the crying need, the vehement demand and the immense subsidies now being paid, and when we compare the results with what was being done with hardly any subsidies, on a very small scale, before the late war broke upon us.

The Prime Minister said in the Debate last week:

'We consider that the 200,000 houses a year is an actual programme, a programme which is being carried out, and it is as nearly
as possible the number of good houses which can be built with the
available resources of labour and materials. . . .'
I must say that I think that statement cast a chill on the party opposite.
On the other hand, it has certainly been endorsed today by the Minister
of Health. He has confirmed it and in every way associated himself
with it. That is his duty, and any exhibition of loyalty on his part to
his chief might well excite approbation even beyond the limits of the
Government Bench.

What a strange position we find ourselves in tonight. The Conservative Party ask for the house building to be raised to a rate of
300,000 a year at the earliest moment. The Prime Minister, supported
by his most ardent champion, declares that 200,000 is the most that
can be done. Our demand, which represents the wish and the will of
the nation, is dismissed in contemptuous terms and brushed aside
with all sorts of aspersions on our motives. One would have thought
it would have been welcome, and it might even have afforded a basis
for common action. The prime basic fact which stares us in the face
tonight is that building at the rate of 200,000 a year in no way solves
the problem. We do not make any progress with rehousing the people.
We only keep level with houses which are already falling or have
fallen into decay. The social evils affecting every aspect of our life,
which are connected with the present housing shortage, are now presented to us by the Government as bound to continue, so far as can
be seen, indefinitely. Sir, that situation is obviously intolerable.

Take the argument about comparing what was done in the five years
after the First World War. There is this great difference between them.
The first is that after the First World War there was no American aid.
[HON MEMBERS: 'Cheap.'] On the contrary, a hard demand was
pressed upon us for the repayment of war debts. The second is that
there was practically no destruction by bombing in the First World
War. Thirdly, the local authorities were virtually without experience
of building in 1918. This time they had all the practical experience
gained by the pre-war slum clearance and other municipal housing
schemes. And finally, far more preparations were made by the wartime Government on this at the end of this war than were ever thought
of in 1917 or 1918—[Interruption.] I am talking of the National Coalition Government and, on this occasion, there are still one or two
representatives of it on the Front Bench.

What stood out dramatically at the end of this war was the need to
rehouse the people after the devastation of the bombing. We all

recognized it in the National Coalition. I will read to the House what I wrote at the time to some of my colleagues—on 5 April 1944:

'The whole of this emergency housing scheme must be viewed in relation to a ten-years' plan for the steady, full-time employment of a considerably enlarged building trade for permanent houses instead of a fever for three or four years and then a falling off. The building trade should have a broad and steady flow giving all its members a good assurance of employment and thus encouraging piece-work.'

Everyone realizes, of course, that what is given for one purpose may, to some extent, have to be taken from others. The Government supporters naturally seek to obtain from us a list of reductions or economies which we would make in order to use these for electioneering purposes. That is quite natural in the unhappy conditions in which we have lived for a year and which seem likely to continue. I have no intention of making any piecemeal propositions. [*Laughter.*] I have a feeling, listening to the debates and watching hon Members opposite, that their anxious consciences find relief in laughter. No one would grudge them any solace they can get from giggling.

Naturally, I have no intention of making piecemeal propositions. There is no obligation on a party in opposition, without access to Government machinery, to produce a detailed scheme. That can only be done where they have the power to act. But it is on such a definite, general design alone that changes of a large character of this kind can be judged. It may well be that a general design for an increase in housing would contain some features unpopular in themselves, but when presented in its entirety and harmony it would be greatly in the interests of the nation and would be generally welcomed.

In this matter of housing there are two questions: first to get the houses, and second to allot them. Do not let us quarrel too much about the second point. Do not let us quarrel so much about it as to prevent us from achieving the first, without which the second would not arise. Mrs Beeton and, I believe, her predecessors in the Cookery Book, begins the recipe for jugged hare, 'First catch your hare.' One of the reasons for the Minister of Health's failure is that he mixes up these two processes. In order to make sure that nobody who was well-to-do could get a house, he has in fact prevented large numbers of houses being built for the ordinary wage earners.

I listened to the speech of the right hon Gentleman tonight with sorrow, because—here I make an admission—I do not believe he is as bad as he makes himself out. But I will say this to him. Hate is a bad guide. I have never considered myself at all a good hater—

though I recognize that from moment to moment it has added stimulus to pugnacity. People who have been denied an opportunity in life are deeply embittered, but the Minister of Health does not belong to that class. No man's services in the war were accorded such a wonderful reward as he received. With the mood, and the need, and the ruins in the country glaring at us all from day to day, and with the piling up of arrears of house-building, could there have been a task so plain and so inspiring as that which was offered to him? It was one which any man of vitality and vigour, in the prime of life, and gifted with abilities of a high order and Parliamentary gifts, would have embraced with joy, and gratitude to the land in which he lived. With the immense powers at his disposal under wartime regulations and with the long five years which have been granted to him, he might have left a mark upon the social life of the British people, and rendered them a service which would have made his name at once famous and beloved. I cannot understand how this did not appeal to him, and how it did not drive out all hampering passions and prejudices, the indulgence of which have led to the present unhappy plight that he is in.

It is not only a question of building houses—not only a question of numbers—but the cost has risen to a point which, despite subsidies on an enormous scale, involves rents which many of those in most need of houses cannot afford. The rents charged to the tenants have risen remorselessly. Before the war the average rent of a local council house was 7s. a week. [HON MEMBERS: 'No.'] In many places now £1 a week rent is charged. In some cases, 25s. is charged by councils.

MR BEVAN rose——

MR CHURCHILL: No, I really cannot give way. [HON MEMBERS: 'Give way.'] I do not want to be—[HON MEMBERS: 'Give way.'] We can always shout each other down. I do not want to be involved in a personal altercation. We gave the right hon Gentleman a patient and courteous hearing. There is no use in having a state of rowdiness, as if rowdiness paid any party. I do not want to be involved in an altercation with the right hon Gentleman. However, if there is a point on which I am in error and upon which I am open to correction I will gladly give way.

MR BEVAN: I am very much obliged to the right hon Gentleman for giving way. I am not anxious to engage in a personal altercation. I only want to get the facts correct. The right hon Gentleman has compared the net rent of a pre-war house with the gross rent of a post-war house.

MR CHURCHILL: No.

Mr Bevan: Yes. As representatives of local authorities who saw me the other day will confirm—and there are hon Members now sitting on both sides of the House who were present with the deputation—the average rentals in Great Britain upon which the subsidies are based are rents of between 14s. and 15s., including the repair allowances, as against the net—[*Interruption.*] Perhaps hon Members will just listen. The rents upon which subsidies are paid are net rents, and the 7s. compares with the 14s. to 15s. post-war rents.

Mr Churchill: The other day the Chancellor of the Exchequer showed us how all the rise in the cost of living was a delusion. The Minister of Health now proceeds to show us that there is no appreciable rise in rents. I am told that in some cases they have gone up to 25s. and 27s. a week, and that is clearly a level which ordinary working people cannot pay out of their wages. So much for the cost, which has certainly greatly increased in housing.

When we complain that houses have not been supplied in the necessary quantities it is said: 'Half a loaf is better than no bread.' But half a house is not a good plan. We could usefully use more two-bedroomed houses, and more small flats for old people enabling them to move out of their large houses to make room for families. Any habitable house is better than no house at all, or a house so dear that the poorest class, for which it is built, cannot afford to pay the rent which the local authority is bound to charge. There are many cases of that of which we know, and the richer class of people take the houses because those for whose needs they were specially designed and intended are unable to reach the level of rent. It is no service to the lower income group to offer them prizes which are beyond their reach; indeed it is a mockery. Before the war, the size of a house was 800 square feet. The Government raised it to 1,050 square feet. That is more than the figure that rules in the United States, whose economic position is vastly more powerful than our own, and from whom we have received such immense assistance. The amount of space is less important than how it is used. I am assured that there may well be scope for improved design within the existing compass of housing.

It is necessary also, I think, for the Government to understand the peculiar position of house-building labour. I said some time ago how a bricklayer and his mates engaged in building a house were like people living on a raft of which they had every day to burn a plank or two to cook their dinner. That is the feeling which is in their minds. They ask themselves what is going to happen to them when it is finished. In the present circumstances there is a field of employment for the house-builders unlimited for many years except by Government decision. As I said earlier, I thought that we should give them an assurance of a ten-years' guaranteed programme. Free from the anxiety that their work may end with the job, they could go ahead with piece work without fear or stint and all the incentives, including the bonus system, could apply. Here alone might be a 20 or 25 per cent increase in the building effort. There is really no reason why the output per man in the building trade should be lower than pre-war or so much lower than in the United States. Make them a fair and attractive proposition and we will get surprising results, but this policy of the Prime Minister that 200,000 is the limit, endorsed by the Minister of Health—I daresay to his regret—is bad for the rate of output—even within that limit.

There is no trade in the country which can more readily adapt itself to a static condition than the building trade. They would like a progressive condition but they are quite ready, after the rough time which they have had in the last generation—I have seen it: the first to be called up for mobilization and so on and the first to be turned off when building slackens and so on—[*Interruption.*] I am the author of the labour exchanges and the first Unemployment Insurance Act. I was in these matters years before many hon Gentlemen opposite were able to take an adult interest in them. I say that they are quite ready, after their experiences, to settle down into a static condition.

The Government limit of 200,000 houses—it was only 175,000, as the Minister reminded us, until this new Parliament forced the restoration of the cut—undoubtedly has most evil and discouraging effects. How long it is to last, we cannot tell. The late Chancellor of the Exchequer, whose absence from our councils we deeply regret and still more the reason for it, told us in the Budget that this limit would last for three years. Such a limit, or anything like it, must reproduce the deterrence of efforts, enterprise and piece-work which ruled in the days when the building trade had always an unabsorbed tail of unemployment.

Therefore, when I endorsed as a resolute aim of the Conservative Party the raising of the rate of building to 300,000 a year, I did not mean that to be the static limit. We shall thrust towards it with all our life, strength and wit, but once this figure gleams upon our horizon— 'forward again' must be the policy and the order. So much for the Government's policy and the Prime Minister's statement. I am sure that the Prime Minister's statement represents the rigid attitude of planners who understand only about half of what is really going on.

Now I come to the question whether the proposal we make is possible and practicable, or whether it is all moonshine. [HON MEMBERS:

'Hear, hear.'] I am glad to carry Members opposite with me. I said that 100,000 houses would cost £150,000,000 a year from an annual income of over £10,000,000,000. The Prime Minister's reply is that houses are not built with money. Money, of course, is only a fairly well-known method of expressing effort and resources. I am surprised it has not occurred to the Prime Minister, because it has been known about in quite a lot of countries for quite a long time. Let us look at the additional effort and resources required. Judgment on this kind of enterprise depends on two conditions: are they so big that they are beyond our power, and, secondly, if they are within our scope, are there bottlenecks which prevent them? Several constructive speeches have been made today. We have also made, in our own research department, a considerable examination. My personal experience of Government machinery is considerable, and I must say that I have never seen a major task which I was more sure of as being within practical limits. I would not fear to take responsibility for this achievement. I offer my assurance that it is a reasonable objective, and that, should we be called upon to exercise power, it would receive the highest priority and the most vehement effort jointly with national defence.

That is what I have to say on the proportion, but let us now look at the bottlenecks. My hon Friend the Member for Wallasey [Mr Marples], in his admirable speech today, dealt with these details. I was very glad that with his technical knowledge he was able to put this subject before the House as a practical matter of detail and on its merits, instead of trying to reduce it to the ordinary bang and slam on one side and the other of party politics. I was sorry that my hon Friend, a private Member speaking from a back bench, should have been made the victim for so prolonged a personal attack by the Minister of Health. I really thought that the Minister would have done himself much more good—though he is the judge of that—if he had devoted himself to the merits of the question, and tried to give the House the feeling that his heart was burning to conquer in this struggle to find homes for the British people. I shall not attempt to go into details. [HON MEMBERS: 'Go on.'] If I did so, I would trespass on the reply to this Debate.

THE SECRETARY OF STATE FOR SCOTLAND [MR MCNEIL]: If another five minutes would furnish the House with any details, I should be delighted to give up that time.

MR CHURCHILL: 8,000 million bricks were made before the war, but we are now making a little over 6,000 million. Of this 6,000 million a little more than 3,000 million are used for the construction of the traditional brick dwelling-house. Out of them are built about 160,000 houses. To build another 100,000 houses would need about 2,000 million more bricks. That is well within the range of the pre-war brick-fields. If these had not been restricted and jogged about by changes of policy, there would be plenty of bricks. But the brick-fields are already running at 80 per cent of their pre-war capacity, and there should be no great difficulty or delay in restoring them to their pre-war normal output. So much for bricks.

More cement will also be needed to achieve our target, but this need present no great problem. An extra 900,000 tons would produce 100,000 houses. The industry already produces 10,000,000 tons, and it would be producing more if it had been allowed to go ahead with the expansion plans it had in 1945. Next year this industry plans to produce 10,500,000 tons. As a temporary measure, we could, if necessary, reduce for a time the exports, which are running at a rate of 1,600,000 tons. Certainly by the end of next year the cement industry, if not nationalized, will have caught up with all our demands, including rearmament.

Then there is timber. We have been told that if no timber can be got from sterling area countries like Norway, it will affect the dollar position. But here again I am sure that the quantities and proportion would have their say. I am assured that about £9,750,000 worth of dollars or less than half of our last year's tobacco bill, would give all the dollars necessary to buy from Canada the extra timber. I do not believe it would be necessary to go so far, because I am sure a good deal can be got within the sterling area. Far greater elasticity will come from the abolition of bulk buying by officials. Anyhow, the whole timber transaction is one well within our compass. The improvement in the dollar exchange would more than justify such a step. We lose at home by the higher prices for raw materials, but in the exchange we gain, especially by the sale of tin and rubber. It may well be that we could find a partial compensation for Britain at home in using our improved dollar position to buy more timber, and thus help to solve the housing question.

I am asked: 'Are you for or against controls?' But what a crude and absurd way to state the issue. Government speakers talk as if there were no middle course between the universal regulation of a Socialist State administering all the means of production, distribution and exchange and what they call the anarchy of the jungle. But the vast majority of the human race dwell in the temperate zones which lie between the burning heat of the equator and the freezing cold of the polar regions. Our belief is that the fewer the controls the better;

that the more freedom and enterprise can play their part the more chance there is of a fertile, prosperous and progressive community.

We also think that private management is far more economical and resourceful than management by State officials. We are sure that the completion of the Socialist aim of substituting State industry for every form of private industry would reduce our standard of life and would reduce the present number of our population. In the United States, where a capitalist competitive system prevails and where wartime regulations were practically swept away until recently—[HON MEMBERS: 'Ah.'] Well, there is a war in Korea. What about that 'Ah' now? The United States have three times our population, so, according to Government standards, they ought to be building 600,000 houses a year. They are actually building more than 1,000,000.

Now, when rearmament casts its shadow upon the world and upon our country, there must evidently be a maintenance or even a renewal of some wartime regulations. We have agreed that the Supplies and Services Act should be renewed on an annual basis, but our hope of establishing full freedom under the well-known and long-established laws of our country remains our goal. The difference between the two sides of the House is that the Socialists aim at the maximum of controls and the Conservatives aim at the minimum. Both seek to progress in those opposite directions for different reasons as far as they possibly can. Can we now accept that as a summary of the differences between us?

If we apply that mood of thought to the position of the building industry at the present time it means that we should, of course, use the local authorities as well as the private builders, and that we should only alter the system of licences step by step. The Minister of Health has suggested that under a Conservative Government a great number of houses would be built for sale to the well-to-do by speculative builders and that few houses would be built to let for the ordinary man. It is our intention that, under a Conservative Government, the priority given to houses built by local authorities will be maintained. This obligation will be scrupulously honoured in our house-building programme.

MR BEVAN: In what proportion?

MR CHURCHILL: We want the local authorities to be able to reduce their waiting lists and to resume the process of slum clearance which was interrupted by the war.

MR BEVAN: The right hon Gentleman has made a very important statement. In what proportion would the right hon Gentleman maintain local authority house-building?

MR CHURCHILL: I said that I had no intention of stating exact details. Give me the power and I will give you the figures. We have to indicate our principles, and I am indicating some very clear principles. Over and above that commitment, to which we are all pledged, we should expand output so as to make it possible for free enterprise and renewed impulse to build large numbers of additional houses, both for sale and to let. So long as the housing shortage continues, the Government must restrict the ceiling on price or size of houses built for sale, and this must be dependent upon the prevailing, and sometimes upon the local, conditions. We shall take steps to prevent the diversion to any kind of luxury building, whether public or private, of the resources of men and materials—a great deal of them is being taken for public building—which could be devoted to the housing of the people.

I listened to the speech of the noble Lady the Member for Anglesey [Lady Megan Lloyd George] [HON MEMBERS: 'Hear, hear.'] I hope that the applause from the other side of the House will assure her of any immunities which she may be seeking. I need not say that I speak as a life-long friend of her father and her family, but I feel that she should have verified the facts before making the statement about the Carlton Club claiming a licence to rebuild the bomb-damaged premises. We have given up all hope of ever rebuilding the Carlton Club and no application for a licence has ever been made. The site is being disposed of. Speaking as one who lived in her father's generation, I do not consider that prefixing the words 'I am informed that' relieves one of all responsibility.

LADY MEGAN LLOYD GEORGE: I am sorry to interrupt the right hon Gentleman, but when I was informed that that was not the case I withdrew the statement. [HON MEMBERS: 'No.'] Certainly I did so.

MR CHURCHILL: I was here at the time but I suffer a little from deafness and did not realize that the charge had been withdrawn.

LADY MEGAN LLOYD GEORGE: I said that I was very glad that it was so and that no licence had been granted.

MR CHURCHILL: Honour is completely satisfied on both sides. We say that the emphasis should be placed upon new houses. In 1935 new housing absorbed 48 per cent of the building industry's output. In 1947 the figure was only 34 per cent, and in 1948 31 per cent. We have no later figures, but I am informed—[Laughter]—I must be careful—that it might well be only 30 per cent today.

I think that the Government have been at once ambitious and in-effectual in their building plans. They have dispersed, instead of concentrating, their resources. They have been very loose in their application of principles of selection in regard to their objectives. The need above all is to establish in this sphere, as in many others, the right priorities. They ask, for instance, whether we would cut the new power stations. The answer is 'No'. Without power we cannot build houses, carry out our defence programme or expand our industrial output. But the question of whether the necessary electrical supply could not be obtained with fewer bricks subtracted from the housing programme is still open, and my hon Friend the Member for Wallasey drew our attention to American practice on this subject, which certainly seems to deserve study.

I am grateful for the five minutes extra which the right hon Gentleman has granted me, and I shall draw to a conclusion the remarks I have ventured to offer to the House. We must not let this 'wiping the floor' mood of the Prime Minister and the Minister of Health blot out from our minds the pathos and the tragedy of the shortage of houses. The life of the nation and the happiness and virtue of the human race are founded upon the family and upon the home. Empire, ideologies, party struggles, class warfare, all present their attractive temptations to the active mind, but the foundations of all our health and honour lie in the home and the family.

It was John Bright who spoke of his supreme pleasure in seeing little children playing upon the hearth. I cannot understand why this result should not be won. Let us have less chatter and planning and scheming for future Utopias. Let us get on with this imperative job of housing the millions who ask so little and get so little for all their efforts. The family requires a home and the home requires a house or, if you like it, an 'accommodation unit'—something, at any rate, where a man has his own front door. Outside is the great, bewildering, tumultuous world; inside, the family can plan what is best for themselves, what it is best to aim for, what is wisest to give up. And in so deciding they create at once the foundation and the motive power without which all the super-planners are only chasing shadows. Where does the family start? It starts with a young man falling in love with a girl. No superior alternative has yet been found! Look at the number of couples whom the statistics show either cannot get married because they cannot get a house to live in, or have to live with their parents, or jam up in the sort of collectivist squalor of Communist lands. I see that a judge in Plymouth said the housing shortage was the principal cause of divorces. Then what of the health? There is no doubt that tuberculosis thrives on bad housing conditions. In Scotland it has actually gone up since the war. Then comes the sharp issue of children not having a home they love, or a family circle which commands their loyalty, and of the many forms of consequential juvenile misconduct of which we read.

The Minister of Health cannot brush all this aside and escape from this Debate without incurring blame and condemnation outside for not having offered us a constructive statement and words of encouragement. All his critics will not be on one side of the House. I have a number of quotations, some very moving, from speeches made last week from the Benches opposite, one particularly from the hon Member for Kirkdale [Mr Keenan] who said:

'What is the good of having fine schools or even fine hospitals if there is no home in which the children can rest? . . . I believe in bedrooms before schoolrooms. . . . It is certainly a fact that not all building-trade workers who are capable of house-building are engaged on house-building.'

It astounds me that the House has not rallied to this proposal which we make and resolved that it shall be carried into effect by every priority to other issues except self-preservation.

But, sir, you may be sure that the nation will not endure this mismanagement and misdirection much longer. They will not agree to a system of British life and society which means that no progress is being made to overtake the housing arrears, that as many houses are falling into decay every year as are being built, that slum clearance is static like all the rest of it, that all the personal stresses now endured by hard-working couples are to continue, and that even to raise these issues in the House of Commons is to incur the insulting charge of vote-catching and partisanship.

Early last week there came across my mind some lines about our island life which Charles Masterman used to repeat to me. Oddly enough, while I was seeking to verify the quotation it was used in the House by the hon Member for Oldham West [Mr Leslie Hale]. The poet and the teacher, as he was—William Watson—speaking of the hard social conditions of the life of the people, asked:

'Is there no room for victories here,
No fields for deeds of fame?'

But I have found another verse of William Watson, which I remembered at the same time:

'The England of my heart is she,
Long hoped, and long deferred,
That ever promises to be,
And ever breaks her word.'

Why should she always break her word to those who love her so well and defend her safety and honour with their lives? Now is the time, here is the occasion, and this housing issue is the deed to sweep that hard reproach away.

---

14 *November—Foreign Office announce the offer of a credit of £3,000,000 to Yugoslavia to help to relieve the existing food shortage there due to disastrous summer drought.*

15 *November—Mr Shinwell, Minister of Defence, announces in the House of Commons that measures are to be taken to raise a Home Guard in the event of an emergency.*

16 *November—King Farouk's speech read from the Throne by Nahas Pasha, the Egyptian Prime Minister, declares that the Egyptian Government will insist upon the abrogation of the Anglo-Egyptian treaty of 1936, on the evacuation of British troops from Egypt, and on the unification of the Nile Valley under the Egyptian Crown.*

20 *November—Mr Bevin states in the House of Commons that despite Egypt's attitude to Britain, as set out in the speech from the throne on 16 November, the Government intends to send to that country the Centurion tanks which she has paid for.*

22 *November—Due to strong opposition from all parties in the House of Commons, the Foreign Under-Secretary (acting in Mr Bevin's absence) agrees to a temporary suspension of the shipping of tanks to Egypt.*

21–23 *November—Queen Juliana and Prince Bernhard of the Netherlands pay State visit to London.*

[30 *November* 1950

I hope that the level calm of yesterday's debate will be regarded as an example of our composure in times of danger and not as an instance of any failure on our part to realize its gravity. Perhaps the calm in all its aspects represents various characteristics in our national character. Certainly we are in danger, but the danger is not new. It was visible in all its terrible potential from the moment when the armies of democracy dispersed and melted away in the hour of victory while the armies of the Soviet oligarchy were maintained at an enormous strength and were re-equipped to a very high degree and when, on top of this, Russian imperialism, clothed in a new garb, advanced to carry the creed of Communism and the authority of the Kremlin forth in every direction until some solid obstacle was reached.

This danger became apparent to some of us before the war ended and was recognized widely throughout our confidential circles. It began to be realized by much larger numbers of people in Britain and the United States when the first conference of the Council of the United Nations took place at the beginning of 1946. Up till then for the great masses of the people all had been softened and shrouded in the Western democracies by the comradeship of the great struggle, by their relief in hard-won victory and by their admiration of the valour and sacrifices of the Russian armies. However, I must remind the House that already at the beginning of 1946 the Foreign Secretary felt himself forced to describe, to his face and in public, Mr Vishinsky's statements as lies. I am not blaming the Foreign Secretary, but it showed how rapidly, in the course of a year, we had been disillusioned, or the outer world had been disillusioned. Since then, the increasing realization by the Western democracies of the danger in which they stood and stand has been continuous.

There were two major differences between the state of the world after the First and after the Second World Wars. The sour aftermath of triumph in arms, however complete, brought with it in both cases many troubles, but here are the two differences. After the First War, when the victors had disarmed the Germans and their allies, no powerful organized army remained upon the scene except the French Army. After this war the armed might of Russia has emerged steadily year by year, almost month by month, as a rock shows more and more above an ebbing tide. The second difference, which arose out of the realization of the first, was that the United States, instead of retiring into isolation, instead of demanding full and prompt repayment of debts and disinteresting herself in Europe and even in the League of Nations, of which she had been one of the founders, has come forward step by step as the knowledge of the situation has dawned upon her and has made the great counterpoise upon which the freedom and the future of our civilization depends. This fundamental change in the policy of the United States constitutes, in my view, the best hope for the salvation of Christian civilization and democracy from Communist and Russian conquest and control. I hope, therefore, that we shall regard it as our first objective not to separate ourselves in action or in understanding or in sympathy in any degree, however slight, that can be avoided from the United States.

But the favourable policy of the United States after this last war, which has been so helpful to us in so many ways, did not affect the military disparity caused by the maintenance of immense Russian armies year after year and the development of their armoured forces, their air power and their submarines. We did not come to terms with them at the moment of German surrender while we, too, had the weapons in our hands. The Western Allies abandoned the whole of Eastern Germany, including an immense area of which they stood in occupation, to Soviet control, and Russia remained the overwhelming armed Power, towering up in Europe and in Asia, avid for the expansion of her creed and her rule. The war had liberated Russia from her two preoccupations—Germany and Japan. Both these warlike nations have inflicted terrible defeats and injuries upon Russia in this present twentieth century. Now both have ceased to be military factors and the years that have followed our victory have brought enormous increases of power and territory to Soviet Russia. In one form or another they have gained control of half Europe and all China without losing a single Russian soldier. They have every right to be encouraged by the progress they have made, but they show no signs of being in any way satiated or satisfied or even contented with it, and we can perceive no limits at present to their aims.

So much for the past. Let me now, in the very few minutes I shall detain the House, look to the present and the future. I hoped myself—and my view was shared by my colleagues at that time—that a lasting settlement might be reached with Russia before we evacuated our portion of Central and Eastern Germany, and before the United States' armies were demobilized and dispersed. Later, in 1948, I hoped that we might come to terms with them before they gained the secret of the atomic bomb. Now I hope that we may come to terms with them before they have so large a stockpile of these fearful agencies, in addition to vast superiority in other weapons, as to be able to terrorize the free world, if not, indeed, to destroy it.

Let us look at the time factor. In some aspects it is in our favour: in some it is adverse. The Soviets, under the restraint of the immense United States' superiority in the atomic sphere, and also by the consolidation of the rapid and immense gains which they have made and are still making in many directions without incurring any direct risk—under these two opposite forces—have hitherto been under restraint and control.

They have repeatedly been assured that the United States would not fight what is called a 'preventive' war. The United States have expressed the general opinion of the civilized world upon that aspect. On this basis the war, if ever it comes—which God forbid—will come at the moment of Russian choice. It, however, should be noted that the two restraining or consoling arguments which I have mentioned are both diminishing. The Soviet stockpile of atomic bombs is growing.

How fast, I have no idea. I do not know whether the Government have knowledge. At any rate, we have none. And the Soviets must expect, while this stockpile is growing in their favour behind them, more resistance to their further expansion, and they will not find their progress so easy as it has been in the past. It is impossible to prophesy what they will do, or when, or how they will do it. One can only judge these matters by estimating what is their interest. The great Duke of Marlborough quoted a saying in his day: 'Interest never lies'; and there is no doubt that trying to put oneself in the position of the other party to see how things look to him is one way, and perhaps the best way, of being able to feel and peer dimly into the unknowable future. It is, at any rate, the only guide—and it does not include accident, passion, folly or madness, madness which may arise from some error, some blunder, or from the results of some internal convulsion. All that can be said is that it certainly does not seem to be in the Russian interest to begin a major struggle now.

We are told that it is provocative to organize an Atlantic army, with, as I see it, a European army inside it and a German contingent, on honourable terms, inside that. We are told that that is provocative. It does not seem likely, however, that anything that we can do in the next two years in Europe will reverse the balance of military power. We may be stronger, but not strong enough in that time to deter, still less to prevail. There is plenty of room for us to get much stronger without altering the situation in Europe decisively. Therefore, while it is right to build up our forces as fast as we can, nothing in this process, in the period I have mentioned, will deprive Russia of effective superiority in what are called now the conventional arms. All that it will do is to give us increasing unity in Europe and magnify the deterrents against aggression, and, perhaps, give us the means of gradually approaching the situation when relations between world Powers may express themselves in normal terms and not only be measured in the strange and novel methods of the atomic age.

Dangerous as it may be to make such a prediction—I make it in all good faith, and without official knowledge—I would venture to express the opinion that a major attack by Russia in Europe is unlikely in the near future, and that it will not be provoked or produced by the modest measures of defence now being so slowly, so tardily and ineffectively developed up to the present by the Atlantic and Western Powers. Even if our preparations developed more rapidly, a long period must elapse before they could offset the Russian superiority, even if the Russian strength itself were not increased meanwhile. It is upon this that I found my hope that we still have time, that there is

still a breathing space for us to pursue the policy of seeking an understanding, and for us to also pursue the essential counterpart and
foundation of any such hope, namely, the building up of a more
reasonable measure of defensive strength. This may be a vain hope.
I may live, perhaps, to be mocked at if proved wrong by events. It is,
at any rate, the working hypothesis of my thought in these anxious
and agonizing times.

Therefore I am in favour of efforts to reach a settlement with Soviet
Russia as soon as a suitable opportunity presents itself, and of making
those efforts while the immense and measureless superiority of the
United States atomic bomb organization offsets the Soviet pre-
dominance in every other military respect and gives us the means to
talk together in a friendly and dignified manner and, at least as equals.
I think that we are all agreed with what my right hon Friend the
Member for Warwick and Leamington [Mr Eden] said yesterday
about the kind of answer we should make to the Russian proposals
for a Four-Power conference. I was very glad to hear the Foreign
Secretary fully endorse the suggestion which he made for drawing up
an agenda, which should no doubt be done in the first instance by
competent officials.

I hope, however, that at the right and best time, especially after
matters are stabilized in the Far East, a conference will arise which
will not merely be like those of which we have had too many in the
past, of two sides arguing against each other in the glare of publicity,
but that the decisive conversations will take place in confidence, in
privacy and even in secrecy, and will be conducted at the highest
levels. It is what I asked for at Edinburgh six months ago. I agree
that much has happened since then, particularly these great developments in the Far East and also the immense and active leadership now
assumed by the United States, with whom we must march, or walk,
hand in hand and to whom we must give all the help and goodwill
which our power and experience allow. Much has happened since
then, but I do not think we should exclude from any of the discussions
which may take place, perhaps after the present unhelpful crisis has
passed away, the personal touch between those who have the right
and the power to speak for the great States involved. That is only what
I said at Edinburgh. I fully agree that time and the new circumstances
which have come into view must influence, and even perhaps govern,
our action.

This brings me to the crisis in Korea and China. We all find much
that is disquieting in it, but I do not see that what is happening in the
Far East should make the Soviets in a hurry to depart from their

present policy of expansion by means of the cold war and of using others to advance their aims. The Foreign Secretary asked yesterday: Is this move of the Chinese into Korea part of a grand strategy for a definite purpose?

'Is there a Russo-Chinese conspiracy on a world-wide scale?' They were very proper questions for the right hon Gentleman to ask, and to ask himself out loud. He said that he did not know the answers. I do not know who does. If it were true, that certainly would not suggest that the Russians contemplated an immediate violent action in Europe. We can only use the facts as they are known to us and endeavour to deduce conclusions from them.

On the contrary, the plan would evidently be to get the United States and the United Nations, so far as they contribute, involved as deeply as possible in China, and thus prevent the reinforcement of Europe and the building up of our defensive strength there to a point where it would be an effectual deterrent. It is one of the most well-known—almost hackneyed—strategical and tactical methods, to draw your opponent's resources to one part of the field and then, at the right moment, to strike in another. Military history shows countless examples of this and of variants of it. Surely, however, the United Nations should avoid by every means in their power becoming entangled inextricably in a war with China. For this reason I had hoped that General MacArthur's advance in Korea—and I paid my tribute to him the other day, and to the extraordinary skill with which the operations had been handled, up to the point which we had then reached—would stop at the neck or wasp waist of the peninsula and would leave the country between the neck and the Yalu River and the Chinese frontier as a kind of no-man's-land which Allied air power would dominate. Under this cover there might have been constructed an ever-stronger fortified line across the neck, wherever it might be found suitable. Of course, to hold such a line it is essential that the approaches to it should also be commanded, and therefore such a line cannot be exactly along the imaginary lines which are drawn on the maps to indicate the parallels. To take a practical guide, the shortest space might be chosen and the strongest defence made there, with a hinterland or neutral space before it—or if not neutral, a no-man's-land, a disputed no-man's-land—which would give the necessary facilities to the defence.

Whether this will be possible now depends upon the result of the great battle which is at this moment raging. I suppose we shall know in a few days what the results are. I am sure, however, that the whole House feels that the sooner the Far Eastern diversion—because, vast as it is, it is but a diversion—can be brought into something like a static condition and stabilized, the better it will be for all those hopes which the United Nations have in hand. For it is in Europe that the world cause will be decided. As my right hon Friend the Member for Warwick and Leamington [Mr Eden] said yesterday, it is there that the mortal danger lies. I am sure that we all agree with that. Perhaps we are biased by the fact that we live there or thereabouts. But none the less, one cannot conceive that our natural bias has in any way distorted the actual facts.

There is another reason why we should be very careful not to indulge in criticisms of the United States or their commanders, or do anything which could weaken, even by gusts of opinion, the vital ties that bind our fates together. We fight in the name of the United Nations. That gives a great moral sanction to our action, but in Korea and the Far East the burden falls almost entirely on the United States. It is important to get the proportions right. The Minister for Defence read us out yesterday, or circulated, the British casualties before the recent fighting. I fear that they may have been increased since then. The killed were 51, wounded 175 and missing 5. We have not been told what are the American casualties, but I have heard on good authority that they have lost at least 7,000 or 8,000 men killed and between 20,000 and 30,000 wounded. It may be accurate or inaccurate, but that was before this recent fighting. And therefore I say that we must realize the enormous weight of the burden that rests upon them and of the noble sacrifices they are making in the common cause.

Casualties are no doubt not the only measure of war effort, but they are the supreme and truest measure of the sacrifice and exertion of the brave troops made by any army. Our contribution and that of the other United Nations countries, however precious to us, cannot in any way be compared with that of the United States. Our thoughts are with our own gallant soldiers. We watch their fortunes with the deepest sympathy and confidence that they will do their duty with distinction. But their presence there must be taken as a symbol of our loyalty to the common cause and our main responsibility lies here at home in Europe.

I thought that it was a great pity when at the American suggestion and under American pressure the Combined Chiefs of Staff Committee was allowed to lapse. Contacts have, I fear, been lost which cannot be wholly regained by larger bodies speaking different languages. The Combined Chiefs of Staff Committee was the keystone of our arch of victory. Formally or informally, in one way or another, it should, I am sure, be reconstituted at the earliest moment. It is quite true that when we have so few troops engaged in the existing theatre of war, we cannot expect to exert influence except by reasoned argument. But let us make sure we have full opportunity for that, especially taking place as it would between officers who have been through the great struggle together and who know each other's minds and have confidence in each other's characters. I entirely agree with what my right hon Friend said yesterday that the strongest British representation possible should be available—I mean Ministerial representation—in Washington and if necessary at Lake Success. It should be there in these present anxious and formative weeks. No one must underrate the latent strength of our country or the contribution we are capable of making directly or indirectly to the common cause of the United Nations.

When your friend and ally is bearing almost the whole weight, it is natural that he will have the control. War is little more than a catalogue of mistakes and misfortunes. It is when misfortune comes, however, that allies must hold more firmly together than ever before. Here in Britain, and I doubt not throughout the British Empire and Commonwealth of Nations, we always follow a very simple rule, which has helped us in maintaining the safety of this country: 'The worse things get the more we stand together.' Let it also be seen that the English-speaking world follows the same plan. Nothing will be more helpful in rousing the nations of Europe to coherent measures of self-defence than the feeling that the unity of the English-speaking world and of the free nations of Western Europe is unbreakable, and that the stresses and perils of our position only weld us more solidly together and call forth whatever exertions are necessary for self-preservation.

This also applies in a smaller sphere to our party affairs at home. Had some of the Amendments, or one of the Amendments, on the Paper been moved, we should, of course, have voted with His Majesty's Government. But even if there is no Division—and I understand that is unlikely—the House of Commons has here today by its temper and its attitude an opportunity of making our fundamental unities apparent to the world, and we may be sure that all this process gives the best hope of avoiding a third world war, not by appeasement of opponents from weakness, but by wise measures, fair play from strength, and the proof of unconquerable resolve.

UNVEILING OF A STATUE TO THE EARL OF OXFORD AND ASQUITH

A SPEECH IN THE HOUSE OF COMMONS
6 DECEMBER 1950

---

4 *December—Mr Attlee and Mr Truman meet at White House in Washington for discussions on the Anglo-American policy on Korea, North Atlantic Defence, raw materials, etc.*

5 *December—Report of British Electricity Authority for the year ended 31 March 1950 shows a net consolidated trading surplus of £7,163,236.*

[6 *December* 1950

I am grateful for being asked to unveil this monument to my old chief, Herbert Henry Asquith. I served with him and under him for ten convulsive, formative and momentous years. After having been Home Secretary for three years, and Chancellor of the Exchequer for two, he was Prime Minister for eight.

This was a period of intense political strife here at home, ended only by the outbreak of world war. He guided, and at times corrected, my vagaries in the party bickerings, and entrusted me with the preparation of the Fleet, on which in those days, when the air was but an infant, our national existence depended. Never can I forget the support he gave me in the Navy Estimates of 1913-14. We had more than twenty Cabinet meetings about them and I should never have survived as a Minister but for his commanding authority.

He was a great friend of my father's and, to my youthful eyes, presented the spectacle of one of those great parliamentary personages brought forth in the sunset of the Victoria era. It is always very difficult to discount one's own viewpoint in the changing scenes and proportions of our lives. But I must say that the statesmen whom I saw in those days seemed to tower above the general level in a most impressive way. The tests were keener, the standards were higher, and those who surmounted them were men it was a treat and honour to meet. They were the representatives of an age of ordered but unceasing movement. Liberalism had stricken the shackles off the slave and broken down the barriers of privilege. The road was open to those of the highest natural quality and ability who chose to tread it.

Henry Asquith had neither wealth nor favour to help him; nor did he need them. His outstanding personal force, capacity, precision of

443

mind, and hard-won knowledge raised him swiftly to the high control of national affairs. At forty, with a massive legal record behind him, he was Home Secretary. At fifty he was Prime Minister. He made his way by his distinction in House of Commons debate. Hard, clear-cut, lucid argument, expressed in happy terms with many a glint of humour and flash of repartee, brevity, as well as clarity—these were his weapons in those days of lengthy, sonorous harangues. He was no ebullient orator pouring forth his sentimental or passionate appeal. But few there were who could face him in the tense debating of issues, large or small. Here was a man who dealt in reasoned processes, who placed things in their proper scale and relation, who saw the root of the matter and simplified the tale.

You must not think of him, however, as the embodiment in public affairs only of common sense and goodwill. These were his foundations, but in action he showed himself as hard and as stern as the times required. Henry Asquith was not only a Liberal, he was a Radical. He had made his own way by his talents and driving power. He was determined to broaden the road and break down the remaining barriers so as to enable ever larger numbers of ordinary people to win their place in an expanding society and have a fair share of the show. In this way he was in basic harmony with an age which has brought, and is bringing, ever more millions of men and women to a table which might but for human folly and wickedness be ever more bountifully laden for the whole human race.

He was not in essence an organizer or administrator, nor was he a revolutionary impulsion. As I saw him he was a *Ruler* who, as I have written, 'knew where he stood on every question of life and affairs in an altogether unusual degree. Scholarship, politics, philosophy, law and religion were all spheres in which, at the time when I knew him best, he seemed to have arrived at definite opinions. On all, when the need required, his mind opened and shut smoothly and exactly, like the breech of a gun.

'He always gave me the impression of measuring all the changing, baffling situations of public and parliamentary life according to settled standards and sure convictions. There was also the sense of a scorn, lightly and not always completely veiled, for arguments, for personalities, and even for events, which did not conform to the pattern he had with so much profound knowledge and reflection adopted.'*

I wrote these words nearly twenty years ago, and I am content to repeat them now, because the statue which we shall presently see should express the character of a strong man, not drifting with the

* *Great Contemporaries.*

tide, or trimming his sails to the gusts of popularity, but making his impact on the society in which he lived by pursuing purposes—far above party—which served the causes he had made his own.

Henry Asquith was a patriot, who at all times sought, according to the broad light by which he marched, the welfare of the British people, and the enduring splendour of the British Empire. At no time, in power or out of power, did the clatter and anger of political struggles in a free democracy prevent him from responding to those deep undertones of national honour and of national safety for the country and the people, whom he served or led.

Although I was in a subordinate station—one of his lieutenants— and nearly a generation behind him, I saw him often and knew him well. He had a full and joyous life. His blood bit deep, and he transmitted to his children the untiring courage and far-ranging intellect by which he had himself been upborne. Some of them are here today to see their father's memory proclaimed, and enshrined amid universal respect in the House of Commons, where he shone and which he loved. All his sons of military age fought in the forefront of the First World War. Raymond was killed with the Grenadiers on the Somme. 'Ock' died before his time as the result of wounds received in battle, rising through four years of repeated deeds of prowess from sub-lieutenant to brigadier-general. Brilliant figures stand here with us today who carry on Henry Asquith's lineage and his fame.

Before their eyes, while all salute, I now unveil the statue of their sire.

MR OLIVER STANLEY

A SPEECH TO THE HOUSE OF COMMONS
13 DECEMBER 1950

---

7 *December—The North Atlantic Deputies' Organization announce that they have 'reached a stage in their discussions where they are ready to enter into a meeting with the Military Committee for the joint consideration of the politico-military aspects of the German contribution'.*

13 *December—The North Atlantic Deputies' Organization and the Military Committee announce that they have reached 'complete agreement on political and military recommendations for German participation in an integrated force for the defence of Western Europe'.*

The Chancellor of Exchequer announces in the House of Commons that, due to the good progress by Britain in her economic recovery, her dollar deficit has now disappeared and that agreement has been reached with the United States Government for the suspension of Marshall Aid.

[13 *December* 1950

On this side of the House we are greatly obliged to the Prime Minister for the kindly tribute which he has paid to our late colleague. We are all also very glad that the Government in this matter have not been bound by a narrow view of the precedents for such a tribute. There have been exceptions, and they have been made in accordance with the general feeling of the House, which, in such matters, is probably the safest of guides. The Prime Minister has mentioned two outstanding cases where the exact forms were not observed, but where the feelings of the House desired an opportunity of corporate expression. Oliver Stanley may well be another of these exceptions.

The appreciations published in the newspapers of every hue show how widely understood and admired were his exceptional and outstanding gifts and qualities. Reading them must have been a comfort to his many friends in the House of Commons and throughout the land. He served at the front in the line as a regimental officer through many of the severities of the First World War. He filled great offices of State in peace and war. I regretted very much that I could not persuade him to accept the Dominions Office at the time of the formation of the National Government. He preferred to rejoin his regiment. It was not until two years later that I was able to persuade him to allow me to submit his name as Secretary of State for the Colonies. This delay was not due to any breach in our personal friendship or in our political relations.

Oliver Stanley always set the interests of his country, as he conceived them, far above his personal fortunes or career. In the year before the war he wrote to Mr Chamberlain advising him that the Government should be widened and strengthened in composition, and placing his own office at the Prime Minister's disposal in order to help such a process. I did not know about this for several years afterwards, but it is a remarkable example of his bearing and relationship to public life, and a proof of the high level upon which his actions proceeded.

He was indeed, as so many of us know, a delightful companion. His conversation never lost its dignity, even in casual talk, and he always preserved in it the spark of the unexpected. His memory will long be cherished, and cherished most dearly by those who knew him best. Our keen sympathy, as the Prime Minister has said, goes out to his family and the children he has left behind him.

Oliver Stanley's career has been cut short in its prime. None the less, it is not lacking in the sense of completeness, because we have the presentation in an integral and matured form of his personality, of his gifts, and of his record that endures with us. On this side we have suffered a heavy party loss, and, many of us, a keen personal loss; but, as the Prime Minister has said, the House of Commons as a whole is conscious that Parliament is definitely and seriously the poorer by the untimely removal of this capable, experienced and attractive figure, who adorned our debates with a happy combination of wit and wisdom, and enriched our public life by high character, by disinterested public service, and by a commanding view of wide horizons.

THE INTERNATIONAL SITUATION

A SPEECH TO THE HOUSE OF COMMONS
14 DECEMBER 1950

---

12 *December—During a debate on an Opposition motion of censure Mr Noel-Baker, Minister of Fuel and Power, outlines the Government's plans to increase coal output by means of a vigorous miners' recruiting campaign.*

14 *December—Mr Attlee gives a detailed statement to the House of Commons on his recent visit to Washington and his discussions with Mr Truman on Korean and international affairs.*

[14 *December* 1950

I hasten to associate myself whole-heartedly with the tribute which the Prime Minister has paid to Mr Peter Fraser. His part in the war was in every way worthy of the country he represented and of the magnificent New Zealand Divisions which served with honour in every field.

We are all very glad to see that the military situation for the time being in Korea has somewhat improved. I hope also that there is truth in the reports that a measure of censorship is being established over the dispatches from the front or from Tokyo by the war correspondents of all the United Nations. I should think most of us agree with General Robertson's protest upon this point. When one sees day after day the exact position, numbers, condition and intentions of the United Nations troops, very often unit by unit, set forth, one cannot but feel that it is hardly fair to the soldiers who are fighting that the enemy should be presented with such complete intelligence, whereas so little seems to be known by us about the other side, and such a large measure of ignorance prevails, among the general public at least, about the enemy's disposition, strength and movements. Indeed, the wildest estimates are given on high authority only to be contradicted and reversed a few days later.

One instance, a small one, but not without significance, particularly struck me. A Centurion tank was damaged and left behind. This was immediately published and its importance emphasized. All the secrets were published of the latest British tank. Thus this vehicle, left behind among great numbers of no doubt other broken-down vehicles, in all the litter of retreat amid the snow, acquired instantly, in the enemy's eyes, an exceptional significance. I was very glad to read—I hope it is true—that it had been successfully destroyed from the air. That would have been a very good tale to tell if true after it had happened, but why was it necessary to attract the enemy's attention to this vehicle beforehand? That seems to me a particular illustration. We really must have tighter control over what is published. We all seek to prevent and limit aggression, and one of the additional deterrents which we might impose upon the enemy's aggression would be to tell them that if it goes on much longer we shall cut them off from these invaluable supplies of information.

The Prime Minister's visit to Washington has done nothing but good. The question we all have to consider this afternoon in the House of Commons is, how much good. The Prime Minister spoke of the importance of renewing the series of meetings between the President and the Prime Minister which had taken place during the war and since the war. We all agree with that. We all agree with the advantages of direct discussion to which the Prime Minister has just referred. I must say it seems to me that five years is rather a long interval, and the decision when it came was very suddenly taken. My right hon Friend the Member for Warwick and Leamington [Mr Eden] spoke on 29 November and urged that we should have stronger representation at Washington at the highest level. I endorsed this when I spoke the next day. I did not wish to appear to reflect any more than he did in the slightest degree upon our excellent Ambassador in Washington, and I used the particular phrase 'Ministerial representation'. That very evening we were told that the Prime Minister was going. During the afternoon there was some excitement caused in the House by the accounts of Mr Truman's interview with the Press which appeared on the tape. But I understand that this was not the reason that led to the Prime Minister's decision to go and that this was taken earlier in the day. Certainly the decision was very hastily arrived at after an interval of five years.

Many will think that earlier meetings might have been held. Several recent occasions occur to me. When the Soviet-inspired aggression by the North Korean Government across the 38th Parallel took place, and when the United States intervened vigorously and actively with the approval of the United Nations Assembly and we joined with them at the end of June, that was certainly an occasion which the Prime Minister might have considered for talking matters over with our great Ally and friend.

Again, after General MacArthur's brilliant counter-stroke, which gave us back Seoul and changed the whole aspect of the fighting up to that point in Korea, would have been, it seems to me, a good moment to talk over the next steps. At that moment many issues were open, which would have gained by having that direct discussion face to face between the heads of Governments assisted by their military advisers. It is always easy to be wise after the event, but there were many people in this country who were wise before the event. I am by no means sure that His Majesty's Government and their expert advisers are excluded from that large number. Those who had this view felt that it would be wiser to fortify a line, if not at the 38th Parallel, at the waist or at the best military position in advance of it, thus leaving a broad no-man's-land in which we could reconnoitre and into which we could go with mobile columns and, of course, with the all-powerful air forces available, while building up all the time a strong fortified line which we could hold while, perhaps, conversations went on.

There is much to be said for strong fortified lines. If properly organized in depth, if protected in front by ever-expanding mine-fields and wire entanglements, and if developed week after week by concreted structures and excavations and firmly held with modern fire power, they would prove a terrific obstacle to the advance of infantry. All this becomes greater when both flanks rest upon the sea and the sea is in Allied command and when we have unquestioned mastery of the air. Such a position, once established, about 100 miles long, presents a very different obstacle to the advance and infiltration of masses of enemy infantry than does a moving front in hilly, rocky, scrub-covered country, then broadened to about 300 miles.

I am speaking only of what has happened in the past. I do not attempt to say anything about what may happen in the future. [HON MEMBERS: 'Why not?'] It would be very unwise and unnecessary to do it in military operations. To pierce a properly fortified line not only would masses of artillery have to be accumulated, but there would also have to be very heavy concentrations of armour. These would present admirable targets to overwhelming air power. It certainly seems that the Chinese armies, if they had attacked such a line, might well have renewed on an even larger scale the painful experiences which we our-selves often suffered on the Somme and at Passchendaele and in other bloody battlefields of the First World War. I cannot help feeling that it would have been well if all these matters had been talked over at the right moment and in good time in Washington by the highest authorities in both our countries.

We immediately approved the Prime Minister's decision to go when he did, and I feel sure that no one regrets it now. We welcome and whole-heartedly support the Prime Minister's statement about British and American unity and how their two flags will fly together however the winds may blow. That is indeed the foundation, as he said in his closing words, of our safety and the best hope for the peace of the world and for the survival of free civilization. It is a great comfort in the darkening scene to feel that there are no party differences, or very limited party differences, in this country on this supreme issue, and that the task of trying to drive a wedge between us and the United States is left to the Communists and their fellow-travellers, aided perhaps, no doubt through folly rather than malice, by the usual Ministerial indiscretions.

Another advantage which has come from the Prime Minister's journey has been the renewed explicit declarations by the United States emphasizing the priority of the defence of Europe. We are glad indeed that General Eisenhower is to be appointed to the Supreme Command of the army—however it may be denominated—which is being constituted there. We were led to believe that this appointment would be made many weeks ago. Progress in European defence, which was tardily begun, continues to be lamentably slow. It is more than nine months since I pointed out that no effective defence of Europe was possible without the armed strength of Germany. The movement of opinion in that direction has been continual, but nothing has been done. No agreement has been reached, and meanwhile Germany lies even more undefended than do other European countries under the menace of Communist and Russian aggression.

The months slip quickly away all the time. Several years have already been wasted, frittered away. The overwhelming Russian military power towers up against us, committees are multiplied, papers are written, words are outpoured and one declaration succeeds another, but nothing in the slightest degree in proportion to the scale of events or to their urgency has been done. When we return after our anxious Recess we shall require a full and prolonged debate upon defence, and we shall demand that a portion of it shall be in secret. It was with the danger of Europe in my mind that I said some weeks ago that I hoped that we should not get entangled in China. In order to protect myself from the charge of being wise after the event, I venture to remind the House that on 16 November, before these recent reverses in Korea had taken place, I asked the Minister of Defence a supplementary question, which I do not think he resented in any way:

'. . . whether he and the Foreign Secretary will constantly bear in mind the great importance of our not becoming, and of our Allies

so far as we can influence their actions not becoming, too much pinned down in China or in the approaches to China at a time when the danger in Europe is . . . occupying all our minds?'
I need scarcely say that I hold to that conviction still.

In view, however, of what has happened since then in Korea, and in the United Nations Assembly, I feel it requires to be stated with more precision and refinement. We must not at any time be drawn into urging a policy which would inflict dishonour or humiliation upon the United States or upon the United Nations. Such a course would be at least as full of danger as any other now open to us. We learn from the newspapers that the proposals for a truce or cease fire which were proposed by the thirteen Asiatic and Arab States, have been opposed by the Soviet delegation. They certainly seemed to be very far-reaching proposals from our point of view.

I will not say more about them, but, while the fullest priority should be given to the defence of Western Europe, it would be a great mistake to lose our sense of proportion and cast everything to the winds elsewhere. The only prudent course open to the United States and ourselves is to stabilize the local military position and, if the opportunity then occurs, to negotiate with the aggressors and at least make sure that we negotiate from strength and not from weakness. We shall no doubt hear from the Foreign Secretary tonight how the question of further conversations with Soviet Russia stands. There was, I think, fairly complete agreement in the House that no abrupt negative or merely dilatory action would be appropriate to the Russian request, and from what we have read in the newspapers it does not seem likely that there will be any serious disagreement between us upon the procedure eventually to be adopted.

I am strongly in favour of every effort being made by every means, to secure a fair and reasonable settlement with Russia. I should, however, be failing in frankness to the House, and to some of those who agree with me upon this matter, to whom I am much opposed in many ways, if I did not make it clear at this stage that we must not place undue hopes upon the success of any negotiations which may be undertaken. It is our duty—and a duty which we owe to the cause of peace and to our own consciences—to leave no effort unmade that wisdom and fair play can suggest, and that patience can bring forward. But on this side of the House we have never contemplated that if negotiations failed we should abandon any of the great causes for which we have stood in the past, and for which the United Nations Organization stands today.

The declaration of the Prime Minister that there will be no appeasement also commands almost universal support. It is a good slogan for the country. It seems to me, however, that in this House it requires to be more precisely defined. What we really mean, I think, is no appeasement through weakness or fear. Appeasement in itself may be good or bad according to the circumstances. Appeasement from weakness and fear is alike futile and fatal. Appeasement from strength is magnanimous and noble and might be the surest and perhaps the only path to world peace. When nations or individuals get strong they are often truculent and bullying, but when they are weak they become better mannered. But this is the reverse of what is healthy and wise. I have always been astonished, having seen the end of these two wars, how difficult it is to make people understand Roman wisdom, 'Spare the conquered and war down the proud.' I think I will go so far as to say it in the original: *Parcere subjectis, et debellare superbos.* The modern practice has too often been, punish the defeated and grovel to the strong.

Unhappily, except as regards the atomic bomb—about which I shall have a word to say before I sit down—we are in a very weak position and likely to remain so for several years. As I have repeatedly said, it is only the vast superiority of the United States in this awful weapon that gives us any chance of survival. The argument is now put forward that we must never use the atomic bomb until, or unless, it has been used against us first. In other words, you must never fire until you have been shot dead. That seems to me undoubtedly a silly thing to say and a still more imprudent position to adopt. Moreover, such a resolve would certainly bring war nearer. The deterrent effect of the atomic bomb is at the present time almost our sole defence. Its potential use is the only lever by which we can hope to obtain reasonable consideration in an attempt to make a peaceful settlement with Soviet Russia. If they had superiority, or even something like equality in this weapon with the United States, I cannot feel any assurance that they would be restrained by the conscientious scruples or moral inhibitions which are often so vocal in this country. It would certainly be a poor service to the cause of peace to free them from all cause of apprehension until they were in every respect ready to strike.

The Soviet power could not be confronted, or even placated, with any hope of success if we were in these years of tension through which we are passing to deprive ourselves of the atomic bomb, or to prevent its use by announcing gratuitously self-imposed restrictions. Of course, when we say 'we', we must not forget that we have been unable to make the atomic bomb ourselves. Our failure during five years of peace has astonished me very much when I remember how far we were advanced, not only in knowledge but in initiative, in 1942 and 1943.

In the communiqué published last week by the President and the Prime Minister, President Truman stated that it was his 'hope that world conditions would never call for the use of the atomic bomb', and he undertook to keep His Majesty's Government informed of developments 'which might bring about a change in the situation'. This assurance by the President contained in the joint communiqué is in very general terms. There is no guarantee in that assurance even of consultation. But in wartime we were on equal terms with the United States in the whole business of atomic research. Today the Prime Minister used a new phrase when he said that full weight will be given to any representations we may make. In 1943 I made an agreement with the President. Since then I understand other arrangements have been made. The Prime Minister tells us today that the same spirit and the same background are there in the present understanding, but he and one or two of my friends and former colleagues on both sides are the only ones in the House to know exactly what this means. I am sure that the Government would be wise to make a fuller statement upon this subject than we have yet heard.

MR SYDNEY SILVERMAN (Nelson and Colne): Would the right hon Gentleman allow me——

MR CHURCHILL: No, I would rather not, thank you very much. One can always take examples from what happens. The President of the United States the other day let himself be cross-examined freely during a Press conference on this very topic. In my opinion, one ought not to say anything upon the subject one has not very carefully considered beforehand. I certainly do not intend to be cross-examined by the hon Gentleman, because I have considered carefully what I should say. I am strongly of opinion that the Government should make a fuller statement upon this subject, and that this would be beneficial both to our own position and to our relationship with the United States. After all, this matter has become one of very real and vital consequence to us since the decision of the Government to afford the United States the bomber base in East Anglia, which makes it all the more necessary that the position in which we stand should be clearly defined.

We are debating this afternoon matters of supreme importance to ourselves and to the whole Empire and Commonwealth of Nations. We do so at a time when, on domestic questions, parties are evenly balanced and deeply divided. A continuance of these conditions is harmful to our national strength. The responsibility lies in the first instance upon the Government and in a special degree, of course, upon the Prime Minister. They decide the movement of our affairs. We respond to the action which they take in these matters. The Prime Minister has taken marked steps to increase the differences in home politics. I ask him, even now, if he will not reconsider—[*Interruption.*] Hon Members opposite can get ready to howl. They have not had much at which to cheer during the speech to which they listened earlier; now, perhaps, they will have their chance. I ask the Prime Minister, even now, whether he will not reconsider his decision to force the Steel Nationalization Act upon us in the midst of all these storms and dangers. Not only should he consider that an abatement of domestic quarrels would be advantageous, but he should also consider the injury that will be done to our rearmament programme by taking this industry from the competent hands in which it now rests and placing it under the imperfect and inexperienced State management by which it is threatened. It really is not a matter for mere hilarity for uneasy minds and unsettled consciences below the Gangway.

The Prime Minister spoke about raw materials and the arrangements which were being made for them, but steel is the mainspring of all effective rearmament measures. We wished the right hon Gentleman well upon his Transatlantic mission, and we have recognized the advantages which it has secured, but I will say now that if he persists in his present attitude on steel nationalization, he will fail in his duties to the country as a whole. Although we approved of the visit of the Prime Minister to the United States, although we lent him full support on his mission, although the results have been helpful so far as they go, we cannot in these circumstances feel confidence in the loyalty of the Government to the people of this country. The Prime Minister is counting on our support, which will not be withheld on issues of national importance abroad, while at the same time he is seeking to placate his political tail by acts of party faction at home.

MR FREDERICK ELWYN JONES (West Ham, South) *rose*——

MR CHURCHILL: It is very doubtful whether these——

HON MEMBERS: Point of order.

MR SPEAKER: Does the hon Member wish to raise a point of order?

MR FREDERICK ELWYN JONES: Is it in order for the Leader of the Opposition to question the loyalty of His Majesty's Government?

MR SPEAKER: That is a matter for the right hon Gentleman and not for me. That is not a point of order.

MR CHURCHILL: As my voice was drowned by hon Members opposite, I might repeat the sentence on which I closed—namely, that we think it is very doubtful whether——

MR S. SILVERMAN *rose*——

MR CHURCHILL: If there is any one man in this House who should hang his head in shame—[*Interruption*]—it is the hon Gentleman, who won cheers by abusing the United States as shabby moneylenders.

MR SILVERMAN *rose*——

HON MEMBERS: Sit down.

MR SPEAKER: Is this another point of order?

MR CHURCHILL: —and now has to applaud with all his strength the tributes paid by the leader——

MR SILVERMAN: Mr Speaker——

MR SPEAKER: Does the hon Member rise to a point of order?

MR SILVERMAN: Yes, sir.

MR SPEAKER: Then will the hon Member put it?

MR SILVERMAN: I want to ask you, sir, whether it is in order for the Leader of the Opposition to use his great opportunity on an historic occasion to accuse everybody in the world except himself of disloyalty.

MR SPEAKER: That is not a point of order. Hon Members must not waste the time of the House by these mere party accusations.

MR CHURCHILL: As the hon Gentleman went out of his way to interrupt me in what I was hoping would be the closing sentence that I should have to utter, I thought it right to point out what he had said in the past and to draw his attention to the very different sentiments which have been put forward today. I regret very much that the Prime Minister—[*Interruption*]—I beg hon Gentlemen opposite not to interrupt any expression of their feelings which they may desire to make, because it does not trouble or worry me in the slightest. It only prevents my getting on with what I have to say.

MRS BRADDOCK: If your gang had been in control, we would have been at war by now.

MR CHURCHILL: I am quite determined to utter my last sentence if I have to stand here half an hour. What I say is that I very much regret that the Prime Minister has not risen to the heights of his national responsibility, and I predict that he will encounter misfortunes and reproach on the discordant course to which he has devoted himself.